ABORIGINAL RELIGIONS IN AUSTRALIA

ABORIGINAL RELIGIONS IN AUSTRALIA

A Bibliographical Survey

TONY SWAIN

Bibliographies and Indexes in Religious Studies,
Number 18

Gary E. Gorman, Series Adviser

Greenwood Press
New York • Westport, Connecticut • London

Library of Congress Cataloging-in-Publication Data

Swain, Tony.
    Aboriginal religions in Australia : a bibliographical survey /
Tony Swain.
        p.   cm.—(Bibliographies and indexes in religious studies,
    ISSN 0742-6836 ; no. 18)
    Includes indexes.
    ISBN 0-313-26044-3 (lib. bdg. : alk. paper)
    1. Australian aborigines—Religion—Bibliography. 2. Australia—
Religion—Bibliography. I. Title. II. Series.
Z7834.A8S82   1991
[BL2610]
016.299'92—dc20   91-2153

British Library Cataloguing in Publication Data is available.

Library of Congress Catalog Card Number: 91-2153
ISBN: 0-313-26044-3
ISSN: 0742-6836

First published in 1991

Greenwood Press, 88 Post Road West, Westport, CT 06881
An imprint of Greenwood Publishing Group, Inc.

Printed in the United States of America

The paper used in this book complies with the
Permanent Paper Standard issued by the National
Information Standards Organization (Z39.48-1984).

10 9 8 7 6 5 4 3 2 1

for Mum and Dad

Contents

Foreword

"I did not perceive that they did worship any thing"—so said William Dampier of the Australian Aborigines following his two visits to New Holland at the end of the seventeenth century.[1] By the 1920s, after decades of 'modern' ethnographic research, this view had altered very little: "Australia is the present home and refuge of creatures, often crude and quaint, that have elsewhere passed away and given place to higher forms. This applies equally to the Aboriginal as to the platypus and the kangaroo."[2] While it would be incorrect to assume that such base ignorance has characterized all understandings of Aboriginal cultural life, it has been the norm until comparatively recent times. Even the notable achievements of Durkheim were constrained by the lingering positivism of early twentieth century anthropology. Consequently, Aboriginal religions most typically have been viewed as simple and primitive (in contrast to primal) in form and content.

By the middle of the century, however, attitudes were beginning to change, with Aboriginal religions being viewed far more positively. Ironically, such change is best seen in relation to events of the dominant White culture. The accession of Queen Elizabeth, for instance, was marked in part by a groundswell of popular interest in the Aborigines, and this was accompanied by a more positive attitude towards their culture. "Our Aborigines, far from being reviled as 'the lowest form of humanity' and 'more akin to beasts than man', are now, following the testimony of the world's leading anthropologists, renowned for intelligence and morality which our materialism has been slow to appreciate."[3] (The reference to "our" Aborigines, though, continues to reinforce an attitude of cultural imperialism.) This attempt to be more understanding took concrete form

---

[1] Quoted in Richard White, *Inventing Australia: Images and Identity 1688-1980* (Sydney: George Allen and Unwin, 1981), p. 3.

[2] Baldwin Spencer, *The Arunta: A Study of a Stone Age People* (London: Macmilllan, 1927), vol. 1, p. vii.

[3] Rex Ingamells, *Royalty and Australia* (Melbourne, 1954).

in the early 1960s with the establishment of the Australian Institute of Aboriginal Studies; from then the scene was set for an unprecedented burgeoning of invaluable scholarly research, which has continued into the present.   Outstanding contributions have been made to genuine understandings of Aboriginal culture and religions by a panoply of notable scholars, including the Berndts, Strehlow, Elkin and many others. Despite the advances in our understanding of Aboriginal religions- and there have been many, as the volume in hand affirms- they still tend to be studied in isolation from other primal religions. Beginnings have been made in seeking to comprehend Aboriginal religions in a comparative sense, particularly among members of the Australian Association for the Study of Religions, but overwhelming emphasis remains on the discrete and the anthropological rather than the comparative and the philosophical.

Along with this somewhat one-eyed approach to the study of Aboriginal religions there remains a tenacious lack of interest among many who might contribute valuable insights to our understanding of Aboriginal culture. Once again a primarily White event is best evidence of this—the 1988 Bicentenary of European settlement of Australia. Leading up to this incredibly chauvinistic celebration was a massive burst of publishing activity; this resulted in many valuable and interesting reviews of Australian life in the last two centuries, but for the most part Aboriginal contributions were ignored. Typical of this in relation to religious studies were Mol's *The Faith of Australians* and O'Farrell's otherwise insightful essay on religious ambivalence—neither even mentions Aboriginal religions.[4]   As Max Charlesworth, himself one of a miniscule band of philosophers with an identifiable interest in Aboriginal religions, has pointed out, "for the most part...these writers are ethnographers and anthropologists and...it is a pity that very few scholars with interests in the philosophy of religion or comparative religion have attempted to work in the area of Aboriginal religion with a view to discussing it in a wider context."[5] Perhaps scholarship is poised just now to jump into these deeper waters. Certainly, Tony Swain in the present volume holds such a view, suggesting that scholars of Aboriginal religions over the years have been asking a series of interrelated and increasingly complex questions, most recently "what does their religious life mean?" Today, we are on the threshold of asking genuinely comparative questions. "With the emergence of Aborigines," Swain says, "writing about their own traditions and their experience of colonization we are, after two hundred years, only now perhaps ready for the next question: what are we going to say to one another?"

---

[4] Patrick O'Farrell, "The Cultural Ambivalence of Australian Religion." In *Australian Cultural History*, ed. by S.L. Goldberg and F.B. Smith, 7-14 (Cambridge: Cambridge University Press, 1988).

[5] Max Charlesworth, "Introduction." In *Religion in Aboriginal Australia: An Anthology*, ed. by M. Charlesworth et al. (St. Lucia: University of Queensland Press, 1986), p. 12.

To answer this adequately, it is important to know where we have been, what we have learned, and what remains to be learned. *Aboriginal Religions in Australia* does just that, serving as a guide to the burgeoning literature on Aboriginal religions. In it the author aims to have included every published work "with a substantial section on Aboriginal religion and which intends to be an accurate documentation." Within these careful parameters it is clear to me that the work is far more exhaustive than the author's scholarly diffidence permits him to declare (at least in public). For this reason alone Swain will stand as a landmark in the bibliography of Aboriginal religions for decades to come. Beyond that, the work also presents three masterful surveys of scholarship in the history of the study of Aboriginal religions, the major themes in these religions and their regional distinctions. It is my firm conviction that Tony Swain, of the Department of Religious Studies at the University of Sydney, has produced a child of inestimable value to the various scholarly communities with an interest in Aboriginal religion. As a step-parent I am more than a little pleased with this work and have no reservation whatever in commending it to a wide readership.

G.E. Gorman
Charles Sturt University

Preface

This is not a book about Australian Aboriginal religions. It is a book about *literature* on Australian Aboriginal religions. The difference is far from merely semantic.

From the outset I was faced with a choice. Should I classify and order entries according to Aboriginal traditions or Western academic interpretations of those traditions? The decision was made almost instantly. To attempt something even approximating an 'Aboriginal' (presuming there is such a thing) arrangement of published material on their cultures would be an impossible task. In contrast, once we accept categories like 'myth', 'initiation', 'magic', or 'totemism', the data very readily falls into place.

There is no point in ignoring the Western signature of my taxonomy. This is not to say this is a desirable state of affairs, and I for one hope the continuing dialectical relationship between Aborigines and scholars will lead to the ordering of our conceptions in a manner more faithful to Aborigines' own understandings. This, however, will be a long and living process, not one that will be completed with the scalpel-like stroke of a reviewer's pen. I do hope, nonetheless, that this work will go some way towards helping us take stock of both the virtues and failings of what we have achieved after studying the religions of the first Australians for a full two centuries.

The narrative section of this book is designed to provide the historic and analytic contexts for the cataloguing that follows. Each bibliographical entry is subject to a double classification. The major sections are geographical (South-East, Central Desert, Tasmania, etc.), but each region has sub-sections that order material by theme (Myth, The Arts, Birth, Women, etc.). For someone whose primary interest is thematic it should be a simple matter to locate particular themes in each of the sub-sections within the geographically defined sections. More specific investigation of select topics can be pursued through the four indexes which, besides offering an alphabetical listing of all titles and authors, provides a "tribes and places" index as well as a general subject index.

Beside thematic and regional classifications, each entry provides another piece of information whose significance should not be underestimated: its date. A reader familiar with the history of the study of Aboriginal religions will be able to anticipate many of the pre-conceptions which underlie a publication merely by knowing when it was written.

The three narrative chapters thus in turn explore the three pieces of information which accompany each entry in the bibliography: its date, thematic sub-section, and geographic section. Chapter one is a history of the study of Aboriginal religions which shows how a succession of theories, conceptions and blatant prejudices have moulded the way writers have approached the traditions of the Aborigines. Chapter two then teases out those themes scholars have felt useful in analyzing Aboriginal religions, placing their emergence in historical perspective and discussing their usefulness as conceptual tools. Finally, the third chapter highlights the unique features of the ten regions used as the primary categories of classification, describing possible historic forces which have shaped their particular forms.

Having now stated what this book is about and how it is ordered, one other introductory matter needs to be addressed: What's in it? Or, more to the point, what has been excluded?

The positive form of the answer is this: I have included *every published work of which I am aware with a substantial section on Aboriginal religion and which intends to be an accurate documentation.* This perhaps sounds exhaustive, but in fact it excludes quite a lot of material. To answer in the negative, the following are excluded:

* *unpublished* sources.

* works *not intended to be accurate*, including juvenile books or books like C. Mountford and A. Roberts' well known *Dreamtime* series. Translations of Aboriginal children's myths, however, are included (e.g. Berndt, 0414).

* *insubstantial publications*. With two exceptions (0342, 0553), this has excluded all newspaper articles and most journal articles less than about 1,000 words in length. (If the information is unique, I have sometimes included shorter pieces.) I also exclude many comparative studies which do not sustain sections on Aboriginal religion, even if they do refer to it frequently throughout the publication. I am here thinking pre-eminently of the "amongist" style of early anthropological books which jump from region to region across the globe in providing examples for their theories saying "among the such-and-such, we observe... etc."

* various *translations* (I give preference to the English translation, where possible) and *reprints with differing titles*.

* works that *say little or nothing about religion*. This seems self-evident, but some publications are deceptive. I have, for example, omitted all missiological pieces which only state what Aborigines *should* believe and *should* do (in contrast to reports of actual Aboriginal Christian beliefs

and practices, which are included); and the many works on Aboriginal art which fail to explain the religious significance of the pieces illustrated.

Finally, a comment on the entries themselves. If the work is something of an anthropological note, and most of these are less than about 2,000 words in length, then I merely state in as few words as possible its subject matter. All other entries are examined on their merits as coherent and ethnographically sound pieces. Most of my annotations are of roughly the same length, and aim at giving a feel for the publication as a whole. I always specify the main subjects covered and the people being referred to, but beyond this do not attempt an exhaustive compendium of every detail of the book or article. Rather, I consider the intentions of the author, his or her thesis, and the quality of the material. Whatever its length, I attempt to respect the 'integrity of the text' as a whole and evaluate it accordingly. This is not, of course, to say that I applaud every publication listed in the bibliography, and in many cases I have recorded my criticisms in the annotations. This is particularly true for the opening bibliographical chapter which contains works generalizing, often sweepingly, about Aboriginal religion continent-wide, an area where many scholarly angels have feared to tread.

Acknowledgments

My thanks to Gary Gorman for suggesting I write this book and his careful editorial advice; Adrian Marrie, fellow bibliographer, whose knowledge was a great help; the librarians of the Barr Smith Library in Adelaide, Fisher Library in Sydney, and The Australian Institute of Aboriginal Studies Library in Canberra, who were courteous and helpful in aiding my research; John and Jane Foulcher and their children, who transformed two tedious weeks of work in Canberra into a time I will always recall fondly; Garry Trompf, who made this a more complete book; Eric Sharpe, who cast·an expert eye over my spelling in various languages; and lastly, most importantly, and as always, Dany Falconer-Flint.

*

Some of the material contained in chapters 1 and 3 was originally drafted in "A Bicentenary of the Study of Australian Aboriginal Religions," *Religion* 21 (1991): 165-195, and in "Aboriginal Religions in Time and Space," in *Religion in Australia*, ed. Alan W. Black (Sydney: Allen & Unwin, 1991): 151-165.

Part One

Narrative Survey

1

The History of the Study of Australian Aboriginal Religions

The Western world has been interested in the Australian Aborigines because of what these peoples reveal about the nature of our own place within humanity. They have been a mirror in which we have found our own being not only reflected but also highlighted and contoured in bold relief. It is thus not surprising to discover that there really is no demarcation between ancient myths about the inhabitants of the Great South Land and the earliest reports of savage scenes in newly 'discovered' Australia. From those first encounters until today there has been a dialectic interaction between the realities of Aboriginal life and our own lavish expectations about what a people might be like who were once believed - and in some circles still are believed - to represent the germinal bud of humanity. The literature on Aboriginal religion could be called an unhappy conflation of 'science' and 'myth', but like Feyerabend I am not convinced there is a difference.[1] I see the growth of knowledge about Aborigines as a scientific mythopeic process; a quest to define the sustaining truths about ourselves and 'others' in terms of the ever-changing rules of scientific discourse.

The literature included in this bibliography reveals our changing perceptions of ourselves *vis à vis* Aborigines and their religions since 1798 (beginning with Collins, 0927), but the story properly begins long before this in the formation of Western intellectual constructs and early ideas of the nature of humankind. I will, therefore, begin in the ancient world.

BEFORE COLONIZATION (1788). Both Graeco-Roman and Judaeo-Christian traditions prepared the West for its encounter with Aborigines. Expectations of a Great South Land were common since the Pythagoreans deduced the earth's sphericity and Crates of Mallos (second century B.C.) developed the widely accepted view that the world was

---

[1] P. Feyerabend, *Against Method* (London: Doubleday, 1975).

divided into four major land masses by two oceans.[2] As equatorial regions were considered to be uninhabitably hot, and hence an impossible barrier for Adam's descendants, Christians, like St. Augustine, deemed it a 'fable' that there were humans in the antipodes.[3]

Nonetheless, sailors safely navigated to southern waters where in the fourth, unknown, *Terra Incognita*, said Isidore, "the antipodeans were fabulously said to dwell".[4] Some located the Isles of the Blest, where the dead and infernal gods dwelt, in the south. Another view, dating back to the fourth century B.C.E. forecast the extreme height of the southerners - an idea Abel Tasman could still entertain when he said in the seventeenth century that "the natives here must be of very tall stature" because he had observed notches made by Aborigines to climb trees were five feet apart.[5]

Many of the 'Marvels of the East'[6] came to be transferred to the South Land, thus said to be populated by various monstrous races. A Portuguese map probably depicting Australia details what a journalist described in 1886 as "a symbolic prophecy of Darwin's theory" as, of the three kinds of humans shown, one had a dog's head, another that of a monkey.[7] This was of course a cartographer's fabrication, but when the Dutch captain Van Carstel sighted Aborigines he readily affirmed "that in appearance they were more like monsters than human beings".[8]

The initial Dutch response was fired not only by centuries of speculation, but also by the political turmoil of the time, the outward imperialist race that emerged from inward European struggles, and the twin intellectual impacts of Calvinist Christianity and Hobbesian social thought.[9] Willem Jansz's description of the Torres Strait Islanders as "savage, cruel, black barbarians",[10] would have both confirmed to Calvinists that these were not amongst the elect and reinforced Hobbesian dogma that in the 'state of nature', the human lot was a life "solitary, poore, nasty, brutish and short".[11] When the Englishman William Dampier reached Australia's western coast he conceded Dutch opinion, saying these

---

[2] G.A. Wood, "Ancient and Mediæval Conceptions of Terra Australis." *The Australian Historical Society Journal and Proceedings* 3 (1916).

[3] St. Augustine, *The City of God.* Trans. M. Dodds (NY: Modern Library, 1950), p. 532.

[4] cit. J.K. Wright, *The Geographical Lore in the Time of the Crusades* (NY: Dover, 1965), p. 157.

[5] A.J. Tasman, *The Journals of Abel Jansz Tasman* (Adelaide: Australia Heritage Press, 1898), p. 26.

[6] R. Wittkower, "Marvels of the East: A Study in the History of Monsters." *Journal of the Warburg and Coutauld Institutes* 5(1942).

[7] *Sydney Morning Herald* 15th April (1886).

[8] cit. J.E. Heeres (ed), *The Part Borne by the Dutch in the Discovery of Australia* (London:Luzae, 1899), p. 29.

[9] see D.J. Mulvaney, "The Australian Aborigines 1606-1929: Opinion and Fieldwork." *Historical Studies* 8(1958): 134.

[10] cit. Heeres (ed), *op. cit.* p. 6.

[11] T. Hobbes, *Leviathan* (London: Dent and Sons, 1975[1651]), p. 65.

Aborigines were the most miserable people on earth "and setting aside their Humane shape, they differ but little from Brutes".[12]

These initial responses painted a hardly less exotic picture than the fantastic imaginings of the ancients. Indeed, in 1655, Isaac de la Peyrère went so far as to pronounce the heretical view that these people "did not descend from Adam".[13] Others, however, were of an entirely different opinion, no less unconfirmable but more humane. For them the southern world held a new utopia. The Spanish explorer, Fernandez de Quiros, saw the people he encountered as "a decent people, clean, cheerful, and reasonable"[14] and named this new region *Australia de Espiritu Sancto*, "South Land of the Holy Spirit". There was also from the late seventeenth century a spate of allegedly factual accounts of explorers reaching Australia to find the southern utopia populated by anything from Deists to vermilion androgynies.[15]

In all of these accounts we learn much of European peoples' own changing vision of the world but nothing of Aboriginal beliefs, and though typically captains were ordered to learn of the religion professed, they could only report along with Dampier "I did not perceive that they did worship anything".[16]

1788-1820. The first thirty years of colonization did little to rectify this state of ignorance. When Captain Cook claimed Australia for George III in 1770, he had brought the doctrine of the Noble Savage to its antipodean climax with a famous piece of poor grammar: "these people may be truly said to be in the pure state of nature, and may appear to some to be the most wretched upon Earth: but in reality they are far more happier than we Europeans".[17]

On the arrival of the First Fleet, however, such romantic notions soon gave way to an ideology more congenial to the interests of land appropriation. The idea of progress became increasingly entrenched and Aborigines comfortably fitted European notions of humanity's most savage and primitive state. It was, of course, anticipated that their 'superstitions' - their beliefs and practices being deemed unworthy of the word 'religion' - would also display this rudimentary character, and so accord with the

---

[12] W. Dampier, *A New Voyage Around the World* (London: Adam and Charles Black, 1937[1697]), p. 312.

[13] cit. J.S. Slotkin (ed), *Readings in Early Anthropology* (NY: Wenner-Gren Foundation for Anthropological Research, 1965), p. 81.

[14] C. Markham (ed), *The Voyages of Pedro Fernandez de Quiros 1565 to 1606* (London: Hakluyt Society, 1904), vol. 2, p. 486.

[15] W.P. Friedrich, *Australia in Western Imaginative Prose Writings 1600-1960* (North Carolina: Uni. of North Carolina Press, 1967).

[16] Dampier, *op. cit.*, p. 314.

[17] J.C. Beaglehole, *The Journals of Captain Cook* (London: Cambridge Uni. Press, 1955) Vol. 1, p. 508.

theories of those like David Hume and Charles de Brosses who insisted "the savage tribes... are all idolators. Not a single exception to this rule".[18]

At this stage there was little enough actual evidence to support claims of any kind about Aboriginal religion. David Collins produced the first account of consequence in 1798, describing and illustrating mortuary and initiation rites but understandably comprehending little of what he witnessed (0927). There were other snippets of conjecture here and there, with reference to obvious bodily operations or beliefs which flattered the colonialists self-image by suggesting Whites were Aborigines' deceased kin, but in the main all were forced to admit, with Watkin Tench: "To their religious rites and opinions I am... a stranger".[19]

One potentially highly significant episode in 1800 turned out a bizarre disaster. In that year the first ethnographic expedition, sponsored by the French *Sociéte des Observateurs des l'Homme*, sailed with Nicolas Baudin to the southern parts of Australia. A memoir written for the occasion by Joseph-Marie Degerando and entitled *Considerations on the Various Methods to Follow in the Observations of Savage Peoples* contained an exhaustive list of questions to be answered on Australian beliefs,[20] but the chosen ethnographer, François Péron, was so taken by his apparently self-ordained role of spying on the colony for Napoleon that he virtually ignored his research duties. He did claim, however, to have scientifically refuted primitivist theory by using a dynamometer to measure the respective strength of the English, French, mainland Australian and Tasmanian Aborigines. Rousseau had predicted people in a 'state of nature' would be physically superior but Péron found the first Australians to be markedly weaker and so he could scientifically counter the fatal eloquence of those inciting "sensible men... to tremble at the progress of civilization, and to sigh for that miserable condition illustrated in our days by the seductive title of a state of nature"[21] - Strong words indeed for a man who omitted to explain to Aborigines the purpose of the exercise, and who in passing confesses that he had perhaps misread the dynamometer scale.

1820-1870. From the beginning of the third decade of the nineteenth century our knowledge of Aboriginal 'customs' ('culture' was not yet an English word) at last began to widen. The more valuable reports on Aboriginal religions from this period came largely from three kinds of people. Firstly, this was the period of venturing into the interior of Australia and explorers not only found themselves making long

---

18 D. Hume, "The Natural History of Religion." In *Hume on Religion*, edited by R. Wollheim. (London: Fontana, 1969) ,p. 31.

19 W. Tench, *A Narrative of the Expedition to Botany Bay* (London: J. Debrett, 1788),p.66.

20 J. M. Degerando, *The Observation of Savage Peoples* (London: Routledge and Kegan Paul, 1969[1800]).

21 F. Peron, *A Voyage of Discovery to the Southern Hemisphere...* (London: Richard Phillips, 1874), p. 331-2.

acquaintance with their Aboriginal guides but also witnessing communities relatively untouched by the brutalities of colonial life and introduced disease. The journals of C. Sturt, T.L. Leichhardt, G. Grey and T.L. Mitchell contain many scattered references to Aborigines and while their perceptions were superficial, the data helps to fill the many gaps in our information. These works are not listed in this bibliography as they never sustain discrete sections on Aboriginal religions but E.J. Eyre's journals (0931) are listed for their nine separate chapters on the first Australians.

The second important category of informants for this period was missionaries. The first missionary to the Aborigines was William Walker, appointed to this position in 1821 by the Wesleyan Missionary Society.[22] Scholars such as D.J. Mulvaney have insisted that missionaries "stressed the abomination of savage society and spared no thought of investigating its past or recording its present"[23] but the entries in this bibliography clearly reveal that in reality our most serviceable information for this period comes from missionaries. The writings of James Manning (0985), Lancelot E. Threkeld (in Gunson 0936), H.E.A. Meyer (0950), C.G. Tiechelmann (0894) and Rosendo Salvado (0669), though impoverished by today's research standards and at worst highly condescending, were in the vanguard of charting an unknown territory. Furthermore, while admittedly they did stress "the abominations of savage society", they were mostly more enlightened than their fellow colonialists who claimed Aborigines were sub-human. Missionaries were of necessity obliged to at least concede they were dealing with a people capable of being Christianized and civilized.

The third group who provide us with some slight information for this period are the Aborigines' 'Protectors'. Useful but minute pieces of data were collected by Assistant Protector Edward Parker, but his writings, usually cited briefly by others, are not substantial enough to include below. One suspects he knew far more than he recorded for posterity, as he refuted the belief that Aborigines lacked religious sentiments once he had discovered that "a traditional mythology exists among them".[24]

The Protectors were more significant as precursors of modern anthropologists than for what they actually achieved. The Aborigines Protection Society had a primary function of protecting the rights of the indigenous peoples in British colonies but this was seen to be logically posterior to another duty. As the Society once wrote to its Australian branch, a necessary first step was to cultivate "a personal knowledge of the natives... and with that view these officers should be expected to acquire an

---

[22] see J. Woolmington, "'Writings on the Sand': The First Missions to Aborigines in Eastern Australia." In *Aboriginal Australians and Christian Missions*, edited by T. Swain and D. Rose. (Adelaide: Australian Association for the Study of Religions, 1988).

[23] Mulvaney, *op. cit.* p. 7.

[24] cit. J.H. Braim, *History of New South Wales* (London: Richard Bentley, 1846) Vol. 2, p. 241-2.

adequate familiarity with the native language".[25] For some members of the society this securing of knowledge became an end in itself, and from this beginning, and through a series of metamorphoses which I will not document here, there emerged what is today the Royal Anthropological Institute of Great Britain and Ireland.[26]

It is not surprising that forerunners of French and British anthropology had at an early stage looked to Australia, but more unexpected is the arrival of the American Horatio Hale, who was collecting comparative ethnographic data from the Pacific. His pupil, the pre-eminent American anthropologist, Franz Boas, once said Hale "contributed more to our knowledge of the human race than perhaps any other single student".[27] In his *Ethnography and Philology* volume of the reports of the United States Exploring Expedition (1838-1842), Hale wrote a section on Aborigines and what he says of their religion is brief but for its time enlightened (0937).

The fragments of data on Aboriginal traditions from this period rarely illuminate their religious life. Indeed, most writers refused to concede they had anything worthy of the word 'religion'. The terms we encounter are 'customs', 'superstitions' and 'myths'. What Collins wrote in 1798 was still acceptable by 1870. "It has been asserted... that no country has yet been discovered where some traces of religion was not to be found. From every observation and inquiry that could be made among these people, they appear to be an exception to this opinion" (0927:301). Again, in 1864, in an article in the *Anthropological Review*, F.W. Farrar provides this collage of negative opinion from Australia. "Mr. Schmidt says, 'they have no idea of a Divine Being' and Mr. Parkes, 'that they have no words for justice or for sin', and Dr. Laing [sic], 'they have no idea of a Superior Divinity, no object of worship, no idols, nor temples, nor sacrifices, nothing whatever in the shape of religion to distinguish them from the beast".[28]

There were a few dissenters such as Salvado (0669), Archdeacon Günther (cit. Thomas 1064:51), and Manning (0985), who felt they had discovered a belief in an Aboriginal Supreme Being. This evidence, deemed by some to be documentation of an Aboriginal 'religion', was used in early European anthropological debates over the unity of the human species. As religion was universally acknowledged as an exclusively human attribute, proof of Aboriginal religiosity was equally proof of their humanity. The blatantly racist polygenists took great pains to discredit

---

[25] in J. Woolmington (ed), *Aborigines in Colonial Society:1788-1850* (Melbourne: Cassell, 1973), p. 107.

[26] G.W. Stocking, "What's in a Name?: The Origin of the Royal Anthropological Institute." *Man* N.S., 8(1971).

[27] cit. J.W. Gruber, "Horatio Hale and the Development of American Anthropology." *Proceedings of the American Philosophical Society* 3(1967); 34.

[28] F. W. Farrar, "On the Universality in the Belief in God and a Future State." *Anthropological Review* 2(1864): ccxvii.

reports of an Aboriginal Supreme Being, arguing they represented mission-inspired ideas of which Aborigines really had "no comprehension".[29]

Another less racist yet deeply ethnocentric view was that Aborigines were fully human but that it was their very superstitions which, in Eyre's words, inhibited their "better feelings or impulses implanted in the human heart by nature" thus "for ever prevent[ing] them from rising in the scale of civilization" (0931:vol. 2, 384). Here we see a theme recurrent in the period from 1820 to 1870. The notion that Aborigines were in a 'state of nature' had vanished. Now they were slaves to customs which inhibited humanity's true nature, a nature which only emerged in a civilized state. There was no hope for the Aborigine, said Grey, while "complex laws... bind him down in a hopeless state of barbarism, from which it is impossible to emerge, so long as he is enthralled in these customs".[30] From this view of the relationship between custom and progress it was but a small step to the next phase in the following period of evolutionary social anthropology.

1870-1905. From 1870 until around the turn of the century, there was a huge acceleration in the accumulation of information about Aboriginal religions. The reason behind this growth was the emergence of theories of the evolution of human culture which looked to Australia as the place where they might find the key to their locked theoretical problems. E.B. Tylor, founder of modern anthropology, said the Aborigines "stand before us as a branch of the Negroid race illustrating the condition of man near the lowest known level of culture".[31] His American contemporary, Lewis Henry Morgan, said "Australian humanity... stands on as low a plane as it has been known to touch the earth".[32]

The Australian Aborigines have a prominent place in early theoretical studies of religion, such as those to be found in Herbert Spencer's *Principles of Sociology*, E.B. Tylor's *Primitive Culture*, John Lubbock's *Origins of Civilization*, and James George Frazer's *The Golden Bough*. One searches in vain, however, for more than a few sentences in a row of Australian data in their tomes. They do not write about Aboriginal religion so much as use a generous peppering of Aboriginal examples in their universalist comparative schemes. Such fragmented references to Aborigines make these works unsuitable for inclusion in this bibliography, but where these authors turn to focus on the Australian material in more

---

[29] G. Pouchet, *The Plurality of the Human Race* (London: Beavan, 1864), p. 67.

[30] G. Grey, *Journals of Two Expeditions of Discovery in North-West and Western Australia...* (London: T. and W. Boone, 1841) Vol. 2, p. 217-8.

[31] E.B. Tylor "Preface" to H. Ling Roth, *The Aborigines of Tasmania.* (Halifax: King and Sons, 1899) p. v.

[32] L.H. Morgan, *Ancient Society.* (Chicago: Charles H. Kerr, N.D.[1877]), p. 385.

detail, their publications are rightly given a place (e.g. Frazer 0028, 0029, 0084, 0085).

As the assumptions about Aborigines and religion which these scholars popularized were incredibly influential on fieldwork in Australia, it is necessary here to note at least some of their ideas. The hallmark of these notions will be found in many entries in the bibliography (even, alas, in relatively recent ones) and the new student should learn to identify and most critically evaluate them:

1. Their working assumption was that Aboriginal religions were virtually unevolved and hence had *remained unchanged* for millennia. This is demonstrably false.

2. A corollary to this was the alleged correspondence *between European peoples' pre-historic ancestors and 'primitive' peoples* in the modern world. This is a crude technological reductionism which assumes similar tools mean similarities in all domains. There is nothing to suggest Aboriginal religions are like those of prehistoric peoples.

3. 'Primitiveness' or 'lack of evolution' was said to be evinced by *simplicity*, often expressed by saying Aborigines and their cultures were *childlike*. In C.S. Wake's words "the aborigines... are yet in the condition of children".[33] This is racist nonsense and Aboriginal religion and social organization are as complex as those of any other people.

4. It was assumed Aboriginal religious beliefs were the product of childlike *reason*. This emphasis on *rationality* was doubly faulty. Firstly, their understanding of what was 'rational' was so culture-bound that Aboriginal beliefs were inevitably said to be due to erroneous thinking processes. All the earliest theories of the origin of religion assumed this. Religion began with mistaken interpretations of dreams or with over-hasty attribution of causality. Secondly, it presupposed religion was primarily an intellectual phenomena, ignoring its affective, moral, social and many other dimensions.

However unsubstantiatable these anthropological dogmas might be they were so widely accepted that they appeared as virtual truisms. The voluminous theoretical speculation in turn guided a new generation of amateur anthropologists in Australia. Even missionary researchers like G. Taplin (0893) and Carl Strehlow (0794) were constantly being interrogated by letters from abroad, and hence found themselves pressured to look for answers to secular academics' questions. The most noted fieldworkers from this period, however, happily fully identified themselves with the goals and principles of evolutionary thought.

Among the many notable ethnographers and compilers of the period are Brough Smyth who produced two volumes on Victorian Aborigines (0958), W.E. Roth, who did some very valuable research in

---

[33] C.S. Wake, "The Mental Characteristics of Primitive Man as Exemplified by the Australian Aborigines." *Journal of the Anthropological Institute of Great Britain and Ireland* 1(1872): 82.

Queensland (0315), Fraser, who confined himself to New South Wales (0934), and J. Curr, who edited four volumes of data from across the entire continent (0020). R.J. Flanagan (0933) and J. Mathew (0044) are also important figures from this era. Katherine Langloh Parker (later Katherine S. Stowe) should here be singled out as the first prominent woman researcher to give some interesting glimpses into Aboriginal women's religious life (0952).

The most famed researchers from this time, however, are W. Baldwin Spencer and Alfred Howitt. R.H. Mathews in fact provides far more of my entries than these two men combined, but while he produced a great deal of invaluable data, I sometimes wonder if he wrote over thirty articles on Aboriginal religion or wrote one article and changed his examples over thirty times!

Howitt is an excellent instance of how ethnography of this period was guided by overseas theory. By the time his interest in Aborigines first awakened he had read the works of Darwin, Lubbock and M'Lennan, but his initiation into fieldwork was guided by Morgan's investigations into the emergence of systems of kinship and marriage. Later, after Morgan's death, it was Tylor's theories of the evolution of religion which inspired his research into Aboriginal beliefs and rituals, and his mentors' opinions are clearly reflected in Howitt's findings (0938).[34]

Spencer too was greatly influenced by Tylor, but later he found an even closer alliance with Frazer, and the two men's correspondence reveals precisely how the armchair anthropologist guided the worker in the field. Spencer readily conceded that *The Golden Bough* had frequently directed the type of research questions he asked but then, in something of an inductivists' afterthought, added he had directed his colleague F. Gillen to read "no one else's work [but Frazer's] so as to keep him quite unprejudiced in the way of theories".[35]

These observations are made not to dismiss the publications from around the turn of this century but rather to alert readers to the type of mental editing needed to get the most from them. Spencer and Gillen's books on central Australia (0790, 0791, 0792) will always have an important place for students of religion, while Howitt's book on South-East Australia (0938), although imperfect, can now never be surpassed.

1905-1926. The two decades to which I now turn were a period of transition for both anthropological theory and the Western world. The two were of course interrelated. Just as social theory has undeniably been used as an imperialist weapon so too changes in Western socio-political domains have led to shifts in the social sciences. World War I is the centre

---

[34] D.J. Mulvaney, "The Ascent of Aboriginal Man, Howitt as Anthropologist." In *Come Wind, Come Weather* by M. Howitt Walker (Melbourne: Melbourne Uni. Press, 1971).
[35] R.R. Marett and T.K. Penniman (eds), *Spencer's Scientific Correspondence With Sir J.G. Frazer and Others* (London: Oxford, 1932), p.9.

of these decades under consideration and though it presented the final blow to the already waning confidence in the inevitability of a utopian conclusion to evolutionary processes, even before 1914 anthropological theory was in a state of disarray.

Reflecting the intense theoretical instability of the time - Kuhn would call it a time of scientific revolution[36] - studies of Aboriginal religions gave priority to rethinking old data rather than collecting new. Some of the previous generation, like Spencer and Mathews, continued to record and publish information, but with less enthusiasm than in their earlier works. New research, like that of G. Horne and G. Aiston (0890), and J.W. Gregory (0888) in Lake Eyre, was of a poorer quality than that of their predecessors. With the exception of A.R. Radcliffe-Brown, to whom I shall return presently, the ethnography of Aboriginal religions from 1905 until 1930 was in a recession.

Yet it was in the middle of this slump that there emerged the theoretical inspiration for the next wave of research. In 1912, Emile Durkheim published the *Elementary Forms of the Religious Life* (0079), a work which brilliantly and freshly reinterpreted the published accounts of Aboriginal religions. R.M. Berndt rightly says this book "has dogged anthropological studies on this topic" (0007: fascicle 1, p.1). In the following year, Freud ventured into anthropological territories with *Totem and Taboo*, which likewise has stimulated an immense amount of research in Australia.

To appreciate the liberating effects of such theoretical works we must begin by referring to evolutionary anthropology's antithetical opponents with whom they had come to a stalemate. Problems began when the Scottish journalist Andrew Lang began to publish a series of relentless attacks on the principle ideas of theories about the development of religion. Australian data was carefully considered by Lang (see 0093, 0094, 0095), and he felt forced to conclude that the most 'primitive' Aborigines actually were the people amongst whom students were most likely to discover High Gods. Lang was really doing no more than argue the evolutionary case backwards but when his ideas were taken up by Father Wilhelm Schmidt, it was not merely the stages of development but evolution itself which was then attacked. The German *Kulturkreise* (culture-circles) school were concerned to trace the historic spread of cultural matrixes throughout the world and when Schmidt devoted some six hundred pages of his massive *Der Ursprung der Gottesidee* to advocating the presence of an Australian Aboriginal Supreme Being (0995), anthropology and Christian apologetics came very close to merging. (The same was true for E.O. James' analysis of Aboriginal 'High Gods' (0038) in this same period.) Schmidt wrote extensively on Australia (e.g. 0061, 0181, 0788) and it is not surprising that many of his followers also turned their theoretical gaze upon these parts. Ehrlich, for example, expends considerable effort in refuting

---

36 T. Kuhn, *The Structure of Scientific Revolutions* (Chicago: Uni. of Chicago, 1970).

various theories before turning to his defence of the Schmidtian understanding of the origins of Australian beliefs (0022), while Haekel considers totemism in terms of *Kulturkreise* assumptions (0089), as do Hellbusch (0034), Milke (0101), Nieuwenhuis (0102), and Vatter (0114).

The problem with diffusionary theory was that it was no less wildly speculative than the evolutionary paradigm which it challenged. So it was that Durkheim's assertion that the quest for "the very first beginning [of religion]... has nothing scientific about it, and should be resolutely discarded" (0079:20) fell on very receptive ears. Durkheim's "functionalist" solution was to seek out "the ever-present causes upon which the most essential forms of religious thought and practice depend" (*loc. cit.*) and as is well known he discerned that ever-present cause to be a society's experiencing of its own collective existence, which, he said, was indeed an encounter with a transcendent entity. Aboriginal totems were thus no more nor less than emblems of the social group. "The god of the clan, the totemic principle, can therefore be nothing else than the clan itself, personified and represented to the imagination under the visible form of the animal or vegetable which serves as totem" (*ibid.*, 236).

These words were written at a time when the two men who were to champion functionalist anthropology, Bronislaw Malinowski and A.R. Radcliffe-Brown, were in the formative years of their careers. Both had studied and written on the Australian Aborigines but, ironically, at this point Malinowski was the armchair theorist while Brown (as he was then named) had already taken to the field.

Malinowski's "The Economic Aspects of the Intichiuma Ceremonies" (0849) and the *Family Among the Australian Aborigines* (1913) indicate that already he was moving towards a Durkheimian perspective on the role of anthropological research. By 1913, Radcliffe-Brown's views were also maturing along these lines. In 1910 he had replaced Baldwin Spencer as the leader of an expedition to Western Australia, thus becoming the first professional anthropologist to undertake fieldwork in Australia. The results of that expedition were published as "Three Tribes of Western Australia" (0668), and Durkheim wrote to the author stating the publication revealed their accord as to the general principles of their science.[37]

By 1913, the stage was set for the next phase of research into Aboriginal religions. In the following year the Australian Association for the Advancement of Science met with their British colleagues and plans were made to finance extensive fieldwork and the teaching of anthropology in Australia. Both Malinowski and Radcliffe-Brown were part of the very prestigious line-up at that conference, but World War I interrupted their designs and it was not until the Second Pan-Pacific Science Congress of

---

[37] J. G. Peristiany, "Durkheim's Letter to Radcliffe-Brown." In *Emile Durkheim: 1858-1917*, edited by K.H. Wolff (Columbus: Ohio State Uni. Press, 1960), p. 318.

1923 that their ambitions began to be fulfilled. The Congress resolved in words representative of that epoch:

> In view of the great and peculiar interest of the Australian aboriginals, as representing one of the lowest types of culture available for study, of the rigid and inevitable diminution of their numbers and the loss of their primitive beliefs and customs under the influence of higher culture, the Pan-Pacific Science Congress urges that steps should be taken, without delay, to organize the study of those tribes that are, as yet, comparatively uninfluenced by contact with civilization.[38]

As a consequence of this resolution, in 1926 Radcliffe-Brown became Australia's first professor of anthropology. He also chaired the Research Committee on Anthropology of the Australian National Research Council, and his recommendations in this capacity put approximately one dozen researchers into the field. To publish their findings he founded the journal *Oceania* in 1929. This, then, was the beginning of a new and intensive phase of research into Aboriginal religions which was guided by the concerns of functionalist anthropology.

1926-1960. Between the establishment of Australia's first anthropology department and the outbreak of World War II there came a frenzy of research which was directed towards 'salvaging' ethnographies of traditional Aboriginal societies. A.P. Elkin, who was later to fill Radcliffe-Brown's position, began his research in the Kimberley in 1927 (0081) although, like his pupils Ronald and Catherine Berndt subsequently, he did research in a range of regions (e.g. 0695, 0378). Some of the more prominent figures of this period (not all based with the Sydney Department, however, and referring only to their first field expeditions) include Phyllis Kaberry (0565), Andreas Lommel (0569), and Helmut Petri (0575) who worked in the Kimberley; W.E.H. Stanner (0393), W. Lloyd Warner (0397), and Norman Tindale (0394) in Central-North Australia; Ursula McConnel (0321), Donald Thomson (0320), and Lauriston Sharp (0322) in Cape York; Ralph Piddington (0711), Olive Pink (0783), T.G. H. Strehlow (0795), Géza Róheim (0787), and Charles Mountford (0723) in Desert regions; and Caroline Kelly (1057) and Mary Reay (1060) in South-East Australia.

With the exceptions of Lommel and Petri, who were influenced by German historicist traditions, and Kelly and Reay who were located in the radically changed environment of the South-East, these scholars were more concerned with the hypothetical pre-contact state of Aboriginal societies than in living realities. Stanner later reflected that "under the influence of Radcliffe-Brown and Malinowski I had been taught to turn my back on the

---

[38] *Proceedings of the Second Pan-Pacific Congress* (1923)Vol. 1: 36.

speculative reconstruction of the origins and development of primitive institutions", and one consequence of this functionalist approach to the operations of social systems and structures was an unfortunate neglect of dynamic processes and change. Stanner continues: "Where a society was breaking down... we thought it our task to salvage pieces of information and from them try to work out the traditional social forms".[39] While I will not pursue this matter here it should at least be noted that this focus on traditionalism largely undermined Aboriginal attempts to remodel their own societies, so there is a good measure of truth in the claim that functionalist anthropology accommodated colonialist interests and largely went to support the *status quo*.

Functionalist studies of Aboriginal religions have reflected the theoretical position of the two great advocates of that approach. The Malinowskian tradition was best represented by Piddington, Kaberry, Elkin and the Berndts. Piddington, for instance, endorsed Malinowski's broad understanding of the role of religion, stating it served "to provide psychological safeguards against failure, methods of controlling the incalculable, expressions of collective optimism, explanations for failure and disaster, and ways of securing and enforcing socially oriented co-operation."[40] Kaberry's pioneering book with substantial sections on Aboriginal women's religious life maintained a theoretical stance which was "substantially in agreement with that formulated by Professor Malinowski" (0625:xiii) and looked towards the psychological function in individual lives of donning the armour of religion. Again, readers of Elkin's well known introduction to Aboriginal societies will realize sub-headings such as "The Meaning and Social Function of the Rites", "The Value and Function of Initiation Ceremonies" or "Function of Black Magic" owe much to Malinowski's influence (0025).

Perhaps the most apparent influence of Malinowski's theories was in the analysis of mythology. Kaberry, Piddington, and in particular the Berndts, have maintained that myths are models for correct social behaviour. As the Berndts state, "myths in aboriginal Australia...are myths in the classic anthropological sense- what Malinowski called 'charters', guides to actions" (0005:83; see also 0119, 0120, etc.).

The impact of Radcliffe-Brown's ideas was at first less pronounced, in part because they were not so readily applied in a field context. More sophisticated thinkers like McConnel, Warner and Stanner nonetheless inclined towards the 'structural-functionalist' position while Radcliffe-Brown's later writings, as interpreted by Lévi-Stauss, eventually came to inspire a new generation of studies of Aboriginal religions.

Radcliffe-Brown's own writings on Australian Aboriginal beliefs and practices began very much in the Durkheimian vein. Initially, he saw

---

[39] W.E. H. Stanner, *After the Dreaming* (Sydney: ABC, 1969), p. 14.
[40] R. Piddington, *An Introduction to Social Anthropology* (London: Oliver and Boyd, 1950 and 1957) Vol. 2 :366.

himself as doing little more than writing a post-script to the great French scholar's study of Australian totemism by trying to ascertain why, short of resorting to the thesis of the arbitrary flag, certain species were chosen to represent social groups.[41] His conclusion has been dubbed the position that totems are chosen because they are "good to eat"- that is, that totemic animals and plants are things which make the social group feel physically satiated and hence socially euphoric. But even the young Radcliffe-Brown was not so naïve as this and he was well aware that some totemic species were hardly palatable. Already he had a far more cognitive understanding of the processes involved, maintaining that what was fundamental was not so much the foods themselves but rather an overriding philosophy which gave all nature significance in terms of its importance to the human social order (see Swain, 0261: 115-117).

This understanding was amplified in Radcliffe-Brown's allegedly proto-structuralist paper of 1951. Taking the widespread Aboriginal myth of Eaglehawk and Crow, he proceeded to show that the similarities and differences between the two birds mirrored the relationship between the social groups with which they were symbolically linked. Certainly there are implications for structuralist thought here but there is no radical break with the author's earlier thesis. In 1929, he summarized Australian totemism as "a mechanism by which a system of social solidarities is established between man and nature".[42] In 1951, he was merely re-affirming the mechanisms through which "the world of animal life is represented in terms of social relations similar to those of human society" (0107:21).

Radcliffe-Brown's interest in the links between human, natural and symbolic domains influenced Warner's famous analysis of 'Murngin' (Yolngu) society; the first full-length monograph on an Aboriginal community by a trained anthropologist (0937). The volume is rich in ethnographic detail on eastern Arnhem Land myth and ritual, and the theoretical stance taken is, for its time, refreshing. Rejecting the fashionable logical positivist understanding of language and symbol, Warner attempted to show the internal coherency of Aboriginal religious thought. "Murngin logic... is verifiable and grounded in reality, provided one grants them their choice of symbols" (*ibid.*:400). Not brave enough, however, to completely endorse relativism, Warner ultimately retreats into a distinction between empirical logic and social logic, and thence argues Aboriginal ritual strives to actualize what technology cannot achieve.

Ursula McConnel also leans heavily upon Radcliffe-Brown in her study of Wikmungkan myth (0330), but perhaps more significant was her attempt at *rapprochement* between the treatment of symbol in functionalist anthropology and psychoanalytic theory (0099, 0327). This brings us to

---

[41] A.R. Radcliffe-Brown, "The Sociological Theory of Totemism." In *Structure and Function in Primitive Society* (London: Routledge and Kegan Paul, 1952), p. 126-7.
[42] *ibid.*, p. 131.

the other significant scholar of this period, Géza Róheim, prolific on the subject of Aboriginal religions and the only great exponent of Freudian theory in the study of Australian Aboriginal cultures. While thorough, Róheim's first armchair analysis of *Australian Totemism* (0108) merely reiterated Freudian orthodoxy. In 1928, however, he travelled to Australia to undertake field-work, primarily with the Aranda and Bidjandjadjara. From this time on his publications depart increasingly from Freud's notion of 'totemic' religions springing from a primordial patricide inherited somehow through a race memory, and look rather towards the actual practices of child-raising in Aboriginal families. While his later theories are excessive and take huge leaps of faith in the interpretation of symbols, his data was often exceptionally useful because of the questions he asked as a consequence of his psychoanalytic position. In particular, he sheds considerable light on religious themes in Aboriginal dreams, the sexual element of mythology, the symbolism of androgyny and other all too often neglected topics.

With the exception of Róheim, functionalist thought prevailed in the study of Aboriginal religion until 1945. There was an inevitable interruption to research during the second World War, and while from its end until 1960, some good research was done (e.g. Meggitt, 0779), there was nothing suggesting a clear break with earlier studies. The 1960s, however, were a different case.

1960-1990. World War II sowed many seeds of change for the study of Third and Fourth world peoples. The War itself removed any glory from the notion of 'empires' and imperialist régimes, and one consequence of the strife of that time was a shift in power in Third World countries. People once powerless objects of study began to take over the important position of 'gatekeeper' for those wishing to write about their culture. While the process of internal-colonization is somewhat different, increasingly Aborigines too have been able to influence the type of research anthropologists perform in their communities. Again, World War II provides a point of reference, and since that time Aboriginal people have received social services, voting rights, award wages, and the freehold title to large tracts of their traditional lands.

Academics have thus been progressively forced to acknowledge the human rights of those they study. The concern with issues of ethics, given momentum by scandals like Project Camelot in the 60s[43] and, more relevant to Australia, Project Thailand in the 70s,[44] is one feature of scholarship since 1960. Complementing this has been the search for theoretical approaches which move away from the positivist ideals

---

[43] K. Gough, "World Revolution and the Science of Man." In *To See Ourselves* edited by T. Weaver (USA: Scott Foresman, 1973).

[44] P. Flanagan, *Imperial Anthropology: Thailand.* AICD Occasional Paper No. 2 (Sydney: AICD, 1971).

modelled on the natural sciences toward a humanistic and even humanitarian perspective.

At the same time there have been explosions in the number of institutions teaching subjects related to Aboriginal studies, a proliferation of Australian anthropological journals,[45] and most importantly, the formation of the Australian Institute of Aboriginal Studies in 1964. The most recent phase in the study of Aboriginal religions is marked therefore by an increase in research and the hunt for new ways of interpreting the ever-accumulating data. Some writers, such as the Berndts (0378), Tonkinson (0708), Peterson (0854), and Strehlow (0795), give priority to recording data, and while they are often insightful they could not be said to be particularly theoretically innovative. Most publications, however, tend to display the imprint of one of several recent trends in anthropological thought. The element common to each of these positions is the concern to transcend the paradigm of positive social science.

Until very recently, the most influential school of thought in the interpretation of Aboriginal religions was that of Lévi-Strauss' particular brand of structuralism. Lévi-Strauss wrote at length on Aboriginal kinship,[46] 'totemism' (0098) and mentality (0097). Taking Radcliffe-Brown's last paper on Aboriginal totemism, he sought to push the author's interpretation to what Lévi-Strauss saw as its logical conclusion: myths about Eaglehawk and Crow and 'totemic' arrangements were no more nor less than reflections of a particular mode of thought; of intellectual and philosophical systems. Mythic thought, he said, builds up structures by fitting together and binarily juxtaposing fragments of events and perceptual images in such as way as to overcome in narrative or in social order contradictions for which reality offers no solution. This much sounds promising, but in practice Lévi-Strauss' treatment of Australian (and other) data is so cavalier that he ends up, as he cheerfully admits, making his own myths about other peoples' myths.[47] Without dwelling on analytic details, I might briefly mention his well-known interpretation of the binary structure of the Yolngu *Wawalak* myth. Here he sees *Yulunggur*, the python, as representing masculinity, sacrality, superiority, and the bad (monsoonal) season while the *Wawalak* sisters stand for female qualities, profanity and the good season. It is not necessary to follow the way in which Lévi-Strauss resolves the paradox of why the 'superior' men are associated with an inferior season, as every ethnographic detail upon which this alleged dilemma is based is faulty. The monsoonal season is not seen by the Yolngu as bad or inferior, the women of that area are not profane (nor the

[45] P. Hinton and G. McCall, "The Great Australian Anthropological Periodicals Explosion." In *Anthropology in Australia* edited by G. McCall. (Sydney: The Anthropological Society of NSW, 1982).

[46] C. Lévi-Strauss, *The Elementary Structures of Kinship* (London: Eyre and Spottiswoode, 1969).

[47] C. Lévi-Strauss, *The Raw and the Cooked* (London: Allen and Unwin, 1970), p. 6.

men purely sacred), one cannot suggest men are regarded as superior, and, when all is said and done, the snake *Yulunggur* is probably female (not male, as Warner, Lévi-Strauss' source, had said), and hence not exclusively associated with men (see Berndt, 0413).

Despite his excesses, Lévi-Strauss' theories began what can only be called a fad in the study of Aboriginal traditions. This is clearly evident in the volume edited by L.R. Hiatt on Aboriginal mythology (0126), a collection Wendy O'Flaherty must have had in mind when she wrote: "A book that applies Claude Lévi-Strauss's technique to Australian mythology is looked to for proof or disproof of structuralist's formulations rather than new insights into Australian mythology."[48] Maddock has been the strongest advocate of the structuralist approach to Aboriginal religion (e.g. 0131, 0436, 0437), but Lévi-Strauss' influence is clearly evident in a host of studies from those of Berndt (0072), to von Brandenstein (0074); from Hiatt (0251) to Turner (0447). Of such works it is safe to say that as a rule their value increases the more critical and flexible they are in their use of their Parisian-born methodology.

Structuralist interpretations of myth are concerned with their meaning, and this is an orientation shared with several other post-60s approaches to Aboriginal religion. In his introduction to what is to date the most coherent general introduction to Aboriginal religions, Mircea Eliade puts forward the ideal of considering "the understanding of the meaning of a particular culture, as it is understood and assumed by its own members" (0023:xviii) and concludes that "the ultimate goal of the historian of religions is not to point out that there exist a certain number of types of patterns of religious behaviour... but rather to understand their meanings" (*ibid.*:200). Attempts have been made to reveal how Eliade's studies of religion are rooted in Husserlian phenomenology,[49] but others claim he reverts to Platonism and Jungianism[50] - his treatment of Australian High Gods perhaps tending to support the latter opinion.

Related to Eliade's *Australian Religions* is Nancy Munn's influential *Walbiri Iconography*, published in the same series in the same year, and informed by the theories of the phenomenological sociologist Alfred Schutz (0840). Munn maintained the entire Waljbiri cosmology was encoded by two graphic motifs. The circle represented the fertile site where ancestral essences 'went in' to the country, and also women's childbearing abilities. In contrast, the line is masculine, conveying mobility in space along tracks between sites. Time, too, is involved as the past is made available to the present through the 'coming out' and 'going in' cycle. There is thus a

---

[48] W. D. O'Flaherty, *Women, Androgynes and Other Mythical Beasts* (Chicago: Uni. of Chicago Press, 1980), p.3.

[49] D. Allen, *Structure and Creativity in Religion: Hermeneutics in Mircea Eliade's Phenomenology and New Directions* (The Hague: Mouton, 1978).

[50] Å. Hultkrants, "The Phenomenology of Religion: Aims and Methods."*Temenos* 6(1970):77.

continuity between the social relation of female and male, the geographic qualities of inside and outside, and the cosmological past and human present, each communicated and brought into iconographic unity by the circle and the line. This determination to extrapolate rich meaning from seemingly simple representations has spilt over not only into Morton's (0815, 0816), and Dubinska and Traweek's re-evaluations of her thesis (0828) but also into the study of Aboriginal arts more generally.

Since Munn's pioneering work, the study of Aboriginal art forms has been increasingly swayed by phenomenological and hermeneutic concerns, although this is often diffused and passes unacknowledged by writers. (This is only fair, as Husserl never made it public that Aboriginal mythology revolutionized his own thinking![51]) Layton, however, is explicit. While his earlier studies of Arnhem Land, following de Saussure, argued that myth was *langue* and ritual *parole*, his writing on Kimberley iconography has approached myth and art as text in the Ricoeurian sense (0433, 0605). Broadly speaking, the 'hermeneutics' of Aboriginal arts have focused on trying to locate the source of meaning. On one hand, this has led to an emphasis on unintentional ambiguity in Aboriginal designs which allows them to easily assume new religious significances in an ever-changing world (eg. 0606). On the other - and perhaps raising the question: how do we differentiate 'unintentional' Aboriginal ambiguity from ethnographers' ignorance? - there have been some sophisticated studies in the tradition of Munn which emphasize deliberate ambiguity and multivalent symbolism in Aboriginal art and language. Keen suggests Yolngu ritual language is 'ambiguous' in both senses; there are esoteric and exoteric meanings, but meaning is open-ended and there is always room to create deeper 'inside' interpretations (0487). Others have revealed how often we fail to appreciate the subtle, deliberately veiled, but highly significant embodiments of religious meaning in the Aboriginal arts. Like the Vitalist sculptors, they warn it is not only form but space that must be observed. Thus, says Moyle, it is the pauses *between* dances and songs that provide the rhythm for initiatory rituals (0834). Thus, say Morphy and Taylor, it is cross-hatching *within* figures that manifests the power of ancestors (0470, 0471, 0475). And thus, says Ellis (evoking Merleau-Ponty), it is the melodic contour and not the words of a song which summons specific ancestors and produces a feeling of iridescence which transposes performers into the realm of the eternal (0731).

Akin to phenomenological investigations of meaning in Aboriginal traditions are a range of analytical works which cannot be located within a single category but which share a focus upon ontology. The finest amongst them is still W.E.H. Stanner's brilliant study of Murinbata religion (0393). Frustrated when trying to pass beyond the "anterooms of meaning"

---

[51] Noted by M. Merleau-Ponty, 'Phenomenology and the Sciences of Man', in *Phenomenology and the Social Sciences,* edited by M. Natanson. (Evanston: Northwestern Uni. Press, 1964), p.102.

(*ibid*.:60), Stanner turned to the model of sacramentality in order to penetrate an alien understanding of the world. From here his investigations of myth and rite, which bear a superficial resemblance to structuralist methodology, led him to the formulation of a dozen propositions summarizing Murinbata ontology (*ibid*.:151 ff.). The basic orientation of that ontology was "the celebration of a dependent life which is conceived as having taken a wrongful turn at the beginning, a turn such as the good life is now inseparably connected with suffering" (*ibid*.:39).

Stanner's orientation has not been pursued until very recently. D. Rose's study of cosmologies in the Victoria River District has revived some of his concerns (0576, 0654), as have my own writings (0260, 0885) and those of Glowczewski (0803). Each of us, furthermore, have found ourselves, at least in part, in accord with Turner's stimulating studies of the underlying logic of Aboriginal societies. In a conscious inversion of Lévi-Strauss' position (and that of Hegel and Marx), Turner has proposed that the foundation of Aboriginal life is a view of existence which actually opposes the tendency to find syntheses to oppositions and rather nurtures ways of achieving on-going plurality (0112, 0396).

The various attempts to understand the 'meaning' of Aboriginal religious traditions rest upon a growing respect for the intrinsic value of the world-views of the first Australians. Structuralists, phenomenologists, and 'ontologists' have each been willing to accept that the Western world might learn from Aboriginal truths. While this is certainly an implicit statement of human equality, others have turned more explicitly to theories oriented towards the liberation of oppressed peoples.

Marxist studies of Aboriginal religion have unfortunately been poorly conceived. Mainstream Marxists (e.g. Mannzen, 0042) or Marxist-Leninists (e.g. Kabo, 1069) have seen religion as an ideology of those seeking to control the production and distribution of economic resources, and often lapse into evolutionary arguments long rejected in non-Marxist circles. Even Bern's relatively recent study of "Ideology and Domination" has suggested that religion is the oppressive belief structure of a gerontocracy designed to control youths and so gain exclusive rights to the means of (re-)production - women (0193). That Marxist thought need not be so simplistic can be seen in Langton's Althusserian reply to Bern, which claims he misused his theoretical sources to produce a highly androcentric interpretation (0203). More sophisticated use of Marx's concepts can be seen in Godelier's very brief re-interpretation of Yolngu mythology (0428) and most importantly, Myers' excellent studies of Pintubi society (esp. 0203).

While Marx was concerned with the liberation of subjected peoples, his legacy in the interpretation of Aboriginal religions has tended to paint a negative picture of their beliefs and practices. But Marxism has also been very influential upon feminist thought, which has produced more satisfying studies.

Feminism must be acknowledged as a discrete approach to Aboriginal religions. It should not be confused with the study of Aboriginal women's religious life (discussed in the next chapter) which has by no means always been undertaken from a feminist perspective (e.g. Róheim, 0871, Kaberry, 0625, Munn, 0840). Bell, for instance, argues that not only were earlier male researchers androcentric in their research but also that women researchers tended to internalize this model of the anthropological enterprise (in 0018:232-3). Gross too has attacked androcentric interpretations and proposes instead an 'androgynous' methodology giving women the same status as subjects as men (0198, 0199).

A central issue in feminist informed studies is the relationship between Aboriginal men's and women's domains. Bell argues that before colonization Aboriginal women were in many ways independent of men and sustained a virtually autonomous parallel culture. Women's religious life gave them direct access to the Dreaming and hence, *contra* Bern, it could not be said they had taken on men's ideological constructs (0865). Hamilton too recognizes that women have separate domains which are largely self-contained (0200), but also acknowledges that men do control women's labouring and appropriate women's ability to reproduce in their own ceremonies. She has thus recently accused Bell of romanticizing pre-colonial Aboriginal women's life and ignoring sexual domination in power relationships (0201). Others, such as White, see Aboriginal myths as reflecting male sexual aggression and hence a society which clearly acknowledges male dominance (0763). In such an uncharted area, this diversity of opinion is both welcome and healthy, and Merlan has admirably ordered the writings in this area to date (0204).

Finally, and most importantly, the period since 1960 has seen the words of Aborigines themselves being given published form. In some cases, such as Langton (0203), it is difficult to distinguish Aboriginal discourse from some White academic views, but in other instances it is clear that we are being presented with a distinct and valuable insight into Aboriginal spirituality. These works almost always reveal the contemporary face of Aboriginal religion, often considerably influenced by Western traditions. They range from co-authored books (e.g. Benterrak, Muecke and Roe, 0560) through to stylistically revised works recorded by non-Aboriginal academics such as Shaw (0577, 0578, 0579) and books of Aboriginal discourse edited by Whites (Yule, 0556). And, of course, there are pieces by Aborigines themselves (sometimes with assistant writers or editors), including those of Paddy Roe (0593), Djiniyini Gondarra (0543), Bill Congoo (0325), Eve Fesel (0236), and many others.

Having brought this survey to the present, I will conclude with a small observation. The history of the study of Aboriginal religions can be seen as a gradual, faltering progression towards the simple realization that

Aboriginal Australians are human beings who, like us, try to give significance to their life. The questions Western writers have asked about Aborigines and their religions have been, in order, as follows:

* Do they exist?
* Are they monsters?
* Do they have a religion to make them human?
* Are their beliefs the most primitive of all human notions?
* What possible function might their religion have?
* What does their religious life mean?

With the emergence of Aborigines writing about their own traditions and their experience of colonization we are, after two hundred years, only now perhaps ready for the next question:

* What are we going to say to one another?

2

The Themes

In the first chapter I concentrated upon the procession of academic paradigms which have been applied to the study of Aboriginal religions. My survey highlighted the changes that have occurred in two centuries of writing about these people in the hope that the reader will thus be guided in making allowances for the bias inherent in any one work from a particular period. But there have also been continuities in scholarship, and the history of certain persistent themes in the Western encounter with Aboriginal religions will be the subject of this chapter.

Today, concepts like totemism, myth, ritual or initiation are so familiar that we assume they are somehow intrinsically connected with the very being of Aboriginal culture. They are not. Rather their reality lies within a Western intellectual heritage and in most cases the concepts we have inherited, like any lens, both sharpens and confines our vision. In recent years, some of these categories have been questioned. Others have thus far escaped scrutiny. By placing the thematic sub-classifications I use in the bibliography in historical perspective, I intend to remind readers that this book employs a system of ordering faithful to literature about Aborigines but not necessarily true to Aboriginal societies themselves. If this helps develop a critical understanding of our academic preconceptions and thus leads to the dismantling of the very concepts whose stories I am about to tell, then I will be entirely satisfied.

GENERAL (on 'RELIGION'). The works located within the sub-classification 'General' of course mean 'Generally on religion'. We might suspect such a broad category would be unproblematic, but in fact the concept of 'religion' sits uneasily with Aboriginal thought. To explain why, it is necessary to briefly tell the history of the concept 'Aboriginal religion'.

The ancient Romans provided us with the word *religio* which initially referred either to a power or powers which as a condition of citizenship people were obliged to obey, or to a person's acknowledgement of such powers. It was only with Greek influence that *religio* emerged as something objective which might be the subject of analysis,[1] while with the advent of the Christian *ecclesia* there arose the notion of religious exclusiveness, of 'our' form of worship against that of others.[2] With Deisism in the seventeenth century there then emerged the idea of 'true' and 'false' religions. By this time, as Cantwell Smith so coherently shows, 'religion' had become "something that one believes or does not believe, something whose propositions are true or are not true, something whose *locus* is in the realm of the intelligible, is up for inspection before the speculative mind."[3]

From the time of the Deists, the implicit definitions of religion were largely those which Lord Herbert of Cherbury had pronounced universal human 'common notions' - the belief in a Supreme Being, the worship of that Being, the moral orientation of worship, the sense of sin that can be expiated, and the belief in a retributive after-life.[4] And it was because Aborigines lacked such beliefs that they were, until the 1870s, said to be totally devoid of a religious life. I have already quoted some contemporary opinions on the absence of Aboriginal religiosity in the preceding chapter. A few further examples highlight the reasons for this conclusion. Eyre, for instance, wrote about Aboriginal ceremonies, sacred objects, 'witchcraft', sorcery, initiation, mortuary practices, belief in the soul and myths, but maintained "they have no religious beliefs or ceremonies"(0931: 355) because they lacked a clear and rational belief in a Creator God. Cunningham opted for exclusion on moral grounds - their body of superstitions "can hardly be called religion, since it neither influenced them to the commission of good actions nor deters them from the perpetration of bad."[5] Others called upon their lack of worship, or their 'indistinct' notion of the after-life.

By 1871, nothing had changed except a definition. The evolutionary ethos of that time constantly sought the origin of 'higher' forms in the 'lowest' state in which they could be found, and religion too was thus studied. All that was necessary was to modify the definition of 'religion' to contain those lower forms. This was first done by that most influential founder of British anthropology, E.B. Tylor, in his book *Primitive Culture*. Having considered many claims that Aborigines (and others) lacked a religion, he saw that this was only due to a rather arbitrary delineation between forms of belief, and chose to offer a new criteria of religiosity. He wrote:

---

[1] W. Cantwell Smith, *The Meaning and End of Religion* (NY: Mentor, 1962), pp. 24-5.

[2] *ibid.* pp. 30-32.

[3] *ibid.* p. 40.

[4] in P. Gray (ed), *Deism: An Anthology* (New Jersey: D. Van Nostrand, 1968), pp. 32ff.

[5] P. Cunningham, *Two Years in New South Wales* (London: Henry Colburn) Vol. 2, p.40.

> The first requisite of a systematic study of the religions of lower races, is to lay down a rudimentary definition of religion. By requiring in this definition the belief in a Supreme Deity or a judgement after death... no doubt many tribes may be excluded from the category of religions. But such narrow definition has the fault of identifying religion with particular developments than with the deeper motive which underlies them. It seems best to fall back at once on this essential source and simply to claim, as a minimum definition of religion, the belief in Spiritual Beings.[6]

From this time onwards (with a few minor dissenters, e.g. Frazer 0029), it emerged quite clearly to observers that Aborigines had 'a religion'. By the turn of the century the idea that there might be non-religious peoples on earth had "gone to the limbo of dead controversies."[7]

There have been, nonetheless, a range of views on exactly what constitutes the essence of Aboriginal religiosity. The early evolutionists, like Tylor himself, saw religion as individual people's beliefs in spiritual phenomena. In contrast Durkheim and his followers emphasized both the social aspect of Aboriginal traditions and the affective qualities of the category of "the sacred" (0079). Others, most notably Stanner, have developed the tradition of Robertson Smith[8] and insisted upon the priority of ritual over belief (0393). What is no longer questioned, however, is that Aborigines do in fact have a religion.

Not questioned, that is, except by Aborigines themselves. Like so many of the members of the 'religions' of the world[9] they recognize the seal of post-Enlightenment Western thought on the concept 'religion'. In traditional contexts the English glosses 'Law' or 'Dreaming' are used almost to the total exclusion of 'religion', while in urban settings 'Spirituality' is the most commonly employed term (cf. Maddock 0255:566). These alternative words can also have unintended connotations to the non-Aboriginal ear, but it is clear that they each attempt to go beyond the narrow secularist concept of religion which we have applied to certain aspects of their culture. Law, Dreaming, and (to a lesser extent) Spirituality, embrace far more than 'religion'. They include the domains of what we might call geography, social relationships, political life, technology, history and many others. (See Swain, 0110).

Ironically, the study of Aboriginal religions must progress beyond the very notion of 'religion' itself. It is a little embarrassing to realize that while Western thinkers felt it was a great honour for Aborigines to be

---

[6] E.B. Tylor, *Primitive Culture* (NY: Harper, 1958[1871])Vol. 2, p. 8.

[7] F.B. Jevons, *An Introduction to the History of Religions* (London: Methuen, 1896), p. 7.

[8] W. Robertson Smith, *The Religion of the Semites* (NY: Schocken, 1972[1889]), p. 20.

[9] see Cantwell Smith, *op.cit.*

ushered into the fold of religious humanity, Aborigines themselves have largely ignored this gesture, considering it at best irrelevant, and at worst, destructive.

PHILOSOPHY AND TOTEMISM. Aboriginal 'philosophy' is a relatively new category, although much of its content has been discussed for over a century. The subject of 'totemism' is one of the main things it incorporates, but in the past few decades this concept has fallen into disfavour and so I have chosen to also reflect more recent thinking in my choice of terminology.

'Totemism', like Aboriginal 'religion', began in the early 1870s. In the first year of that decade, J.F. M'Lennan concluded his articles on "The Worship of Plants and Animals." Drawing on the Journals of Grey[10] for Australian examples to shed light on the practices in the ancient world, he proposed that "the natives represent their family names as having been derived from some vegetable or animal common in the district they inhabited."[11] And thus began the problem of Australian totemism, a problem which, despite Lévi-Strauss' proclamation that it is more illusionary than real (0098), continues even today.

M'Lennan did not publish a theory of the origin of totemism. The first hypothesis of this kind was offered by Herbert Spencer, also in 1870,[12] and again using Australian examples, while it was the Anglican scholar and theologian, F.B. Jevons, who originally suggested that totemism was the germinal form of religion, seeing it as a type of sacrament.[13] This view was initially considered to be unsupportable,[14] but three years later, in 1899, Spencer and Gillen's *The Native Tribes of Central Australia* provided Jevons with his first examples of Aborigines in fact consuming their 'totem' in a 'sacramental meal'.[15] By the turn of the century, Australian 'totemism' was an obsession. Theorists like Frazer constantly directed researchers, in particular Spencer and Gillen, towards data which might resolve totemic riddles and in this case armchair speculator and ethnographer converged to produce a joint theory of Aranda totemism (0802 and 0808). Spencer and Gillen's data was, however, also conscripted to many other theoretical causes. It was writ

---

[10] G. Grey, *Journals of Two Expeditions of Discovery in North-West and Western Australia...* (London: T. and W. Boone, 1841) Vol. 2, p. 228.

[11] J.F. M'Lennan, "The Worship of Plants and Animals." *Fortnightly Review* 6-7(1869-70):411.

[12] H. Spencer, "The Origin of Animal Worship, etc." *Fortnightly Review* 7(1870).

[13] Jevons, *op. cit.*

[14] e.g. E.B. Tylor, "Remarks on Totemism with Especial Reference to Some Modern Theories Concerning It." *Journal of the Anthropological Institute of Great Britain and Ireland* 28(1899):145.

[15] F. B. Jevons, "The Place of Totemism in the Evolution of Religion." *Folk-Lore* 17(1899):380.

large in Andrew Lang's anti-Frazerian theory (0804), a host of German diffusionist studies (e.g. 0034, 0089, 0101, 0102, 0114), both Freud's and the early Róheim's psychoanalytic interpretations (0108), and, of course, Durkheim's monumental functionalist study of Australian totemism (0079).

With the emergence of professional anthropological fieldwork it was inevitable that the notion of Aboriginal totemism would be a part of their scholarly inheritance. In 1933, Elkin attempted to clarify the now totally muddied waters with a typography of totemism*s* (in the plural) throughout Australia. Now we had individual, dream, clan, sex, section, sub-section, and moiety totemisms (0081)! A great deal of the field-research of the early professional phase added to such compendiums, so the Berndts were able later to add local, birth and multiple totems to the list of manifestations (0011).

It is hardly surprising that many began to feel the concept of 'totemism' itself was producing a false fragmentation of the data. As early as 1929, Radcliffe-Brown had stated "it may well be asked if 'totemism' as a technical term has not outlived its usefulness",[16] arguing that "totemism is part of a larger whole."[17] Elkin too had concluded his survey of totemisms by looking toward the philosophic foundation of 'totemism's' many forms (0081). Again, Stanner moved towards a broader philosophical stance, saying "totemism in Aboriginal Australia is *always* a mystical connection... between living persons... and other existents... *within* an ontology of life that in Aboriginal understanding depends for order and continuity on maintaining the identities and associations which exemplify the connection" (0393:225).

In light of this growing dissatisfaction, Lévi-Strauss' famous *Le Totémisme Aujourd'hui*, is not as radical as it first appeared, but it can take credit for making a sustained attack on 'totemism' in an attempt to put the term to rest once and for all. Having carefully analysed earlier positions, and drawing inspiration from Radcliffe-Brown in particular, Lévi-Strauss sought to dissolve the notion of 'totemism' into the the study of modes of thought in Aboriginal and other societies (0098). Original enthusiasts thought the subject was now dead, but this verdict is premature. Peterson's (0103), Hiatt's (0090) and Kessler's (0091) responses, for example, seem to suggest that if anything Lévi-Strauss may have given a last breath of life into what was already a terminally fated subject.

Scholars at present still refer to 'totemism' in Australia, although with ever-decreasing frequency. It is entirely possible to document the beliefs and practices of an Aboriginal community without employing this artificial concept, and as our appreciation of the underlying principles of Aboriginal philosophy becomes more sophisticated it is to be expected that

---

[16] A.R. Radcliffe-Brown, "The Sociological Theory of Totemism." In *Structure and Function in Primitive Society* (London: Routledge and Kegan Paul, 1952), p. 117.
[17] *idem*, "The Definition of Totemism." *Anthropos* 9(1914).

the nineteenth century notion of 'totemism' will be seen as the total anachronism that it is.

MYTH. 'Myth', like 'Totemism', has some very unfortunate connotations, but it seems likely that its usage will continue. 'Story' is perhaps a more neutral term but suffers from being overly inclusive if used without some accompanying adjective. There is also the perennial problem of distinguishing 'myth' from 'legend' and 'folk-tale' (see Hiatt, 0251:1-3). We might dismiss this as a semantic issue, but there is in fact substance to the debate. Aborigines themselves distinguish stories belonging to the class of events known as Dreaming from those which, while fantastic to the Western ear, occurred a long time ago but nonetheless within the ordinary realm of human history. Again, there are demarcations between secret and 'open' stories, cult-based narratives and those without ritual form.

For the purposes of this bibliography, 'myth' includes all stories which have significance to Aboriginal understanding of the foundations of their cosmos. But this is a kind interpretation of some authors' intentions. Many earlier works meant by 'myth' and 'legend' simply that the stories were not true.

Indeed, at first few people felt Aboriginal myths were worth collecting at all, and certainly they were not admitted into the domain of 'religion'. As late as 1911, Sir John Lubbock could say "mythology is not religion. The myths [of Aborigines] are often contradictory, childish, repulsive and blasphemous."[18] Many early investigators who asked Aborigines for stories (usually requesting information on creation and sky-beings in particular) were of a similar opinion. By the turn of the century, however, some researchers had begun to appreciate Aboriginal myth. In 1896, Katherine Langloh Parker gave us the first of her collection of Aboriginal 'legends' and 'fairy tales' collected from New South Wales (0991) and while her method of recording the texts is deficient by today's standards, it is still remarkable that she produced this data at all. Among her contemporaries, R.H. Mathews' little pamphlet on the *Folklore of the Australian Aborigines* (0987) is the work which comes closest to Parker's in quality, while a few years later the French scholar Arnold van Gennep produced a collection of *Mythes et Légendes* gleaned from the works of those working in Australia (0123).

Books of Australian mythology have of late found a growing popular audience, which causes problems in compiling bibliographies directed towards the serious student. Some, of the calibre of Mountford and Robert's *Dreamtime* series I have simply left out, trusting that readers will appreciate these can hardly be regarded as attempts to be faithful to

---

18 J. Lubbock, *Marriage, Totemism and Religion: An Answer to Critics* (London: Longmans, Green and Co., 1911), p. 154.

Aboriginal traditions. Others, such as for example those of Reed (0138, 0139, 0140, 0141), Thomas (0146) and Cotton(1073), are more likely to be consulted for reliable data and are thus included to warn the inexperienced student.

In fairness to popularists, I should add that academic interpretations of Aboriginal mythology also have a history of unreliability but at least they have in the main recorded their material with care before attempting their analytic ventures. The publications of R. Berndt (0417, 0418), C. Berndt (0412, 0413) and Heath (0431) in Arnhem Land, Capell (0586) in the Kimberley, McConnel (0330) in Cape York, Strehlow in the Central Desert (0845), Hercus in Lake Eyre (0902) and Laade in the Torres Strait Islands (0283), represent a scholarly tradition which has an acceptable degree of reliability, while the Berndts' recent collection of "myth and story", *The Speaking Land* is to date the best attempt to make anthropological expertise from a broad area available to the general reading public (0120).

The interpretation of Aboriginal mythology has occupied anthropologists since their discipline acquired its first Australian department. Functionalist studies in the Malinowskian tradition (esp. Berndt and Berndt, 0005, 0119) presented a rather uninspired image of myths as sanctions for the social orders and not surprisingly researchers have welcomed any more promising methodologies. Psychoanalytic approaches certainly have a great deal of analytical power (which is not synonymous with analytical accuracy) and Freudian ideas have been extensively and often insightfully employed by Róheim (0056, 0057), McConnel (0099), Hiatt (0127), and Morton (0816). Jung's heritage in Aboriginal studies, however, is not at all glamorous (e.g. Bennie, 0493), although Petchkovsky's work shows some promise (0389, 0442).

Once again, however, it is Lévi-Strauss who has had the most substantial impact on interpreting Aboriginal mythology. His is a Midas touch, which is a good or bad thing depending on whether one prefers analytic wealth or ethnographic life. Certainly any myth he touches will always bear his mark. Eaglehawk and Crow, since Lévi-Strauss (0098) reinterpreted Radcliffe-Brown (0107), has become a structuralist's gold (e.g. Blows, 0969) while the *Wawalak* myth seems now to be more Lévi-Straussian than Yolngu. After Lévi-Strauss (0097) lifted the myth from Warner (0397), we have been inundated with analyses of the story by Munn(0441), C. Berndt (0413), Layton (0433), Knight (0432), Hargrave (0429), Godelier (0428) and Buchler (0425).

More promising to my mind are some recent and less self-consciously methodological understandings of Aboriginal stories, foremost amongst which are the collaborative work by Benterrak, Muecke and Roe (0560), and the studies by D. Rose of post-colonial Aboriginal narratives about Captain Cook and Ned Kelly (0652, 0655). Besides placing myth within a broader and more realistic context than is usual in scholarly studies, such works have a dialogical stance which gives them an authenticity that lifts them out of the sometimes sterile and indeed incestuous academic discussion which has plagued the subject of 'myth'.

ART. Art does not have an independent existence in traditional Aboriginal societies, but a vast amount has been written on their Arts as Art - i.e. music, poetry, song, and visual art. All of these forms have a 'religious' context, but I have in no way tried to include everything written on these subjects. For extensive listings on Aboriginal visual art, the reader is referred to Marrie (0256).

My criterion for inclusion is 'meaning'. All Aboriginal 'arts' have meaning, but this meaning is not self-evident. It requires exegesis. An arrangement of stones, a carved tree, a non-representational composition of dots and lines, an engraved stone in themselves will tell us little, yet many studies confine themselves to merely describing observable and physical features. I have only included studies which give substantial information on the religious significance of the 'art' form.

The visual arts in particular lend themselves to descriptive accounts which are virtually devoid of information on their meaning. This is perhaps unavoidable in the study of some types of rock art which are no longer associated with cultic practice, although Brandl (0458), Lewis and Rose (0606), Carroll (0459), and Wright (0684) show that this is not a desideratum, while Palmer (0681) has even attempted to produce some interpretation of stone arrangements.

'Living' visual arts have been more fully documented, especially in Arnhem Land and Desert regions. Elkin, Berndt and Berndt's volume on Arnhem Land art (0464) pioneered attempts to provide serious accounts of the religious significance of iconography, a tradition which has as its highlights the works of T.G.H. Strehlow (0843), Nancy Munn (0839, 0840, etc.) and Howard Morphy (0470, 0471). General texts on art, such as those of Lommel (0160) or Black (0156) contain some useful commentary, while Berndt's iconographic introduction to Aboriginal religion obviously gives prominence to the belief and ritual accompanying art works (0007).

Of late, the subjects of Aboriginal 'song', 'poetry' and 'music' have been increasingly explored, the categories reflecting the expertise of researchers more than any real demarcations within Aboriginal thought. 'Song' and 'Poetry' require linguistic competence to be adequately represented, and, while this did not stop Harney and Elkin (0430), the results of well-qualified research can be readily appreciated. It is true especially of von Brandenstein and Thomas' delightful collection of *Tabi* verse (0689) and Strehlow's unsurpassed *Songs of Central Australia* (0845). Although to my mind of slightly lesser quality, R.M. Berndt's translations of cult (0418, 0481) and love (0454) songs have without doubt had the most impact on both academic and literary opinion.

Ethnomusicologists have only recently begun to tackle in earnest Aboriginal traditions (while dance as a subject is still in an embryonic stage). Alice Moyle has surveyed briefly the history of opinion on Aboriginal music (0163), and among the scholars who have particularly added to our understanding of the relationship between music and religion, mention should be made of the work of R. Moyle (0738, 0835), Ellis (0731, 0757), Payne (0739), and Wild (0846, 0847).

Visual art, song and music, however, mostly find their expression within a ritual context, which is our next thematic category.

CEREMONY. The study of Aboriginal ceremonial life is one area where academic thought has the potential to converge with lived religious life. Aboriginal classification of their beliefs is largely determined by their ritual context. Maddock writes:

> The popularity of the cult for study stems from the fact that it is in many ways a natural whole - it seems to be self-bounding. Commonly it has a name... one or more cycles of songs, and has attached to it a body of myths and tangible symbols, such as a musical instrument. (0255: 567)

Here we see many of our previous categories - myth, song, music, art - having their deeper roots in the ritual domain. Yet as Maddock also correctly notes, researchers have been reluctant to allow the cult to retain its integrity. Berndt, for example, discusses the *Kunapipi* cult with the main emphasis on the myths associated with it (0481). Others neglect the songs, or the social or geographical context of the performances. Maddock continues:

> In spite of seeming to be the natural unit of study, no cult has yet been the subject of a truly comprehensive published work... It is as though the student of a cult is defeated by the sheer abundance of what it offers to eye, ear and mind (0255:568).

There has also been the tendency, partially but not always entirely legitimate, to focus on particular occasions of ceremonial acts. Mortuary or initiatory ceremonies, for example, appear as discrete categories in much of the literature, and yet the songs and ritual sequences of the performances are shared with other aspects of cult life. I have nevertheless attempted to acknowledge a demarcation perpetuated by literature between rites of passage (birth, initiation, the 'higher degree', and death), and other rituals. The body of writing on each stage of passage is furthermore substantial enough to warrant separate consideration.

The general heading of 'ceremony' itself also includes a range of ritual forms. At one extreme are exchange ceremonies, most conspicuous in the north of Australia, and perhaps made more spectacular by contacts with Indonesians. Thomson (0491), Stanner (0490), and Berndt (0480) have documented these rituals, and more recently Wild has edited a volume devoted to the diplomacy ritual of *Rom* (0492).

This same region has also supported a large number of studies on the Mother cult. Baldwin Spencer was the first to refer to this (0392: 213-218), and it was subsequently documented more fully by Warner (0397) and Berndt (0481). *Kunapipi* is the name of the cult studied by the aforementioned researchers, but it has also been recorded (often in a radically transformed state) in other regions as *Gadjeri* (Meggitt, 0851), *Punj* (Stanner, 0393), and *Kurrangara* (Petri, 0648). While the *Dhuwa* moiety ceremonies of Arnhem Land (such as *Kunapipi*) have been more extensively researched, the *Yirritja Yabuduruwa* (Elkin, 0483; Maddock, 0488) is also worthy of mention here.

Studies of Desert ritual have focused on the inappropriately named 'increase' rituals most widely known by their Aranda term - *Intichiuma* (Spencer and Gillen, 0790), but also as *Banba* among the Waljbiri (Munn, 0840), etc. Their impact is certainly not merely 'magical', as Spencer and Gillen believed, and their pragmatic side in any case is not directed towards 'increasing' so much as maintaining a cosmic balance. Mention might also be made of the Fire ceremonies for the resolution of conflict in this region (Spencer and Gillen, 0855; Peterson, 0854), which have also received a reasonable degree of attention.

Other rituals, such as the South-Eastern initiatory *Bora* cults, will be referred to in later sections. Enough has been said here, however, to indicate the range of ritual forms found in the literature. The classifications commonly used - 'corroboree' (public ceremony), 'increase' ritual, commemorative rites, ceremonial exchange, 'love magic' rites, etc. - are more often than not misleading and at times obscure the data they attempt to illuminate.

There is nevertheless an as yet unfulfilled potential in the analysis of Aboriginal religious performances to develop an approach to their religious life in a way giving more weight to their own understandings of their traditions. This is not to suggest, as Stanner does, that rite is either historically or structurally prior to myth (0393), but merely that Aborigines largely classify religious phenomena in terms of its ritual occasion.

BIRTH. The rite of passage of birth, belonging almost exclusively to the female domain, has been subject to the same neglect that is symptomatic of the study of Aboriginal women's religious life more generally (see below). Parker first described the rituals surrounding birth in South-East Australia (0952), and her account indicated a far more extensive withdrawal from society than is revealed by more recent ethnographies. It has thus been suggested (Gross, 0198) that women's birth ceremonies were originally more extensive than recent accounts would indicate, but given the immense colonial impact that had already occurred in the area about which Parker wrote, this can be no more than speculation.

Even if birth as a rite of passage is, and in pre-contact times was, a relatively modest ceremony in terms of size and duration, the birth process and women's reproductive physiology have become fundamental symbols in Aboriginal transition rites. This is discussed in the following sections of this chapter. Another point to be noted here is the spiritual importance of birth, for whatever the stature of the ceremonies, birth was recognized as of profound religious significance as an essential channel connecting immortal and atemporal ancestral life essences to the world of ordinary life. Which brings us once again to a controversy.

Birth among Aboriginal people has quite correctly been documented in relationship with beliefs about the spirit or soul. But the discussion has lost all proportion and relevance by being sidetracked from the outset by a rather fruitless question - do Aborigines understand the physiological relationship between intercourse and conception and the father's role in providing semen?

The debate began when Frazer, having faithfully summarized the inaccuracies of the available literature, concluded that Aborigines were totally ignorant of physiological paternity. He then offered the theory that totemism was nothing but confusion over the nature of conception (0029: 160), and he used this alleged ignorance as proof of the primitiveness of Central Australian Aborigines in particular. To this, Andrew Lang replied: "denial of procreation is not a 'proof of pristine ignorance', but a philosophic inference from philosophic premises" (0174: 190). The argument, while voluminous, never advanced in quality much beyond this point. Many evolutionists were drawn to the issue, as were psychoanalytic anthropologists like Róheim (0180), who recognized that nescience of the relationship between coitus and birth would undermine the biological foundation for the universality of the Oedipus complex.

By 1937, the data had become so tangled that Montagu devoted an entire book to resolving the controversy, a book which, in its second edition of 1974, ran to over 400 pages (0178). Having thoroughly researched both the theoretical opinions and the ethnographies, Montagu concluded confidently that Aborigines declared intercourse was not the cause of conception, although it may have a preparatory role.

Perhaps the story might then have faded into the obscurity it deserved but alas, a passing remark by Melford Spiro, to the effect of "no, they don't", led to Edmund Leach's "yes, they do" (0175), Spiro's rejoinder ("don't, don't, don't", 0182) and so to Dixon (0346), Kaberry (0616) and a host of others[19] then reviving this tedious debate.

And thus we were inflicted with another book, this time by

Mountford, attempting to convince us that Aborigines really are ignorant of physiological paternity after all. Mountford's volume is far inferior to Montagu's, and Stanner's Foreword to the work as politely as possible tries to warn the reader just how naïve Mountford is if he thinks his publication will end the dispute (0179).

It is unfortunate that so much effort has been wasted in confronting this shadow of a phenomena whose substance has thus largely been ignored (but see Merlan, 0176). This is evident even at the level of the language which surrounds the topic; we have been less concerned with what Aborgines believe than with that of which they are said to be ignorant. How often have Aborigines been pestered by trivial queries about biology when they are attempting to explain to the researcher something far more profound? I conclude with Warner's embarrassing awakening to his own failure to appreciate what he was being told (0397: 23-4).

> An occasion arose in which I could inquire of certain old men just what the semen did when it entered the uterus of a woman. They all looked at me with much contempt for my ignorance and informed me that "that was what made babies." I had not been able to obtain this information earlier because the [Yolngu person] is far more interested in the child's spiritual conception... than he is in the physiological mechanism of conception.

INITIATION. The rite of passage of initiation - what Aborigines often refer to (in the case of boys) in English as "the making of young men" - was one of the first things Europeans discovered about Aboriginal religious life. In 1814, Flinders observed "the most remarkable circumstance... [among the northern Aborigines was] the whole of them appeared to have undergone the Jewish and Mahomedtan rite of circumcision",[20] while even Dampier had commented on the practice of tooth avulsion, a practice of which the explorer, Mitchell, later said "it would be very difficult to account for a custom so general and so absurd otherwise than by supposing it a typical sacrifice."[21] As early as 1798, Collins had published an account of an initiation ceremony he had partially

---

[19] E.G. Schwimmer, "Virgin Birth." *Man* N.S. 4(1969); R. Needham "Virgin Birth." *Man* N.S. 4(1969); H.A. Powell, "Virgin Birth." *Man* N.S. 3(1968); K. Burridge, "Virgin Birth." *Man* N.S. 3(1968).

[20] M. Flinders, *A Voyage to Terra Australis...* (London: G. and W. Nicol, 1814) Vol. 2: 212.

[21] T.L. Mitchell, *Three Expeditions into the Interior of Eastern Australia* (London: T. and W. Boone, 1939) Vol. 2:345.

witnessed two years earlier at Port Jackson, and while he was not admitted to the secret domains, his text and illustrations are testimony to the rapid realization among Europeans that Aborigines at least had such ceremonies.

In the past two hundred years, however, what has been written on initiation has not progressed in sophistication as much as might be expected. Indeed, it has tended to be something of a frontier subject, written about superficially but a great deal when ethnographers first encountered a new region or people, and then becoming less discussed as they became more 'at home' in the area. It is as though initiation becomes an investigator's own rite of passage.

In accord with this observation, we can see that the largest number of studies devoted to initiation are to be found in the early reports on the South-Eastern *Bora* (and cognate terms) cults. Besides the many writers reporting on the occasional ceremonies they had been allowed to witness (e.g. Gunn,1017; Fraser,1016; Cohen,1014), there were also the extensive surveys to be found in the writings of the rivals Howitt and R.H. Mathews. Howitt could stand as a symbol of anthropology of his time. We can piece together biographical details of his 'initiation' into Aboriginal secret cults - his early publications which are those of an outsider (0932:194-199) to his being taught the role of the bullroarer (0938:510) which he in turn used to gain access to secret rituals (*ibid* : 517).[22] Yet his publications at best merely describe the manifest ritual behaviour of the ceremonies, a limitation also present in Mathews' work. Mathews claimed to have a substantial amount of information on the significance of these cults, but if he did they were never published.[23]

The ice-breaking role of the study of initiation is also evident in Spencer and Gillen's Central Australian investigations (0862), the reports of early professional investigations in remote north-western Australia (Elkin, 0618; Piddington, 0753), Cape York (Thomson, 0320), and the Western Desert (Tindale, 0755). (In Arnhem Land initiation is contextualized in the broader major ritual cycles - *Djungguan*, *Kunapipi*, *Ngurlmag* and the *Narra* of the respective moieties.)

There are, of course, other more recent accounts of initiation which form part of larger ethnographies, the best perhaps being that of Meggitt (0779), but even these leave the reader dissatisfied as to their import and religious meaning. For analytic and interpretative accounts one must turn to the general texts, like those of Elkin and the Berndts (0025, 001), where one will find some mention of the significance of the metaphors of death and (re)-birth in initiation ritual, a theme more fully developed by Eliade (0023) and, following him, Hiatt (0127, 0171).

---

[22] see D.J. Mulvaney, "The Anthropologist as Tribal Elder." *Mankind* 7(1970).
[23] A.P. Elkin, "R.H. Mathews: His Contribution to Aboriginal Studies; Part II." *Oceania* 46(1975): 143.

WOMEN. It might seem strange to interpose the theme of 'women' at this point. I am *not* referring to a post-initiatory rite of passage in which men "acquire wives", as marriage is not celebrated as a religious occasion by Aborigines. Rather, at this juncture I wish to redress an imbalance which has been evident in particular in the literature on the preceding three categories, although it less obviously permeates other areas as well. When we read of 'ceremony' or 'initiation', more often than not the text refers exclusively to men's rituals while, remarkably, 'birth' as a category has also tended to focus upon men's beliefs and views on what women do (a subject which Aboriginal men often display obvious discomfort in discussing insofar as it is not their domain).

Feminist anthropology has recently made, and continues to make, a sustained attack on this state of affairs, but a partial redress has occurred simply by the advent of women researchers or the occasional man who wondered what had happened to half the world in publications on Aboriginal religion.

Yet the issue goes deeper than a simple case of oversight. Women were quite explicitly said by some scholars to be barred from the realm of the sacred in keeping with their allegedly generally inferior social position. Warner was a champion of this position, arguing that while men made a life progression through the realm of the sacred, women were bound to the arena of the profane (0397). Predictably, in arguing his case Warner does not present any data on women's religious life, but Róheim's was a more informed misrepresentation. To his credit, he at least offers useful information on Central Desert women's beliefs and ceremonies, but he turned his back on his own data to conclude that these women were virtually devoid of true religion and possessed little more than an elaborate fear of demons (0871).

It was interpretations such as Warner's and Róheim's that Phyllis Kaberry sought to repudiate in her aptly titled volume *Aboriginal Woman: Sacred and Profane*. Obviously, she was not the first to refer to women's religious life. I have noted earlier the work of Parker (0952), and by the early twentieth century Joyce and Thomas could collate a surprising amount of information, albeit garbled, on the traditions of Aboriginal women (0202). What Kaberry undertook that was particularly significant was not merely an entire volume devoted to women, but also consciously to refute common misconceptions about their place in Aboriginal society.

Yet, as Bell notes (in 0018:243), Kaberry assumed a somewhat defensive stance which resulted in her accepting much of the male image of what women's religion might be like. Her understanding of religion was simplistic - "Man [sic] dons the armour of religion because it offers him [sic] a protection against fate and misfortune" (0625:158) - and it was her task to prove women were equally in need of such armour. Kaberry did not satisfactorily explore the unique qualities of women's heritage. Rather, they were merely incorporated into the common paradigm of Aboriginal men's religious orientation.

Other women writers, such as C. Berndt (0624), Goodale (0500), and Munn (0840), do *not* self-consciously develop feminist perspectives. Munn, unlike Kaberry, explored the defining differences between men's and women's religiosity; the former being wider ranging and concerned with the maintenance of broader cosmic structures, the latter focused on the domestic religious domain - a view to which Bell has taken particular exception. We might suspect she would equally oppose Myers' view that men's traditions have greater societal value insofar as they transcend territory and kinship relations in contrast to women's more localized rituals (0703:252-3).

Bell's own position belongs to a class of scholarship which she calls "Towards a Feminist Perspective" (in 0018:244) and which seeks to fathom the origins and mechanisms of the dogma of male dominance. I have already briefly discussed feminist-informed theoretical approaches to Aboriginal religions in the preceding chapter. Suffice it to say that Aboriginal women's religious life is currently a vital topic, theoretically diverse, controversial and destined to retain its prominence for some time to come.

MAGIC. Beyond initiation for young men and women there are, in Aboriginal societies, opportunities for individuals to be further inducted and thus acquire an exceptional degree of spiritual power. Eliade (0211) would call them 'shamans', Elkin, people of 'high degree' (0213). 'Wizard', 'witch-doctor', 'sorcerer', 'medicine-man', and more recently, 'traditional healer', are other cognate terms used at one time or another throughout the two centuries of literature.

The powers of these individuals are, in less spectacular form, accessible to the majority of adult Aborigines; and the most common concept which researchers have used to draw these phenomena together into a manageable form has been 'magic'.

While Frazer's *The Golden Bough* has fallen into scholarly disrepute, we have nonetheless, and largely unconsciously, inherited his concept of magic as a false science resting on erroneous principles of causality. The Aranda, Frazer said - and from his first-hand experience Baldwin Spencer agreed[24] - were magicians *par excellence*. "Roughly speaking, all men in Australia are magicians, but not one is a priest" (0029:162). While Frazer's evolutionary progression from magic through religion to science was readily abandoned, his understanding of what defined magic has been widely employed. It was, for example, very apparent in Haddon's reports on Torres Strait magic (0265, 0266, 0295).

---

[24] cit. R.R. Marett and T.K. Penniman (eds), *Spencer's Scientific Correspondence with Sir J.G. Frazer and Others* (London: Oxford, 1932) p. 75.

While initially offered as an alternative definition, Durkheim's view that magic (*contra* religion) is an individual affair (0079) has tended to be overlaid upon Frazer's views, and while Warner took great pains to refute Durkheim by pointing to the social role of Yolngu magic (0397), the stereotype of the 'magician' has been, and in some cases still is, that of an individual or very small group performing ritualized actions for clearly defined pragmatic results.

And yet, despite this condescending positivist image, there have always been those enchanted and drawn to these Aboriginal practices. It is quite evident, if not actually explicitly stated, that in Eliade's view of Aboriginal 'shamans' (0211) or in Elkin's comparisons of Aboriginal men of high degree with (alas, unreliable) reports of Tibetan supernatural feats, the authors are convinced that there is substance to Aboriginal assertions. McElroy tested the psi capacities of Aborigines but was honest enough to report his negative results (0509). Ronald Rose claimed positive evidence, but the author should have concealed his methods of fabrication with more care (0221), while Thero, I'm sure, made up everything he wrote (0223).

Aboriginal 'magic', now mostly given more respectable but less inclusive rubrics (e.g. 'medicine') is today universally acknowledged to have some real effects, although authors are divided as to whether this be sociological, medical or metaphysical. Psychoanalytical and/or ethnomedical studies, such as those by Reid (0510, 0511), Cawte (0209), and Biernoff (0505), as well as the work of McKnight (0355, 0357), have of late provided much valuable information. This is an area of research destined to expand and, given current demand for non-Western means of healing and New Age enlightenment, to appeal increasingly to (and be written for) a large reading audience.

DEATH. The final rite of passage is death, and it is a subject which has been inadequately investigated. Aboriginal methods of disposing of the corpse have attracted considerable attention, but often little information is provided as to what the ceremonies signify to the participants. In the South-East, early reporters noted that most corpses were burned, but some were cremated. This was mentioned as early as Collin's account of 1798 (0927), while B. Hiatt has mapped the distribution of cremation in the area (0229). Yet we look in vain for convincing explanations for the variation in mortuary practice within this region.

Death is a ritual process which leaves a substantial record for archaeologists, and perhaps it is the archaeological influence on this subject which has in part led to its presentation as a less than vital religious expression, although in fairness one must add that Haglund (1051) and, in particular, Pardoe (1053), have attempted to extract some meaning from the mute records of the past.

Several ethnographic accounts of mortuary practice are particularly outstanding. Warner's is one (0397), while Turner (0395) has an excellent section on Groote Eylandt funerary ritual. Meggitt's chapter on the subject (0779) provides a reliable and thorough chronology of Waljbiri funerals, although it is short on reflection on symbolic processes. Clunies Ross and Hiatt (0518), Keen (0522), and Morphy (0547) provide valuable observations on the role of sand sculptures in the Yolngu socio-religious understanding of funerary ritual. To date, the richest single account of a funeral is that of Morphy which attempts to locate the death of one child of the Madarnpa clan within the network of social and religious relationships constituting the Yolngu world (0523).

Broader interpretations of mortuary practice are found primarily in general survey books. Eliade, for instance, sees death, like birth, initiation and the making of traditional healers, as a ritual process recapitulating cosmogony. "Once again [at death], though for the last time, man does what was done in the beginning by a Supernatural Being. With every new death, the primordial scenario is re-enacted" (0023:171). The Berndts, in partial contrast, emphasize that while death is materially an absolute end, Aborigines are equally concerned with spiritual continuation, even if individual human personalities as such do not endure (0011:488). Maddock in turn pursues the significance of the separation of body and spirit at death and explores the ways Aborigines conceptualize this cardinal human predicament in order to achieve some control over human destiny (0041: chap. 7). Maddock's is arguably the best general overview of death currently available, but is hardly an exhaustive study. This is an impoverished area of study very much in need of fuller investigation.

CHANGE. Everything known by Europeans about Aboriginal religion has been recorded since invasion. Maddock opens his study of Aboriginal society with the statement: "one has... to add L.R. Hiatt's observation that anthropologists in Australia have moved behind the advancing frontier to A.W. Howitt's observation that the frontier in Australia has been marked by a line of blood" (0041:ix). Entire communities were murdered, or died of introduced diseases; many 'tribes' were severely reduced before researchers ever encountered them. In the South-East it is estimated the population had been culled by a staggering 96 percent a full generation before the first serious ethnographic accounts of the region were produced.[25] And yet until the 1960s, virtually every report was written about the alleged nature of 'traditional' Aboriginal societies. Scholars simply ignored the fact the people they consulted lived on missions, stations and government reserves and maintained a radically transformed culture. The theoretical and political reasons for this state of

---

[25]N. Butlin, *Our Original Aggresssion* (Sydney: George Allen and Unwin, 1983).

affairs have been briefly alluded to in the preceding chapter, and here I confine myself to a survey of studies of change in Aboriginal religions.

Writers suspected change long before they would study it. Thus, during the first academic debate concerning the possibility of mission influence on Aboriginal traditions, which began in the mid-nineteenth century, those advocating the existence of syncretism in South-Eastern Australia made such claims only to deem these beliefs polluted and hence inadmissible anthropological evidence (Swain, 0261:34-39, 79-85, 93-98). It was simply unthinkable that this adulterated data itself deserved to be studied.

During the early phase of professional anthropology, those interested in changing traditions were mostly marginal to institutionalized functionalist scholarly circles. Thus Thomson, investigating Melanesian influence on Cape York religion (0320), had his views refuted by McConnel (0339), while Lommel (0646), who advocated European impacts on Kimberley cults, was severely upbraided by R. Berndt (0635). Admittedly, Elkin always maintained an open attitude towards the pressures of diffusion, but he tended to locate these in the distant past and never pursued the actual history of contact.

Some readers might be surprised to discover the majority of new movements appear to occur in the Kimberley, but the truth is that this is simply where the majority of the literature on the subject is based. Petri and Lommel were schooled in German historicist traditions and had a far keener eye for changing patterns. Indeed, much of the literature on religious dynamics came from the hand of writers with continental backgrounds, beginning with Siebert (0892), through Petri and Lommel, to Frederick Rose (0768) and, more recently, Kolig (0639, 0640, 0644) and Glowczewski (0883). This is more than coincidence.

With the 60s and the demise of static functionalist models, change became a fashionable topic. The volume *Aborigines Now: New Perspectives in the Study of Aboriginal Communities* captured the mood of that decade and contained Calley's justly famous piece on Bandjelang Pentecostalism (1055), while at much the same time R. Berndt published the first (and to date only) monograph on an Aboriginal movement inspired by Christianity (0530).

Since the 60s there has been a gradual growth of data on new religious movements. For the Kimberley, Kolig (0644) has produced a substantial work on the Fitzroy Crossing area, while Akerman (0634) and D. Rose (0652, 0654) have likewise considered various aspects of religious reform. Wallace (0772), Tonkinson (0707, 0771), Glowczewski (0883) and I (0885) have each considered new forms of Desert religion, Thompson has written on Cape York Aboriginal Christianity (0368), Bos (0537, 0538) and Morphy (0548) have discussed Arnhem Land, I have re-examined the data for South-East Australia (1062), and Beckett (0300) and

Fitzpatrick-Nietschmann (0304) have analysed the mission impact in the Torres Strait Islands .

Until very recently, however, research into change in religion has been rather piecemeal and unsustained. A symposium on 'Contemporary Aboriginal Religious Movements' was held at the Australian Institute of Aboriginal Studies in 1981, but the proceedings were not published. Kolig (0238) and Wild (0246) have attempted overviews of modern movements, but to my mind there is a lack of insight in both of their pieces. The largest single contribution to this area of study has been a collection of over thirty original articles on the mission impact on Aboriginal cultures which D. Rose and I co-edited (0245), and which hopefully sets the stage for a great deal more research in this vastly understudied area.

LITERATURE. Finally, it is a sign that any field of study has attained a discrete autonomy, although alas not necessarily a mellow and rich maturity, when participants begin to reflect upon that field itself rather than its contents. Aboriginal Studies reached that stage some time ago,[26] but Aboriginal Religion has but recently come to that point. When I published a history of the study of Aboriginal religion in 1985, there was no comparable work (0261) but since then Maddock (0255) and Morphy (0258) have both charted the history of this subject and other more confined studies have also been written. This bibliography itself is of course another contribution to this process of taking stock of scholarly achievement.

---

[26] A.P. Elkin, "The Development of Scientific Knowledge of the Aborigines." In *Australian Aboriginal Studies*, edited by H. Sheils (Melbourne: Melbourne Uni. Press, 1963), is perhaps the best of Elkin's many reviews of the history of Aboriginal Studies. His earliest was "Anthropological Research in Australia and the Western Pacific, 1927-1937"*Oceania* 8 (1938).

3

The Regions

Australian Aboriginal religion? Australian Aboriginal religion*s*? Which is it? The preceding chapters tend towards the impression that the answer should be in the singular. Theoreticians more often than not attempted to interpret and analyse the ritual and belief of the continent as a whole, often totally ignoring the fact that the phenomena of which they spoke were geographically highly confined. Eliade's discussion of High Gods (0023:Chap. 1), for example, is perhaps comparable with the popular stereotypes which see digeridoos, bark paintings and returning boomerangs as something co-terminous with Aboriginality. Clearly there are dangers in this type of thinking. After all, it was not until Europeans circumnavigated the Great South Land and found it a single landmass that the concept of *the* Australian Aborigines began as a possibility. It hardly reflected a pre-colonial sense of identity, although of course today Pan-Aboriginal (and Islander) movements have emerged in response to a changed socio-political environment.

The supposed commonality of Aboriginal religiosity is also reflected in the themes discussed in chapter two. It is often simply assumed that Aboriginal peoples share a core of mythic orientation, ritual and philosophy. The 'Dreaming' is seen as ubiquitous, although it is primarily a Desert concept in its linguistic origin. 'Totemism' is apparently something all Aborigines participate in. Secret male initiation ceremonies are implied to be universal (although in fact there are regions like Groote Eylandt where, in historic memory, there were no secret cults at all [Turner, 0396]). 'Corroboree' is now used to describe all Aboriginal public ceremonies, thus providing them in a single semantic stroke with an unproven unity. Examples could be expanded almost interminably.

I am not saying there is no substance to the claim that Aboriginal religions share a common essence. Frankly, I think it true. The people of a continent traversed by efficient trade networks,[1] yet heavily insulated from the rest of the world during a history of at least 40,000 and perhaps as many as 100,000 years, is bound to have its own distinctive cultural character.   But there are nonetheless differences, indeed, substantial differences, between, and even within, the various 'cultural blocs'.

Demarcating these blocs is itself an issue upon which opinion varies.   Without a doubt climate and ecology play an important role. Peterson has suggested drainage basins provide an accurate guide to the demarcation of culture-areas, but from the point of view of the student of religion his divisions are overly fragmentary.[2]   In contrast, the regions used by the Australian Institute of Aboriginal Studies, while in the main at least being faithful to the often loosely defined divisions found in the literature, at times employ rather arbitrary boundaries.

The lines of demarcation and the subsequent cultural-areas I adopt are something of a compromise between the divisions in natural, cultural and literary worlds.   There is overlap, but never perfect accord.   Like Peterson I have consulted maps of drainage divisions but saw no reason to adopt his fine grading.   The map of drainage divisions in the *Atlas of Australian Resources*,[3] for example, is easily aligned with the language families identified by O'Grady, Voegelin, and Voegelin,[4] the main differences in the latter being a division in the uncoordinated drainage systems of the Western Plateau to separate the Central and Western Deserts, and the addition of several borders in the external drainage areas that skirt the continent from the north-west, via Cape York to the South-East. These occur at 'bottlenecks', where the coast and inland limits of the external drainage regions converge, thus demarcating the Kimberley, the Central-North, Cape York and the South-East.   The main instance where I have ignored both natural and cultural boundaries is in the South-East, in which case I have allowed my main guide to be the rather loose understanding of the limits of that area employed by earlier (and some later) writers (e.g. Howitt, 0938).   This, however, has only meant the convergence of the south-eastern coast and the Murray-Darling areas.

Including the Torres Strait Islands and Tasmania, the result is a total of ten regions.   Using Oates and Oates' linguistic survey of Australia-whose spelling of 'tribal' names I also employ- as a guide,[5] I then plotted

---

[1] F. D. McCarthy, "'Trade' in Aboriginal Australia and 'Trade' Relationships with Torres Strait, New Guinea and Malaya." *Oceania* 9(1939) and 10(1939).

[2] N.Peterson, "The Natural and Cultural Areas of Aboriginal Australia." In *Tribes and Boundaries in Australia* edited by N. Peterson (Canberrra: Australian Institute of Aboriginal Studies, 1976).

[3] in R.F. Warner, "Hydrology." In *Australia: A Geography*, edited by D.N. Jeans (Sydney: Uni. of Sydney Press, 1977), p. 54.

[4] in W.J. and L.F. Oates, *A Revised Linguistic Survey of Australia* (Canberra: Australian Institute of Aboriginal Studies, 1970), p. xii.

[5] *ibid.*

my boundaries on both the maps of Tindale[6] and that of O'Grady, Wurm and Hale,[7] and then located works within this bibliography accordingly. (See map on p. 65).

While a bibliographer must give precedence to the reality of the publications being classified, and while I have thus constantly kept an eye to ensuring the literature itself was well served by the regions I use (i.e. that these are the areas writers see themselves as working within), it is nonetheless evident that each of the various areas has its own distinctive traditions - I have said that climate and ecology play a part, and obviously drainage basins and Aboriginal cultures share boundaries, but we need not thus immediately embrace a theory of environmental determinism. For it was the relatively lush country of the South-East which attracted colonizers to that region. The monsoons of the north brought not only rain but Indonesians. The latitude of Cape York changed the climate, but also put it close to Melanesian peoples. The Deserts, in contrast, are not only a harsher environment for Aborigines, but are also harsher for later comers and further from the coast on which contacts first occur. In brief, climate not only influences Aboriginal cultures but also the process of historical association with non-Aboriginal peoples.

In the following pages I discuss each of the regions in turn in the order in which they are set out in the bibliography. Beginning in the north-east with the Torres Strait Islanders we travel in an anti-clockwise arc, from Cape York across the north and then returning through the Deserts to the South-East and Tasmania. My focus in each case is not only on the (perhaps climatically induced) specific features of the region in question, but also on unique historic influences due to its geographic location and the process of change since the colonial period. In discussing these factors I evaluate the quality of literature for each of the zones in question.

TORRES STRAIT ISLANDS. Except for the fact that Torres Strait Islanders have come under Australian political control and thus are a part of an emergent Pan-Aboriginal and Islander identity, they would not warrant inclusion in this volume. While the Western Islanders have linguistic affinities with Aborigines, their origins, according to their own traditions (Laade, 0282), are Melanesian and Polynesian and their culture too is essentially of that kind. That their rituals include, for example, wooden human effigies (*madub*) associated with the success of their gardens, should suffice to indicate the magnitude of the gulf between them and their hunter and gatherer neighbours. Nonetheless, there are affinities and shared heritage. The Yolngu of East Arnhem Land have one of the

---

[6] N.B. Tindale, *Aboriginal Tribes of Australia* (California: Uni. of California Press, 1974).
[7] O'Grady, Wurm and Hale, "Aboriginal Languages of Australia." Map reproduced to accompany Oates and Oates, *op. cit.*

islands in the Torres Strait as the land of their *Yirritja* moiety dead (Berndt, 0517), while the Hero-cults of Cape York have passed from Papua New Guinea into Australia via the Islands (Thomson, 0320).

Our knowledge of this area's religious life is very unsatisfactory. With the exception of anthologies of myths (Lawrie, 0285; Laade, 0283), we are almost fully dependent upon the reports of the Cambridge expedition to the Islands in 1893. Haddon and Rivers' (0274) investigation of 'totemism' provides one link between the Western Islands and Australia, although the Eastern and Central areas lack this orientation. For the West, they noted that people identify themselves with their 'clans' *augug*, which they are not permitted to kill or consume, and for which they perform 'increase' ceremonies. Haddon considered that the localized 'totemic' traditions were in more recent times overlaid with the Hero-cult. In the Western Islands this was associated with inter-island warfare and 'totemism' remained, but in the East the general and peaceful association with the common cultural Hero was virtually to the exclusion of segmentary religious principles.

The members of the Cambridge expedition had difficulty in eliciting information on traditional religious life. Although the London Missionary Society had arrived only 27 years earlier, much had been suppressed. Islanders themselves say their "heathen darkness" was dispelled in an instant (Beckett, 0300:212-3). This perhaps overstates the case, but the fact remains that pre-contact Islander religions were never observable to Western investigators and the best studies of religion in this area have been those accepting this state of affairs and hence focusing on religion as contemporarily practiced.

Beckett's "Mission Church and Sect" pioneered this approach among the Islanders. He argued for three layers in their Christian history. The first was a mission régime bent on diverting indigenous effort into capitalist labour pools; the second was the Anglican church which was seemingly benign but had a softly oppressive irrelevance; while finally, the Assemblies of God Pentecostal sect is said to have appealed as a religion of dissent and as a radical anti-colonial movement (0300).

Other recent researchers have attempted to illustrate continuity in change. Kitaoji has thus argued from a structuralist vantage point for the contemporary relevance of the myth of the Heroes *Bomai* and *Malu* (0280), while Fitzpatrick-Nietschmann maintains that while Christian ceremonial forms were accepted these were in fact camouflaging a persistent traditional content (0304).

CAPE YORK (AND THE GULF). There have always been affinities between the religion of the Islanders and those of the people in Cape York Peninsula, maintained in the past by trade routes, today by a shared experience of government and church.

Thomson's account of religious life among the Koko Ya'o, for instance, has several points of convergence with Haddon's interpretation of the traditions of the Western Islanders. Haddon had recorded beliefs concerning the culture Hero *Kuiam* who had travelled to the Islands from Australia, and Thomson in turn relates the Cape York narratives of *Iwai* and *Sivirri*, a crocodile and a seagull, who amongst other things are the instigators of the initiation ceremonies in the area (0320:488). According to Thomson, their cults, which share with those of the Islanders and Papuans a great deal of unique - by Australian standards - ritual paraphenalia (e.g. drums and shelters resembling Melanesian clubhouses), migrated to Australia long ago and have evidently overlaid more ancient traditions which approximate those to be found elsewhere in Australia. *Iwai* had not only been incorporated into the 'totemic' order (to adopt Thomson's choice of term) but had been regarded as *tjilbo*, an honorific meaning 'old man', among the Ancestral Beings.

The recognition of Ancestors to whom all people are spiritually linked is one of the most common Aboriginal responses to radically different classes of strangers. The All-Fathers of the South-East and All-Mothers of the north are discussed below in this regard. The Heroes of Cape York never become fully transcendent Beings, however; that is, they were denied the status of being the spiritual parent of all people and with whom all humans thus stood in a single unified relationship. It is because the Hero-cult, despite its wide cultural significance, was localized within one clan that Thomson saw it as being largely brought within the normal 'totemic' scheme. McConnel, who worked further to the south with the Wikmungkan, went so far as to say the Hero-cults were entirely in accord with religious systems elsewhere in Australia and hence largely indigenous in origin (0339), but in arguing this she was unduly reluctant to recognize the important modifications to belief and practice highlighted by Thomson.

In the Cape region, the spiritual affiliation linking people and land was largely patrilineal. Ancestral Beings and the potent essences giving rise to all life were also associated with these places. *Iwai* himself was a part of this order, although his association was apparently more with abstract principles (e.g. 'sexual licence') than specific species (Thomson, 0320: 503). Rites were performed by the people of a land to either increase *or* decrease species populations, thus highlighting the fact that 'increase' ceremony is a misnomer for rites directed towards maintaining the cosmological balance established by Ancestral Beings. In Thomson's data there appears another 'aberrant' feature. Despite the patrilineal association between Ancestors, sites, and living people, a person's own spirit does not emerge from that land. There were apparently no 'spirit children' associated with sacred sites which impregnated women, but rather the *ngorntal* is linked with the mother's country, and what Thomson calls the 'personal totem' is consequently not inherited immediately upon birth (*ibid*.:493ff.). Thomson suspected an older strata of matrilineality being conflated with a later, Islander influenced, patrilineality. Certainly there are conflicting principles at work, but as McConnel found patrilineality in the areas further to the south (0339) - along with the more typical arrangement in which a conception is understood to result from the implantation of a spirit essence from the father's land's sacred centre (*auwa*) - we can hardly attribute patrilineality solely to Islander influence.

By the time of the earliest ethnographies, Cape York culture had already been affected by White Australians. While missionaries were relatively late to arrive, Seligmann was greeted, in 1908, by an Otati 'Bible Story' (0365) while Mjöberg was presented with a myth on the respective origins of Blacks and Whites (0310:408-9). Some have argued that the latest wave of aliens has had little impact. Others, like Sharp, predicted total disruption and no possible future but civilizing and Christianizing (0366). Both views, of course, are naïve.

Christian belief and practice have been accomodated in Cape York, yet it has unique forms clearly revealing the persistence of tradition. At Yarrabah there has been a spate of visions and deliverance rituals with their roots in both Christian and Aboriginal domains (Hume, 0363); the Jir Joront have achieved cosmological and ritual accord between pre-European attitudes and those which have resulted from contact (Taylor, 0367); and among the descendants of the people with whom Thomson observed Islander influence there are now new attempts being made to establish harmony between initiation into the cults of the Heroes and initiation into the Christian church (Thompson, 0368, 0369).

CENTRAL-NORTH. If the Islander-inspired Hero-cults are the most conspicuously unique aspect of religion in Cape York, then in the Central-North of Australia, and particularly in Arnhem Land, the fertility cults of the All-Mother, which were at least partially developed from contacts with Indonesians, are a defining feature.

Among the Yolngu in eastern Arnhem Land, religious belief and practice is ordered by two exogamous moieties. The *Yirritja* moiety's traditions dwell on the various classes of strangers to come to this area. Europeans and Japanese are among the recent groups, but before them were the people of Badu, in the Torres Strait (Berndt, 0517), and in particular, the Macassans from southern Sulawesi, who sailed on the monsoons to Australia's northern coast in search of trepang (see Berndt and Berndt, 0377; Berndt, 0531, F. Rose, 0550, Warner, 0397, etc.). According to Yolngu accounts, however, there was a yet more ancient class of trepang collectors called the *Baijini*. They are said to have brought their families to Australia, built stone houses and established a rice-based agriculture, but no evidence, historical or archaeological, has yet been forthcoming to suggest who these people might have been.[8]

---

[8] C.C. Macknight, "Macassans and Aborigines." *Oceania* 42(1972).

The explicit references to these newcomers in Arnhem Land religious life are of two main kinds. Firstly, they are the subject of extensive song-cycles, which have as yet to be published (for samples, see Berndt, 0533), and a large class of myths (Maddock, 0243; Turner, 0554). Secondly, they are tied in with Aboriginal conceptions of the soul. This includes their representation in ceremonies celebrating the affiliation between individuals and their spirit land, but also particularly in mortuary ritual. Although the *birrimbir* (soul) is said to return to the 'clan well' (Warner, 0397), it is also claimed to travel to the Land of the Dead. In the *Yirritja* moieties' case this is Badu, and the rites for the departure of the soul replicate the Macassan praus setting sail for Sulawesi (0531). Sculptures identified with Dutch custom officials are also used as funerary posts (0456).

The All-Mother cult likewise has clearly alien elements. The Mother, right across the coast of Central-North Australia, is said to have come from a land to the north, and in Arnhem Land some people quite explicitly name her home as Macassar (0376:113). In the famous *Djanggawul* song cycle when the All-Mothers and their brother are getting close to Australia's coast, they smell the *Baijini* on the land and later find these light-skinned trepang gatherers already well-established in their stone house (0418:101-2). Analysis of the available ethnographies and comparisons with traditions from southern Sulawesi provide a strong case for the Mother cult in Australia being a post-Indonesian phenomena, and possibly developing as recently as the early eighteenth century.[9]

The Mother is the heart of the cults in Central-Northern Australia. Most widespread is the *Kunapipi* ('Womb') which appears to have begun in the Roper River area (Berndt, 0481: xxviii), spreading to the north coast, and also westwards from whence it swung both to the north where it was documented as *Punj* (Stanner,0393), and south where it is referred to as *Gadjeri* ('Old Woman') (Meggitt, 0851).

The *Kunapipi* ritual varies considerably under local conditions. Away from the coast the significance of fertility symbolism diminishes, and in differing coastal areas it has become attached to various myth cycles. In east Arnhem Land, for example, it is associated with the story of the *Wawalak* sisters, a narrative which also sustains the *Djunggaun* and *Ngurlmag* rituals in that region. The *Kunapipi* rituals symbolically replicate, among other things, the swallowing of the sisters by the python *Yulunggur* and the life-giving properties of their wombs. These are instances of the commonly paired ritual metaphors of subsumption (swallowing, killing, etc.) and giving birth; of death and life.

The womb is an image central to other cults in northern Australia. The *Dhuwa* moieties' *Narra* rituals focus on the myth of the *Djanggawul*. The grounds represent the womb and the sacred poles (*rangga*) are brought

[9] T. Swain, "The Earth Mother From Northern Waters." *History of Religions* 30, 3 (1991): forthcoming.

forth from the shelter in a manner paralleling the birth of the first people
from the Mother (Warner, 0397). The western Arnhem Land *Mareiin*
(0484) are closely related to these *Narra*, although naturally linked with
different mythic constellations.

In eastern Arnhem Land initiation is set in the context of the four
rituals already referred to, that is, *Djunggaun, Kunapipi, Ngurlmag* and
Narra, while in western Arnhem Land, the *Ubar* and *Mareiin* fulfil these
functions. Women's initiation is far less elaborate but this does not mean,
as Warner suggested (0397), that women are therefore profane. After all,
men appropriate women's bodily functions as symbols of sacrality (0171,
0856), and hence concede that women are *in essence* sacred in their ability
to bring eternal life forces into the temporal world. As the elder
Djanggawul sister said when her brother stole her sacred objects
(themselves symbols of fertility): "I think we can leave that. Men can do it
now... We have really lost nothing, for we remember it all... For aren't we
still sacred... Haven't we still got our uteri... " (0418: 40-1).

Not all northern cults are associated with images of motherhood.
Berndt notes the *Yirritja* moiety *Narra* are primarily associated with the
myth of *Laitjun* and *Banaitja* which emphasizes male principles (0007: fasc.
3, p.3), while Stanner says the myth of *Kunmunggar* and *Jinimin*
symbolically competes with the All-Mother's "mysterious female power"
(0393: 55). In more recent times, the most prominent male mythic figure
is the Christian God. There is currently a very active Christian revival
which began on Elcho Island but has spread throughout the Central-North
of Australia and, indeed, the continent as a whole. The movement focuses
on ecumenicalism as a face of political unity and operates under the banner
of the phrase "Father make us one" (Bos, 0538). Aboriginal theologians
from this area have sought reconciliation between their All-Mother and the
new All-Father (e.g. Yule, 0556; Gondarra, 0542).

Mission influence had made an impact prior to this most recent
revival, although it was poorly documented. Falkenberg (0401) considered
briefly the effects of Catholic missions, and Berndt (0529) recorded a
Christian myth cycle transposed into a Dreaming form long after the
relevant mission was abandoned. The best known development of this kind
was the Elcho Island Adjustment Movement in which previously secret
rangga were placed on public display in association with a crucifix outside
the local church. Berndt has interpreted this in terms of political goals and
deliberate cultural reformulation (0530), but more recently Morphy (0548)
has argued for its significance as a means of educating Europeans in the
ways of Aboriginal land tenure.

KIMBERLEY. Complex historical processes have obviously
been involved in shaping the religious traditions of the areas thus far
discussed, but published accounts often downplay this factor. The
Kimberley, in contrast, is typically depicted as a cross-roads of religious

innovation. In reality, it is probably no more innovative than other northern regions, but the presence of scholars schooled in German historicist traditions in this area has resulted in publications with a concern for documenting change. Elkin (who studied with the British Pan-Egyptian diffusionists) and Capell (introduced to Australian anthropology by Elkin) also consider such factors. Teasing apart the older threads of history is a complex and perhaps ultimately impossible task. Capell, for instance, discerned three layers of mythic traditions. The oldest, a cult of the dead, was followed by the *Wandjina* cult which he suggests has its origins in Timor, and was itself finally overlaid with narratives of the Rainbow Serpent and others (0584). Aboriginal myth does not really help resolve the chronology. According to Ngarinyin cosmogony, for example, the androgynous serpent *Ungud* first emerged from the oceans, created various lands, and then deposited the eggs of the *Wandjina* throughout the area. In other versions, however, the *Wandjina* are self-created (Elkin, 0604; Petri, 0575). Whatever the order of emergence of these cults, we can at least say that the mouthless *Wandjina* have been the most noted element of Kimberley iconography and mythology (e.g. Blundell, 0599; Capell, 0586; Crawford, 0601; Elkin, 0604; Lommel, 0607; Petri, 0575).

The next waves of religious development in the Kimberley came from the east, via the northern Waljbiri at the apex of the Central Desert, and ultimately from Arnhem Land. These were a range of cults of the "Fertility-Mother" genre - *Kunapipi* in Arnhem Land (Berndt,0481), *Gadjeri* among the Waljbiri (Meggitt, 0851) and travelling west (through Balgo, Hall's Creek, Sturt Creek, etc.), taking the forms of *Dingari*, *Kurrangara* and *Worgaia* (Berndt, 0631; Lommel, 0646; Petri, 0648).

Kurrangara is particularly interesting. Although this is the name of one section of the *Kunapipi* rituals in the west, according to Lommel (0646) it had transformed into a cult with a pessimistic eschatology anticipating the destruction of the earth. Petri (0575, 0648) also found this situation, with the elders concerned about a poison accompanying the *Djanba* spirits associated with the cult (cf. Meggitt, 0881). Older men advocated returning to the traditions of the *Wandjina* and Rainbow Serpent as the only means of preventing the disastrous world-end.

By the 1960s the Petris found things had again transformed. The *Kurrangara* and *Wandjina* traditions had to some extent merged, and there had been revivals of *Dingari*. In 1963, there then appeared a full-blown messianic movement. The Ancestral Being leading it was *Jinimin*, already reported by Stanner (0393, 0551), but now equated with Jesus. He was said to have revealed himself to Aborigines, given them a 'new' Law called *Worgaia*, told them to be steadfast in their traditions and that they would then, and only then, defeat the Europeans. They would themselves receive white skin and great wealth from Noah's ark which was filled with gold and crystals and was located in Aboriginal lands (cf. Kolig, 0642). The

boat would also save Aborigines from a second, European-destroying, flood (Petri and Petri-Odermann, 0650, 0651; Koepping, 0636).

While the cults derived from the fertility ceremonies have travelled from the Central-North westwards, a more recent innovation, *Julurru*, has been traded in the opposite direction (Akermann, 0634). Having begun on the west coast (some Aborigines say from as far south as Perth) it has passed across Fitzroy Crossing, through Balgo into the Central Desert. Like the Jesus-*Jinimin* cult it has explicit Christian elements and cargoistic expectations (see Kolig, 0640; Glowczewski, 0883). Yet it is a movement of even wider synthetic parameters, incorporating things from the Christian God to Islamic 'Malay' cultural elements, and from traditional Dreaming tracks to motorbikes and aeroplanes.

There is yet more to the rich religious tapesty of the region, including stories of figures said to be actual historic personalities who were nonetheless of great religious significance. Shaw has recorded the narratives of Boxer, a 'magic' man from Queensland said to have brought *Djamba* traditions with him (0578, 0579; see also Rowse, 0657) while Kolig (0641) and D. Rose (0652, 0655) have documented narratives dealing wih Captain Cook and the bushranger Ned Kelly, showing how they have been located within Aboriginal cosmologies. Kolig (0645) and D. Rose (0653, 0654) have also done much to investigate the impact of Christian missions in this area, although their respective claims for minimal influence to my mind require some qualification.

SOUTH-WEST. The relatively fertile region running south from Port Hedland along the West Australian coast to Cape Pasley on the south coast unfortunately did not receive anything like the research attention it deserved. It is an important and discrete area, the most conspicuously uniting feature of its religious practice being the lack of circumcision and subincision rites. The border between this region and the Western Desert is traditionally defined by scholars by the absence of these rites, although Gray (0691) has documented the spread of circumcision into the northern parts of the area in recent years.

Ironically, many pioneering researchers have worked here: Salvado was among the first of the early missionary writers (0669); Bates was for her time the most knowledgeable of women ethnographers (0660); and Radcliffe-Brown began professional field-work in Australia in this area (0668). But with the exception of the Pilbara area, where von Brandenstein (0663) and Petri (0682) have added to our knowledge, little has been done to fill the vast gaps in our understanding.

Hallman (0676) and Berndt (0661) have attempted to salvage something about religious life in the South-Western corner, but there is not enough data to fully comprehend the unique features of the area. To say that there were intiation rites, 'increase' ceremonies, a body of myth and ritual and traditions surrounding death (Berndt, 0662:84-6) is neither surprising nor informative. Perhaps the most interesting study from that area comes from White (0692) who pieces together the story of how Aborigines of King George Sound incorporated the military ritual of Captain Matthew Flinder's men into their *Koorannup* ceremony - a fitting symbol of the forces that were ultimately to destroy their traditional religious life itself.

WESTERN DESERT. As we now swing back to the east we enter the vast Desert of Central Australia. While borded east and west by regions which have lost much of their pre-contact religious life, the Desert was to some extent a haven for Aborigines precisely because of its inhospitability to European economic pursuits. Yet even here it is impossible to speak of people unaffected by alien life-styles. The exception proves the rule. When, a few years back, a handful of Pintubi who had never before seen whites were encountered the event was so unexpected as to attract considerable media attention.

Within the Desert there have also been degrees of outside influence on religious life. Towards the very heart of the continent there was from an early date not only the overland telegraph line and the station that was the embryo of what is now Alice Springs, but also the Lutheran Mission at Hermannsburg which, while recording useful material (C. Strehlow, 0794), at the same time prohibited the performance of Aboriginal ceremonies. Under such a régime change was inevitable. In other areas, reflected in studies such as Meggitt's work on the Waljbiri (0779) or Tonkinson's on the Mardudjara (0708), the authors can claim to have witnessed traditions showing minimal signs of outside influence, but such contexts do not prevail today. Missions, mining companies and European bureaucracies have become ubiquitous things.

I have followed the academic custom of separating the Western and Central Deserts if for no other reason than it makes a large number of entries more manageable. The division, however, is not absolute, nor easily defined. The Australian Institute for Aboriginal Studies has simply used the state border between Western Australia and South Australia and the Northern Territory, but the matter need not be that arbitrary. A Western bloc can be delineated with a common linguistic and cultural core (Tonkinson, 0708:6-8). The Bidjandjadjara belong to this region but their northern neighbours, the Aranda, differ from them in some important ways. From the Aranda to the Waljbiri, via whom Central-Northern cultural elements passed into the Desert, are then the approximate reaches of the more heterogenous Central Desert cultures.

Desert religious conceptions, in my view, represent the essence of Aboriginal religion throughout the continent, but in other regions historic processes have overlain the general pattern with new motifs. We thus find apparent 'contradictions' or 'redundancies': the spirit of the dead goes to a site-based home but *also* to the Land of the Dead (Badu, Heaven, etc.);

myriad ancestors transform the world but there is *also* a transcendental or quasi-transcendental figure beyond this process (All-Mother, All-Father, etc.). The 'Desert' understanding of the cosmos can thus be seen in non-Desert areas, barely below the surface of new tides of religious thought.

Desert ontology is fundamentally pluralistic, there are no pre-eminent ancestors, nor are there any people with access to more than a small segment of the eternally world-sustaining Dreaming beings. The whole consists in the fabric woven of independent threads, yet even this image is too formal and lends itself to the misunderstanding of a universally acknowledged blueprint. Not a geometric grid but an organic pattern of Dreaming pathways criss-crossing the landscape.

It is readily acknowledged by Aborigines of the Western Desert that no one knows the full body of their Law. While some stories, like that of the Two Men or *Wati Kutjara* (Tindale, 0726; Mountford, 0733; McCarthy, 0721; Berndt,0715) transverse this area and thus link communities together, it is nonetheless understood that people are custodians only for that segment of the Ancestor's spiritual forces which have been localized in their country.

Ritual in this area links living people with the Ancestral order to maintain a balance which can endure. The people spiritually associated with a site at which Dreaming beings are (*not* 'were') manifest perform ceremonies (re-)actualizing sacred events and thus ensuring the balance of those parts of the cosmos for which they are responsible (Berndt and Berndt, 0695; Tonkinson, 0708. On the view of time expressed here, see Barden, 0710; Bain, 0712; Ellis, 0731 and Myers, 0703).

Rites of passage affirm the fact that human beings are ontologically identical with Ancestors. The Ancestor's spirit essence which has become fixed in the country causes pregancy and birth as it becomes incarnate in women (Sackett, 0748; Tonkinson, 0750). Later, novices are inducted into the meaning of their true identity (e.g. Piddington, 0753; Tindale, 0755). Finally, death is a return of spirit essences to their rightful place and no general Land of the Dead is recognized. One might rather speak of the Lands (in the plural) of the potential for life (Berndt and Johnston, 0766, and Elkin, 0767, do not do this issue justice).

Tonkinson has examined what happens in a Western Desert culture when the people are removed from their spirit's lands (0749), while Wallace (0772) and Sackett (0770) have observed the effects the colonial presence had on initiation ceremonies. But considering the extent of change in religious life in this area - the type of change F. Rose (0768) hints at and Tonkinson (0707) provides the context for - the dynamics and history of religious life in this region have been sadly neglected, perhaps because this is the area which tends to attract researchers searching for that unicorn of Aboriginal Studies: Aborigines totally untouched by the non-Aboriginal world.

CENTRAL DESERT. The Central Desert can certainly boast some of the most influential studies of Aboriginal religion. Spencer and Gillen's books (0790, 0791) radically improved the quality of Australian fieldwork; Róheim began his psychoanalytic ethnography in the region (0784, 0787); Meggitt (0779, 0851) and Munn (0840) produced particularly rich monographs with the Waljbiri; Bell opened a new chapter in the study of women's ritual life (0865); and Strehlow translated songs with a linguistic flair not to be equalled (0845).

Since the turn of the century, in some schools of thought the Aranda have become almost synonymous with Aboriginality. Had not no less a scholar than Durkheim found *the* most elementary form of religious life among them (0079)? Have not the Arandic words '*churinga*' (*tjurunga*, inscribed boards or stone slabs) and *Intichiuma* ('increase' ceremonies) found a universal application in discussing Aboriginal religions? Yet in some respects the Aranda are anomalous to Desert culture. Their 'conception totems' which recruited members of 'lodges' in terms of the place where the mother first felt the pangs of pregnancy, were, for example, to some extent at odds with the principles of patrilineal inheritance found elsewhere in the Central Desert (Spencer and Gillen, 0790; Strehlow, 0798). Some scholars, such as Hamilton (0699), have entertained the possibility that this is the original and earliest method of lodge recruitment, but it is impossible to validate such assertions.

To the north of the Central Desert the Waljbiri provide another variation on Desert themes. While remnants of fertility cults have entered the Western Desert via the Kimberley (Berndt, 0694), the Waljbiri *Gadjeri* is far more conspicuous in this regard (Meggitt, 0851). Yet while symbols of women's procreative powers are explicitly evident (Wild, 0856), the mythology of the Mother has been replaced among the Waljbiri by the story of two males known as the *Mamandabari* who traverse a wide range of Waljbiri country and whose exploits can only be recalled in part by the people of any one site-based descent group. In this sense the northern *Gadjeri* has been transposed into a typically Desert segmentary religious key.

In the main, the spiritual aspects of the life-cycle in the Central Desert are of the same kind as those found in the Western Desert. Among the Waljbiri the *guruwari* or life essence deposited in the landscape by an Ancestor is lodged in a woman who passes near the site (Munn, 0840). These *guruwari* are the source of all fertility, animal and human, and a major part of ritual is to ensure their balanced continuation. Unlike the Aranda, however, this conception Dreaming does not determine lodge affiliations, which is regulated by patrilineal descent, and their patri-spirit or *pirlirrpa* is revealed to them upon initiation (Meggitt, 0779).

Not all Central Desert ritual is of the *Intichiuma* (Waljbiri *Banba*) or 'increase' type (see Morton, 0852). *Gadjeri* and initiation ceremonies have already been mentioned and there are also relatively widespread cults associated with celebrating the activities of various ancestors. The serpent *Yarrapiri* is an example. He emerged from Bidjandjadjara country (Mountford, 0817) and among the Waljbiri is associated with Fire ceremonies (Peterson, 0854). While fire ceremonies are frequently connected with *Yarrapiri*, they are found in various other contexts throughout the Central Desert (Spencer and Gillen, 0855) and thus represent yet another genre of ritual to be found.

A further class of ritual is the public ceremony which, despite its entertainment value, is nonetheless of religious significance. The Waljbiri *Purlapa* are often said to be revealed to individuals by Ancestral Beings whilst dreaming. In more recent times God has been counted among these Ancestors, and Christian ceremonies and icons have become a part of Waljbiri and neighbouring religious life (Swain, 0885). The relationship between Christian and other beliefs and practices is a complementary rather than competitive one and Aboriginal people maintain they are upholding 'Two Laws'.

Despite the impact of Christian missions in this region, especially upon the Aranda at Hermannsburg, very little has been done to investigate recent religious innovations. With the exception of my paper on Waljbiri Christianity and Glowczewski's study of *Julurru* among the northern Waljbiri, and a few notes by F. Rose from the southern border of the Central Desert (0768), this remains an uncharted topic. Changes to and within traditional religious life in a post-colonial context has, however, been addressed by Bell(0864), Wild(0847) and others.

LAKE EYRE. While the peoples of Lake Eyre, and the Dieri in particular, were the focus of early missionizing and consequently had their religious life documented by the pioneering proselytizers (Reuther, 0891; Siebert, 0892; Taplin, 0893; Tiechelmann, 0894), colonial pressures weighed heavily upon their traditions and thus, with a few exceptions, little investigation of any quality has been carried out there this century. In many respects Lake Eyre religious life was close to that of the Desert, although it was also influenced by the Gulf and South-Eastern regions. Ancestral Beings (*Muramura*) had transformed themselves at specific sites which became the focus of patrilinear rituals performed by members of the *bindara* or patrilineal clan. This is in keeping with the typical Desert segmentary religious structure.

Two distinctive features, both possibly post-mission innovations, are worthy of note. One is the *toas*, 'guide posts' or 'direction markers' which symbolically refer to particular *Muramura* and, by extension, sites with which they are associated. The antiquity of *toas* has been the subject of debate, and their origin will now probably never be fully understood (Jones and Sutton, 0908).

The second noteworthy feature is the Lake manifestation of the *Molonga* cult. The cult itself came to the area from Queensland (see Roth,

0315) and was also recorded elsewhere in Australia. But in the Lake, according to the missionary Siebert (0892), it was a millennial movement, focusing on a future battle between Aborigines and Whites which would climax with the appearance of *Kanini*, the spirit of "the Great Mother of the Water", who was to swallow all the colonial Australians. Alas for the Aboriginal people of Lake Eyre, she did not come.

SOUTH-EAST. The South-Eastern corner of Australia is the area with the longest and most intense colonial history. Considering the immense disruption to Aboriginal traditions in this region, the body of literature on their religions is surprisingly large. The quality of the publications, however, leaves much to be desired. Most are from the nineteenth and early twentieth centuries and the modern student searches in vain for answers to many of their research questions.

The defining feature of this area is the sky-dwelling transcendental All-Father. There is no reason to hesitate in calling him a Supreme Being. Throughout the region he is the focus of all belief and ritual, and his home, usually said to be somewhere beyond the clouds, is the locus of all power and the paradise to which people aspire upon death.

This religious understanding is so at odds with that of the rest of the continent that it was from an early date the subject of controversy (*supra*). Are we witnessing Christian teachings blended with pre-contact ideas? Or is it the case, as earlier scholars maintained, that the more fertile climate of the South-East had allowed these peoples' beliefs to 'evolve' to a 'higher' level?

My own position (Swain,1062) is a variant of the former view, but I see no real case for the argument that Christian ideas had become 'confused' with tradition. Rather it seems that these Aborigines had deliberately employed and re-worked the cosmology of their invaders in order to come to terms with their own place in a radically changing world.

The first thing to note in this regard is the depreciation of the earth. Although Radcliffe-Brown (0966) could still find remnants of ideas about 'increase' rites and site-based spirit essences, most researchers reported beliefs which indicated the earth was secondary to an unknown heaven. Upon death the spirit no longer returned to its territory but found "its way to the sky-country, where it lives in a land like the earth, only more flexible, better watered, and plentifully supplied with game" (Howitt, 0938: 440). Insofar as the more typically Aboriginal locative notions of earth-bound sites as the eternal homes of spirit essences is discernible in some studies of the South-East (e.g. Mathews, 0948), it seems reasonable to suspect the heavenly scenario was a relatively recent innovation.

Turning to the All-Father himself our suspicions are intensified. The earliest reference to him (as *Baiami*) came from the Wellington Valley Mission, where Rev. James Günther claimed he had found the belief in a God said to be eternal, omnipotent and good (cit. Ridley, 0955:135; also

Hale, 0937). James Manning's account is even more surprising. Several critcs have accused Manning of embellishing his report, but as the author was himself uncomfortable with his data and thus double-checked the details it is quite possible that he faithfully relates what he was told by Aborigines. This was that *Baiami* lives in heaven on a throne of crystal, but because he was lonely made a son whose spirit dwelt on earth from "England to Sydney" (0985:160). Other reports, such as Howitt's, were less anachronistic, but none countered the view that an other-worldly Supreme Being was the key to religious belief in the region.

Ritual in the South-East was dominated by the 'clever men' who officiated at the deities' ceremonies. The cults, most commonly referred to as *Bora*, were intiatory, with the novice being taught of the true powers and attributes of their High God. Howitt, Mathews, and others have left us with numerous accounts of the physical dimension of the rituals, including the ground sculptures and dendroglyphs (carved trees) but what they signify or mean we are mostly not told. It would seem that they were depictions in part of *Baiami's* first camp, and the god was typically portrayed in a recumbent position. But what of the other icons said to depict his benefactions? The majority were of indigenous themes, but there were also cattle (Fison and Howitt, 0932:210, note the god has many cattle) horses, pigs, trains, ships, playing cards (four aces, to be specific), and even effigies of Whites themselves (see Swain, 1062, for extensive references).

Whatever the origin of the All-Father, in more recent years he has come to be associated by Aborigines with the Christian god. Howitt was in fact told *Brewin* (the Kurnai term) was "Jesus Christ" (Fison and Howitt, 0932:255), and similar opinions have been expressed by Aborigines throughout New South Wales and Victoria. In unpublished notes from the 1903s, Elkin referred to data collected from informants initiated around the time of Howitt's and Mathews' field-work.[10] He does not actually acknowledge synthetic elements, although references to "our saviour" with a virgin mother clearly indicate their presence. By the 1950s, when Calley performed his field-work with the Bandjelang, the same myth had been quite explicitly linked with Christian imagery (1055). Variants of this account have been reported by Robinson (0994) and the Holmers (0978), and in each case the site of Christ's grave is located in the nearby landscape.

Beckett (1054), Reay (1061), and Kelly (1057), have also added to our understanding of religious dynamics in the South-East, but the beliefs and practices of urban-based Aborigines has remained totally neglected. Those wishing to pursue this trail will have to consult the poetry, song and art of contemporary Aborigines themselves.

As for the earlier period it seems conclusive that the High God, while probably having some indigenous roots, only came to be an *otiose*

---

[10] "Kattang Inititation" ms. *Elkin Papers*. Fisher Library, p. 130, Box 11, folder 1/3/10.

Supreme Being in the wake of invasion. This is perhaps to argue no more than the Wiradjuri man who said: "He was always among the people long ago... when the white peple came out to Australia, Baiami heard that they were coming. He then got 'frightened', and cleared away" (Berndt, 1047:334).

TASMANIA. I began my survey of the religious heritage of the ten regions employed by this bibliography by considering the relatively peaceful Papuan and Indonesian influences in the north. Desert people in turn were to some extent isolated and protected by the very harshness of their homelands, but the South-East story was brutal. In Tasmania, however, genocide was even more rapid and thorough. Depending on their sensibilities, Europeans either congratulated themselves or lamented the fact that the last Tasmanian Aborigine died in 1876 - a verdict which today's Tasmanian Aborigines (for reasons many Whites seem totally incapable of appreciating) wish to contest! But for all scholarly intents and purposes, these Aborigines were deemed extinct in 1876, and so there field-research came to an end... before it had begun.

Roth wrote an ethnographic obituary for the Tasmanians in 1890 (1071), collecting snippets of data and pasting them into a serviceable collage. Since then a few writers have tried to transcend the huge limitations to the data. Vögler's is the best attempt (1072) but others, like Worms (1074 and 0071: chap. V) and Cotton (1073) are dangerously unreliable.

I can but conclude with a most appropriate quotation to be found in Roth (1071:55): "they recognized a malignant spirit, and attributed strong emotions to the devil... they believe him to be *white* - a notion suggested by their national experience".

Part Two

Bibliographical Survey

4

Trans-Regional

General

0001 Abbie, A.A. (1970) *The Original Australians.* Wellington: A.H. and
        A.W. Reed. 288 pp.
A general introduction to Aboriginal cultures with a strong emphasis on physical
anthropology.   Religious themes are covered in two chapters, treating
cosmology, totemism, spirit beliefs, major rituals, medicine men and mortuary
practice. Emphasis is given to physical manifestation, such as the relatively long
section on bodily mutilation (pp.143-152). Lacks sophistication and the author
makes superficial comparisons with religious beliefs and practices elsewhere in
the world.

0002 Basedow, Herbert (1925) *The Australian Aboriginal.* Adelaide: F.W.
        Preece. 422 pp.
Intended as a general introduction to Aboriginal Australia, but in fact all of the
data comes from South Australia, the Northern Territory, and the Kimberley.
Favours physical and material anthropology, but does contain chapters on
religious ideas, initiation and mortuary practice. Lacks any real insight and
there are a host of errors in some sections. *Altjira* is mistranslated as 'Supreme
Spirit' and *Altjeringa* is given the grotesque gloss of 'the "walk-about" of the
spirit ancestors' (p.279). This, combined with the author's racist views on
Aboriginal mental capacity, make this a book to avoid.

0003 Bates, Daisy (1947) *The Passing of the Aborigines: A Lifetime Spent
        among the Natives of Australia.* 2nd ed. London: John Murray. 258 pp.
Reflections of Australia's most famous female amateur anthropologist from her
sojourns throughout Western and South Australia.   Contains chapters on
initiation and discusses totemism, myth, ritual, spirit beliefs, mortuary rites and
new cults such as the *Molonga* and *Wanji-Wanji.* Despite aiming at a non-
specialist audience there are many snippets of useful information. Intriguing, if
not entirely reliable.

0004   Bennett, Samuel (1982) *Australian Discovery and Colonisation.* Volume
        2. Sydney: Currawong Press. 661 pp. 1st ed. 1865.
The 40 page chapter on Aborgines contains sections on 'superstitions', largely
based on the observations of others. Speculative and confused.

0005 Berndt, Catherine H. and Berndt, Ronald M. (1971) *The Barbarians: An
        Anthropological View.* London: C.A. Watts. 192 pp.
A hodge-podge of a book trying to come to grips somehow with the question:
"What is civilization?" Chapter 4 "In Aboriginal Australia" (pp.43-58) considers
songs, mythic imagery, social foundations of religious tradition, etc., to illustrate
the richness of symbolic life and the centrality of the sphere of the sacred. Some
useful analysis.

0006 Berndt, Catherine H. and Berndt, Ronald M. (1978) *Pioneers and
        Settlers: The Aboriginal Australians.* Carlton, Vic.: Pitman Australia. 150
        pp.

Later reissued as *The Aboriginal Australians: The First Pioneers*, and designed as a general introduction to traditional Aboriginal cutures' relevance to modern Aboriginal issues. Religion as such is not given a separate section but is considered in chapters on "The Future through the Past", "Women and Men", "A Feeling for Rhythm" and "Art Had Meaning". Geared towards the general reader and school student.

0007 Berndt, Ronald M. (1974) *Australian Aboriginal Religion.* Iconography of Religions, section V. 4 Fascicles. Leiden: E.J. Brill. 151 pp. + plates and maps.
At present the best continent-wide single volume study of Aboriginal religion, unfortunately spoiled by its original 4 fascicle form. A general introduction is followed by a four phase geographical survey: South-East, North-East, North and Central Australia. The conclusion suggests some diffusionary patterns of religious complexes within Australia. There is a strong iconographic emphasis throughout and 220 excellent black and white plates. The text is condensed to a high degree making it more of 'specialist' reference than an introductory treatment.

0008 Berndt, Ronald M. (1983) "Australian Aborigines: Religion." In *The Australian Encyclopedia.* 4th ed. Vol. 1, 158-165. Sydney: The Grolier Society.
Briefly signposts most of the main themes of Aboriginal religion, but the discussion is inevitably superficial. Considers general concepts such as: Dreaming, sacredness, the relation between myth and ritual; the rituals of initiation, 'increase', 'love' and larger cults; traditional doctors and healing; and other themes such as women, art, death and change.

0009 Berndt, Ronald M. (1987) "Australian Religions: An Overview." In *The Encyclopedia of Religion*, edited by M. Eliade. Vol. 1, 529-547. New York: Macmillan.
After some general discussion of Aboriginal sacred life this article broadly paints the unique features of the religions of the major cultural blocs of Australia. These are the mobile adaptive cults of the north, the segmentary system based on networks of dreaming tracks for the centre, the South-Eastern tradition of a prominent deity of the All-Father type, and the Cape York Peninsula 'hero-cults' which focus on the spirits of the dead. A dry but solid survey.

0010 Berndt, Ronald M. and Berndt, Catherine H. (1952) *The First Australians*. Sydney: Ure Smith. 144 pp.
Covers much the same topics as the authors' more academic text (0011) but in this case geared towards school students. No more than scratches the surface of topics such as mythology, symbolism, ritual, rites of passage, magic, sorcery and death. Simultaneously too superficial for serious study yet too attached to academic categories for younger students.

0011 Berndt, Ronald M. and Berndt, Catherine H. (1977) *The World of the First Australians*. 2nd ed. Sydney: Ure Smith. 602 pp.

There are several hundred pages on religion in this book, including detailed chapters on rites of passage, totemism and mythology, ritual, magic and sorcery, and death and the afterlife. Also contains data under less obvious headings such as oral literature, art, law and order, etc. The revised edition contains commentaries on the various chapters. Although an awkward way to keep a book up to date, the additional material is valuable and at times provides interesting notes on the development of theoretical issues related to aspects of Aboriginal religious life. A good general introduction.

0012 Berndt, Ronald M. and Berndt, Catherine H. (1988) "Traditional Religions." In *The Australian People: An Encyclopedia of the Nation, its People and their Origins*, edited by J. Jupp, 159-165. Sydney: Angus and Robertson.
An overview of Aboriginal beliefs and rituals. Considers the concept of Dreaming, ancestral travels and shape-changing, conception beliefs, secrecy and the sacred, initiation and mortuary beliefs. There is discussion of the purpose of myth (a guide to action) and ritual (life regulation) and the complementarity of men's and women's religious domains is stressed. Rather dull, and due to length, superficial.

0013 Bleakley, J.W. (1961) *The Aborigines of Australia: Their History - Their Habitats - Their Assimilation.* Brisbane: Jacaranda Press. 367 pp.
This book's main innovation was that it was willing to examine Aborigines in historical perspective. The author, one-time Protector of Aborigines in Queensland, pushes throughout his paternalistic assimilation policies. These even appear in the chapters on spiritual life and magic and medicine. Thus, teaching Aborigines of sexual physiology may help them towards agricultural pursuits (p.33)! The sections on religion are superficial and inaccurate.

0014 Capell, Arthur (1950) "Aboriginal Religious Practice." *Mankind* Occasional Paper No. 1. 12 pp.
Considers Aboriginal understandings of the sacred and the concept of 'totemism' in theory and practice, before discussing generally the social aspects of rites and initiatory ritual. Localized and non-localized cults are referred to and a general plan of ritual processes developed. The core idea is said to be that of the 'sacrament' - the outward and visible sign of an inward and spiritual gift. Not sophisticated and draws dubious analogies with Christian traditions.

0015 Carmody, Denise Lardner (1981) *The Oldest God: Archaic Religion Yesterday and Today.* Nashville: Abingdon. 190 pp.
Chapter 6 examines Aboriginal religions in the context of 'archaic' religions and contains comparisons with American Indians and Africans. Themes include myth, medicine men, and feminine sacrality. The scholarship is superficial and full of errors, ambiguities and over-simplifications. C.G. Jung and Carlos Castaneda loom large.

0016 Carmody, Denise Lardner and Carmody, John (1988) *The Story of World Religions.* California: Mayfield. 491 pp.

Contains a sizeable section on "The Australian [Aboriginal] Religious Story" (pp.45-57), which, having made some general observations, proceeds to "A Creation Story", "An Initiation Story", "A Fertility Story", and some concluding remarks on major 'story' themes. While the book seems to be aimed at lower tertiary (or even younger) students, the superficialities and errors are not thus justified. Confuses localized traditions with common patterns and the accounts of religious episodes of invented Aborigines ('Luke', 'Matthew' and 'Dorca') are simply grotesque.

0017 Charlesworth, Max (1987) "Australian Aboriginal Religion in a Comparative Context." *Sophia* 26,1: 50-57.
Considers how Aboriginal religions have been largely ignored in comparative studies of religion - partly because they appear to belong to the domain of anthropology. Crude comparative methods are rejected but the author nonetheless feels there is no need to deem Aboriginal traditions incommensurable with others. Suggests land mediates the divine/human spheres and hence has the same mediatory role as Jesus in Christian thought. Fails to convince that the research he advocates would deepen understanding.

0018 Charlesworth, Max; Morphy, Howard; Bell, Diane; and Maddock, Kenneth, eds. (1984) *Religion in Aboriginal Australia: An Anthology.* St. Lucia: University of Queensland Press. 458 pp.
A rather disjointed and uneven anthology of previously published material which suffers from having too many editorial agendas. It would simultaneously confuse the beginner whilst failing to inspire the advanced researcher. The contributions, some of them of unquestionable value, span 80 years. The book is in four sections: Myth (edited by Maddock), Ritual (by Morphy), Women (by Bell) and Change (by Charlesworth). Each editor contributes a well presented introduction to their section.

0019 Chauncy, Philip (1876) "Notes and Anecdotes of the Aborigines of Australia." In *The Aborigines of Victoria: With Notes Relating to the Habits of the Native of Other Parts of Australia and Tasmania...*, by R. Brough Smyth, Vol. 2, 221-284. Melbourne: John Currey.
The author's memoirs from various regions since 1841 and particularly south-west Western Australia and Victoria. The section on 'Customs and Superstitions' considers beliefs in Supreme Beings, the soul and death, malicious beings, the idea that Whites are re-embodied Aborigines, traditional healing, initiation and funerary ceremonies. Entries are brief and the author well-intentioned but patronizing.

0020 Curr, Edward M. (1886) *The Australian Race: Its Origin, Languages, Customs, Places of Landing in Australia, and the Routes by which it Spread itself over that Continent.* Vol. 1. Melbourne: John Ferres. 425 pp.
Curr's own contribution to this collection is a 240 page introductory section. Chapter 3 on "Manners and Customs" contains a host of dogmatic assertions, leaning towards the sensational, and usually confused. He considers 'Gods',

'witchcraft', sorcery, rainmaking and healing, taking off on wild flights of fancy on topics like infanticide, cannibalism (Whites taste tough and salty, p. 77) and the 'terrible rite' allegedly used as a contraceptive (subincision). The author's own data, primarily from the Banjerang (South-East) is more valuable but also needs cautious handling.

0021 Dean, Beth and Carell, Victor (1955) *Dust for the Dancers*. Sydney: Ure Smith. 214 pp.
Voyeuristic tourist ethnography with descriptions and all-too explicit photography of secret sites and ceremonies. Many references to ceremonies witnessed, but superficial records.

0022 Ehrlich, Lambert (1922) *Origin of Australian Beliefs*. Vienna: Francis Chamra. 81 pp.
A *Kulturkreise* (culture circle) interpretation of Aboriginal religion in line with German diffusionary thought. Part I reviews evolutionary theories and concludes all unilineal schemes fail as they cannot explain the High Gods. The author advocates the existence of several different cultures within Australia, and in particular emphasizes Melanesian contacts through Cape York. Suggests the South-Eastern High Gods are the oldest stratum of Australian beliefs, and one cannot help suspecting Christian apologetics. Dated references and loose interpretation.

0023 Eliade, Mircea (1973) *Australian Religions: An Introduction*. Ithaca: Cornell University Press. 205 pp.
This book (originally a series of articles) covers themes for which Eliade is famous in the History of Religions - High Gods, mythical geography, initiations, 'medicine men', death and eschatology. At times his comparative categories rest uneasily with the Aboriginal data. The first chapter 'Supernatural Beings and High Gods' is the worst offender. The remaining chapters are better and often insightful.

0024 Elkin, A.P. (1932) "The Secret Life of the Australian Aborigines." *Oceania* 3,2: 119-138.
A dated and at times patronizing article which focuses on the pragmatic necessity of understanding Aboriginal secret beliefs and ceremonies in order to regulate Aboriginal behaviour. He suggests for example (p.137) that exchange of sacred boards could be used as a substitution for wife-exchange, the latter seen as being offensive to missionaries and other civilizing agents. The descriptive accounts of initiation, mortuary, 'historical' and 'increase' rites are of a very general nature.

0025 Elkin, A.P. (1964) *The Australian Aborigines: How to Understand Them*. 4th edition. Sydney: Angus and Robertson. 393 pp. 1st edition, 1938.
The first scholarly anthropological introduction to Aboriginal societies continent-wide, reprinted and revised since 1938. New sections have been added but the structure and content (including superceded ethnography and outmoded theory) has not markedly changed. Religious themes are discussed under the headings of totemism; the secret life and initiation; philosophy, rites and beliefs;

art and ritual; medicine men and magic; and death and what follows. The discussion of 'philosophy' was, when it first appeared, pioneering.

0026 Elkin, A.P. (1965) "Aborigines: Religion." In *The Australian Encyclopedia.* 2nd ed. Vol. 1, 45-52. Sydney: The Grolier Society.
A broad ranging but unsatisfying summary of Aboriginal religious life. Works from a distinction between totemic traditions and the 'god'-based religions of the South-East and Arnhem Land and emphasizes the social functions of myth and initiation ritual. Contains a Cook's Tour of regional cults; the cult-heroes of the South-East, totemic cults of the Deserts, the *Wandjina* of the Kimberley and the Fertility mothers of the north. Finally three themes appear somewhat randomly: art, cannibalism and astronomy.

0027 Elkin, A.P. (1970) "Australia: Myth and Magic of the Aborigines." In *Man, Myth and Magic: An Illustrated Encyclopedia of the Supernatural,* edited by R. Cavendish. Vol. 2, 176-184. New York: Marshall Cavendish.
A popularized overview of some of the basic features of Aboriginal religious life. The concepts of Dreaming and totemism are first discussed as underlying principles. There are then brief descriptions of regional religious traditions: the Sky Heroes of the South-East, the *Wandjina* of the Kimberley, the Fertility Mother of Arnhem Land, etc. Concludes by discussing 'medicine-men'.

0028 Frazer, James G., ed. (1894) "Notes on the Aborigines of Australia." *The Journal of the Anthropological Institute of Great Britain and Ireland.* 24: 158-198.
Reponses to Frazer's "Questions on the Manners, Customs, Religions, Superstitions, etc. of Uncivilized or Semi-Civilized Peoples", geared toward his own theoretical interests and containing references to themes such as rites of passage, magic, religious ideology, spirits and eschatology. The replies are from Samuel Gason (Lake Eyre region), "The Stationmaster" (Central Desert), Lindsay Crawford (Victoria River Downs), W.H. Willshire (Central Australia), E. Hamilton (South Australia), M.C. Matthews (general/unspecified) and Paul Foelsche (Arnhem Land). The result is, inevitably, uninspiring.

0029 Frazer, James G. (1905) "The Beginnings of Religion and Totemism Among the Australian Aborigines." *Fortnightly Review* 1,162-172; 2, 452-466.
A piece of Victorian evolutionary anthropology targeted at Aboriginal religion. The article is an extract from the huge third edition of *The Golden Bough,* highlighting Frazer's thesis that Aborigines maintain the most primitive form of pre-religion practised. "Roughly speaking, all men in Australia are magicians, but not one is a priest" (p.162). Hence, he argues, magic precedes religion. The rest of the article fends off the mass of ethnography clearly contradicting his thesis. With hindsight it is simply silly.

0030 Frazer, James G. (1939) *Anthologia Anthropologica: The Native Races of Australasia.* London: Percy Lund Humphries. 390 pp.

Sir James' notebooks on Australia open this volume (pp.1-44), including material not used in his other works. Regions are covered state by state and, in keeping with his interests, most extracts are on religious themes. The whole consists of quotations and paraphrases of published accounts. Exceptionally dull.

0031 Gibbs, R.M. (1982) *The Aborigines*. Melbourne: Longman Cheshire. 135 pp.
Light-weight and unreliable sections on religion.

0032 Hambly, Wilfrid D. (1936) *Primitive Hunters of Australia*. Chicago: Field Museum of Natural History. 59 pp.
Superficial summary chapters on magic, folklore and totemism etc.

0033 Havecker, Cyril (1987) *Understanding Aboriginal Culture*. Sydney: Cosmos. 101 pp.
Billed as an insight into the spiritual philosophy of Aborigines by a 'blood brother', this book conflates misunderstood material with pure fabrication. With no acknowledgement of local variations, cosmology, magic, totemism, spirits, art and healing are examined in a bizarre manner. Good intentions, New Age agendas, and hopelessly confused data.

0034 Hellbusch, Sigrid (1941) *Einfluss der Jagd auf die Lebensformen der Australier*. Berlin: Ebering. 227 pp.
After a consideration of physical and mental abilities of Aborigines and their economic life comes a long section on totemism, discussing restrictions on killing animals, 'increase' ceremonies, and regulations for obtaining and cooking species. A chapter on 'medicine men' and elders is again followed by the theme of 'totemism', this time in terms of marriage regulations, the position of women, infanticide and initiation. Myths concerning the respective roles of men and women are given. Dated.

0035 Herrmann, F. (1967) *Völkerkunde Australiens*. Mannheim: Bibliographisches Institut. 250 pp.
A general treatment of Aboriginal peoples and cultures with sections on totemism, initiation, the ritual use of sacred objects (bullroarers, *tjurunga*, etc.), beliefs and iconography.

0036 Indriess, Ion L. (1963) *Our Living Stone Age*. Sydney: Angus and Robertson. 224 pp.
Claims to be a non-ethnographic book, a more vibrant, human account which is nonetheless accurate. In practice this means constantly interjecting with well-meant but often ethnocentric comments. The book tends to the sensationalistic, even voyeuristic. The focus on religion relates to sexuality and the more specifically genital side of men's and women's initiation. As, however, the book is based on the author's own observations prior to World War I, some of his data may be cautiously used to supplement other more balanced sources.

0037 Isaacs, Jennifer (1980) *Australian Dreaming: 40,000 Years of Aboriginal History*. Sydney: Landsdowne Press. 304 pp.

They don't come any glossier than this beautifully photographed book. The text deals primarily with myth as Aboriginal history and some of the stories were collected for this volume. Most of the text, however, is drawn from secondary accounts and there is a general lack of insight. Covers cosmogony, celestial myths, the life cycle, death, and Indonesian and European impacts.

0038 James, Edwin O. (1917) *Primitive Ritual and Belief: An Anthropological Essay.* London: Methuen. 243 pp.
An analysis of Aboriginal religions with an apologetic *raison d'être*. Suggests that religion evolves in search of the unknown and infinite, and that there is progressive revelation. To this end Aboriginal 'High Gods' are advocated as "The Beginning of Theism" (chap. XII). The book is devoted largely to Aboriginal traditions because they are "nearest to the primitive type" (p.3), and chapters cover rites of passage, totemism, rain-making, war, 'sacrifice and communions", myth and 'increase' rites.

0039 Keen, Ian (1988) "Aboriginal Religion." In *Many Faiths, One Nation*, edited by I. Gillman, 61-73. Sydney: Collins.
A largely accurate but rather uninsightful overview of Aboriginal religion. Marred by dated concepts ('animistic', 'magical', etc.), and tends towards a summary cataloguing of religious phenomena - myths, procreation beliefs, rituals, initiation, mortuary practice. Refers to social and political significance of religion and concludes with a hasty sketch of regional variations and half a page of generalities on Christian impacts.

0040 King-Boyes, M.J.E. (1977) *Patterns of Aboriginal Culture: Then and Now.* Sydney: McGraw-Hill. 175 pp.
Mainstream academics will find this book bizarre and annoying. Aboriginal religious life is featured in the author's own myth-making process. A sample must suffice: chapter 4: "Creation as Cosmology - Man and Nature" is concerned with concepts of time and space. There are, it is stated, "nine facets of time... each with a distinctive energy" (p.43). Aborigines, apparently, have them all, unlike simplistic Western ontologies. Aboriginal social organisation, art, myth and ritual are likewise eulogized in distorted ways. Beware!

0041 Maddock, Kenneth (1974) *The Australian Aborigines: A Portrait of Their Society.* 2nd ed. Harmondsworth: Penguin. 210 pp.
The chapters dealing with religious issues are, fortunately, less controversial than others in this excellent general introduction to Aboriginal societies. Chapter 5: "The World-Creative Powers" makes a twofold division into i. totemic powers, which belong to a specific social group, and ii. transcendental powers which are available to all. The Rainbow Serpent, a widely diffused mythic figure, bridges these two categories. The other two relevant chapters deal with "the Rites of Life", again with a binary division into 'fertility' and 'initiatory' rites, and "the Fall into Death."

0042 Mannzen, Walter (1949) *Die Eingeborenen Australiens.* Berlin: Gebrüder. 260 pp.

The first mainstream Marxist monograph devoted to Aboriginal Australia. Based on a study of secondary sources, and heavily referenced and documented. His main thesis is that Aboriginal society is designed to maintain the privileged position of old men. Religion, *per se* is relegated to an appendix, where totemism is interpreted as an economic institution for controlling the production and distribution of the means of life. Compare Bern (0193).

0043 Mathew, John (1889) "The Australian Aborigines." *Journal and Proceedings of the Royal Society of New South Wales* 23: 335-449.
This article was later expanded into the author's book (0044).

0044 Mathew, John (1899) *Eaglehawk and Crow: A Study of the Australian Aborigines including an Inquiry into Their Origin and a Survey of Australian Languages.* London: David Nutt. 288 pp.
The title of this book refers to the well-known and widespread myths of two conflicting birds who frequently head moieties. Mathew argues these myths reflect historical processes and the clash of two populations in Australia. This sets the tone of the volume which is frequently highly conjectural. Topics covered include initiation, burial, art, 'corroborees', sorcery, 'superstitions' and religion. The value of the volume is, however, increased by the author's own data from the Kabikabi of Queensland.

0045 Mathew, John (1926) "The Religious Cults of the Australian Aborigines." *Report of the Australian and New Zealand Association for the Advancement of Science* 18: 524-540.
An unreliable attempt at an overview of Aboriginal religious life, covering themes such as solar worship, totemism, sacred objects, belief in an afterlife, 'phallic' ceremonies, myths, etc. Dated orientation.

0046 Micha, Franz J. (1958) "Der Handel der Zentralaustralischen Eingeborenen." *Annali Lateranensi* 22: 41-228.
An extensively researched study of trade that passes through Central Australia from various regions. Considers documentation for trade evinced by myths such as the *Wati Kutjara* and rituals such as the *Molonga* and other 'wandering cults'. Contains useful attempts to link cultic traditions.

0047 Micha, Franz J. (1965) "Zum Geschichte der australischen Eingeborenen." *Saeculum* 16,4: 317-342.
A broad-ranging historical view of Aboriginal society focusing upon cultural variation within Australia, the historic influences in the north-west, Arnhem Land and Cape York, and the spread of ceremonial forms.

0048 Mol, Hans (1982) *The Firm and the Formless: Religion and Identity in Aboriginal Australia.* Waterloo: Wilfred Laurier University Press. 103 pp.
Part of a three volume study of the applicability of the author's 'identity model' of religion to specific religious traditions. Attempts to examine how religion reinforces Aboriginal identity by bolstering wholeness ("the firm") against the threat of formlessness. Beside general interpretations of the available

ethnographic evidence, there is a discussion of the theories of eminent scholars who have studied Aboriginal religion. The result is unconvincing and some reviewers felt the book regressed to an offensive revival of social Darwinism.

0049 Murdock, George P. (1934) *Our Primitive Contemporaries*. New York: Macmillan. 614 pp.
Chapters 1 and 2 are on Tasmanian and Aranda Aborigines summarized mainly from Roth (1071), and Spencer and Gillen (0792) respectively.

0050 Perez, Eugene (1981) *Australian Aboriginal Religions* (Not Given): Artlook. 17 pp.
A horrible style of writing, at times confusing, does not enhance the author's horrible argument. This is a condescending piece of Christian apologetics in the guise of anthropology. Lacks any real understanding of Aboriginal traditions although the thesis is in parts heavily obscure. Particularly considers the processes of "secularisation and re-sacrilisation' but fails to say anything meaningful.

0051 Pitts, Herbert (1914) *The Australian Aboriginal and The Christian Church*. London: Society for Promoting Christian Knowledge. 133 pp.
This book "makes no claim to being... a scientific treatise"(p.ix), which is just as well. Browses through topics such as 'corroborees', magic, 'increase' rites, death, spirit beliefs and myths. Part II then introduces the history of missions, although this is very incomplete and predictably misses the opportunity to look at mission impacts on social life/religion. Little use.

0052 [Radcliffe-] Brown, A.R. (1913) "Australia." In *Customs of the World*, edited by W. Hutchinson, 139-198. London: Hutchinson.
Summarizes the ethnographic data of the time from throughout Australia covering conception beliefs, initiation, marriage, totemism, 'increase' ceremonies, magic, sorcery, vengeance and burial practices. Although Radcliffe-Brown's text is sober enough, the numerous photographs, which are individually quite valuable, collectively create a bizarre effect which can only be a reflection of an editorial fascination with exotica.

0053 Radcliffe-Brown, A.R. (1945) "Religion and Society." *The Journal of the Royal Anthropological Institute of Great Britain and Ireland* 73: 33-43.
An extension of Durkheim's thesis (0079), again relying heavily on Australian data. Attempts to demonstrate correspondence between religious and social forms. Some of the ethnography is confused or superficial: thus Dreaming is rendered a 'world dawn' and clearly synthetic beliefs are argued to be unaffected by contact (p.41). Nonetheless, a thesis and orientation which had a profound influence on Aboriginal studies.

0054 Reclus, Élie (N.D.) *Le Primitif d'Australie ou les Non-Non et les Oui-Oui: étude d'ethnologie comparée, Dayéris, Narrinyéris, Kamilaroïs, Minnal-Yangas, Yirclas, Yarra-Yarras, etc.* (No details given).

A study of Australian ethnography to throw light on the ancient world. A strange and rambling work containing a compendium of seeming exotica on cannibalism, infanticide, initiation, funerals, mummification, and beliefs about the afterlife, spirits, skyworld, etc. The book bears no date but appears to have been written c.1890. It is unstated and unknown if it is based on personal observation, although much data seems highly improbable. Particularly strange and of historical interest only.

0055 Robinson, Roland (1977) *The Australian Aboriginal.* Sydney: A.H. and
       A.W. Reed. 126 pp.
The commentary on the text in sections on religion in this book is superficial and at times simply wrong. Thus (p.18) "to the Aboriginals, Earth is the Great Fertility Mother" confuses a northern tradition with all Australia. The extracts from myths the author has collected, however, are at times of value.

0056 Róheim, Géza (1945) *The Eternal Ones of the Dream: A Psychoanalytic
       Interpretation of Australian Myth and Ritual.* New York: International
       Universities Press. 270 pp.
Using his own information and other published sources the author covers a range of topics: initiatory myths, circumcision and subincision rites, *tjurunga*, bull-roarers, 'phallic' rituals, 'increase' rites, menstrual rituals, love magic, conception beliefs, androgyny, etc. Stresses 'separation anxiety' and the religious life's role in both widening parturition between mother and son and compensating for this loss, through the transfer of youths from the biological mother/son unit to the totemic father/son group. Myths, however, reveal the desire for reunion with the mother, of course!

0057 Róheim, Géza (1950) *Psychoanalysis and Anthropology: Culture,
       Personality and the Unconscious.* New York: International Universities
       Press. 496 pp.
A substantial section on Australia (pp.41-150) tends to reiterate his previous findings (0056, 0786). Examines mother-child relations to determine ambivalence reflected in 'demon lore', underlying a pre-Oedipal hostility. Oedipal development is then examined as revealed in phallic cults, and from this a range of data is incorporated: love magic, magic, symbols of androgyny, subincision, spirit children, rituals, death, mourning. A post-Freudian *tour de force* of Aboriginal society and religion.

0058 Róheim, Géza (1952) *The Gates of the Dream.* New York: International
       Universities Press. 554 pp.
Although scattered references to Aborigines appear, the main reference, a theoretical appendage to (0056), is on pp.101-117. He notes Aranda myths end with ancestors dying, and becoming *tjurunga* or phalloi. The penis re-enters the mother. The *Wandjina*'s sexuality is next argued. Fragmented thesis.

0059 Rose, Frederick G.G. (1976) *Australien und seine Ureinwohner: Ihre
       Geschichte und Gegenwart.* Berlin: Akademie. 172 pp.
Brief section on religion.

0060 Schidloff, B. (1908) *Das Sexualleben der Australier und Ozeanier.* Leipzig: GMBH. 314 pp.
Victorian voyeurism with sections on Aboriginal initiatory operations, love magic, etc.

0061 Schmidt, Wilhelm (1909) "Die soziologische und religiös-ethische Gruppierung der Australier." *Zeitschrift für Ethnologie* 51: 328-377.
A dated attempt at developing a sequential order of Aboriginal cultures by examining sex-totems, local totems, patrilineality/matrilineality, circumcision, subincision, etc.

0062 Spencer, W. Baldwin (1914) "The Aborigines of Australia." In *Commonwealth of Australia Federal Handbook* (no details given): 33-85.
A solid summary of Australian ethnography at the time, mostly dealing with religion. Totemism, as was the fashion , is dealt with in its social, ceremonial, and magical aspects; initiation is surveyed and beliefs in 'reincarnation', 'superior beings' (High Gods) discussed. Also contains sections on traditional healers and death rituals. Bears witness to many evolutionary controversies, although these are not explicitly acknowledged. The very graphic plates, mostly from the Central Desert, are themselves most valuable.

0063 Spencer, W. Baldwin (1928) *Wanderings in Wild Australia.* 2 vols. London: Macmillan. 455 pp.
A popular account of the author's ethnographic life from the Horn expedition of 1894 onwards, and from Lake Eyre through the Central Desert to the Central-North. Contains a wealth of early descriptions of ceremonies, beliefs, magic, etc. To some extent repeats information of 0392, 0790 and 0791, but often adding new data or detail.

0064 Stanner, W.E.H. (1965) "Religion, Totemism and Symbolism." In *Aboriginal Man in Australia: Essays in Honour of Emeritus Professor A.P. Elkin,* edited by R.M. Berndt and C.H. Berndt, 207-237. Sydney: Angus and Robertson.
Contains three main sections. The first examines the history of the misconception that Aborigines lacked a religious life. The second sketches 7 key elements of Aboriginal religion, with the emphasis on symbolism and the underlying 'philosophy of assent'. The final section focuses on the concept of totemism defined as a symbolically expressed mystical connection between living persons and certain species existing within a specific ontology in which continuity of life depends upon maintaining totemic associations. These 'philosophical' and symbolic interpretations were pioneering.

0065 Stanner, W.E.H. (1976) "Some Aspects of Aboriginal Religion." *Colloquium* 9,1: 19-35.
Suggests the 'architectonic' idea of Aboriginal belief is that people are patrilineally linked with ancestors through territory and totems and takes this tetrad (people, countries, totems/ancestors) as the foundation of his discussion. Contains a 7 point summary of the nature of Aboriginal religion and a listing of 6 ideas which Stanner considers to be "authentically Aboriginal". This is

followed by a discussion of the nature of Aboriginal ritual and finally a foray into the issue of Aboriginal 'philosophy', although here Stanner's main concern is to divorce himself from the writings on the topic by Elkin (0083).

0066 Strehlow, T.G. H. (1971) "Religions of Illiterate People: Australia." In *Historia Religionum: Handbook for the History of Religion*. Vol. 2. Religions of the Present, edited by C.J. Bleeker and G. Widengren, 609-627. Leiden: E.J. Brill.
A concise and in most respects, a well-balanced introduction to the common features of Aboriginal religions. The first section on totemic ancestors and creative epochs provide some valuable corrective linguistic insights into the (mis)conception of 'dream time'. Other sections cover topics such as procreation, ritual, and Aboriginal views on death and eschatology. Favours central Australian religious manifestations.

0067 Thomas, Northcote W. (1906) *The Natives of Australia*. London: Archibald Constable. 256 pp.
For its time a rather sound introduction to Aboriginal society, although obviously limited by current standards. The chapter on 'religion' is largely devoted to the All-Fathers of the South-East but other sections on myths and tales, magic, disposal of the dead and initiation broaden the book's horizon. Buried in the chapter "the pleasure of life" is information on two millennial cults (*Molonga* and that associated with *Mindi*) and other anti-White performances, although their significance is missed by the author.

0068 Tindale, Norman B. and Lindsay, H.A. (1963) *Aboriginal Australians*. Brisbane: Jacaranda. 143 pp.
A superficial book only redeemed by Tindale's photographs and some data from his numerous research trips to Desert regions and northern Australia. Stories, totemism, initiation, and mortuary practice are considered briefly and unsatisfactorily.

0069 Tokaren, S.A. (1968) *Die Religion in der Geschichte der Völker*. Köln: Pahl-Rugenstein. 734 pp.
Pages 41-77 cover the religion of Aboriginal Australia (including Tasmania). The discussion of initiation and 'increase' ceremonies, taboos, myth, *tjurunga* and other icons is atrociously researched, and the theoretical terms in which the discussion is couched are equally inadequate.

0070 Worms, Ernest A. (1963) "Religion." In *Australian Aboriginal Studies: A Symposium of Papers Presented at the 1961 Research Conference*, edited by H. Sheils, 231-255. Melbourne: Oxford University Press.
A general overview which states in 8 points the essential features of mainland and Tasmanian Aboriginal religions. These are totally imbalanced and at times simply wrong (e.g. universality of a personal sky-being and traces of sacrifice and prayer). The author's suggestions for further research which he develops from his general statements are consequently flawed. A separate section on 'Tasmania', while welcome, is extremely speculative. Strehlow's 'commentary' and the 'discussion' gently attempt to steer Worms towards ethnographic reality.

0071 Worms, Ernest A. [and Petri, Helmut] (1986) *Australian Aboriginal Religions*. Translated by M.J. Wilson, D. O'Donovan, M. Charlesworth. Richmond: Nelen Yubu. 231 pp.

First published posthumously in German in 1968, when Helmut Petri prepared the text and interposed some of his own data. It was translated into French in 1972 and from the later version this English translation was made. German studies of Aboriginal religion, so frequently ignored, are well represented in this volume but the English edition was born outdated and lacking vitality. Half of the content is devoted to sacred objects. The rest examines deities, initiation, the afterlife and, as an afterthought, the Tasmanian Aborigines. More a catalogue of Aboriginal religious phenomena than a description of living religious traditions.

See also: 0079, 0123, 0193, 0247.

Philosophy and Totemism

0072 Berndt, Ronald M. (1970) "Two in One and More in Two." In *Échanges et Communications: Mélanges offerts à Claude Lévi-Strauss*, edited by J. Pouillon and P. Maranda, 1040-1068. Paris: Mouton.

Reviews aspects of Lévi-Strauss' views on Australian totems (0098) which, says Berndt, Australian anthropologists had also been independently exploring. By 'two in one' he refers to Lévi-Strauss' interpretation of Aboriginal social sub-systems (moieties, sections and sub-sections) as being purely 'totemic' arrangements which operate in a different sphere to marriage rules. "More in Two" refers, somewhat obliquely, to the relationship of a person to their totemic species and further, to the phenomenon of 'multiple' totemism.

0073 Berndt, Ronald M. (1987) "The Dreaming." In *The Encyclopedia of Religion*, edited by M. Eliade, vol. 4, 479-481. New York: Macmillan.

Defines the major features of the Dreaming, relates it to the concept of 'totemism' and reviews previous scholarly opinion on the topic.

0074 Brandenstein, C.G. von (1974) *Names and Substance of the Australian Subsection System*. Chicago: University of Chicago Press. 199 pp.

Argues that the solution to the substance of moieties, sections and subsections will uncover the principles ruling Australian totemism. Extensive (tedious?) linguistic analysis 'reveals' the meaning of the classificatory groups. Moieties are based on the opposition of 2 temperamental dispositions: quick and slow. Sections compound this opposition with another: warm and cold, producing four possible combinations. Finally, subsections introduce a further binary criteria, Round (big) and Flat (small), giving a total of 8 categories. These 3 types of classification, he says, are basis of the Aboriginal World Order.

0075 Broadribb, Donald (1972) "Aboriginal Totemism." *Milla wa-Milla: The Australian Bulletin of Comparative Religion* no.12: 20-35.

A generalist approach to Australian totemisms lamenting the 'vast confusion', to which the author happily adds with superficialities and poor research. Róheim is misrepresented, other Freudians attacked, and Jung eulogized as totemism is revealed to be "a system of symbols used by the Aboriginal peoples to link themselves with the archetypal realm of existence" (p.35).

0076   Doolan, J. K.   (1979)   "Aboriginal Concept of Boundary: How Do Aboriginals Conceive 'Easements' - How Do They Grant Them?" *Oceania* 49,3: 161-168.
Some brief comments on the mythological foundations of land 'ownership' and the Dreaming establishment of 'easements'.

0077   Dupré, Wilhelm   (1975)   *Religion in Primitive Cultures: A Study in Ethnophilosophy.* The Hague: Mouton. 366 pp.
A disjointed book working towards a linked understanding of culture and religion which the author speaks of, grandiosely, as ethnophilosophy. The general overview of Australia (pp.96-9) and the more extensive study of Australian totemism (pp.223-233) do not really manage to go beyond previous studies.

0078   Durkheim, Émile   (1900-1)   "Sur le Totémisme." *L'anne sociologique* 5: 82-121.
An interpretative study of totemism and social organisation deriving its main ethnography from the Aranda writings of Spencer and Gillen (0790). Historical interest only.

0079   Durkheim, Émile   (1965)   *The Elementary Forms of the Religious Life*, translated by J.W. Swain.   New York: The Free Press. 507 pp.   1st English ed: 1915.
This interpretation, primarily of Spencer and Gillen's (0790) study of the Aranda, has had more theoretical influence on studies of Aboriginal religion than any other book. The thesis is that totemic objects are powerful and sacred because they are a tangible manifestation of a society's collective existence. *Intichiuma* ceremonies are analysed as a means of promoting group solidarity. Concludes by establishing implications for the sociology of knowledge at a broader level. Evolutionary pre-suppositions and dated ethnography have not deterred followers of this brilliant sociologist.

0080   Durkheim, Émile and Mauss, Marcel   (1963)   *Primitive Classification.* London: Cohen and West. 96 pp.
This important essay, published first as "De Quelques formes Primitives de Classification" in 1901-2 devotes 2 chapters to Aboriginal Australian classifications (pp.10-41). While the evolutionary insistence on the simplicity of Aboriginal classification is untenable the attempt to search out the logistics of their socio-cosmological structure was pioneering. Considers the general application of social classification to the realms of totemism and mythology, drawing on examples from throughout Australia to substantiate their thesis.

0081   Elkin, A.P.   (1933)   *Studies in Australian Totemism.*   The Oceania Monographs, No. 2.   Sydney: The Australian National Research Council. 147 pp.

Consists of 5 articles, the first 3 providing a broad ethnographic survey of totemism in the Kimberley. Following this is a brief examination of other forms of totemic manifestations elsewhere in Australia. The presence of moieties, sections or subsections are used as classificatory criteria. Finally, Elkin generalizes regarding the various forms of totems - individual, dream, sex, clan, section, sub-section and moiety - and notes some functional and philosophic aspects of totemism. A dated but ethnographically valuable book.

0082 Elkin, A.P. (1967) "Religion and Philosophy of the Australian Aborigines." In *Essays in Honour of Griffithes Wheeler Thatcher 1863-1950*, edited by E.C.B. MacLaurin, 19-44. Sydney: Sydney University Press.
An adventurous but somewhat disappointing attempt to examine Aboriginal religious beliefs in terms of their philosophical content. A central theme is the tension between the segmentary nature of totemism and the universality of the Dreaming. Elkin relates this to Indian Upanishadic thought as well as the philosophies of Lucretius, Bergson and Leibniz. The comparisons, alas, are rather haphazard and lack depth.

0083 Elkin, A.P. (1969) "Elements of Australian Aboriginal Philosophy." *Oceania* 40,2: 85-98.
Concludes that the essential difference between Western and Aboriginal epistemologies is that the latter lacks linear measuring and numbering units and is further rooted in the ontology of the Dreaming which does not seek causal explanations. To arrive at this conclusion he examines Aboriginal 'philosophy' as cosmology and epistemology, the latter including the themes of causation, time, space, number and ownership. Elkin's analysis is theoretically simplistic and makes too many uncritical comparisons with Western philosophy.

0084 Frazer, James G. (1910) *Totemism and Exogamy: A Treatise on Certain Early Forms of Superstition and Society.* Vol. 1. London: Macmillan. 579 pp.
Volume 1 of this 4 volume work reprints Frazer's article on the origins of Aboriginal totemism and religion (0029) as well as providing 400 pages of ethnographic summary of totemism in central, South-Eastern, north-eastern and western Australia. Dated theory and interminable but rather pointless detail. See also 0085.

0085 Frazer, James G. (1937) *Totemica: A Supplement to Totemism and Exogamy.* London: Macmillan. 518 pp.
Old thinking updated with some 250 pages of new Australian examples. A collation of the results from the new era of professional fieldwork in Australia, but in the form of something of a huge footnote to (0084). If used critically, may provide a convenient summary of data on Australian totemism to the mid '30s.

0086 Friedberg, Claudine (1979) "Classifications Rituelles, Classifications Profanes: Les Examples Australiens, à propos des Classifications Dualistes

en Australie d'Alain Testart." *Journal d'Agriculture traditionelle et de Botanique Appliqué* 26,2: 147-159.
Uses Testart's thesis of dual classification (0111) to critically suvey other works dealing with Australian Aboriginal classification, including Worsley (0408) and Brandenstein (0674).

0087 Gale, Irma F. (1980) "Aboriginal Time: Dawns of Many Winters." *Folklore* 91,1: 3-10.
A superficial and frequently incorrect examination of Australian Aboriginal and Native American views of time. Although supposedly Aboriginal views form a major part of her arguments, Gale only cites one of Mountford's books, written for a 'coffee table' market.

0088 Gennep, Arnold van (1920) *L'état Actuel du Problème Totémique.* Paris: Ernest Leroux. 363 pp.
Contains scattered references to Aborigines as well as a focused review of specifically Australian theories of totemism (pp.125-140).

0089 Haekel, Josef (1950) *Zum Individual- und Geschlechtstotemismus in Australien.* Vienna: Herald. 75 pp.
An in-depth study of Australian totemism attempting to cast light upon its diffusion. Geographic regions are considered and historically ordered before examining the themes of individual, sex and group totemism, spirits and dream children. Tied into issues of patriarchy and matriarchy, German 'culture-circle' debates and other outmoded ideas. Suggests possible non-Australian origins of Australian totemic ideas.

0090 Hiatt, L.R. (1969) "Totemism Tomorrow: The Future of an Illusion." *Mankind* 7,2: 83-93.
Takes issue with Lévi-Strauss' thesis (0098) that 'totemism' is a false category. Suggests that Lévi-Strauss creates a paradox by arguing that totemism is an illusion and yet simultaneously that what was called 'totemism' has identifiable fundamental features. With the Australian data in mind, Hiatt defines totemism as a form of classification or symbolism in which social groups are signified by natural species and suggests that so defined, it constitutes a genuine phenomenon for inquiry. See Kessler (0091).

0091 Kessler, Clive S. (1971) "Is 'Totem' Taboo?" *Mankind* 8,1: 31-6.
Agrees with Hiatt (0090) that 'totemism' is a term that need not be proscribed but feels Hiatt's reasons are unfounded. In particular argues that Lévi-Strauss did not maintain the position ascribed to him and that his actual views are resilient to Hiatt's objections. He joins with Hiatt, however, on other short-comings in Lévi-Strauss' view stressing the need for a pluralist approach.

0092 Kolig, Erich (1988) "Australian Aboriginal Totemic Systems: Structures of Power." *Oceania* 58,3: 212-230.
Summarizes theories of Australian totemism before arguing that section, subsection and moiety classification are ways of ordering to gain magical power. Crude comparisons are made with Taoist and European alchemy to arrive at

little more than a slightly qualified version of Lévy-Bruhl's thesis that 'like affects like' through 'mystical participation'. Nineteenth century anthropology with a recent and full bibliography.

0093 Lang, Andrew (1905) *The Secret of the Totem.* London: Longmans, Green and Co. 215 pp.
The evolutionist (or devolutionist) approach to totemism exemplifying all its faults. A range of theorists are disposed of; 'group marriage' is (rightly) denied; the Aranda are said at length to be less primitive than Aborigines of the east coast; and the author at last gives his explanations in terms of a primitive cyclopedian family and the magic of names being transmitted from people to obejcts. A wealth of useless information on totemic emblems, myths and divisions.

0094 Lang, Andrew (1905) "The Primitive and Advanced in Totemism." *The Journal of the Anthropological Institute of Great Britain and Ireland* 35: 315-336.
Anti-evolutionary (degenerationist) attempt to prove that South-Eastern Aborigines were more primitive than central Australian Aborigines in order to further the author's thesis that High Gods are a belief found with the origin of religion. Indicative of problems of the study of Aboriginal religion at the turn of the century, totally unverifiable and theoretically obsolete.

0095 Lang, Andrew (1913) "Mr. Andrew Lang's Theory of the Origin of Exogamy and Totemism." *Folk-Lore* 24: 155-186.
A posthumous extract from a book in the making which summarizes the author's final views on totemism, relying mainly on Australian evidence. The thesis is similar to that of his previous work (0093). Depends upon a range of fanciful suppositions from a primordial horde with a dominant male, through mystical connections between people and names, to thoroughly conjectural history of social development. Quite dead.

0096 Láng, János (1963) "A 'totemizmus' alapjai és kialakulása." *Különlenyomat az Ethnographia* 74: 374-401.
A horrible resuscitation of nineteenth century theory tinged with Pavlovian psychology. Drawing almost exclusively on Aboriginal ethnographic data he argues that the totemic ceremonies developed from the wanderings of real ancestors who took possession of the land from the local groups. Knowledge of traditions is thus seen as a right to the land. A range of evolutionary preconceptions are brought in to justify this thesis.

0097 Lévi-Strauss, Claude (1966) *The Savage Mind: The Nature of Human Society.* London: Weidenfeld and Nicolson. 290 pp.
La Pensée Sauvage is a continuation of the line of thought in (0098). Here he advocates the famous thesis that "mythical thought is... a kind of intellectual 'bricolage'"(p.17). Aboriginal data forms the core of two chapters (3 and 8). Examines variations and transformations of 'totemic' ancestors throughout Australia and makes a well-known analysis of the Yolngu *Wawalak* myth (pp.91-

96), as well as considering the theoretical relationship between sacrifice and 'increase' ceremonies. Controversial.

0098 Lévi-Strauss, Claude (1969) *Totemism.* Harmondsworth: Penguin. 190 pp.
This famous essay attempted to put an end to the 'totemic illusion'. Australian data forms the bulk of the author's evidence and he takes to task Elkin's (0081) study of totemism in particular. Developing Radcliffe-Brown's thesis (0107), Lévi-Strauss steps into the realm of pure intellect arguing 'totemism' is no more nor less than a manifestation of a mode of thought. Totemic species are chosen because they are 'good to think'. Far from ending 'totemism', the author revived its defendants, such as Hiatt (0090) and Peterson (0103).

0099 McConnel, Ursula H. (1933) "The Symbol in Legend." *Psyche* 13: 94-137.
The legend of Eden and a Koko-janju moon myth are analysed, as are general concepts of 'totemism' throughout Australia in an attempted rapprochment between psychological, sociological and historical investigations of symbolism. Suggests totems are kinship 'tags' and as economic conditions became more difficult, kinship becomes more tightly organized, and that, as with the Aranda, reincarnation beliefs and locality based totemic affiliations take prominence (p.106). Ambitious, eclectic, disjointed, unsatisfying.

0100 Makarius, Raoul and Makarius, Laura (1961) *L'origine de l'exogamie et du totémisme.* Paris: Librairie Gallimard. 362 pp.
Australian data is very well represented in the author's survey of incest taboos and kinship obligations, said to be linked with 'increase' rites and a range of food restrictions. (Does not the absence of a mouth in *Wandjina* indicate a food taboo?) Forms of totemism are discussed as well as the 'giving' of totems in 'myth' and reality. Dubious.

0101 Milke, Wilhelm (1936) "Totemzentren und Vermehrungsriten in Australien und Ozeanien." *Zeitschrift für Ethnologie* 68: 211-227.
In the tradition of the German *kulturhistorische* school, attempts to relate Australian and Papuan totemism. Argues for the wide distribution of the *tabu* type of fertility rites in Australia which are also located in the Torres Strait but *not*, significantly, in Papua New Guinea. Suggests, *contra* Schmidt (0788), that Australian totemism is not of Papuan derivation but perhaps the inverse is true, or possibly both are of Indonesian origin. Goes beyond reasonable inference.

0102 Nieuwenhuis, Anton W. (1928) "Der Geschlechtstotemismus an sich und als Basis der Heiratsklassen und des Gruppentotemismus in Australien." *Internationales Archiv für Ethnographie* 29: 1-52.
A broad, tedious survey of 'sex-totemism' in Australia arguing that its primary place is in the South-East where it probably arose. Sex totemism is compared with group totemism of central Australia and the marriage class system of central Queensland in order to establish historical sequences. The whole is in line with Schmidtian diffusionary theories and is totally dated.

0103 Peterson, Nicolas (1972) "Totemism Yesterday: Sentiment and Local
      Organisation Among the Australian Aborigines." *Man* NS 7,1: 12-32.
Critiques Lévi-Strauss (0098) for ignoring the affective side of totemism. In
particular stresses people's affiliation with sites and land which, he suggests,
predates (on logical grounds) other social divisions. Concludes that clan
totemism is a territorial spacing mechanism which employs the human
psychological tendency to have sentimental attachments to places. Dated views
on Aboriginal territorial organisation and a restricted view of totemism.

0104 Petri, Helmut (1950) "Kult-totemismus in Australien." *Paideuma* 5,1/2:
      44-58.
An Australian-wide statement drawing on the works of Elkin, Tindale, Strehlow
and Howitt but especially relying on the author's own Ngadatjara, Nyigina,
Ngarinyin, Karadjeri and Bard data. Considers the journeys of mythological
figures (e.g. the *Wati Kutjara*, see Tindale 0726; *Djarmar*, see Worms 0595,
etc.) and the association of these heroes with what Petri refers to as 'cult
totemism'.

0105 Petri, Helmut (1963) "Totemismo." In *Enciclopedia Universale
      Dell'arte*, vol. 14. colums 50-55. Venezia: Instituto per la Collaborazione
      Culturate.
Brief overview of Australian totemism, emphasizing totemic art.

0106 Petri, Helmut (1965) "Traum und Trance bei den Australiden." *Bild der
      Wissenschaft* no. 4: 277-285.
A conservative view of Aboriginal ontology stating that although there may be
changes, the substance of their world does not alter. The author's observations
in 1954-5 and 1960-1963 in the Canning Basin discerned no loss of 'totemic
conceptions' originating in dream and trance. Raises the open question of
whether dreams and trances - visual hallucinations - are the origin of 'totemic'
conceptions. Rather lightweight and speculative.

0107 Radcliffe-Brown, A.R. (1951) "The Comparative Method in Social
      Anthropology." *Journal of the Royal Anthropological Institute of Great
      Britain and Ireland* 81: 15-22.
An article immortalized by Lévi-Strauss (0098) who saw it as anticipating
structuralism. Notes widespread occurence of paired bird myths in Australia and
then relates a western Australian eaglehawk and crow version. Argues that those
particular birds are mythologized because they have features of similarity and
difference corresponding to the social relationship between moieties - that of
'oppposition'.

0108 Róheim, Géza (1971) *Australian Totemism: A Psycho-Analytic Study in
      Anthropology*. 2nd. ed. London: Frank Cass. 487 pp. 1st ed. 1925.
A thoroughly researched book based on studies of Australian totemism up to
1924 and using psychoanalytic theories to interpret the data. Detailed surveys of
sex-totems, individual totems, conception and 'class' totems and totemic taboos.
Also examines 'increase' ceremonies and Dreaming myths. Finally there is an
extensive reconstruction of an hypothetical development of totemism along

orthodox Freudian lines. Predates Róheim's field-work, and he himself later repudiated some of the views in this volume.

0109 Stanner, W.E.H. (1957) "The Australian Aboriginal Dreaming as an Ideological System." *Proceedings of the North Pacific Science Congress* 3: 116-123.
Frequently republished as "The Dreaming" this deservedly famous article was largely responsible for giving this Aboriginal concept its prominence. Stanner attempts to render Aboriginal 'poetic' philosophy into a form intelligible to readers. He sees it as at least 3 things - a narrative about the basis of the world, a charter for what constitutes valid knowledge, and a foundation for moral law. The Dreaming is, finally, a metaphysic affirming a 'mood of assent'.

0110 Swain, Tony (1989) "Dreaming, Whites and the Australian Landscape: Some Popular Misconceptions." *The Journal of Religious History* 15,3: 345-350.
Attempts to clarify concepts misused by those who look to Aboriginal religious life for spiritual inspiration. In particular, 'Dreaming' is argued not to be an affective quality of 'religious feeling' for the landscape, as often alleged, but an intellectual construction of a Law embracing environmental, social and religious domains.

0111 Testart, Alain (1978) *Des Classifications Dualistes en Australie: Essai sur l'Evolution de l'Organisation Sociale.* Lille: l'Université de Lille. 222 pp.
Examines oppositions (such as eaglehawk and crow), and associations (for instance, oppossum with eagle), in Aboriginal mythic thought. Argues that these occur more frequently in tribes with matrilineal moieties than in those with patrilineal moieties. This is, without reasonable explanation, argued to prove that matrilineality is more ancient. The 'logic' of dual classification is then linked to an opposition between violator and non-violator, which, once again unconvincingly, is said to evidence the priority of matrilineal societies.

0112 Turner, David H. (1987) *Life Before Genesis: A Conclusion: An Understanding of the Significance of Australian Aboriginal Culture.* 2nd ed. New York: Peter Lang. 181 pp.
An original, thought-provoking and personal book which interprets the Book of Genesis in light of an analysis of the 'redemptive' features of Andiljaugwa (Groote Eylandt) society, and the 'fallen' Bidjandjadjara (and Canadian Indians). Focuses on the concepts of 'federation' and 'incorporation' as revealed in Aboriginal mythology. Turner's analytical methods are essentially those of Lévi-Strauss but he arrives at very different conclusions.

0113 Vatter, Ernst (1925) *Der Australische Totemismus.* Hamburg: Mitteilungen aus dem Museum für Völkerkunde. 158 pp.
130 different 'tribes' have their 'totemic' life considered, although the western part of the continent receives scant attention. Social aspects of totemism are emphasized, as are the categories of individual, sex and sub-totems. Central Australian data is given special examination. The tedious debate of the earliest

form of totemism is then taken up, weighing the many theories, contrasting evolutionists and diffusionists positions, etc.

0114 Vatter, Ernst (1926) "Karten zur Verbreitung totemistischer Phänomene in Australien." *Anthropos* 21: 566-579.
'Totemism' as a continent-wide phenomenon is divided into its manifestations (e.g. individual, class, phratrie and section totems) and their respective distribution is plotted onto 10 maps. Useful only to the extent to which the artificial categories can be considered significant.

0115 Webster, Hutton (1911) "Totem, Clans and Secret Associations in Australia and Melanesia." *The Journal of the Royal Anthropological Institute of Great Britain and Ireland* 41: 482-508.
A reinterpretation of the ethnographic data on totemism and initiation from eastern and central Australia as well as the Western and Eastern Torres Strait Islands. These are further compared with Melanesian data in an attempt to argue that secret societies have emerged from totemic-type clan-focused initiation most clearly evidenced in central Australia. Speculative evolutionary theory.

See also: 0029, 0034, 0061, 0064, 0065, 0167, 0174, 0257, 0259.

Myth

0116 Berndt, Catherine H. (1980) "Australia." In *Mythology: An Illustrated Encyclopedia*, edited by R. Cavendish, 284-291. London: Orbis.
A brief selective overview singling out the All-Father, All-Mother and Rainbow Serpent themes as specific examples of Aboriginal mythology. Discusses the territorial base of myth, the stories' link with social and environmental realities and the relationship between the sexes as revealed in the famous *Wawalak* myth.

0117 Berndt, Catherine H. (1987) "Rainbow Snake." In *The Encyclopedia of Religion*, edited by M. Eliade, Vol. 12, 205-208. New York: Macmillan.
Briefly describes this mythic figure's manifestations throughout Australia and explores its symbolic significance.

0118 Berndt, Catherine H. (1987) "Australian Religions: Mythic Themes." In *The Encyclopedia of Religion*, edited by M. Eliade, Vol. 1, 547-562. New York: Macmillan.
Portrays myth as a charter for the 'practical' concerns of life, addressing human interaction within natural and social environments. Regional variations and widespread mythic themes are considered and their affiliation to local topography and social groups underlined. The process of interlocking of mythic episodes to form a complex network is discussed. Throughout the emphasis is on the function of myth in establishing models for life.

0119 Berndt, Ronald M. (1979) "A Profile of Good and Bad in Australian Aboriginal Religion." *Colloquium* 12: 17-32.

Attempts to define the essence of Aboriginal religious life. Diverges from Stanner's view that Aborigines see life as something which had taken an 'immemorial misdirection' and argues that good and bad are seen as unavoidable components of life. Focuses on myth, particularly those of Arnhem Land but also those associated with the Western Desert *Dingari*, arguing that they are charters for correct social behaviour and that inevitable consequence are shown to follow actions.

0120 Berndt, Ronald M. and Berndt, Catherine H. (1988) *The Speaking Land: Myth and Story in Aboriginal Australia.* Melbourne: Penguin. 438 pp.
An anthology of 195 traditional myths and stories (from about 50 to 60 storytellers from central Australia and Arnhem Land) translated from the vernacular languages. The organisation is thematic and each myth is placed in context by the Berndts. Their understanding of Aboriginal myth is functionalist in the Malinowskian sense, seeing it as an exemplar of both good and bad actions, in each case with inevitable consequences. There is a tension in trying to make localized stories accessible to a wide audience, but nonetheless a very rich collection.

0121 Campbell, Alastair H. (1967) "Aboriginal Traditions and the Prehistory of Australia." *Mankind* 6,10: 476-481.
A revival of the 'myth as history' thesis (see Hiatt, 0251) which argues that Aboriginal mythic reference to different sea levels, climates and animals indicates a retention in oral traditions of events occurring 8-10,000 years ago. The data is sketchy, selective and now dated.

0122 Dixon, Roland B. (1964) *Oceania.* Vol. 9 of The Mythology of All Races, edited by L.H. Gray. New York: Cooper Square. 364 pp.
While the author of this book, which first appeared in 1916, claims to have avoided prejudicing data with interpretation, the very presentation is heavily weighted. A major section is devoted to "Myths of Origin and the Deluge" which, while present, are hardly a central theme in Australia. There is also a rather non-Aboriginal bias for celestial myths. Attempts to plot cultural regions within Australia and trace northern diffusionary processes.

0123 Gennep, Arnold van (1906) *Mythes et Légendes d'Australie.* Paris: Librairie Orientale et Americaine. cxvi + 188 pp.
A long introduction of 116 pages is followed by the actual 'Myths and Legends of Australia' which are French translations from the works of Smyth, Curr, Howitt, Parker, Roth, and Spencer and Gillen. The introduction is divided into 10 chapters, which deal with general issues of Aboriginal biology and sociology before considering religious themes such as beliefs in conception and 'reincarnation', totemism, supernatural Beings, magic and religion, the relationship between myth and ritual, and the content of the myths.

0124 Haines, Ros (1989) "Dreamtime Astronomy." In *Guide to Australian Astronomy*, edited by J. Fairall, 40-47. Alexandria: Federal.
Considers the pragmatic, social and philosophical significance of Aboriginal astronomy. Devoted mainly to a collage of myths from across the continent, and

argues that the humanizing of the cosmos helped overcome a sense of helplessness. Journalistic and hardly profound.

0125 Harney, W.E. (1959) *Tales from the Aborigines.* London: Robert Hale. 189 pp.
Northern Territory Aboriginal stories from the north coast to the Deserts classified under the sections 'Tales of "Fantasy", "Imagination", "Caution and Observation" and "Contact". Horribly over-edited and often highly unreliable. The final chapter 'The Symbols of Uluru' which portrays Ayer's Rock as the Earth Mother is a good example of misinterpretation.

0126 Hiatt, L.R., ed. (1975) *Australian Aboriginal Mythology.* Canberra: Australian Institute of Aboriginal Studies. 213 pp.
A volume of analytical studies of Aborginal mythology drawing heavily on structuralist and other interpretative methodologies. The contents are: Hiatt (0251), Blows (0969), van der Leeden (0434), Maddock (0436), White (0763), Hiatt (0127), Beckett (0297), and translated excerpts of van Gennep (0123).

0127 Hiatt, L.R. (1975) "Swallowing and Regurgitation in Australian Myth and Rite." In *Australian Aboriginal Mythology*, edited by L.R. Hiatt, 143-162. Canberra: Australian Institute of Aboriginal Studies.
Analyses various accounts of serpents who devour and later regurgitate other Dreaming Beings. Maintains there is a connection between such myths and rites of initiation in which neophytes are hidden (swallowed) from women and re-born (regurgitated) into the society of men. Argues a Freudian interpretation is valid insofar as the symbolism is connected with the removal of young males' libido from 'mothers', but he goes further, following Eliade, to suggest the myths also have a cosmological interpretation.

0128 Kolig, Erich (1978) "Aboriginal Dogmatics: Canines in Theory, Myth and Dogma." *Bijdragen de Taal-, Land- en Volkenkunde* 134: 84-115.
Dogs have usually been said to have been domesticated by Aborigines for economic reasons. Kolig says it was a symbolic move, and expends many words rejecting both the ecological and emotional catharsis theories. His thesis is that the dog is an ambivalent animal, with some sinister airs but spiritually useful in guarding the world against supernatural dangers. Taboos on killing are noted along with the negative symbolism of dog-ness in speech and myth. The dog is thus the anti-creator and the symbol of a social chaos.

0129 Lèvy-Bruhl, Lucien (1983) *Primitive Mythology: The Mythic World of the Australian and Papuan Natives.* St. Lucia: University of Queensland Press. 332 pp.
First appeared in 1935 as *La Mythologie Primitive.* Refurbishes the author's thesis (dating back to 1910) of a pre-logical mode of thought with new Australian and Melanesian ethnography. In this region, he says, myth is the core of the sacred, and from this premise he moves on to examine mythic beings in their human/animal duality, totems, kinship, the power of myth and the principle of participation in initiation which binds myth and magic together. Theoretically dated.

0130 Löffler, Anneliese, ed.   (1981).   *Märchen aus Australien: Traumzeitmythen und -geschichten der Australischen Aborigines*. Düseldorf: Eugen Diederichs. 284 pp.
A retelling of the Aboriginal myths taken from an assorted, and qualitatively mixed, group of published works. Some order is given by a geographical listing, but in terms of states rather than cultural areas.

0131 Maddock, Kenneth (1970) "Myths of the Acquisition of Fire in Northern and Eastern Australia." In *Australian Aboriginal Studies: Modern Studies in the Social Anthropology of the Australian Aborigines*, edited by R M. Berndt, 174-199. Nedlands: University of Western Australia Press.
Analyses 23 myths of the acquisition of fire, from western Arnhem Land, Cape York, the east Coast and Tasmania. Finds a correlation between fire myths and beliefs concerning the spirits of the dead. Those who have lost life in the flesh are seen as being on a lower physical plane than embodied people. Likewise those who have lost fire in myths are portrayed as lower than those who steal fire (often birds). Although the correlation is stronger in the southern areas, Maddock concludes, *à la* Lévi-Strauss, that losers of life in the flesh: possessors of life in the flesh:: losers of fire: takers of fire.

0132 Mountford, Charles P.   (1978)   "The Rainbow-Serpent Myths of Australia." In *The Rainbow Serpent: A Chromatic Piece*, edited by I.R. Buchler and K. Maddock, 23-97. Paris: Mouton.
Surveys the forms of Rainbow-Serpent myths throughout Australia, providing a valuable, although by no means exhaustive, overview.   Detects four main regions: 1) the Central and Western Deserts, where the serpent has no significance other than that of a Dreaming ancestor, 2) the east of Australia, which is characterized by special links between medicine men and the serpent, 3) Arnhem Land, where the serpent is almost a 'Supreme Being', and 4) the Kimberley where the Rainbow Serpent beliefs are replaced by the *Wandjina* cult.

0133 Partington, Geoffrey (1985) "The Australian Aborigines and the Human Past." *Mankind* 15,1: 26-40.
Attempts to dispel the notion that Aboriginal mythic thought is totally devoid of historic reflections upon their human past, a view the author attributes to the functionalist view of myth. Maintains, in contrast, that Aborigines do indeed have a sense of historical time, albeit shallow and that this is something Aborigines should be developing. Focuses unduly on the supposed negativeness of ahistoricity and neglects the positive dimensions of such an ontology.

0134 Pettazzoni, Raffaele (1948) *Miti e Leggende: I: Africa, Australia*. Turin: 480 pp.
Translations into Italian of the mythology of Africans and Aboriginal Australians. The preface gives Pettazzoni's views, as an historian of religions, on myth and legend, insisting that myth is *not* false history. Represents a major scholarly achievement but nonetheless contains important errors of fact. Thus, for example, the map which correlates beliefs with social organisation did not accurately represent academic knowledge at the time.

0135 Poignant, Roslyn (1985) *Oceanic and Australasian Mythology*. 2nd ed. Middlesex: Newnes. 144 pp.
Offers a brief overview of Aboriginal religious and mythic principles, before exploring some diversity in myths throughout the continent. The South-East Sky Heroes, a moon myth from Cape York, the Dieri *Muramura*, various Desert myths, the Kimberley *Wandjina*, and the Arnhem Land Lightning Brothers, *Yulunggur*, the *Djanggawul* and the *Wawalak* are all present. Adds nothing new, but a usable, popular, well-illustrated introduction with few (but some) errors.

0136 Radcliffe-Brown, A.R. (1926) "The Rainbow Serpent Myth of Australia." *Journal of the Royal Anthropological Institute of Great Britain and Ireland* 56: 19-25.
A survey of the evidence for a huge serpent associated with the rainbow. The account runs north to south through eastern Australia, then turns to the west coast, the Deserts and concludes with the Kimberley. There are a few brief notes on this 'practically universal' mythic figure's association with rain-making, quartz-crystals, 'medicine men' and totemism.

0137 Ramsay-Smith, William (1930) *Myths and Legends of the Australian Aboriginals*. London: George C. Harrap. 356 pp.
The only order to this book is a five-fold division of myths: origins, animal, religious, social and personal. There is no sensitivity to geographic variations or social contexts of myths, nor references to sources. Imbalanced, inauthentic and confused, the book is only saved by some reasonable monochrome photographs and some hilariously inappropriate colour paintings. Comic relief only.

0138 Reed, A.W. (1965) *Myths and Legends of Australia*. Sydney: A.H. and A.W. Reed. 256 pp.
See (below) 0141.

0139 Reed, A.W. (1965) *Aboriginal Fables and Legendary Tales*. Sydney: A.H. and A.W. Reed. 144 pp.
See (below) 0141.

0140 Reed, A.W. (1978) *Aboriginal Legends: Animal Tales*. Sydney: A.H. and A.W. Reed. 141 pp.
See (below) 0141.

0141 Reed, A.W. (1978) *Aboriginal Myths: Tales of the Dreamtime*. Sydney: A.H. and A.W. Reed. 142 pp.
The author/publisher of this and the preceeding 3 well-known books has no first-hand experience with the people whose stories intrigue him so. The first two books implicitly differentiate, unsatisfactorily, between myth, legend and fable, while the latter pair are distinguished by one focusing on animal narratives, the other on cosmogonic myths - again, an unhappy division. As they merely retell previously published and paraphrased or translated accounts, they add nothing for the researcher's use.

0142 Robinson, Roland (1966) *Aboriginal Myths and Legends*. Melbourne:
       Sun Books. 218 pp.
With a few exceptions the 56 narratives were collected, in Aboriginal English,
by the author and transcribed in a way that is not overly intrusive. Robinson's
own material from Arnhem Land and the Central and Western Deserts, focusing
on traditional themes (ancestors, Rainbow Serpent, fertility, law), may fail to
conform to anthropological rigours, but the final section on the South-East
region happily adds to our knowledge in an areas where anthropologists were
then remiss.

0143 Robinson, Roland (1968) *Wandjina: Children of the Dreamtime:
       Aboriginal Myths and Legends*. Milton: Jacaranda. 112 pp.
Myths on many subjects - except *Wandjina*! Contains hideous illustrations,
absurd title, bland introduction and disorganized text with no references to
sources. Most stories are available elsewhere in Robinson's books and many of
them are in themselves of value and interest. The presentation and lack of
contextualisation largely destroys the data.

0144 Robinson, Roland (1970) *Altjeringa and Other Aboriginal Poems*.
       Sydney: A.H. and A.W. Reed. 80 pp.
Nearly all of the data for first section of this book was collected from the
Aboriginal communities of NSW, and the value of the stories is that they do not
hide the effects of contact. Percy Mumbulla's "Captain Cook" is a South-Eastern
version of northern Cook myths (see Kolig 0641, Rose 0652, etc.); Alexander
Vesper's "The Sermon of the Birds" explicitly parallels tradition with "the
prophecy of Christ". Despite the verse formatting, there is much that is
authentic in this collection.

0145 Robinson, Roland (1976) *The Shift of Sands: An Autobiography 1952-
       62*. Melbourne: Macmillan. 375 pp.
Autobiography of a poet who spent much of his life collecting Aboriginal myths.
Contains extensive quotations from his mythic records. Includes some material
on northern fertility cults but is perhaps most useful in the South-East where he
makes no attempt to edit contact influence - thus the three brothers who create
Australia come in a sailing ship (pp.277-8), which is why Aborigines recognized
Captain Cook when he arrived. Non-professional ethnography at its best.

0146 Thomas, J.W. (1939) *Some Myths and Legends of the Australian
       Aborigines*. Melbourne: Whitecombe and Tombs. 75 pp.
I suspect the author made up as much as he gleaned from published sources (not
one of which is acknowledged). A horrible mishmash of romanticism and
condescension set the tone for the introduction and the myths themselves are
arranged without order or purpose. Useless.

0147 Triebels, L.F. (1958) *Enige Aspecten van der Regenbogsslang: Een
       Vergelijkende Studie*. Nijmegen: Drukkerij Gebr. Janssen. 141 pp.
Originally a doctoral thesis comparing serpent myths and examining the
relationship with 'medicine men' in Australia, China, India and other areas.

Aboriginal Rainbow Serpents are considered from published accounts throughout the continent on pp. 36-49.

0148 Wilpert, Clara B. (1970) *Kosmogonische Mythen der australischen Eingeborenen: Das Konzept der Schöpfung und Anthropogenese.* München: Klaus Renner. 380 pp.
Published Ph.D. dissertation examining cosmogonies and their representation of the origins of nature and society, using cultural-historical methods (particularly reveals the influence of H. Petri). Examines data region by region, often in terms of particular 'tribes'. Generalizes regarding cultic heroes and creative processes. Concludes by suggesting cosmogonies establish the environmental prototypes akin to Platonic 'forms', and also by indicating gaps in the data. Suggests possible external influences on cosmogonies.

0149 Worms, Ernest A. (1957) "Australian Mythological Terms: Their Etymology and Dispersion." *Anthropos* 52: 732-768.
A linguistically dubious continent-wide examination of terms which ventures into areas in which the author has no background (especially the South-East). Mythological terms are categorized by 35 different roots. Concludes that the basic cult of Australia is that dealing with ghosts and the dead, and that other developments, such as the *Wandjina, Ungud, Maianjari* and *Djamba* of the Kimberley are of recent origin.

See also: 0055, 0107, 0111, 0153, 0154, 0159, 0196, 0251, 0254, 0995.

The Arts

0150 Adam, Leonhard (1954) *Primitive Art.* Melbourne: Penguin. 3rd ed. 247 pp.
First published in 1940, containing some detail on religious belief and practice associated with art.

0151 Adam, Leonhard (1958) "Anthropomorphe Darstellungen auf australischen Ritualgeräten." *Anthropos* 53: 1-50.
Describes *tjurunga* and the common designs found on wood and stone objects. Considers style, shape and ceremonial use. Some analysis is made of naturalistic and geometric types' associated myths and interpretations. Draws parallels from Papua New Guinea. Illustrations and plates taken from Kimberley and Desert regions are given and comparisons are made with rock art of the Musgrave Ranges. The focus is on anthropomorphic forms.

0152 Adam, Leonhard (1963) "A Parallel Between Certain Ritual Objects of the Ainu and of the Australian Aborigines." In *Congrès International des Sciences Anthropologiques et Ethnologiques, 6th, 1960,* 9-13.
Compares Aboriginal and Ainu art and ritual object forms, suggesting historical contacts.

0153 Berndt, Catherine H. (1983) "Australian Aborigines: Oral Literature."
       In *The Australian Encyclopedia*. 4th ed. Vol. 1, 171-173. Sydney: The
       Grolier Society.
Considers myths briefly as a form of oral literature.

0154 Berndt, Catherine H. and Berndt, Ronald M. (1982) "Aboriginal
       Australia: Literature in an Oral Tradition." In *Review of National
       Literatures: Vol. 11; Australia*, edited by L.A.C. Pobrez, 39-63. New
       York: Griffon.
Considers the role of the sacred in Aboriginal song-poetry and other forms of
oral literature. Briefly gives the *Djanggawul* and *Wawalak* myths as well as
excerpts from the Western Desert *Djilbi Gandju* (Old Man) myth complex and a
Dieri myth. Argues that myths are mirror images of real life. Considers
Macassan influence on song-cycles as a part of the process of innovation and
creativity.

0155 Berndt, Ronald M. (1983) "Images of God in Aboriginal Australia." In
       Representations of Gods. Visible Religion: Annual for Religious
       Iconography, edited by H.G. Kippenberg et al., vol. 2, 14-39. Leiden:
       E.J. Brill.
Wisely emphasizes the difficulties of generalizing about the innumerable
Aboriginal views on 'gods'. Trying to hierarchically organize such beings, he
says, is futile. The iconographical context is equally problematic as 'gods' have
various shapes. They are intrinsically associated with geographic formations,
specific species and individual groups, and their depiction reflects these
affiliations. Indeed, as a deity's essence can be transformed into the land,
animals, living humans and sacred objects, icons are not images of god but *are*
the beings themselves.

0156 Black, Roman (1964) *Old and New Australian Aboriginal Art*. Sydney:
       Angus and Robertson. 175 pp.
Attempts to place art in its socio-religious context. There is the standard survey
of styles with some relevant mythic episodes. Interesting is the focus on
changing traditions; thus on p.14 are rock-poundings of automobiles and White
people, on pp. 50-53, Macassans are portrayed and discussed in context of the
Djanggawul myth, while p. 58 has a panel of Jesus crucified by Royal Australian
Air Force people. Sacred and ceremonial objects and designs are considered,
although here the commentary is thinner.

0157 Davidson, Daniel S. (1951) "The Thread Cross in Australia." *Mankind*
       4,7: 263-273.
Discusses distribution but with little consideration of religious significance.

0158 Godden, Elaine and Malnic, Jutta (1982) *Rock Paintings of Aboriginal
       Australia*. French's Forest: A.H. and A.W. Reed. 128 pp.
Contains a brief chapter on "Dreamings", referring to Rainbow Serpents, All-
Mothers and All-Fathers (drawing heavily, it would seem, on Maddock 0041),
but not detailed. Also discusses 'the power of places' and includes a chapter on
regional variations in art and associated stories, singling out the Kimberley, Cape

York, Arnhem Land and 'the South' (including Desert regions). Accompanied by good colour plates, which are poorly annotated.

0159 Laade, Wolfgang (1975) *Musik der Götter, Geister und Menschen: die Musik in der mythischen, fabulierenden und historischen Überlieferung der Völker Afrikas, Nordasiens, Amerikas und Ozeaniens*. Baden-Baden: Valentin Koerner. 344 pp.
A survey (pp.313-366) from Cape York to Arnhem Land and the Kimberley through the Deserts to the South-East describes (from published accounts and the author's own material) Aboriginal myths relating to music and musical instruments. This is followed by a section on the origin of new songs and a selection of extracts from Aboriginal songs with translations.

0160 Lommel, Andreas and Lommel, Katharina (1959) *Die Kunst des fünften Erdteils Australien*. München: Staatliches Museum für Völkerkunde. 183 pp.
Based on fieldwork in 1954-5 this continent-wide survey is strongest on the Kimberley region. The 'stagnancy' of Aboriginal art is proposed and mythology and beliefs for the north-west, especially the Wunambal, are described. The relation between art and religion is explored. Speculates on the influences on Aboriginal art, some of the claims being rather extravagant.

0161 Morphy, Howard (1987) "Iconography: Australian Aboriginal Iconography." In *The Encyclopedia of Religion*, edited by M. Eliade, Vol. 7, 14-17. New York: Macmillan.
Summarizes briefly the mythic origins of Aboriginal art, its methods of encoding meaning and the ways in which this meaning is revealed. All examples are drawn from central Australia and Arnhem Land.

0162 Mountford, Charles P. (1938) "A Survey of Australian Aboriginal Pearl and Baler Shell Ornaments." *Records of the South Australian Museum* 6,2: 115-142.
Examines the distribution of bailer shell and pearl oyster shell ornaments throughout Australia, indicating their ceremonial and decorative functions. Briefly considers the myths associated with the shells and their use in attracting lovers, healing, rainmaking, etc. Well illustrated, but lacking in exegesis.

0163 Moyle, Alice M. (1977) "Music and Dance: Mastersingers of the Bush." In *The Moving Frontier: Aspects of Aboriginal European Interactions in Australia*, edited by P. Stanbury, 63-75. Sydney: A.H. and A.W. Reed.
A survey of European impressions of public ceremonies or 'corroborees'. Draws mainly on the views of early explorers, missionaries and settlers and focuses largely on NSW. Later parts will be of more interest to ethnomusicologists but the earlier sections also consider 'corroborees' in their ritual setting. Examines the innovation and travel of new 'corroborees' and their roles in terms of a range of comparisons from opera to rites of passage.

0164 Odermann, Gisela (1959) "Holtz- und Steinsetzungen in Australien." *Paideuma* 7,2: 99-114.

A continent-wide survey, with superior data for the Kimberley (where the author had first-hand experience) and includes descriptions of wood and stone arrangements, platform burials, 'increase' ceremony sites, burial posts, etc.

0165   Rose, Frederick G.G.   (1969)   *Die Ureinwohner Australiens: Gesellschaft und Kunst*. Leipzig: Koehler and Amelang. 228 pp.
Pages 38-62 consider 'beliefs and art of primitive society' and explains how Aboriginal people see their art as a form of their beliefs. The bulk of the book is a regional survey, but more interesting perhaps is the section on innovation in tradition-based art, ranging from figures of missionaries, through to a black Jesus being executed by RAAF staff, *Kurrangara* cult innovations, and a central Australian potential cargo-cult. A good introduction.

0166   Sutton, Peter   (1987)   "Mystery and Change." In *Songs of Aboriginal Australia*, edited by M. Clunies Ross, T. Donaldson and S.A.Wild, 77-96. Sydney: Oceania Monographs.
Documents both the regularity and 'anomalies' in fit between songs/myths and actual rights of people to sites they sing about, using data from the Wik of Cape York Peninsula and the Mudbara and Djingilu of the Central Desert. Suggests apparent anomalies are in fact an important part of a cultural ideology maintaining a tension between stability and change. 'Anomalies' provide avenues for change without threatening the overall logic of the cosmology.

0167   Sutton, Peter   (1988)   "Dreamings." In *Dreamings: The Art of Aboriginal Australia*, edited by P. Sutton, 13-32. Ringwood: Viking.
Attempts to explain how the concept of Dreaming infuses Aboriginal art. A cautious yet accessible exposition linking ancestors, stories and art to the Dreaming or Law, showing how the latter differs from ontologies in other societies. Dichotomies of spiritual/material, sacred/secular, natural/supernatural, are shown to be inappropriate and the essential unity of land, symbol, stories and people is stressed.

0168   Walsh, Grahame L.   (1988)   *Australia's Greatest Rock Art*. Bathurst, N.S.W.: E.J. Brill/Robert Brown. 312 pp.
A beautifully photographed survey of rock art throughout Australia. The introductory chapter on "The Dreaming" (pp.35-38) is not profound and the 100 sites which are documented do not (and could not) always have information on the associated mythic traditions. At best, Walsh's commentary briefly summarizes current opinion as to the religious significance of sites.

See also: 0007, 0603.

Ceremony

0169   Baal, J. van   (1973)   "The Cult of the Bull-Roarer in Australia and Southern New Guinea." *Bijdragen tot de Taal-, Land- en Volkenkunde* 119: 201-14.

Claims similarities between southern Papuan and Australian bull-roarer cults. Australian examples considered are the Yolngu *Djanggawul* and *Kunapipi* and Aranda ceremonies. Argues these are primarily phallic cults, *rangga*, *tjurunga*, etc. and mythic beings (including the All-Mother) being given phallic interpretations. Considers what this symbolism signifies for procreation beliefs. Does not explore historical contacts, but see Leeden (0496).

0170 Barker, Graham (1976) "The Ritual Estate and Aboriginal Polity." *Mankind* 10,4: 225-39.
Distinguishes the 'range' - the tract of land over which a group has economic access - from the 'estate', the land with which people are ritually affiliated. The bestowal of a ritual property is shown to represent an essential aspect of individual and group politics. In rituals, furthermore, people's assumed credentials are publicly asserted, and, if contested, are necessarily resolved before the performance can be completed.

0171 Hiatt, L.R. (1971) "Secret Pseudo-Procreation Rites Among the Australian Aborigines." In *Anthropology in Oceania: Essays Presented To Ian Hogbin*, edited by L.R. Hiatt and C. Jayawardena, 77-88. Sydney: Angus and Robertson.
Tries to answer two questions: why are Aboriginal men concerned with procreative rites? and why are these kept secret from women and children? Hiatt builds on suggestions put forward in psychoanalytic theory (e.g. Róheim 0108 and 0056; Bettelheim 0184), concluding that the rites are a means whereby men delude themselves that they are masters over domains in which women have natural advantages (reproduction), whilst simultaneously attempting to mystify and intimidate the women.

0172 Hiatt, L.R. (1979) "Queen of Night, Mother-Right, and Secret Male Cults." *Musicology* 5: 191-204.
Secret men's cults among the Aranda and Waljbiri of Central Australia and the Mara and Murinbata of the Central-North are examined and the theme of symbolic re-birth emphasized, as is the ambivalent attitude of men regarding women's mythic and contemporary sacred status. These principles are finally applied to an interpretation of Mozart's opera *The Magic Flute*, and its Masonic representation of the cult of Isis and Osiris.

0173 Shapiro, Warren (1988) "Ritual Kinship, Ritual Incorporation and the Denial of Death." *Man* NS 23,2: 257-297.
Argues that spirit-finding is a form of ritual kinship rather like godparenthood, while ritual lodges are pseudo-procreative corporations akin to the Roman Catholic Church. These are but two comparable instances of a common human symbolic creativity springing from the 'denial of death'. Aboriginal denial of death is achieved (in the case of men) by dissolution of the carnal self into the eternal ritual object, and this is briefly compared to Merina tombs, Bororo name sets and Buddhist Nirvana. Challenging and already controversial.

See also: 0014, 0197, 0200, 0237.

Birth

0174 Lang, Andrew (1907) "Australian Problems." In *Anthropological Essays Presented to Edward Burnett Tylor In Honour of his 75th Birthday, Oct. 2, 1907*, by H. Balfour et al., 203-218. Oxford: Clarendon.

Addresses two Australian 'problems'. The first relates to totemism as an institution regulating marriage. The second is the thorny issue of Aboriginal ignorance of physiological paternity. Pioneered a position which now has a strong following: Aborigines do not *lack* physiological understanding so much as subsume these beliefs to their spiritual explanations which are "a logical result of their animistic philosophy"(p.212). Other aspects of Lang's argument leave much to be desired, however.

0175 Leach, E.R. (1966) "Virgin Birth." *Proceedings of the Royal Anthropological Institute* 39-49.

A lecture provoked by a comment by Melford Spiro suggesting Aborigines were ignorant of physiological paternity. Leach marshalls available data to argue that while it is a cultural belief that conception is caused by the presence of a spirit child entering a woman this does not preclude a knowledge of physiological processes of procreation. Leach, unfortunately, allows the argument to descend into a personal brawl with Spiro. See Spiro (0182), Kaberry (0616) and Dixon (0346).

0176 Merlan, Francesca (1986) "Australian Aboriginal Conception Revisited." *Man* NS 21,3: 474-93.

Argues that the 'spirit child' debate which has focused on the issue of knowledge of physiological paternity is misconstrued. Re-examines the ethnographic data suggesting a new way of framing the question in terms of identity construction. The social conditions under which spirit child beliefs might arise are said to be in gender-constituting institutions where women are defined as 'bestowable' and as having 'exchange value'. Aboriginal conception beliefs, it is suggested, express continuity and are used in claims to rights.

0177 Montagu, M.F. Ashley (1941) "Ignorance of Physiological Maternity in Australia." *Oceania* 12,1: 75-78.

A reply to critics of his view that Aborigines are ignorant of their blood tie with their mother.

0178 Montagu, M.F. Ashley (1974) *Coming into Being among the Australian Aborigines: A Study of the Procreative Beliefs of the Australian Aborigines*. 2nd. ed. London: Routledge and Kegan Paul. 426 pp.

Attempts to use exhaustive documentation to solve the problematic question: were Aborigines ignorant of physiological paternity and maternity? The first half of the book is a geographical survey of procreative beliefs in Australia. The remainder examines some past controversies and looks at some theoretical implications of his findings. Montagu was convinced the evidence supported the view that Aborigines declared intercourse was *not* the cause of conception.

0179 Mountford, Charles P. (1981) *Aboriginal Conception Beliefs.*
Melbourne: Hyland House. 72 pp.
Mountford's last book, written in part to refute the views of those who still
believed that perhaps, after all, Aborigines did know of the connection between
copulation and conception. In particular, Leach (0175) is singled out.
Mountford suggests a "simple uncontentious survey"(p.12) will finally solve
decades of dispute. This is indeed naïve, and the book is far too summary and
uncontextualized. The 42 brief descriptions given cover most of central and
northern Australia.

0180 Róheim, Géza (1938) "The Nescience of the Aranda." *British Journal of
Medical Psychology* 17: 343-360.
Aborigines (allegedly) deny the relationship between coitus and childbirth but,
says Róheim, they reveal in symbolic form a clear understanding of the process.
This indicates repression. This is (despite the title) a continent-wide survey of
mythical beliefs about human conception and an examination of their veiled
acknowledgement of physiological processes. As only the eternal Dreaming
Fathers can give rise to birth, physiology is being denied so that a man can
finally identify with his father and hence, his Oedipal wishes.

0181 Schmidt, Wilhelm (1952) "Die Konzeptionsglaube Australischer
Stämme." *International Archives of Ethnography* 16,1: 36-81.
Critiques the findings of Montagu (0178) suggesting the so-called ignorance case
rests primarily on Aranda evidence and that they represent the newest stratum of
Aboriginal Australia. The more 'ancient' South-Eastern tribes did not lack such
knowledge, nor did those of the north of the continent. Some of Schmidt's
protests are indirectly linked to his search for an Australian 'primitive
monotheism'.

0182 Spiro, Melford E. (1968) "Virgin Birth, Parthenogenesis and
Physiological Paternity: An Essay in Cultural Interpretation." *Man* NS
3,2: 242-261.
A reply to Leach (0175) defending the position that Aborigines lack knowledge
of physiological paternity. Not convincing, however.

See also: 0089, 0169, 0173, 0210.

Initiation

0183 Basedow, Herbert (1927) "Subincision and Kindred Rites of the
Australian Aboriginal." *The Journal of the Royal Anthropological
Institute of Great Britain and Ireland* 57: 123-155.
A thorough examination of the literature on subincision, detailing tools used, the
actual perforation of the uretha, after-care and post-subincision appearance.
Subincision is related to circumcision and 'fire-stick circumcision'. Speculations
that have been offered for the rite's origin are listed. The actual ceremonies,

their mythic significance and Aboriginal understandings of subincision however, are not discussed.

0184 Bettelheim, Bruno (1955) *Symbolic Wounds: Puberty Rites and the Envious Male*. London: Thames and Hudson. 286 pp.
A post-Freudian interpretation of circumcision and related rites which argues they are not imposed nor do they threaten castration. Rather they are men's attempts to be more complete human beings by symbolically appropriating women's reproductive organs. Considers myths of origins of circumcision, subincision, fire in initiation and *Kunapipi*. In these he sees men adopting rituals which give them a 'business' as important as that of women. A thesis with merit, although at times somewhat cavalier with the data.

0185 Davidson, Daniel S. (1928) *The Chronological Aspects of Certain Australian Social Institutions: As Inferred from Geographical Distribution*. Philadelphia: (No Publisher Given). 148 pp.
An overly ambitious study of the diffusion of various forms of social organisation and marriage regulations into and across Australia. Also includes a discussion of the distribution of forms of initiatory practice - circumcision, subincision, tooth avulsion, scarification, etc., comparing these with practices in Fiji, Tonga and Brazil.

0186 Eliade, Mircea (1958) *Birth and Rebirth: The Religious Meaning of Initiation in Human Culture*. London: Harvill. 175 pp.
Sections on Aborigines are repeated, in part verbatim, in Eliade (0023).

0187 Montagu, M.F. Ashley (1937) "The Origin of Subincision in Australia." *Oceania* 8,2: 193-207.
Rejects the contraceptive theory of subincision firstly, because it in fact has no contraceptive value, and secondly, because, in his view Aborigines are ignorant of physiological paternity. The purely diffusionist explanation for the rite is also rejected. In Montagu's opinion the practice originated as a means for men to emulate menstruation. It provides a magico-religious means for disposing of 'bad humours of the body' which are believed to accumulate during powerful rituals.

0188 Purcell, B.H. (1893) "Rites and Customs of Australian Aborigines." *Zeitschrift für Ethnologie* 25: 286-289.
Brief superficial notes on circumcision, etc.

0189 Róheim, Géza (1943) "Transition Rites." *Psychoanalytic Quarterly* 2: 336-374.
A comparative study of birth and intiation ritual. Relies heavily on Australian data, including his own Aranda, Bidjandjadjara, etc., material. Gives detailed descriptions of circumcision ceremony which he compares with northern rites. The structure of gerontocracy is said to restrict the elders themselves. Re-opening of old men's initiation wounds thus relates to re-living their own initiation. Initiation is argued to be based on incestuous desire for one's mother and subsequent Oedipal guilt. A Freudian reading of rites of passage.

0190 Singer, Philip and De Sole, Daniel (1967) "The Australian Subincision Ceremony Reconsidered: Vaginal Envy or Kangaroo Bifid Penis Envy." *American Anthropologist* 69: 355-358.
Suggests subincision is designed to make the human penis resemble that of a kangaroo. See Cawte (0859) and (0860).

0191 Stuart, T.P. Anderson (1896) "The 'Mika' or 'Kulpi' Operation of the Australian Aborigines." *Journal and Proceedings of the Royal Society of New South Wales* 30: 115-123.
Documentation, complete with photographs, of the physiology of the practice of subincision with some very shaky conjectures as to its origin and function. Perhaps a wound provided the idea? People would then have noticed a reduction in seminal fluid entering the vagina. Hence it was a form of population regulation? Quite unfounded.

See also: 0115, 0127, 0171, 0210.

Women

0192 Bell, Diane (1982) *Aboriginal Women and the Religious Experience.* The Young Australian Scholar Lecture Series. Bedford Park: Charles Strong. 16 pp.
Smoothly explores a large range of issues in the study of Aboriginal women's religious life. Ethnographic examples from central and northern Australia are offered to show women's religious roles as nurturers of people, relationships and land through ritual. Documents the history of the study of Aboriginal women's religion from the early 'man equals culture' approach through the 'anthropology of women' (e.g. Kaberry, Berndt and Goodale), to the 'feminist perspective' which she advocates.

0193 Bern, John (1979) "Ideology and Domination: Toward a Reconstruction of Australian Aboriginal Social Formation." *Oceania* 50,2: 118-132.
Extends his Marxist interpretation of ethnographies from throughout Australia to argue that religion is the ruling ideology of a gerontocracy which, through initiation, controls society's youths and through reproductive ceremonies, the fertility of women and the environment, and hence the process of production itself. Women (unlike uninitiated youths) are in a position to construct a 'counter consciousness' but their own ritual life has failed in this respect. Women accept subordination. For a critique, see Langton (0203).

0194 Berndt, Catherine H. (1965) "Women and the 'Secret Life'." In *Aboriginal Man in Australia: Essays in Honour of Emeritus Professor A.P. Elkin*, edited by R.M. Berndt and C.H. Berndt, 238-282. Sydney: Angus and Robertson.
Discusses firstly the flexibility, adaptation and spread of women's secret ceremonies. Secondly, there is an examination of some mythical views that women once had a stronger, even superior (to males) religious role. This is

located in the context of the contemporary division of the sexes. Finally, Berndt restates the view of Kaberry (0625) that the equation male: female:: sacred: profane is mistaken. Women, like men, are both sacred and profane.

0195 Berndt, Catherine H. (1981) "Interpretations and 'Facts' in Aboriginal Australia." In *Woman the Gatherer*, edited by F. Dahlberg, 153-203. New Haven: Yale University Press.

A general survey of misrepresentations of the life of Aboriginal women. The nature of, and the omissions in, the data are discussed, and the place of women in Aboriginal religious life given. In particular, she criticizes the views of Elkin, Maddock, Warner and Róheim who each understated women's sacred role. The author opts for an "independence and interdependence" relationship between the sexes which, she suggests, is evident in mythology.

0196 Berndt, Catherine H. (1983) "Mythical Women, Past and Present," In *We are Bosses Ourselves: The Status and Role of Aboriginal Women Today*, edited by F. Gale, 13-23. Canberra: Australian Institute of Aboriginal Studies.

The double-edged title refers both to European 'myths' about Aboriginal women and Aboriginal women's roles as expressed in mythology (in the latter case the exclusive use of northern Australian examples without doubt skews the overall picture). It is further argued that myths reflect the interrelations of everyday life and she rejects White's (0763) view that males see women primarily as sexual commodities. Berndt opts for a model of contrast and cooperation.

0197 Brock, Peggy, ed. (1989) *Women, Rites and Sites: Aboriginal Women's Cutural Knowledge*. Sydney: Allen and Unwin. 141 pp.

This solid collection began as a set of reports commissioned by the South Australian government. Despite belonging to one state, the papers cover 3 cultural areas: Western Desert, Lake Eyre and the South-East. Brock's introduction critiques the over-emphasis of male initiation as the seat of Aboriginal religiosity, pointing to other domains where women's role is greater. The articles are Berndt (0756), Ellis and Barwick (0758), Payne (0762), Gibson (0759), Jacobs (0912), Hercus (0911), and Gale (1046).

0198 Gross, Rita M. (1977) "Menstruation and Childbirth as Ritual and Religious Experience in the Religion of the Australian Aborigines." *Journal of the American Academy of Religion* 45,4 supplement: 1147-1181.

Critiques androcentric studies of Aboriginal women's religious life. The author advocates an androgynous methodology, treating women as subjects in their own right, and concludes that Aboriginal women embody a different order of sacredness to men. Her data is focused on menstruation and childbirth as sacred ritual experiences and the fact that men, symbolically, use these very processes as a central part of their own sacred life.

0199 Gross, Rita M. (1987) "Tribal Religions: Aboriginal Australia." In *Women in World Religions*, edited by A. Sharma, 37-58. New York: State University of New York Press.

Examines Aboriginal data to illustrate the need for non-androcentric procedures in studying religion. Inadequately reviews the scholarship on Aboriginal women before examining Aboriginal women's secret rituals, men's use of mythic women and female symbolism in their own cults and the participation of men and women in joint ceremonies. While menstruation and childbirth receive adequate attention as ritual processes, the section on women's secret ceremonies is unbalanced.

0200 Hamilton, Annette (1981) "A Complex Stategical Stituation: Gender and Power in Aboriginal Australia." In *Australian Women: Feminist Perspectives*, edited by N. Grieve and P. Grimshaw, 69-85. Melbourne: Oxford University Press.
Reviews a range of recent women's views on the position of Aboriginal women and avoids both the 'equal but separate' model and that of total male power. She notes women's autonomy in some domains, but recognizes men-as-a-group retain control. Ritual is given especial attention, women's secret life stressed, but men's qualified ritual dominance affirmed. The paradox that men use women's bodily symbols is raised. Homosociality is stressed, but where this breaks down male dominance takes over.

0201 Hamilton, Annette (1986) "Daughters of the Imaginary." *Canberra Anthropology* 9,2: 1-25.
Reviews and critiques Bell (0865) (via J. Lacan's psychoanalytic theory) who is accused of romanticizing pre-colonial Aboriginal women's life as being one which was autonomous, self-sufficient and largely independent of men. This, Hamilton suggests, not only ignores a larger domain of women's lives, but also undermines feminist anthropology by not acknowledging sexual domination in power relationships.

0202 Joyce, T. Athol and Thomas, N.W., eds. (ND) *Women of All Nations: A Record of Their Characteristics, Habits, Manners, Customs and Influence.* Vol. 1. London: Cassell, 208 pp.
While pp. 130-150 of vol. 1 on Aboriginal women may be bizarre, it is more surprising that it exists at all in this early twentieth century book. Religion is writ large, giving traditions about birth and child bearing, the initiation ('mutilation') of girls, mortuary roles and their 'assistance' in 'corroborees'. 'Witchcraft' and burials are also discussed. The Torres Strait Islanders receive similar coverage (along with other Melanesians) in the following chapter. Pioneering but unreliable.

0203 Langton, Marcia (1985) "Looking at Aboriginal Women and Power: Fundamental Misunderstandings in the Literature and New Insights." In *Aboriginal Perceptions of their Heritage: Papers Presented at the ANZAAAS Festival of Science,* 92-111. Melbourne: Aboriginal Research Centre.
Critiques Bern (0193) in order to assess Marxist theory in relation to Aboriginal Australia. Her three main critiques are firstly, that Bern is epistemologically and theoretically confused, secondly, that Bern's position is androcentric, and thirdly that his survey of ethnographic literature is highly selective. On the latter point

she examines the findings of Hamilton (0200, 0699) and Bell (unpublished), to suggest an alternative position.

0204 Merlan, Francesca (1988) "Gender in Aboriginal Social Life: A Review." In *Social Anthropology and Australian Aboriginal Studies: A Contemporary Overview*, edited by R.M. Berndt and R. Tonkinson, 17-76. Canberra: Australian Aboriginal Studies.
An excellent overview of studies on Aboriginal women's status. While much of the discussion considers social structural constraints and rights, there is constant implicit reference to issues relevant to religion and a good discussion of the socio-religious construction of gender, the ritual domains of men and women and the restriction on cross-gender participation. Concludes both complementary and hierarchical understandings of gender have tended to isolate issues from their broader social contexts. Useful bibliography.

See also: 0042, 0171, 0184, 0187.

Magic

0205 Berndt, Ronald M. and Berndt, Catherine H. (1965) "Aborigines: Magic and Sorcery." In *The Australian Encyclopedia*, 2nd ed., Vol. 1, 65-70. Sydney: The Grolier Society.
Three forms of magic are identified - productive, protective and destructive. Rain-making, love magic and sorcery are discussed as examples. Traditional doctors are discussed in relative detail, focusing on their status, initiation and skills. Suffers from divorcing magic from its social context and other religious phenomena.

0206 Bramell, Elsie (1936) "Magic Among Primitive Peoples." *Australian Museum Magazine* 6,4: 112-118.
Brief and superficial notes on Aboriginal magic.

0207 Cawte, John E. (1965) "Medicine Man - Medical Man: A Note on Faith in the Doctor as Exemplified by Australian Aborigines." *The Medical Journal of Australia* 2,3: 134-136.
Kimberley and Waljbiri doctors' skills as social healers briefly considered.

0208 Cawte, John E. (1971) "Australia 10,000 Years B.P.: Mental Health in Primitive Societies." *Mental Health in Australia* 4: 60-67.
A chatty look at the powers of mental healers which relies on anecdotal descriptions of doctors the author met in Arnhem Land, the Kimberley and Deserts. Considers magical powers but emphasizes the social role of curing and the healer as socio-psychotherapist.

0209 Cawte, John E. (1974) *Medicine is the Law: Studies in Psychiatric Anthropology of Australia's Tribal Societies*. Adelaide: Rigby. 260 pp.

A collection of studies, some previously published (e.g. 0352, 0860) focusing on the psychology of illness and the role of traditional doctors. The author has first-hand data from the Central Desert (Waljbiri), Kimberley (Bagu) and Gulf region (Lardil). The social and religious functions of doctors are examined, Aboriginal concepts of disease noted, and the symptoms of sorcery victims analysed. Also of note are the chapters on *Malgri*, a spirit-intrusion sickness related to territorial organisation and intrusion.

0210 Eastwell, Harry D. (1982) "Overview: Australian Aborigines." *Transcultural Psychiatric Research Review* 19: 221-247.
Discusses literature and views on Aboriginal mental life. Considers 'sexual' themes dealing with knowledge of physiological paternity and rites of circumcision-subincision. Stresses cultural relativism of psychotic disturbance and ideas of 'Voodoo Death'. Traditional healing practices are noted and the new illnesses and medical environment of Aborigines considered as part of a changing tradition.

0211 Eliade, Mircea (1964) *Shamanism: Archaic Techniques of Ecstasy.* Princeton: Princeton University Press. 610 pp.
Brief sections on Australia (pp.45-50, pp.135-139) largely repeated in Eliade (0023).

0212 Elkin, A.P. (1935) "Primitive Medicine Men." *Medical Journal of Australia* Nov. 30: 750-757.
An early overview of methods (massage, trephining, blood-letting), roles and the making of medicine men. Also examines beliefs concerning disease which structure Aboriginal medical ideas. Although the parameters of the article go beyond Australia there is a predominance of Aboriginal data, in particular from the east of the continent. Dated comparative and historical perspectives.

0213 Elkin, A.P. (1977) *Aboriginal Men of High Degree.* 2nd. ed. St. Lucia: University of Queensland Press. 185 pp.
Aboriginal 'medicine men' had received little attention when this book first appeared in 1945. Elkin drew together available data to document the process of initiation into the 'higher degree' of Aboriginal religious life. The book is marred by hasty comparisons with Egyptian mummification ritual and yogic practices in Tibet. Part 2 makes a continent-wide survey of 'medicine-men's' initiation. The third part examines the role of traditional Aboriginal healers in the context of their contact with contemporary Australian society.

0214 Jaqua, Mark (ND) "The Magical World of the Australian Aborigine." *T.A.T. Journal* no. 10: 10-22.
New Age inaccuracies abound. Useless.

0215 Jung, Karl E. (1877) "Schamanismus der Australier." *Zeitschrift für Ethnologie* 9: 16-22.
Proposes to show that magical beliefs and practices in Australia correspond to the Shamanism of the Kaffirs, Papuans, Patagonians and others. Based in part on personal observations and considers the preparation of sorcery bones, counter-

magic and retaliation in the Murray River area and among the Dieri. Also considers dreams and initiations in association with malevolent spirits, healing, beliefs about the dead and other traditions from Sydney to west of Port Augusta.

0216 McCarthy, Frederick D. (1953) "Aboriginal Rain-Makers." *Weather* 8: 72-77.
Brief overview of practices to ensure the arrival of rains. Notes variety from individually dreamed methods to socially maintained ceremonies. Local variations connected to the cult of the Rainbow-Serpent, *Wandjina* and other mythic beings are noted. Lacks detail.

0217 Maddock, Kenneth and Cawte, John E. (1970) "Aboriginal Law and Medicine." *The Proceedings of the Medico-Legal Society of N.S.W.* 4: 170-192.
Maddock's section rests heavily upon his Beswick reserve data emphasizing rights and responsibilities of kinship, sanctions of homicide and the demarcations between accidental death and sorcery. Cawte considers past studies in terms of the models of the 'mystic', 'sociopathic', and 'altruistic' healer. A brief continent-wide survey is given. The social functions of healing are stressed. Two piecemeal pieces.

0218 Petri, Helmut (1952) "Der Australische Medizinmann." *Annali Lateranensi* 16: 159-317.
Considers the genesis, function and nature of 'medicine men'. Takes as a model the Kimberley region where Petri's own research was done, especially with the Worora, Ngarinyin and Wunambal. The making of healers is examined along with their powers, travels, and means of curing. *Kurrangara* doctors (and *Djanba*) are discussed in relation to the 'old way'. There follows a broader survey of the vocation, genesis and powers of healers in Australia; their totem's 'dream journeys', transformations and second sight. Reference to changing social contexts is pursued throughout.

0219 Róheim, Géza (1925) "The Pointing Bone." *The Journal of the Royal Anthropological Institute of Great Britain and Ireland* 55: 90-114.
A thoroughly researched but highly speculative study which attempts to locate the origin of the notion of the magical power of pointing. Pointing came from the central areas of Australia, he argues, where delayed burial provided the fibula of the deceased, the prototype of pointing objects. All others were substitutes for human fibula. Contains map of Australian magical pointing techniques.

0220 Róheim, Géza (1972) *Animism, Magic and the Divine King*. New York: International Universities Press. 390 pp.
First published in 1930, this book explains magic in terms of castration anxiety and contains scattered sections on Aborigines.

0221 Rose, Ronald (1957) *Living Magic*. New York: Rand McNally. 240 pp.
Allegedly a book based on experimentation and field-work, exploring the powers of telepathy, psychokinesis, etc., of the Bidjandjadjara and the Aboriginal people

of the Woodenbong Aboriginal Settlement in NSW. The experiments, which give positive results, are dubious and take up a minute fraction of the volume. The remainder is a B-grade, half-fabricated travelogue.

0222   Sinclair, Jeff (1980) "Of Dreaming and Clever Men." *Horizons* 2: 6-10.
Elkin (0213) married to Joseph Campbell and pop-mysticism.

0223   Thero, E. Nandisvara Nayake (1987) "The Dreamtime, Mysticism, and
          Liberation: Shamanism in Australia." In *Shamanism: An Expanded View
          of Reality*, compiled by S. Nicholson, 223-232. USA: Quest Books.
The author is billed as a Buddhist monk, Ph.D., one-time professor of Comparative Religion and recent member of an anthropological expedition to Australia. The article, from beginning to end, is unmitigated nonsense. Some more spectacular sillinesses are: that the only vegetables Aborigines eat are mushrooms and sacred herbs, that dead ancestors are reincarnated as chiefs, and that they never use spears to fight or ever shed human blood.

See also: 0029, 0147.

Death

0224   Bendann, E. (1930) *Death Customs: An Analytical Study of Burial Rites.*
          London: Kegan Paul, Trench and Trubner. 304 pp.
A theoretically eclectic and dated suvey of death customs relying on now inadequate sources. In each thematic section ('origins of death', 'causes of death', etc., etc.) Australian data is given its separate coverage.

0225   Berndt, Ronald M. and Berndt, Catherine H. (1965) "Aborigines:
          Disposal of the Dead." In *The Australian Encyclopedia*, 2nd ed., Vol. 1,
          70-75. Sydney: The Grolier Society.
A brief discussion of forms of disposal, such as interment, dessication, cremation, exposure and hollow log burial. This is followed by comments on burial and mourning rituals, again paying attention to regional variation. Inquest and revenge are examined and finally the fate of the deceased's spirit is treated. Of introductory value only.

0226   Davidson, Daniel S. (1948) "Disposal of the Dead in Western Australia."
          Proceedings of the American Philosophical Society 93,1: 71-97.
Abandonment, burial, cremation, platform exposure and secondary disposal had been well documented for the east and centre of Australia but this was the first systematic study of their place throughout Western Australia. Field research and published data are combined to determine burial alone occurs in the far west, while other methods are found to the east of the state. Continent-wide comparisons are then made. A useful survey.

0227   Dawson, Warren R.   (1928)   "Mummification in Australia and in
        America." *The Journal of the Royal Anthropological Institute of Great
        Britain and Ireland* 58: 115-138.
Surveys available information and specimens of mummies from north Australia,
Queensland and Adelaide, and argues, following the pan-Egyptian diffusionists,
for their cultural origin in 21st dynasty Egypt.

0228   Haglund, Laila   (1976)   *Disposal of the Dead Among Australian
        Aborigines: Archaeological Data and Interpretation.* Theses and Papers in
        North-European   Archaeology   No. 5.   Stockholm: Institute of
        Archaeology, University of Stockholm. 65 pp.
Briefly summarizes the author's other monograph on the Broadbeach burial
ground (1051) before exploring some of the interpretative problems and
methods in studying Australian disposal of the dead.   The archaeological and
ethnographic records are surveyed and there is a substantial résumé of the place
of mortuary practice within Aboriginal religious thought, but this does not
greatly add to previous opinion.

0229   Hiatt, Betty (1969) "Cremation in Aboriginal Australia." *Mankind* 7,2:
        104-19.
Examines both ethnographic and archaeological evidence for cremation
throughout Australia.   Records sites for cremation noting that it was a major
form of disposal in Tasmania and the South-East.   Three hypotheses are offered
for its equal significance in these regions: independent invention, cultural
borrowings, and thirdly, the author's own view that it is a survival from a time
when they shared a common culture.

0230   Hiatt, L.R. (1966) "Mystery at Port Hacking." *Mankind* 6,7: 313-317.
The bulk of the article is concerned with ethnographic data on the disposal of the
dead throughout Australia.   Draws a broad South (simple disposal) - North
(compound disposal) distinction, and argues that ritual cannibalism is an extreme
manifestation of the desire to retain the corpse while cremation is an extreme
expression of the fear of the deceased's body.

0231   Meehan, Betty (1983) "Australian Aborigines: Disposal of the Dead." In
        The Australian Encyclopedia, 4th ed., vol. 1, 197-199. Sydney: The
        Grolier Society.
A brief overview with both an archaeological and ethnographic emphasis and a
useful bibliography.

0232   Thomas, Northcote W. (1908) "The Disposal of the Dead in Australia."
        Folk-Lore 19: 388-408.
Working from the assumption that Australian Aborigines belong to two broad
groups, Thomas looks at mortuary practice to see if this sheds any light on racial
mixtures.   Argues that complex burial is the cultural accompaniment of the 'old
Australians' of the South-East.   The thesis is followed by a survey of burial
practice which lacks real cohesion.   There is a useful map of Australia with
references to sources of information for each region but Thomas' own
interpretation of the data is uncritical.

Change

0233 Berndt, Ronald M. and Berndt, Catherine H. (1988) "Body and Soul: More than an Episode!" In *Aboriginal Australians and Christian Missions: Ethnographic and Historical Studies*, edited by T. Swain and D. Rose, 45-59. Adelaide: Australian Association for the Study of Religions.
An overview of mission influences on Aborigines based largely on the authors' own field research. Contains sections on the impact of missions on traditional religious practices as well as synthetic developments such as the Elcho Island Adjustment Movement, Miriam-Rose Ungunmerr Baumann's paintings and the *Julurru* cult. Argues missionaries were concerned with the 'body' (welfare) and 'soul' (conversion) but neglected the 'mind'.

0234 Bos, Robert (1986) "The Congress: A New Movement in Aboriginal Christianity." In *The Cultured Pearl: Australian Readings in Cross-Cultural Theology and Missions*, edited by J. Houston, 166-175. Melbourne: The Joint Board of Christian Education.
Examines the major concerns of the Uniting Aboriginal and Islander Christian Congress. Themes discussed are Aboriginal ecumenical unity, freedom from church oppression and to develop Aboriginal theologies, and the desire of Aborigines to conduct their own mission. There is also a brief history of the Congress from 1982-1985, and further directions are noted. Neither critical nor analytical in its approach.

0235 Elkin, A.P. (1933) "Civilized Aborigines and Native Culture." *Oceania* 6,2: 117-146;.
An uninspiring examination of the effects of 'Civilization' on Aboriginal culture with an underlying agenda of finding a policy for bringing Aborigines to a Christian and European way of life. Argues that although the socio-economic aspects of Aboriginal life have been largely abandoned, their ceremonial and 'philosophic' base has been resilient. Evidence is provided from domains such as 'the secret life', burial practice, inquests, magic, belief in pre-existence, totemism and initiation.

0236 Fesel, Eve Mungwa D. (1989) "Religion and Ethnic Identity: A Koorie View." In *Religion and Ethnic Identity: An Australian Study (Volume II)*, edited by A. (I) W. Ata, 5-11. Burwood: Spectrum.
An Aboriginal paper overviewing 'Koorie' religion which tends to dwell on the negative images of early non-Aboriginal writers rather than what Aboriginal religion actually is. The latter, when addressed, is intriguing, but the reader should be conscious of the fact that the prominent 'Our Mother - The Land' image is a rather recent pan-Aboriginal construction.

0237 Kolig, Erich (1982) "An Obituary for Ritual Power." In *Aboriginal Power in Australian Society*, edited by M.C. Howard, 14-31. St. Lucia, Queensland: University of Queensland Press.
Power, says Kolig, is only an ideological construct. The paper compares Aboriginal and Western ideologies of power and their historical interaction. In

the traditional Aboriginal ideology ritual knowledge was power - over nature, the universe and humanity. Western society is based on an ideology of power as the control of things themselves. Aborigines are said to be now in the process of internalizing the Western power ideology in both its intellectual and militant forms.

0238 Kolig, Erich (1987) "Post-Contact Religious Movements in Australian Aboriginal Society." *Anthropos* 82: 251-259.
A useful survey of new religious movements in Australia, quite well researched but bogged down in uninspired theoretical discussions. Maintaining that religion must not be out of balance with lived experience, various attempts to reformulate Aboriginal religions are discussed. South-Eastern High Gods, the widely spread *Molonga* cult, the Kimberley *Kurrangara* (see Petri 0648) are considered along with some more obviously post-contact traditions.

0239 Kolig, Erich (1988) "Religious Movements." In *The Australian People: An Encyclopedia of the Nation, Its People and Their Origins*, edited by J. Jupp, 165-167. Sydney: Angus and Robertson.
A concise overview of various new religious movements. Localized cults, such as the Elcho Island Adjustment Movement (see Berndt 0530) receive little attention, but travelling cults, such as the *Molonga*, the *Kunapipi* of Arnhem Land, and the *Kurrangara*, Jesus/*Jinimin*, *Worgaia* and *Julurru* of the Kimberley are discussed in more detail. Speed of spread, change in leadership structure and pan-Aboriginal tendencies of movements are stressed.

0240 Lommel, Andreas (1962) "Oceanien und Australien." In *JRO - Völkerkunde: Afrika- Amerika- Asien- Australien- Ozeanien: Tradition und Kulturwandel in Ansturm der modern Zivilisation*, edited by A. Lommel and O. Zerries, 151-162. München: JRO.
Pages 159-162 briefly consider new cults.

0241 McCarthy, Frederick D. (1939) "'Trade' in Aboriginal Australia and 'Trade' Relationships with Torres Strait, New Guinea and Malaya." *Oceania* 10,1: 80-104.
Pages 83-86 have a useful summary of possible diffusion of the *Molonga* cult.

0242 Maddock, Kenneth (1985) "Gli Aborigeni Australiani e il Capitano Cook: Quando il Mito Incontra la Storia." *Materiali Filosofici* 14: 57-70.
Considers the Aboriginal appropriation of Captain Cook as a Dreaming figure, sometimes associated with the bushranger Ned Kelly, from published accounts from the Kimberley (Kolig 0641), the Victoria River Downs region and Cape York. Examines some of the significant changes in the Aboriginal versions in contrast to 'historical' facts. Cf. Maddock (0243).

0243 Maddock, Kenneth (1988) "Myth, History and a Sense of Oneself." In *Past and Present: the Construction of Aboriginality*, edited by J.R. Beckett, 11-30. Canberra: Aboriginal Studies Press.
A structural analysis of myths dealing with intruders into Aboriginal Australia. Ten Captain Cook myths and Macassan myths are given (sometimes

unsatisfactorily truncated) and comparisons made. He shows that land and material goods are mythic preoccupations but that there are never balanced exchanges. The Cook myths dwell more on theft, the Macassan on non-accepted gifts, but in neither case do Aborigines manage to appropriate the other's material culture.

0244 Petri, Helmut (1950) "Das Weltende im Glauben Australischer Eingeborener." *Paideuma* 4: 349-362.
An important paper correcting the assumption that Aborigines lack eschatological traditions. Most data comes from the Kimberley - the Ngarinyin, Worora, Wunambal and others, and includes beliefs that if *Wandjina* art is not re-touched the end will come, and a new vision, associated with the *Kurrangara* cult, that the end is imminent. For the South-East, similar views are found associated with the All-Fathers. In both regions the end is precipitated by neglect of traditions in post-colonial times.

0245 Swain, Tony and Rose, Deborah B., eds. (1988) *Aboriginal Australians and Christian Missions: Ethnographic and Historical Studies.* Adelaide: Australian Association for the Study of Religions. 489 pp.
Not all of the 33 original articles in this volume consider the impact of missions on Aboriginal religious life (those that do are listed separately), but all are relevant to understanding the contemporary contexts of Aboriginal traditions. The editors' introduction considers the neglect in studying mission impacts in Australia, offering scholastic and political reasons for this state of affairs.

0246 Wild, Stephen A. (1987) "Australian Religions: Modern Movements." In *The Encyclopedia of Religion*, edited by M. Eliade, Vol. 1, 562-566. New York: Macmillan.
A neglected theme which deserved a better coverage. The author indicates part of the range of change in Aboriginal religions. The well-known cases of Bandjelang Pentecostalism (Calley, 1055), the Arnhem Land Adjustment Movement (Berndt 0530), and the *Kurrangara* cult (Lommel, 0646), form the backbone of the article. It concludes with the author's observations of movements at Lajamanu (Waljbiri people), which are rather superficial.

See also: 0046, 0156, 0213, 0541, 0542, 0543.

Literature

0247 Berndt, Ronald M. and Berndt, Catherine H. (1946) "The Eternal Ones of the Dream." *Oceania* 17,1: 67-78.
Review article of Róheim's book (0056). The Berndt's applaud many of Róheim's insights but object to the idea that religion is based on fantasy or dream. Their own view is that religion indeed derives from the needs for food and sex, but not a "morbid... Oedipus situation"(p.68). The review's real value is the additional data on sexual symbolism in Aboriginal religious belief drawn

from their own field-notes for Arnhem Land, the Kimberley, the Central Desert and the South-East.

0248   Craig, Beryl F. (1969) *Central Australian and Western Desert Regions: An Annotated Bibliography.* Australian Aboriginal Studies No. 31. Canberra: Australian Institute of Aboriginal Studies. 351 pp.
2205 items, including unpublished and very short pieces, up to 1969. Covers both Central and Western Deserts, and provides uncritical annotations listing the main topics covered. Contains subject and tribal indexes.

0249   Craig, Beryl F. (1970) *North-West-Central Queensland: An Annotated Bibliography.* Australian Aboriginal Studies No. 41. Canberra: Australian Institute of Aboriginal Studies. 137 pp.
A listing of materials, including brief publications and unpublished data, from the Gulf regions, across the north of the Lake Eyre district into the north of the South-East. 775 entries are descriptively but not critically annotated, up to 1970 inclusive.

0250   Greenway, John (1963) *Bibliography of the Australian Aborigines and the Native Peoples of Torres Strait to 1959.* Sydney: Angus and Robertson. 420 pp.
Contains 10,283 unclassified, unannotated entries listing books and periodicals, but not unpublished manuscripts or newspaper articles. A very thorough bibliography to 1959, with a detailed index.

0251   Hiatt, L.R. (1975) "Introduction." In *Australian Aboriginal Mythology*, edited by L.R. Hiatt, 1-23. Canberra: Australian Institute of Aboriginal Studies.
A useful analysis of four theoretical orientations in studying Aboriginal mythology. These are: myth as history, advocated by J. Mathew (and others); myth as charter, which is linked primarily with the Berndts; myth as dream, connected of course with Freud and Róheim; and myth as ontology, which was championed by Eliade and Stanner. There is also a brief discussion on the way mythology has been distinguished from other aspects of Aboriginal 'oral literature'.

0252   Keen, Ian (1986) "Stanner on Aboriginal Religion." *Canberra Anthropology* 9,2: 26-50.
A careful analysis of Stanner's famous study (0393) in terms of its broader theoretical applicability. Keen provides an accurate summary and highlights Stanner's understanding of a theory of action, rite, myth, and ontology. His contention that Stanner has understressed the social aspects of religion is fair, but to my mind Keen does Stanner a disservice by judging his rather cavalier and often intuitive approach in terms of those seeking an exhaustive theoretical programme.

0253   Koepping, Klaus-Peter (1981) "Religion in Aboriginal Australia." *Religion* 11: 367-391.

Reviews some important studies of Aboriginal religion since the 1960s. Included are works by R.M. Berndt, Buchler, Elkin, Hiatt, Maddock, Mountford, Munn, Petri, Stanner, T.G.H. Strehlow, and Worms. Stanner unquestionably receives the most space and praise. Koepping's main criticism is that Australian anthropology is parochial. A comparative input, he argues, would help promote the view that Aborigines are part of a wider common humanity.

0254 Maddock, Kenneth (1978) "Introduction." In *The Rainbow Serpent: A Chromatic Piece*, edited by I.R. Buchler and K. Maddock, 1-21. Paris: Mouton.

Surveys the history of the study of Aboriginal Rainbow Serpents in terms of two analytical orientations. The first approach was instigated by Radcliffe-Brown (0136) and adopted by most succeeding scholars. This was to study serpentine diversity itself. This, says Maddock, is a fruitless task, and he then turns to ethnographies which reveal the 'Serpent' as but one rendering of a transformation of spiritual essences into mythic form. Suggests it is more profitable to address the significance of the deeper strctures and the underlying thought-processes than the many transitory shapes.

0255 Maddock, Kenneth (1987) "Australian Religions: History of Study." In *The Encyclopedia of Religion*, edited by M. Eliade, Vol. 1, 566-570. New York: Macmillan.

The study of Aboriginal religion is depicted as a growth from the study of the objective 'other' to the subjective 'other'. Three broad phases are identified: 19th to early 20th century ethnographies; early professional anthropology following Radcliffe-Brown's appointment in the mid 1920s; and a third phase roughly from the 60s, associated with greater institutionalisation. This chronology is highly summary.

0256 Marrie, Adrian (1988) *A Topical Bibliography of Australian Aboriginal Visual Arts, Including a Bibliography Concerning Aboriginal Heritage Issues*. Adelaide: ASTEC. 73 pp.

Over one thousand unannotated references to published and unpublished sources on Aboriginal art. Index includes a section on "Art and Dreaming" as well as regional divisions compatible with the one adopted in this bibliography. Supplements the present bibliography insofar as it lists short newspaper references, papers which do not actually discuss the religious aspects of obviously religious art, and unpublished sources.

0257 Mol, Hans (1979) "The Origin and Function of Religion: A Critique of, and Alternative to, Durkheim's Interpretation of the Religion of Australian Aborigines." *Journal for the Scientific Study of Religion* 18,4: 379-389.

Critiques Durkheim's (0079) exclusive focus on clans in his analysis of totemism. Mol identifies 6 totemic forms: tribe, moiety, clan, manhood, femalehood and personhood - and argues that totemism reinforces the boundaries of all these 'identities'. Not all of Mol's assertions are totally groundless, but he is plagued by a tendency to choose inappropriate expressions and at worst seems to embrace the more offensive aspects of 19th century anthropology.

0258 Morphy, Howard (1988) "The Resurrection of the Hydra: Twenty-five Years of Research on Aboriginal Religion." In *Social Anthropology and Australian Aboriginal Studies: A Contemporary Overview*, edited by R.M. Berndt and R. Tonkinson, 241-266. Canberra: Aboriginal Studies Press.
A very useful overview of the study of Aboriginal religion since the 1960s as it has attempted to rise beyond the Durkheimian paradigm. In particular, the themes of meaning, as explored by those developing the approaches of Stanner and Lévi-Strauss, and social reproduction, are emphasized. Issues such as the status of the relationship between religion and art, politics, and social change are briefly considered. Many references to individual scholars and a solid bibliography make this a valuable article.

0259 Stanner, W.E.H. (1967) "Reflections on Durkheim and Aboriginal Religion." In *Social Organization: Essays Presented to Raymond Firth*, edited by M. Freedman, 217-240. London: Cass.
Firstly reviews Durkheim's study of Aboriginal religion (0079), examining both its intellectual and ethnographic antecedents. The second half examines, in light of Aboriginal practice, Durkheim's dichotomy of the sacred and the profane. Stanner shows that not only do these (and other) binary polarities not exist as such but also that in Aboriginal thought there is, at the very least, the need for a third category, of things neither sacred nor profane (the 'mundane').

0260 Swain, Tony (1985) *On 'Understanding' Australian Aboriginal Religion.* The Young Australian Scholar Lecture Series No. 6. Adelaide: Charles Strong. 14 pp.
Examines theories of Aboriginal religion since the 60s which have sought to come to terms with 'meaning' in Aboriginal religion. Places structuralist (Lévi-Strauss 0097), phenomenological (Eliade 0023), and ontological studies in the context of anthropology's attempt to reconstruct a post-positivist epistemology. In particular supports the concern of Stanner (0393) and aligns his work with a Wittegensteinian notion of 'meaning'.

0261 Swain, Tony (1985) *Interpreting Aboriginal Religion: An Historical Account.* Adelaide: Australian Association for the Study of Religions. 156 pp.
A concise history of interpretations of Aboriginal religion from the 17th century until the present. Looks at the influence of ideas about 'religion', 'noble and ignoble savages', 'nature', 'culture', and 'race' on initial interpretations. There is then an examination of the 19th century with particular attention to racist ideology, and the notions of Supreme Beings and totemism. The final section does not do justice to modern anthropological studies of Aboriginal religions. (Cf. Morphy, 0258).

0262 Swain, Tony (1989) "Belonging to the Emperor: An Australian Perspective on the Encyclopedia of Religion." *Australian Religion Studies Review* 2,3: 91-99.
A review article examining the structural implications of including localized Aboriginal religious traditions within an encyclopedic work. Argues the resultant distortion reflects certain imperialist elements which have emerged with

Western scholarship. Also reviews individual articles on Aboriginal religion such as Berndt, 0009; Berndt, 0118; Wild, 0246 and many others.

See also: 0022, 0048, 0163, 0178, 0192, 0200, 0201, 0203, 0204, 0408, 0659.

5

Torres Strait Islands

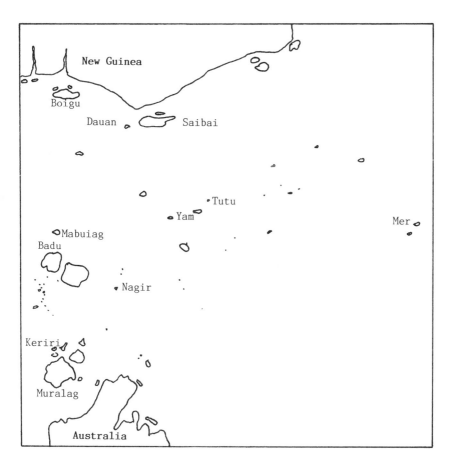

General

0263 Finch, Noel (1974) *The Torres Strait Islands: Portrait of a Unique Group of Australians.* Townsville, Queensland: School Library Association of Queensland. 106 pp.
Brief, superficial sections on religion.

0264 Haddon, Alfred C. (1890) "The Ethnography of the Western Torres Straits." *Journal of the Anthropological Institute of Great Britain and Ireland* 19: 297-440.
Information collected during a botanical expedition. The first part is a general account of the Western Islands, the second records more idiosyncratic features of certain islands. While much of this long article is in the negative, there is nonetheless piecemeal information on magic, rites of passage, taboos, spirits and souls, totemism and supernatural beings. At the time of recording (1888) many of the traditions were already partly forgotten.

0265 Haddon, Alfred C. (1907) "The Religion of the Torres Straits Islanders." In *Anthropological Essays Presented to Edward Burnett Tylor In Honour of His 75th Birthday Oct. 2, 1907*, by H. Balfour et al., 175-188. Oxford: Clarendon Press.
A dated and dull application of data Haddon presents more satisfactorily elsewhere (e.g. 0266, 0295 etc.), hampered by questions of origins. Following Frazer, distinguished 'magic' from 'religion'; his own evidence undermining the division. 'Totemism' is discussed as an intermediate stage. 'Religion' proper is exemplified by the hero-cults which Haddon suggests were borrowed from Papua New Guinea.

0266 Haddon, Alfred C. (1908) "Religion." In *Reports of the Cambridge Anthropological Expedition to Torres Straits: Volume VI: Sociology, Magic and Religion of the Eastern Islands*, edited by A.C. Haddon, 241-280. Cambridge: University Press.
Following Frazer, defines religion as a propitiation or appeal to supernatural powers, associated with taboos and moral injunctions. Despite this taxonomic hallmark of Victorian anthropology, contains some serviceable information on concepts of religious power, ghosts and spirits, totemism, ancestor cults, omens, divination, initiation and several cults which are each documented in a rather superficial manner.

0267 Haddon, Alfred C. (1932) "The Religion of a Primitive Culture." In *The Frazer Lectures 1922-1932 by Divers Hands*, edited by W.R. Dawson, 212-230. London: Macmillan.
Repeats what Haddon has said elsewhere (e.g. 0265) and lacks vitality. Covers the various regions of the Torres Strait, classifying the data in an outmoded way. 'Magic' is discussed prior to 'religion' and then a mixture of evolutionary and diffusionary ideas are used to plot development from the Western 'totemic' tribes to those of the East with more centralised socio-religious organisation.

This, says Haddon, opened the way for the northern hero-cults to invade the area. Uninspired.

0268 Haddon, Alfred C. (1935) *Reports of the Cambridge Anthropological Expedition to Torres Straits: Volume I: General Ethnography.* Cambridge: University Press. 421 pp.
This last published volume of reports gives a more general account of topics covered in previous volumes and also places them in the context of surrounding regions. In this respect his use of Thomson's studies of Cape York (0320) are worth noting. Much of this work merely restates previous volumes' material however, and it is doubtful whether the repetition is justified.

0269 Haddon, Alfred C.; Seligmann, C.G.; and Wilkin, A. (1904) "Magic and Religion." In *Reports of the Cambridge Anthropological Expedition to the Torres Straits: Volume V; Sorcery, Magic and Religion of the Western Islanders*, edited by A.C. Haddon, 320-378. Cambridge: University Press.
A rag-bag of a chapter which includes material that had not comfortably fitted into other chapters in the volume. Ranges from magical training, through sorcery and love magic, on to consider fishing and agricultural magic. Also contains a listing of various types of supernatural beings and notes on omens, dreams, divination, purification, totemism and ancestor worship. There is, finally, an important section on the hero-cults, which deserved fuller consideration.

0270 Hunt, Archibald E. (1898) "Ethnographical Notes on the Murray Islands, Torres Straits." *The Journal of the Anthropological Institute of Great Britain and Ireland* 28: 5-19.
A missionary's ethnography from the Eastern Islands reflecting the questionnaire-type research of the period. Contains sketchy information on religious ideas, totems, the soul, eschatology, sorcery, divination, taboos, marriage ceremonies, rituals related to menstruation and childbirth, death and burial. Highly summary but adds to our scant knowledge of this region. Ends with four myths recounted in reasonable detail.

0271 Kitaoji, Hironobu (1978) "Culture of the Torres Strait People." *Arena* no. 50: 54-63.
Briefly considers the cultural and social integrity of the Torres Strait Islands and the common core of myth and world-view. Affirms the role of traditional rituals, fertility ceremony, magic and love charms today, although noting changing circumstances and the new role of Christianity. Argues for a theocratic organisation.

0272 Moore, David R. (1979) *Islanders and Aborigines at Cape York: An Ethnographic Reconstruction Based on the 1848-1850 "Rattlesnake" Journals of O.W. Brierly and Information he obtained from Barbara Thompson.* Canberra: Australian Institute of Aboriginal Studies. 340 pp.
O.W. Brierly was the artist of *Rattlesnake* and kept a journal, here reproduced, which contained information from Barbara Thompson who had lived with the

Kaura'reg for 5 years. Her information is of particular value in establishing links between the Torres Strait Islands and Cape York. Moore makes a systematic analysis of the Journals in light of supplementary material. Pages 286-300 consider myth, initiation, magic, medicine men and funerary rites.

0273   Moore, David R. (1984) *The Torres Strait Collections of A.C. Haddon: A Descriptive Catalogue.* London: British Museum. 109 pp. + plates.
Religious material culture forms a major part of this collection. The narrative (pp.30-35) merely locates the ritual function of objects. 'Hero Cults' notes myths associated with ceremonial regalia. 'Initiation' is directed toward a range of ritual objects. 'Funerary Rites' includes the use of human remains, masks and other items, while 'Magic and Medicine Men' has numerous material culture examples. The text on religion, while short, ensures this is more than a mere hardware collection.

See also: 0302.

Philosophy and Totemism

0274   Haddon, Alfred C. and Rivers, W.H.R. (1904) "Totemism." In *Reports of the Cambridge Anthropological Expedition to Torres Straits: Volume V; Sociology, Magic and Religion of the Western Islanders*, edited by A.C. Haddon, 153-193. Cambridge: University Press.
Introductory comments are followed by a compendium of totems of each of the Western Islands and a biological classification of totemic species. Social aspects of totems are considered: their relation to clans and the inheritance of totemic affiliation. More detailed examinations of important totemic species of Mabuiag (and, briefly, other islands) are given. Concludes by specifying the magical and religious significances of totems.

Myth

0275   Haddon, Alfred C. (1890) "Legends From Torres Straits." *Folk-Lore* 1: 47-81, 172-196.
Similar to Haddon's later articles (0276, 0277), but lacking the depth of their data. In this case the myths are arranged geographically from north to south for the Eastern 'tribes', which are more strongly represented (17 myths), and then the Western 'tribes' (5 myths). Contains some concluding notes on the myths. The myths were recorded in English, but Haddon refrains from excessive editorial liberties.

0276   Haddon, Alfred C. (1904) "Folk-Tales." In *Reports of the Cambridge Anthropological Expedition to Torres Straits: Volume V; Sociology, Magic and Religion of the Western Islanders*, edited by A.C. Haddon, 9-120. Cambridge: University Press.

An extensive compilation of myths from Muralug, Mabuiag, Badu, Nagir, Yam and Saibai. Recorded in English but not overly edited. Myths are classified by theme into culture myths, totem myths, spirit myths, tales about *Dògais* (female spirits), narratives about people and comic tales. Summaries of plots and anthropological incidents are provided. Some variations of myths are given; others are mere fragments.

0277 Haddon, Alfred C. (1908) "Folk-Tales." In *Reports of the Cambridge Anthropological Expedition to Torres Straits: Volume VI; Sociology, Magic and Religion of the Eastern Islands*, edited by A.C. Haddon, 1-63. Cambridge: University Press.
Maintains the same structure as the study of Western Island myths (0276) and includes a few myths from his earlier general study (0275). Categorised as nature myths, culture myths, religious myths, tales about people and comic tales, complete with a concluding section which provides abstracts of the mythic plots. Collected in English but compare Ray (0287) who transcribes interlineally some of the same stories.

0278 Haddon, Alfred C. (1908) "Mythic Beings." In *Reports of the Cambridge Anthropological Expedition to Torres Straits: Volume VI; Sociology, Magic and Religion of the Eastern Islands*, edited by A.C. Haddon, 314-316. Cambridge: University Press.
A few notes on the status (marital, social, etc.) of mythic beings.

0279 Hamlyn-Harris, R. (1913) "Ethnographical Notes of Torres Strait." *Memoirs of the Queensland Museum* 2: 1-6.
Brief notes on the myth of *Sidor*.

0280 Kitaoji, Hironobu (1977) "The Myth of Bomai: Its Structure and Contemporary Significance for the Murray Islanders, Torres Strait." *Japanese Journal of Ethnology* 42,3: 209-24.
The myth of *Bomai* is concerned with two gods, *Bomai* and *Malu*. Deals with *Bomai*'s navigations, his violation of the women of Kabur, who take revenge, but *Bomai* becomes a Supreme Being. The myth is interpreted in terms of structuralist analysis to reveal a concern with universal problems - the private vs. the collective, individual vs. social, human vs. divine, life vs. death. Historical mythic elements are also considered. The full text is in Japanese.

0281 Laade, Wolfgang (1967) "Further Material on Kuiam, Legendary Hero of Mabuiag, Torres Strait Islands." *Ethnos* 32,1-4: 70-96.
Kuiam, unlike most heroes, comes from the Australian mainland. Further, while those from New Guinea introduced cults, laws and food, *Kuiam* is a sorcerer and killer. *Kuiam* is said by some to be the *Sivirri* of Cape York traditions (Thomson 0341). Laade adds his own versions of the myth from field research and the Islands-Cape York link is analysed; raising as many questions as are answered. A useful attempt to discern cultural contact patterns and influences.

0282 Laade, Wolfgang (1968) "The Torres Strait Islanders' Own Traditions about their Origin." *Ethnos* 33,1-4: 141-158.
Summarises the Islanders' stories about their origin and the origins of the ancestral beings. Papuan explanations are evident, especially for the Eastern Islands, but so are Polynesian accounts, and it is suggested that the latter populated southern Papua New Guinea and then either they or their descendents, having intermarried with the Papuans, peopled the Islands. Also contains brief notes on introduction of Papuan cults into the Islands.

0283 Laade, Wolfgang (1971) *Oral Traditions and Written Documents on the History and Ethnography of the Northern Torres Strait Islands, Saibai-Dauan-Boigu: Volume I: Adi- Myths, Legends, Fairytales.* Holland: Franz Steiner. 125 pp.
The first major study of Island mythology since Haddon's expedition of 1898. Includes Saibai, Dauan and Boigu stories collected by the author in the field (1963-5) and from previous publications and the unpublished notebooks of J.R. Beckett and Rev. W.H. MacFarlane. Variations of myths are included. Some Islander words are used, but there are few verbatim records of the myths. Brief notes are provided to contextualise the myths.

0284 Laade, Wolfgang (1974) *Das Geistgerkanu: Südseemythen und-Märchen aus der Torres-Strausse.* Kassel: Erich Roth. 176 pp.
A collection of myths from the Torres Strait and Papua New Guinea, drawing mainly on the data of his other work (0283).

0285 Lawrie, Margaret (1970) *Myths and Legends of Torres Strait.* St. Lucia: University of Queensland Press. 372 pp.
This lavishly illustrated book contains translations of 166 Islander myths and legends arranged geographically, giving the narrator and date of recording. Although aiming at a non-academic (and perhaps even juvenile) audience, the author adds data to our scanty knowledge of this area. The translations lack sophistication and though Papuan New Guinea data was consulted for comparative purposes, Cape York is alas not thus considered.

0286 Marlow, K.T. (1941) "The Story of the Binibin: A Legend of Torres Strait." *Mankind* 3,1: 14-16.
A paraphrase of the legend is given without commentary of any kind.

0287 Ray, Sidney H. (1907) *Reports of the Cambridge Anthropological Expedition to Torres Straits: Volume III; Linguistics.* Cambridge: University Press. 528 pp.
Contains chapters on the literature of the Western and Eastern Islands. This material was collected orally by Ray but most valuable are the translations from the *writings* of two Islanders, Ned Waria of Mabuiag and Pasi of Mer. The transcriptions with interlinear translations of extracts of these two handwritten books are given, providing valuable mythic information from the earliest unassisted literary works from either the Torres Strait or Aboriginal Australia.

See also: 0289, 0297.

Ceremony

0288 Haddon, Alfred C. (1893) "The Secular and Ceremonial Dances of
    Torres Straits." *Internationales Archiv für Ethnographie* 6: 131-162.
The festive and war dances of the Torres Strait were 'secular' and women
sometimes participated in the former. Ceremonial dances were 'sacred' and
were performed by men alone. They include initiation dances, seasonal dances,
the turtle procession and funeral ceremonies. Various mythical references and
accounts contextualising ritual dances are given and variations between practices
on various islands noted.

0289 Haddon, Alfred C. and Myers, C.S. (1908) "The Cult of Bomai and
    Malu." In *Reports of the Cambridge Anthropological Expedition to
    Torres Straits: Volume VI; Sociology, Magic and Religion of the Eastern
    Islands*, edited by A.C. Haddon, 281-313. Cambridge: University Press.
A description of the hero-cult associated with *Bomai* and *Malu*. Their mythic
origin in Papua New Guinea and subsequent wanderings are related. This is the
foundation of a secret cult into which neophytes were inititated. Ritual designs
and objects are described and song sections (with transcriptions and dubious
translations) are given. Using oral and material culture as evidence, an attempt
is made to reconstruct the rituals, but uncertainty and incompleteness are
symptomatic of the account.

Birth

0290 Haddon, Alfred C. (1908) "Birth and Childhood Customs, and
    Limitations of Children." In *Reports of the Cambridge Anthropological
    Expedition to Torres Straits: Volume VI; Sociology, Magic and Religion
    of the Eastern Islands*, edited by A.C. Haddon, 105-111. Cambridge:
    University Press.
Notes on pregnancy, food taboos, childbirth, population control, twins and post-
natal care.

0291 Seligmann, C.G. (1904) "Birth and Childhood Customs." In *Reports of
    the Cambridge Anthropological Expedition to Torres Straits: Volume V;
    Sociology, Magic and Religion of the Western Islands*, edited by A.C.
    Haddon, 194-200. Cambridge: University Press.
Considers some of the traditions related to pregancy, birth, contraception and
child-raising. The Saibai *bid* - a shredded sago-leaf skirt symbolising the foetus
- is illustrated and discussed, and the process of naming examined. Food taboos
are noted, and the treatment of the afterbirth and the birth of twins described.

Initiation

0292 Haddon, Alfred C. (1890) "Manners and Customs of the Torres Straits
    Islanders." *Nature* 42: 637-642.

Pages 639-41 contain notes on initiation.

0293 Haddon, Alfred C. (1904) "Initiation." In *Reports of the Cambridge Anthropological Expedition to Torres Straits: Volume V; Sociology, Magic and Religion of the Western Islands*, edited by A.C. Haddon, 208-221. Cambridge: University Press.
Description of some initiatory practices from Tutu, Nagir, Mabuiag, Saibai and Muralug with comparative notes from Cape York and Papua New Guinea. Descriptions cover the handing of the boy to his instructors, the rites of initation, the separation from the community, the training in Islander Law, and the rituals of return. The ceremonies were not witnessed and we are only provided with sketches, at times very superficial, of the rites.

Women

0294 Seligmann, C.G. (1904) "Women's Puberty Customs." In *Reports of the Cambridge Anthropological Expedition to Torres Straits: Volume V; Sociology, Magic and Relgion of the Western Islands*, edited by A.C. Haddon, 201-207. Cambridge: University Press.
Discusses seclusion traditions on various Islands. Seclusion may be in a corner of the house (Mabuiag), the bush (Saibai, Tutu), or the seashore (Muralug). The latter practice is compared with girls' rites of passage on northern Cape York. Taboos on foods, seeing daylight and men, touching the ground, etc., are noted. Finally mentions the belief that the moon deflowers girls at puberty while they sleep.

Magic

0295 Haddon, Alfred C. (1908) "Magic." In *Reports of the Cambridge Anthropological Expedition to Torres Straits: Volume VI; Sociology, Magic and Religion of the Eastern Islands*, edited by A.C. Haddon, 192-240. Cambridge: University Press.
A compendium of Mer 'magical' practices using J.G. Frazer's definition of magic and sub-types of magic. Classifies magic into four groups, defined by the object the magic controls: the elements, vegetable life, animals or humans. Sorcery (*maid*) and healing are covered in a final section written by C.S. Myers. Lacks any real location of magic in its wider religious or social contexts.

0296 Simeon, George (1976) "Ethnomedicine in the Torres Strait." *Acta Ethnographica Academiae Scientiarum Hungaricae* 25: 398-400.
Brief notes from field research on current ethnomedical belief and practice.

Death

0297 Beckett, Jeremy (1975) "A Death in the Family: Some Torres Strait Ghost Stories." In *Australian Aboriginal Mythology*, edited by L.R. Hiatt, 163-182. Canberra: Australian Institute of Aboriginal Studies.
An analysis of the Western Torres Strait myth of *Aukam* and *Tiai*. This involves *Tiai* being murdered by one of his brothers and his mother's (*Aukam*) search for his spirit which, unawares, was still living with humans. *Tiai* finally accepts his death and departs for the domain of ghosts, thus beginning the separation of the living and the dead. Beckett sees here a Lévi-Straussian dialectic in which a contradiction between life and death is mediated by the survival of the spirit.

0298 Haddon, Alfred C. (1904) "Funeral Ceremonies." In *Reports of the Cambridge Anthropological Expedition to Torres Straits: Volume V; Sociology, Magic and Religion of the Western Islands*, edited by A.C. Haddon, 248-262. Cambridge: University Press.
As traditional funeral practice had been banned by the government, this is a reconstruction. Considers the announcement of the death to relatives, the preparation of the body and its erection on the platform, the paraphenalia and procedures of mourning, the decoration and ritual presentation of the skull and the 'death-dance'. Most of the exposition relates to Mabuiag. Tutu, Nagir, Muralug and Keriri are but briefly mentioned.

0299 Myers, C.S. and Haddon, Alfred C. (1908) "Funeral Ceremonies." In *Reports of the Cambridge Anthropological Expedition to Torres Straits: Volume VI; Sociology, Magic and Religion of the Eastern Islands*, edited by A.C. Haddon, 126-162. Cambridge: University Press.
An extensive catalogue of Mer traditions surrounding death, largely devoted to describing rituals focusing on the spiritual essence of the deceased (*keber*). Also considers the treatment of the corpse, platform exposure, mummification, and final disposal. Mourning rituals are discussed, including mutilations of mourners' bodies, the disposal of the deceased's property and alimentary customs. A final selection considers changes consequent to colonial government.

See also: 0304.

Change

0300 Beckett, Jeremy (1978) "Mission, Church and Sect: Three Types of Religious Commitment in the Torres Strait Islands." In *Mission, Church and Sect in Oceania*, edited by J.A. Boutlier et al., 209-229. Ann Arbor: University of Michigan Press.
Examines the colonial contexts of three types of Christianity among Islanders living at home and in Queensland. The London Missionary Society is shown to be a theocracy aiding government plans to harness indigenous labour. In the post World War II period, the Anglican church is said to have failed to adapt to

Islander lifestyles. Mainland Islanders thus took refuge in the Assemblies of God, while their kinfolk at home adopted a form of Pentecostalism which stresses political dissent.

0301 Beckett, Jeremy (1985) "Whatever happened to German Wislin?" In *Metaphors of Interpretation: Essays in Honour of W.E.H. Stanner*, edited by D.E. Barwick, J. Beckett and M. Reay, 53-73. Sydney: Australian National University Press.
German Wislin was a mythical hero of a cargo cult that flared briefly in 1913-14. In 1958, Beckett visited the Islands and sought to find any vestiges of the movement. Information was reluctantly revealed, and there was indeed a cult of sorts which focused on the cemetery. However, the author's prime concern is his position in the field. His knowledge of previous ethnographies (0303) convinced people of his own supernatural powers and non-academic interests in German Wislin.

0302 Beckett, Jeremy (1987) *Torres Strait Islanders: Custom and Colonialism*. Cambridge: University Press. 251 pp.
This book opens on Christmas, 1976, when Islanders return to Mer for a tradition-based/Christian-officiated 'tombstone opening' ceremony. This is a book where anthropology and history converge. The story of the London Missionary Society is told in its colonial context and chapter IV, 'Reflections in a Colonial Mirror', looks at Islander internalisation of colonial values in their 'July One' ceremony. A pioneering study.

0303 Chinnery, E.W.P. and Haddon, Alfred C. (1917) "Five New Religious Cults in British New Guinea." *The Hibbert Journal* 15: 448-463.
The last three pages by Haddon briefly document the synthetic 'German Wislin' cult of Saibai. See Beckett (0301).

0304 Fitzpatrick-Nietschmann, Judith (1981) "Tombstone Openings: Cultural Change and Death Ceremonies in Torres Strait, Australia." *Kabar Seberang* 8 & 9: 1-15.
Death ceremonies are used to illustrate social dynamics in post-European Mabuiag Island. Marble headstones have replaced decorated skulls, etc., but while many substantial changes are noted the analysis is reluctant to accept these as 'real' changes. Tombstone opening ceremonies are thus argued to provide an element of continuity and a buffer to innovation by making explicit pre-existing social relations, rules and cultural values. A valuable study.

0305 Passi, Dave (1987) "From Pagan to Christian Priesthood." In *The Gospel is not Western: Black Theologies from the Southwest Pacific*, edited by G.W. Trompf, 45-48. New York: Orbis Books.
Written by an Islander Anglican priest, this paper argues that Anglican missionaries brought a message to fulfil, but not destroy, traditional religious beliefs and practices. Draws parallels between traditional and Anglican beliefs, rituals and social practices but concludes by highlighting some aspects of pre-mission life which, he feels, are best abandoned as incompatible with Christianity.

0306 Rechnitz, Wilhelm (1961) "Language and Languages in the Torres Strait Islands." *Milla wa-Milla: the Australian Bulletin of Comparative Religion* 1: 45-54.
Island reponses to missions, use of hymns etc. Anecdotal.

6

Cape York Peninsula
(and Gulf Region)

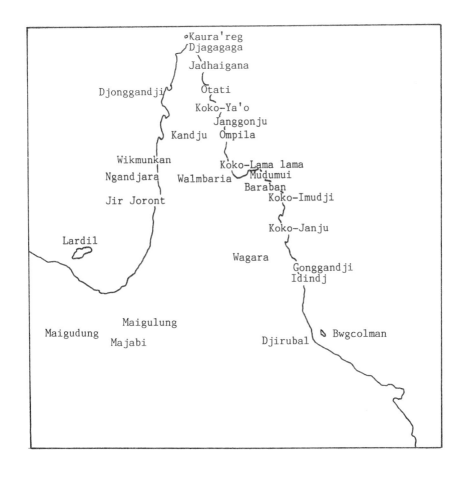

General

0307 Cannon, Richard (1885) *Savage Scenes from Australia.* Valparaiso:
      Imprenta del Universo de G. Helfmann. 32 pp.
A short history of Sommerset in Cape York and the Djagagaga, Jadhaigana and
other peoples. Initiation is described as "a lot of strange mummery" (p.18).
Contains superficial notes on death, belief in spirits, and a 'corroboree' attended
by Papuans and Whites, with dances of the crocodile and horse. Totally
unreliable.

0308 Hale, Herbert M. and Tindale, Norman B. (1933-4) "Aborigines of
      Princess Charlotte Bay, North Queensland." *Records of the South
      Australian Museum* 5,1: 63-116; 5,2: 117-172.
A long but sketchy account of the Mudumui, Walmbaria, Koko-Lama lama and
Baraban. The article tends to be a catalogue of material culture but does contain
brief accounts of religious life. Initiation is disposed of in less than two pages.
Other public ceremonies ('corroborees') are noted as are magic, death,
mourning and burial. Socio-religious processes are largely ignored.

0309 Lumholtz, Carl (1890) *Among Cannibals: An Account of Four Years'
      Travels in Australia and of Camp Life with the Aborigines of
      Queensland.* London: Murray. 395 pp.
Contains brief and superficial notes on taboos, ritual decorations, public
ceremonies, mortuary practices, spirit beliefs and magic.

0310 Mjöberg, Eric (1918) *Bland Stenåldersmänniskor I Queenslands
      Vildmarker.* Stockholm: Albert Bonnier. 584 pp.
Based on the author's experiences and attempts to add to knowledge about
spiritual life. A simultaneously romantic yet condescending view of Aborigines.
Their 'animism' is discussed, and there are conjectures about their higher beings
and beliefs in souls. Contains snippets of myths on a range of themes from
various species to the first Whites. Also considers conception and birth beliefs.
Useful addition for the area, despite weakness of ethnography.

0311 Mjöberg, Eric (1925) "Beiträge zur Kenntnis der Eingeborenen von
      Nord-Queensland." *Archiv für Anthropologie* 20: 108-134.
Ethnographic data from a scientific expedition of 1910-14 containing confused
and brief sections on religion (pp.112-114).

0312 Palmer, Edward (1884) "Notes on Some Australian Tribes." *The
      Journal of the Anthropological Institute of Great Britain and Ireland* 13:
      276-334.
Notes on Aboriginal peoples of the Gulf region - Majabi, Maigudung,
Maigulung, etc., (and briefly, those of the south coast of Queensland). Considers
'corroborees', initiation ceremonies, beliefs concerning the afterlife and spiritual
being, traditional healers, stellar myths, rituals for producing rain, and
mortuary practice. Lacks detail but useful as an early account from the Gulf
region.

0313 Richards, Francis (1926) "Customs and Language of the Western Hodgkinson Aboriginals." *Memoirs of the Queensland Museum* 8,3: 249-265.
Brief notes on Wagara public ceremonies, initiation, traditional healers and burials.

0314 Robertson, William (1928) *Coo-ee talks: A Collection of Lecturettes upon Early Experiences Among the Aborigines of Australia, Delivered from a Wireless Broadcasting Station, by 'Bring-ga'.* Sydney: Angus and Robertson. 198 pp.
The author's radio lectures based on his experiences in central and northern Queensland. Contains chapters on folk-lore, healing and sorcery, initiation, ritual and mortuary practice. At best popularistic, at worst, confuses data from various regions (presumably, from secondary sources) and entertains wild diffusionist theories.

0315 Roth, Walter E. (1897) *Ethnological Studies among the North-West-Central Queensland Aborigines.* Brisbane: Government Printer. 199 pp.
A major pioneering study of the Gulf region Aborigines. 'Religion' *per se* is not considered and religious themes are to be found under rather strange headings. Chapter 8 on 'Recreation' discusses 'corroborees' and contains a major section on the *Molonga* cult (see Siebert 0892). Sections on disease, sorcery, healers, magic and mortuary ritual, are to be found. A final chapter, tellingly labelled 'ethno-pornography', considers rites of passage, love magic and traditions accompanying childbirth and menstruation.

0316 Roth, Walter E. (1903) *North Queensland Ethnography: Bulletin No. 5: Superstition, Magic, and Medicine.* Brisbane: Government Printer. 42 pp.
An important early ethnography of Cape York covering, briefly, a wide range of subjects. Considers beliefs about the sky, earth, sea, fire, plants, animals and humans. Notions of conception are discussed as are those concerning the human soul and consciousness. Rituals described relate to rain-making, love magic, women's puberty and curing by medicine men.

0317 Roughsey, Dick (Goobalathaldin) (1971) *Moon and Rainbow: The Autobiography of an Aboriginal.* Sydney: A.H. and A.W. Reed. 168 pp.
Roughsey is an initiated member of the Lardil people, traditional owners of Mornington Island. His was the first attempt by an Aborigine to write the story of his people. A delightful book discussing myth, initiation, sorcery (*puri-puri*) and a flood-ceremony for drowning enemies. Considers these in the context of contemporary life, referring to changes and the presence of missionaries.

0318 Sharp, R. Lauriston (1934) "Ritual Life and Economics of the Yir-Yoront of Cape York Peninsula." *Oceania* 5,1: 19-42.
The first, large section on this Jir Joront ethnography is entitled 'Totemism' but in fact covers many other themes - cosmology; views on the origins of children; the giving of names; 'increase' rites; commemorative rites for important ancestors (e.g. Rainbow Serpent); initiation, and other topics. There is then a

section on 'Death and Magic', including discussions on the nature of the human spirit and a few notes on traditional healing.

0319 Stretton, W.G.   (1893)   "Customs, Rites and Superstitions of the Aboriginal Tribes of the Gulf of Carpentaria, with a Vocabulary." *Transactions of the Royal Society of South Australia* 17: 227-253.
Dated and shallow as this study may be when discussing birth, initiation, death and magic, it is nonetheless intriguing as an early attempt to examine Indonesian influences on Aboriginal traditions. A pioneering flop.

0320 Thomson, Donald F. (1933) "The Hero Cult, Initiation and Totemism on Cape York." *Journal of the Royal Anthropological Institute of Great Britain and Ireland* 63: 453-537.
A lengthy, valuable, but disjointed account based on fieldwork in 1928-9 with the Koko-Ya'o and, to a lesser extent, Ompila and Janggonju. Begins with a detailed description of the exploits of the culture hero *Iwai*, and his associations with the drum, secret places and initiation. Totemism (personal and clan), knowledge of physiological paternity, and *kunta* (strong or dangerous power) are discussed. The conclusion that the hero-cult was borrowed from the Torres Strait was questioned by McConnel (0339).

See also: 0268, 0272, 0364.

Philosophy and Totemism

0321 McConnel, Ursula H.   (1930)   "The Wik-Munkan Tribe: Part II, Totemism." *Oceania* 1,2: 181-205.
A general description of Wikmunkan totemism containing information on associated myths, rituals, economies and social organization. Adopts the Durkheimian thesis that 'totems' are symbols of clans, arguing: firstly that totems are drawn from objects of social importance; secondly that totems come to symbolize and regulate the clans; and thirdly, that clan sentiments are linked with exaggerated memories of forebears to form associated myths. Despite such conjectural theorizing contains useful ethnographic data.

0322 Sharp, R. Lauriston   (1939)   "Tribes and Totemism in North-East Australia." *Oceania* part I, 9,3: 254-275; part II, 9,4: 439-461.
Totemic systems of Cape York had been recently enlightened by McConnel (0321, etc.), Thomson (0320), and Sharp himself. This article attempts to systematize the data by classifying totemism in the Peninsula into 9 types, categorized by rules of social organization and descent, as well as by features such as the presence of individual totems. In each case the general description of the defining characteristics is followed by a brief discussion of relevant religious beliefs and practices.

0323 Sharp, R. Lauriston (1943) "Notes on Northeast Australian Totemism." In *Studies in the Anthropology of Oceania and Asia*, edited by C.S. Coon and J.M. Andrews, 66-71. Papers of the Peabody Museum of American Anthropology and Ethnology, Harvard University, Vol. 20.

Divides the peoples of the Cape York region into nine totemic groups differentiating various totemic forms (patrilineal, matrilineal, social, cult, etc.). Provides some observations on the nature of totems, beliefs associated with them, and the relationship between the individual and their totem.

0324 Thomson, Donald F. (1946) "Names and Naming in the Wik Mongkan Tribe." *The Journal of the Royal Anthropological Institute of Great Britain and Ireland* 76: 157-168.

Considers the neglected theme of the significance of names, in this case among the Wikmunkan. Examines clan names derived from totemic ancestors, taboos on the names of the dead, and the ritual significance of personal names - for instance the 'navel name' which establishes special social bonds marked by a ceremonial presentation of the child to its namesake.

See also: 0318, 0320, 0327, 0339, 0348, 0358, 0366, 0367.

Myth

0325 Congoo, Bill (1981) *Stories from Palm Island.* Townsville: Townsville Cultural Association. 18 pp.

Bwgcolman stories told by one of that peoples' descendants. Truncated mythemes mainly interesting as examples of change in oral traditions - including a Captain Cook story.

0326 McConnel, Ursula H. (1930) "The Rainbow-Serpent in North Queensland." *Oceania* 1,3: 347-349.

Brief, sketchy account of *Yero*, a mythic Rainbow Serpent figure known in several places in north Queensland.

0327 McConnel, Ursula H. (1930) "Symbolism as a Mental Process." *Psyche* 12,2: 37-51.

A theoretical analysis of the type of data in McConnel (0321). Particularly criticizes the psychoanalytic neglect of social context in the study of symbolism and then looks to her study of Wikmunkan totemism. Argues that symbolism is active where adaptation to the world is imperfect but it is a *conscious* social co-operative process. Sections on *pulawaiya* (totemic ancestors) are relatively brief and point to their communal nature.

0328 McConnel, Ursula H. (1931) "A Moon Legend from the Bloomfield River, North Queensland." *Oceania* 2,1: 9-25.

This myth was originally a part of the Koko-Janju's initiation ceremonies (*ngalandja*). Recounts the mythical activities of *Gidja* (moon/man) and others, relating his travels to the actual geographical formations of the area and linking sites with the divisions of moities. It is argued that the myth simultaneously served as a moral exemplar for social organization and enhanced social cohesion. See also McConnel (0329) and Thomson (0349).

0329 McConnel, Ursula H. (1935) "Myths of the Wikmunkan and Wiknatara Tribes: Bonefish and Bullroarer Totems." *Oceania* 6,1: 66-93.
The bulk of this article consists of transcripts and literal and free translations of three myths from western Cape York. The first concerns *Wolkollan*, a bonefish/human, who entered a body of water to cause the emergence of bonefish thereafter. The other two refer to bullroarers called *moiya* (young girl), *pakapaka* (mature girl), and *moipaka* (a husband and wife pair). The myths are briefly related to their rituals and comments are made regarding symbolism.

0330 McConnel, Ursula H. (1957) *Myths of the Mungkan.* Carlton: Melbourne University Press. 173 pp.
The Wikmunkan stories presented in free translation are said to reveal myths as mirrors of social systems. A general introduction is followed by 36 stories. Each has a brief general orientation preceding the text. The first, for instance, is introduced in terms of its evidence for cultural contact with the Torres Strait Islands. Although accessible and aimed at the general reader, the conclusion attempts to align data with structural-functionalist theory.

0331 Thomson, Donald F. (1940) "Sharks and Shark Lore." *Wildlife* 2,3: 14-17.
Brief notes on beliefs concerning sharks.

See also: 0099, 0281, 0320, 0335, 0339, 0344, 0350, 0362.

The Arts

0332 Dixon, R.M.W. (1984) "Dyirbal Song Types: A Preliminary Report." In *Problems and Solutions: Occasional Essays in Musicology Presented to Alice M. Moyle*, edited by J.E. Kassler and J. Stubington, 206-227. Sydney: Hale and Iremonger.
Djirubal-speaking Aborigines recognize five distinct song types, two of them 'corroboree songs' (*Gama, Marrga*), the remainder 'love songs' (*Jangala, Burran, Gaynyil*). This article examines songs in light of their linguistic context by reference to lexicon, grammar and metre. Some examples, with interlineal and free translations are given. The results are preliminary, emphasizing the full use songs make of grammatical resources.

0333 Flood, Josephine (1989) "Animals and Zoomorphs in Rock Art of the Koolburra Region, North Queensland." In *Animals into Art*, edited by H. Morphy, 287-300. London: Unwin Hyman.
Mainly descriptive, but with some attempts to postulate the religious meaning of the art.

0334 McCarthy, Frederick D. (1964) "The Dancers of Aurukun." *Australian Natural History* 14,9: 296-300.
Sketchy notes on mythic and totemic significance of dances.

0335 McConnel, Ursula H. (1932) "Totem Stories of the Kantyu Tribe, Cape York Peninsula, North Queensland." *Oceania* 2,3: 292-295.
Brief notes on Kandju myths.

0336 McConnel, Ursula H. (1935) "Inspiration and Design in Aboriginal Art." *Art in Australia* No. 59: 49-56.
A collection of shields, swords, ceremonial cross-boomerangs and paddles are illustrated by plates. They belong to Gonggandji and Idindj people of the Yarrabah reserve. The meanings of designs are recorded and as far as possible the associated stories are related. Designs refer to belief in the *buleru* which were responsible for creating the designs and who impregnated icons with their spirits.

0337 McConnel, Ursula H. (1953) "Native Arts and Industries on the Archer, Kendall and Holroyd Rivers, Cape York Peninsula, North Queensland." *Records of the South Australian Museum* 11,1: 1-42.
Concerned primarily with material culture of Cape York (various regions but mostly Wikmunkan) and in particular to show how these reflect Torres Strait and Papuan influence. Religious foundations are prominent (for instance, *Sivirri*, the seagull, is said to have introduced various objects). The ritual use of art is discussed and cults associated with the collection are briefly described, viz. the cults of *Wolkollan* and of the Bull-roarers.

0338 von Sturmer, John (1987) "Aboriginal Singing and Notions of Power." In *Songs of Aboriginal Australia*, edited by M. Clunies Ross, T. Donaldson and S.A. Wild, 63-76. Sydney: Oceania Monographs.
Highlights the relationship between Ngandjara song, dance and power seeking to articulate the connection between song power and the ownership of songs. Refers to some major social divisions and variations in ceremonial song types in the region, and postulates that social power can be regulated by the ability of songs to define interpersonal relationships.

See also: 0166.

Ceremony

0339 McConnel, Ursula H. (1936) "Totemic Hero-Cults in Cape York Peninsula, North Queensland." *Oceania* Part I, 6,4: 452-477; Part II, 7,1: 69-105.
By moving northwards from the Wikmunkan, aims to evaluate increasing Papuan and Islander influence. Thompson (0320) argued hero-cults revealed alien impact. McConnel, in contrast, suggests these are indigenous and in keeping with religious cults found elsewhere in Australia. Presents an account

of the 'totemic' hero-cult forms in this area. Her material is primarily mythic, although there are a few incomplete references to rituals. Each part concludes with translations of important myths.

0340   Thomson, Donald F. (1932) "Ceremonial Presentation of Fire in North Queensland: A Preliminary Note on the Place of Fire in Primitive Ritual." *Man* 32: 162-166.
Notes on ritualized fire use in marriage, mourning and inter-tribal meetings.

0341   Thomson, Donald F. (1934) "Notes on a Hero Cult from the Gulf of Carpentaria, North Queensland." *Journal of the Royal Anthropological Institute of Great Britain and Ireland.* 64: 217-235.
Develops his previous claim (0320) for Papua New Guinean influence on Cape York cults. The hero-cult of *Sivirri* among the Djonggandji is described along with affiliated material culture. Much is made of the fact that *Sivirri* departs to the Torres Strait Islands and comparisons are made with Haddon (0276). Ceremonial grounds, initiation houses, drums, and outrigger canoes are all argued as evidence of contact.

0342   Thomson, Donald F. (1938) "The Secret Cult of I'wai, the Crocodile: An Australian Aboriginal 'Mystery' of Papuan Origin, Revealed to a White Man, and Photographed." *Illustrated London News* July 23: 166-169.
Sensationalizes the Papuan influence on the cult of *Iwai*, describing and mapping diffusion.

0343   Thomson, Donald F. (1956) "The Masked Dancers of I'wai'i: A Remarkable Hero Cult which has invaded Cape York Peninsula." *Walkabout* 22,12: 17-19.
Brief description of initiation ceremony (*okainta*) associated with *Iwai*, a cult hero of 'Papuan origin'.

0344   Thomson, Donald F. (1957) "Sivirri and Adi Kwoiam: A Culture Hero from Western Cape York who Invaded Torres Strait and Died a Warrior Hero." *Walkabout* 23,1: 16-18.
Identifies *Sivirri* with the Islander *Kuiam* cult and briefly describes associated ceremonies.

0345   Thomson, Donald F. (1966) "Masked Dancers of the Crocodile Cult." *Hemisphere* 10,8: 24-28.
Notes on Papuan and Islander influence on the cults of *Iwai* and *Sivirri*.

See also: 0320, 0351, 0358.

Birth

0346   Dixon, R.M.W. (1968) "Virgin Birth." *Man* NS 3,4: 653-4.

Some linguistic insights into Djirubal procreative beliefs in support of Leach (0175) and against Roth (0316).

0347 Montagu, M.F. Ashley (1937) "Physiological Paternity in Australia." *American Anthropologist* 39: 175-183.
Having briefly surveyed the history of debate, Montagu turns a critical eye upon Thomson's claim (0349) that 'ignorance' of physiological paternity is a suppression of such knowledge by later spiritual ideas. Compares Thomson's views with others, advocating contact with Papuans and Whites as the cause of Thomson's 'aberrant' data.

0348 Pearn, John and Sweet, Judith (1977) "The Origins of Pregnancy Superstitions Relating to Congenital Malformations." *Oceania* 48,2: 146-153.
Based on interviews with people of Lardil (and other) descent living on Mornington Island. Lists three types of explanation for congenital malformations: 1) maternal impression, perhaps due to transgression of food taboos; 2) totemic identification; and 3) less commonly, the influence of spiritual beings. Conjectures regarding the origins of pregancy 'superstitions' detract from the article.

0349 Thomson, Donald F. (1936) "Fatherhood in the Wik Monkan Tribe." *American Anthropologist* 38,3: 374-393.
Argues knowledge of physiological paternity, (perhaps a Papuan influence), is widespread in the Cape and gives Wikmunkan statements, transcribed and translated, on pregnancy and childbirth. Birth and the ceremonial presentation of the child to the father are described, and the social/symbolic concept of fatherhood is discussed. Sites of fertility essences are noted and a moon myth showing recognition of the place of semen in fertility is presented (cf. McConnel, 0328). A solid and careful discussion.

See also: 0320, 0356.

Initiation

0350 Laade, Wolfgang (1970) "Notes on the Boras at Lockhart River Mission, Cape York Peninsula, North-East Australia." *Archiv für Völkerkunde* 24: 273-309.
Thomson (0320) had written the only serviceable account of *Bora* in Cape York and this is meant as a supplement to the earlier text. Includes Otati, Koko-Ya'o, Janggonju, and Ombila data from Lockhart River. Gives mostly verbatim transcriptions of Aboriginal English statements on the saga of *Iwai*, the *Bora* procession, the history of Lockhart *Boras*, the *Okainta* ceremonies and *Bora* justice. A valuable and authentic account.

0351 Roth, Walter E. (1909) "On Certain Initiation Ceremonies." *Records of the Australian Museum* 7,3: 166-185.

Substantial notes on observable behaviour in dances performed, bodily decoration and ritual paraphenalia, as well as some comments on relationships between initiation ceremonies and totemic ritual. Includes data from McIvor, Bloomfield and Tully River areas, as well as Princess Charlotte Bay and Rockhampton.

See also: 0293, 0320, 0369.

Magic

0352 Cawte, John E.   (1968)   "Malgri: A Phenomenon in Transcultural Psychiatry." *Image* 28: 29-32.
Malgri disorder on Mornington Island discussed in terms of territoriality and 'taboo'. See (0209).

0353 Hamlyn-Harris, R. (1915) "On Certain Implements of Superstition and Magic: Illustrated by Specimens in the Queensland Museum Collections." *Memoirs of the Queensland Museum* 3: 3-9.
Brief general notes on use of 'death bones', quartz crystals, sorcery splinters, etc.

0354 McKnight, David (1975) "Men, Women, and Other Animals: Taboo and Purification among the Wik-Mungkan." In *The Interpretation of Symbols*, edited by R. Willis, 77-97. London: Malaby.
In Wikmunkan society stepping over objects, oath-taking, faeces, menstrual blood and death can all produce 'taboo' (*ngaintja*). This paper examines these taboos and associated purification rites in the context of social relationships. There is then a sortie into the classification of men, women and animals to examine their respective levels of taboo. Ethnoclassification based on means of reproduction and defecating are highlighted along lines of similar to Mary Douglas' famous *Purity and Danger*.

0355 McKnight, David (1981) "Sorcery in an Australian Tribe." *Ethnology: An International Journal of Cultural and Social Anthropology* 20,1: 31-44.
Based on research in 1966-8 among the Lardil, making a first attempt to analyse the relationship between sorcerer and victim. Describes sorcery beliefs and practices and gives details of 37 cases. Determines sorcery accusations are directed at affines and classificatory brothers and often revolve around women and the bestowal and treatment of wives. There are some concluding comparative and theoretical statements about sorcery.

0356 McKnight, David (1981) "The Wik-Mungkan Concept of Nganwi: A Study of Mystical Power and Sickness in an Australian Tribe." *Bijdragen tot de taal-, Land- en Volkenkunde* 137: 90-105.
The Wikmunkan *'nganwi'* can be used to refer to a range of phenomena: a man's unseen child, sickness, initiation ceremonies, a child's first teeth, etc. Its prime

reference is to the Rainbow Serpent. Having discussed illness caused by visiting strange territories, a man's unseen child, and gossip using names, the ties between various conceptions are linked. Ideology of parenthood is said to be central; particularly the men's claim that they are spiritually both the bearers and begetters of children.

0357 McKnight, David (1982) "Conflict, Healing and Singing in an Australian Aboriginal Community." *Anthropos* 77: 491-508.
Analyses conflict in Wikmunkan society. Sorcery and healing techniques are discussed, stressing that gossip and use of personal names can cause illness. The sociology of healing is explored, with the *nhuyin* being shown to employ skills of social reconciliation. The name as symbol is interpreted in a psychoanalytic sense, but unlike the Western therapist, the *nhuyin* must search for the meaning of a *publicly* recognized symbol of the patient.

0358 Thomson, Donald F. (1934) "The Dugong Hunters of Cape York." *Journal of the Royal Anthropological Institute of Great Britain and Ireland* 64: 237-262.
Study of the traditions surrounding dugong hunting on the central eastern coast of Cape York. Including a section on dugong "Magic and Ritual." Describes the *mänka* , a lump of beeswax used in semi-secret magic to make dugongs sluggish; the rites which are said to make boys good hunters; dugong totemic roles and 'increase' ceremonies; and taboos to avoid misfortune in hunting.

See also: 0209.

Death

0359 Hamlyn-Harris, R. (1912) "Mummification: And Other Customs as Practiced by the Queensland Aborigines, and Exemplified by Specimens in the Queensland Museum Collections." *Memoirs of the Queensland Museum* 1: 7-22.
Contains but brief sections on actual beliefs and practices associated with mortuary ritual.

0360 McConnel, Ursula H. (1937) "Mourning Ritual Among the Tribes of Cape York Peninsula." *Oceania* 7,3: 346-371.
Primarily focuses upon the Wikmunkan. Much of the information is based on informant's recollections, for example, of the practice of ritual cannibalism. Also discusses disposal of the dead, preservation by disembowelling' and dessication, mourning rituals, cremation and beliefs concerning death and the afterlife. Contains transcriptions and literal translations of four myths associated with death. Concludes with conjectures upon the psychological significance of these beliefs.

0361   Roth, Walter E. (1907) *North Queensland Ethnography: Bulletin No. 9:*
       Burial Customs and Disposal of the Dead. Brisbane: Government Printer.
       [365-] 403 pp.
A survey paper organized geographically by Queensland districts. A general
introduction, in Victorian anthropological style, explains the place of ignorance
and fear in motivating the procedures of propitiation, cannibalism, etc. The
accounts for regions vary in quality, the most authentic, for Cape Belford, has a
Koko Imudji text with interlineal and free translations. Accompanying plates
are explicit. A usable though piecemeal source.

Change

0362   Bruno, Jack (1988) "Elegy." In *Aboriginal Australians and Christian*
       Missions: Ethnographic and Historical Studies, edited by T. Swain and D.
       Rose, 11-17. Adelaide: Australian Association for the Study of Religions.
A powerful piece of Aboriginal oratory in both Jir Joront and English. Contains
significant synthetic elements.

0363   Hume, Lynne (1988) "Christianity Full Circle: Aboriginal Christianity
       on Yarrabah Reserve." In *Aboriginal Australians and Christian Missions:*
       Ethnographic and Historical Studies, edited by T. Swain and D. Rose,
       250-262. Adelaide: Australian Association for the Study of Religions.
Interesting data on the 'new' Christianity at Yarrabah, although the sociological
analysis does not always tie into the data. Describes the visionary activities in
the area in which Biblical figures are seen in 'butterfly' paintings, clouds, etc.
The new Christianity is said to have helped overcome problems of alcohol and
drug abuse and to have widened social networks and aided social mobility.

0364   Labumore, [Elsie Roughsey] (1984) *An Aboriginal Mother Tells of the*
       Old and New, edited by P. Memmott and R. Horsman.
       Fitzroy/Kingswood: McPhee Gribble/Penguin. 245 pp.
This edited autobiography of a Lardil woman contains many valuable insights
into religion in a changing world. There are reflections on traditional beliefs
about healing, illness, death and mortuary practice. The chapter 'The first
people to create the world' is mainly a claim that these people knew of God
before Whites arrived, even if 'His' name was not known. The closing pages
align Christian and Aboriginal thought. The editors' touch is light.

0365   Seligmann, C.G. (1916) "An Australian Bible Story." *Man* 16: 43-44.
An Otati Adam and Eve myth.

0366   Sharp, R. Lauriston (1952) "Steel Axes for Stone-Age Australians."
       Human Organisation 11,1: 17-22.
What effects will changes in Jir Joront material culture have on their life?
Taking a simple case of the steel axe, Sharp argues for total transformation. The
symbols of stone axes and their place within a totemic order is discussed. It is
argued that the totemic system was not capable of accomodating European

intrusion. Western Christian religiosity would thus encounter little resistance. For a follow-up see Taylor (0367).

0367 Taylor, John (1988) "Goods and Gods: A Follow-Up Study of 'Steel Axes for Stone-Age Australians'." In *Aboriginal Australians and Christian Missions: Ethnographic and Historical Studies*, edited by T. Swain and D. Rose, 438-451. Adelaide: Australian Association for the Study of Religions.
Sharp's article (0366) suggested that new technology would destroy Aboriginal religious traditions. Taylor follows up Jir Joront religion some 50 years later to find myths and rituals have retained a large traditional core but have managed to accomodate new cultural items, beliefs, and life-styles. This is explained in terms of an alternative view on the nature of 'totemism'.

0368 Thompson, David (1985) *'Bora is Like Church': Aboriginal Initiation and the Christian Church at Lockhart River, Queensland.* 2nd. ed. Sydney: Australian Board of Missions. 48 pp.
Briefly discusses initiation ceremonies (*Bora*) of the Koko-Ya'o and Ompila at Lockhart River before offering a theologian's view of *Bora*. Argues that initiation ceremonies and beliefs are compatible with Christian institutions. Unfortunately there is little insight into how Aboriginal people themselves perceive this co-existence, despite a few tantalising glimpses into this domain.

0369 Thompson, David (1988) "Bora, Church and Modernization at Lockhart River, Queensland." In *Aboriginal Australians and Christian Missions: Ethnographic and Historical Studies*, edited by T. Swain and D. Rose, 263-276. Adelaide: Australian Association for the Study of Religions.
Compares traditional religious practices and Christianity at Lockhart River arguing that, while the two systems are to some extent discrete, they do interact. Traditional *Bora* ceremonies are described, as is the coming of the Anglican mission and the processes of secularization and government administration. Social problems such as alcoholism are said to be hindering religious revival in the face of secularism, but the author raises hopes of a synthetic revival. Somewhat disjointed.

See also: 0317, 0325.

Literature

0370 Craig, Beryl F. (1967) *Cape York.* Occasional Papers in Aboriginal Studies No. 9. Canberra: Australian Institute of Aboriginal Studies. 233 pp.
A comprehensive bibliography of literature on Cape York Aborigines, up until 1966. Each entry is uncritically annotated, and subject and tribal indexes are provided. Unpublished and very brief pieces are also listed.

See also: 0249.

7

Central-North

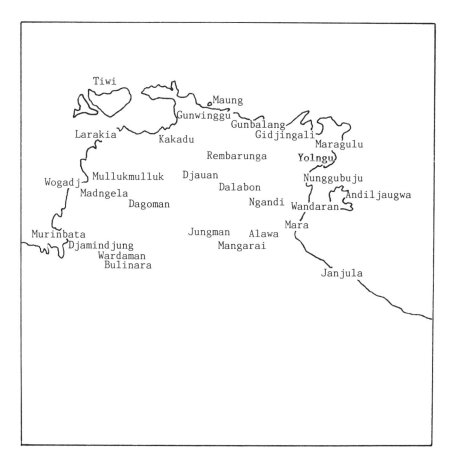

General

0371   Basedow, Herbert   (1907)   "Anthropological Notes on the Western Coastal Tribes of the Northern Territory of South Australia." *Transactions and Proceedings and Report of the Royal Society of South Australia* 31: 1-62.

Notes collected on the Aborigines of the west coast of the Central-North, with emphasis on the Larakia and Wogadj.   There is a description of a funeral ceremony, partial descriptions of men's and women's initiation ceremonies, and references to iconography.   Lacks any real understanding and the author's predisposition to studying material culture is more his forte.

0372   Basedow, Herbert   (1913)   "Notes on the Natives of Bathurst Island, North Australia." *The Journal of the Royal Anthropological Institute of Great Britain and Ireland* 43: 291-323.

Two sections examine Tiwi religion.   Under the heading 'corroborees' is some unsophisticated description of public ritual, and the reference to a dance imitating naval regimentation is interesting (c.f. White 0692).   Secondly, there are notes on burial methods based on observations while exhuming a skeleton. There is no reference to indigenous exegesis at all and the entire paper is based on 9 days of research.

0373   Bern, John   (1987)   "Ngukurr Religion."   In *The Encyclopedia of Religion*, edited by M. Eliade, Vol. 10, 420-424. New York: Macmillan.

While focusing on traditional Aboriginal religious life at Ngukurr, this concise article also considers Christian impacts.   Emphasizes social aspects of *Yabuduruwa* and *Kunapipi* cults, and the power relationships between men, uninitiated boys, and women.   Examines changes to traditional ritual and its possible future.

0374   Berndt, Ronald M.   (1951)   "Aboriginal Religion in Arnhem Land." *Mankind* 4,6: 230-41.

Primarily a selective account of certain religious phenomena at Yirrkala with specific reference to *Djanggawul* and *Wawalak* myths.   These serve as backdrops for a discussion of the *Kunapipi* cult.   Contains some brief comments on the general qualities of Aboriginal religious ecology and the influence of European culture upon it.   For detail see Berndt 0418 and 0481.

0375   Berndt, Ronald M.   (1964)   "The Gove Dispute: The Question of Australian Aboriginal Land and the Preservation of Sacred Sites." *Anthropological Forum* 1,2: 258-295.

A very detailed mapping of the sacred sites of Gove Peninsula, wasted on the general reader.   There are, however, useful introductory notes on economic and religious affiliations with land in this area.   Several hundred sites are named, and there are some brief allusions to the mythic significance of site-names. Concludes by examining some implications of destruction of sites for Aboriginal heritage.

0376 Berndt, Ronald M. and Berndt, Catherine H. (1951) *Sexual Behaviour in Western Arnhem Land.* New York: Viking Fund Publications in Anthropology. 247 pp.
In-depth study of sexuality on Goulburn Island. Religious themes are given prominence. Fertility Mother beliefs are discussed in detail and the *Ubar* (hollow log) ritual and myths are documented. Other mythic themes are considered and in each case, extensive translations are given. 'Love-magic' is treated rather summarily. Finally, there is a large section, with transcriptions and translations, of 'Gossip songs' which have a supernatural reference.

0377 Berndt, Ronald M. and Berndt, Catherine H. (1954) *Arnhem Land: Its History and Its People.* Melbourne: F.W. Cheshire. 243 pp.
Examines Aboriginal relations with pre-Macassans, Macassans, Europeans and Japanese. Chapter 2 provides an overview of religious practice. Chapters presenting Aboriginal views of contact (5-9) make use of evidence from song-cycles, totems and rituals. The *Baijini* (light skinned trepang harvesters) have been mythologized in particular, but Macassan influences are also noted. At times, tends to shy from examining religious influences but nonetheless notes extensive innovations.

0378 Berndt, Ronald M. and Berndt, Catherine H. (1970) *Man, Land and Myth in North Australia: The Gunwinggu People.* Sydney: Ure Smith. 262 pp.
A general ethnography of the Gunwinggu based on research from 1945 to 1968. Focuses on the relationship between the land, people and mythology. Argues that interpersonal relationships and the interaction of people with their environment are symbolically sorted and codified in the mythic sphere. Discusses myths and five important rites, as well as themes such as magic, sorcery and death. The penultimate chapter examines change.

0379 Chaseling, Wilbur S. (1957) *Yulengor: Nomads of Arnhem Land.* London: The Epworth Press. 173 pp.
A missionary's simple introduction to Yolngu life. Discussion of clan wells, healing, magic, and mortuary practice are not ethnographically sophisticated but often provide interesting details. There are also myths of the *Djanggawul* (cf. Berndt 0418), the *Wawalak* and others. A final chapter on 'stone age religion' is superficial and apologetic. A.P. Elkin's "Introduction" provides some background references.

0380 Dahl, Knut (1926) *In Savage Australia: An Account of a Hunting and Collecting Expedition to Arnhem Land and Dampier Land.* London: Allan. 326 pp.
Information based on the author's expedition from Darwin, via the Victoria River area, to Roebuck Bay in 1894. Contains some uninsightful descriptions of magic, religious beliefs, conception ideology and initiation.

0381 Foelsche, Paul (1881) "Notes on the Aborigines of North Australia." *Transactions and Proceedings of the Royal Society of South Australia* 5: 1-18.

Contains some sections on religion repeated verbatim in his 0382.

0382 Foelsche, Paul (1895) "On the Manners, Customs, Etc., of Some Tribes
      of the Aborigines, in the Neighbourhood of Port Darwin and the West
      Coast of the Gulf of Carpentaria, North Australia." *Journal of the
      Anthropological Institute of Great Britain and Ireland* 24: 190-198.
Notes from 14 'tribes' in the Central-Northern region. The section on 'Origin
and the Future State' is either hopelessly confused or represents post-contact
beliefs (reference to a guardian of the dead who *writes* down Aborigines'
misconduct suggests the latter). Also considers birth, initiation, death, inquests,
etc. Untrustworthy, but at times an intriguing early account.

0383 Goode, William J. (1951) *Religion Among the Primitives*. Illinois: The
      Free Press. 321 pp.
Considers the relationship between religious structure and economics, political
action and the family, in each case giving 'Murngin' (Yolngu) examples based on
Warner (0397). Argues religion is action rather than belief, and that it helps
create political unity. Structural-functionalism at its dullest.

0384 Hart, C.W. and Pilling, Arnold R. (1960) *The Tiwi of North Australia*.
      New York: Holt, Rinehart and Winston. 118 pp.
Contains a brief section on religious activities among the Tiwi (pp.87-95),
categorized into 3 classes: taboos, beliefs, and rituals associated with death and
initiation. The emphasis is on the concept of *Pukimani* which refers to anything
sacred, forbidden or set apart: mourners, neophytes, dead bodies, or women
who have just given birth. A useful account, albeit lacking detail.

0385 Lockwood, Douglas W. (1962) *I, the Aboriginal*. Adelaide: Rigby. 240
      pp.
A biography of Waipuldanya (Phillip Roberts) of the Alawa people, based on
material from interviews and inauthentically told in the first person by
Lockwood. Includes information on rites of passage, the *Yabudurawa* (see
Elkin, 0483), and *Kunapipi* (see Berndt, 0481) rituals, magic, women's
ceremonies, after-life, etc. Over-edited.

0386 Mirritji, Jack (1976) *My People's Life*. Milingimbi, N.T.: Milingimbi
      Literature Centre. 72 pp.
Jack Mirritji was born at Japirdijapin in the 1930s. When in his teens, he went
to Darwin where he taught himself to read and write. Although edited by
unnamed Whites, the text is largely authentic and contains segments on the
Wawalak sisters myth, initiation, revenge sorcery, mortuary practice and
traditional healers. Sections on Macassans have a legendary quality also. Not
detailed but a valuable and interesting variation on academic versions of these
themes.

0387 Mountford, Charles P. (1958) *The Tiwi: Their Art, Myth and
      Ceremony*. London: Phoenix House. 185 pp.
Based on the 1954 National Geographic Society Expedition to the Tiwi.
Cosmologies are paraphrased. The myth of *Pukimani* (the founder of *Pukimani*

ceremonies of the same name) is related in detail (cf. Goodale 0500). Songs are given in 'literal translation' although no transcriptions are offered. The *Kulama* (yam) ceremony is also outlined (cf. Goodale 0544), as are beliefs about spirit people. Despite imperfections in recording, the fullest account of Tiwi religious life.

0388 Parkhouse, Thomas A. (1895) "Native Tribes of Port Darwin and its Neighbourhood." *Report of the Australasian Association for the Advancement of Science* 6: 638-647.
Contains brief notes on rites of passage, etc., mainly for the Larakia.

0389 Petchkovsky, Leon and Cawte, John E. (1986) "The Dreams of the Yolngu Aborigines of Australia." *Journal of Analytical Psychology* 31: 357-375.
Paraphrases of nine Yolngu dreams arguing that while dream functions are largely identical with those of Western people, the content and social accord given them differs markedly. In particular, religious themes are prominent in the dreams. Taboos, portents, visits from dead souls and a Christian revival are among the subjects which are given with Jungian interpretations. While at times lapsing into archetypal 'just-so' statements, has many valid insights.

0390 Schmidt, Wilhelm (1953) "Sexualismus, Mythologie und Religion in Nord-Australien." *Anthropos* 48: 899-924.
Drawing on published accounts of Arnhem Land, Bathurst, Melville and Goulburn Islands, considers forms of sexuality and marriage in sacred and secular domains. Using Berndt (0481), and Berndt and Berndt (0376), discusses cults associated with the *Wawalak* and *Djanggawul*, as well as practices of circumcision, subincision and beliefs concerning spirit children.

0391 Spencer, W. Baldwin (1912) *An Introduction to the Study of Certain Native Tribes of the Northern Territory.* Melbourne: McCarron Bird. 57 pp.
Pamphlet discussing initiation, totemism, ancestral Beings, conception beliefs and mortuary customs, each more fully treated in 0392.

0392 Spencer, W. Baldwin (1914) *Native Tribes of the Northern Territory of Australia.* London: Macmillan. 516 pp.
Based on research carried out while Spencer was Special Commissioner for Aboriginals and Chief Protector in 1911-12. A generalized ethnography covering a wide area from Melville and Bathurst Islands to the Gulf of Carpentaria, and southwards to Newcastle Waters. Covers initiation, totemism, sacred objects, mortuary practice, magic, healing and procreation and the All-Mother (*Imberombera*). The detail is not as rich as in Spencer's previous works and there tends to be an Aranda reading of Northern traditions. A useful early account nonetheless.

0393 Stanner, W.E.H. (1959-61) *On Aboriginal Religion..* The Oceania Monographs No. 11. Sydney: University of Sydney. 171 pp.

A sensitive and inspired analysis of Murinbata religious life. Systematically analyses the structure of myths and rites suggesting they reveal a common underlying ontology celebrating a dependent life that has taken an initial wrongful turn. This conclusion has been criticized (see Berndt 0119), as has Stanner's use of sacramentality as a basis for understanding Murinbata religion. His focus on the 'philosophical' aspects of beliefs and rituals was, however, pioneering and with all its shortcomings this remains the finest study of an Aboriginal community's religious life. (See Keen 0252).

0394 Tindale, Norman B. (1925-6) "Natives of Groote Eylandt and of the West Coast of the Gulf of Carpentaria." *Records of the South Australian Museum* 111,1: 61-102; 111,2: 103-134.
A museum-like catalogue predisposed towards material culture but with brief and superficial descriptions of Andiljaugwa initiation and mortuary ritual.

0395 Turner, David H. (1974) *Tradition and Transformation: A Study of the Groote Eylandt Area Aborigines of Northern Australia.* Australian Aboriginal Studies No. 53. Canberra: Australian Institute of Aboriginal Studies. 224 pp.
Focuses on the Bickerton Island Aborigines of the Angurugu Mission describing their life under conditions of increasing White influence. Part I considers the broader context of totemism, and part II focuses on their response to death. Mortuary songs are transcribed and translated and innovations - in particular the equation of Biblical events with local sites - are discussed. A rich account.

0396 Turner, David H. (1989) *Return to Eden: A Journey Through the Promised Landscape of Amagalyuagba.* New York: Peter Lang. 299 pp.
A stimulating, highly original analysis of the sacred geography of Bickerton Island. Establishes the principles linking people with their particular 'promised land', arguing Aborigines work from an understanding which inverts the Western historical urge towards monism, and rather strive to maintain plurality through the formation of federated countries and peoples. Spiritual domains are given prominence in this study, and Christian and Indonesian influences on Aboriginal beliefs and practices are discussed.

0397 Warner, W. Lloyd (1958) *A Black Civilization: A Social Study of an Australian Tribe.* USA: Harper. 618 pp.; 1st ed., 1937.
A fine general ethnography of the 'Murngin' or Yolngu. Magic, totemism and mortuary rituals are richly documented and interpreted in terms of their socio-symbolic significances. Includes his pioneering ethnography of the *Wawalak* myth cycle (including *Djungguan, Kunapipi, Ulmark* and *Marndiella* ceremonies) and the *Djanggawul* myths and rituals. Not to be ignored are the extensive appendices discussing myths, dreams and Malay influence on the Yolngu culture.

0398 Williams, Nancy M. (1986) *The Yolngu and Their Land: A System of Land Tenure and the Fight for Its Recognition.* Canberra: Australian Institute of Aboriginal Studies. 264 pp.

Compares and examines European and Yolngu views on land and their historic interrelation. Background on the Dreaming (note also appendix pp. 234-237) and its implications for Aboriginal concepts of time and place (land) through cosmology is very serviceable. Also considers the importance of ancestral wanderings in myth for land affiliation and the religious foundations of land tenure. A good introduction to the Yolngu spiritual understanding of place.

See also: 0252, 0464, 0523, 0566, 0778.

Philosophy and Totemism

0399 Biernoff, David (1974) "Safe and Dangerous Places." In *Australian Aboriginal Concepts*, edited by L.R. Hiatt, 93-105. Canberra: Australian Institute of Aboriginal Studies.
Examines dangerous places in the area surrounding Yirrkala. Places become dangerous because of Dreaming powers, ritual activity, historic events or recent death or illness. Danger is shown to be relative to the relationship of the individual to a site, to the level of religious development of a person, and to the occasion on which the place is approached.

0400 Borsboom, A.P. (1974) "Dreaming Clusters Among Marangu Clans." In
Australian Aboriginal Concepts, edited by L.R. Hiatt, 106-119. Canberra: Australian Institute of Aboriginal Studies.
An analysis of how the Maragulu classify species into 'Dreaming clusters'. After a preliminary discussion of their social relations, 13 Dreamings are named and briefly described and then related to their place in ceremonial life. Common themes and patterns are identified.

0401 Falkenberg, Johannes (1962) *Kin and Totem: Group Relations of Australian Aborigines in the Port Keats District*. Norway: Oslo University Press. 272 pp.
While primarily a study of changing Murinbata social organization, religion is also examined. The shift towards moiety systems had rendered cult totems unnecessary, new Dreamings had been adopted, and mission influence was associated with the emergence of universal totems (p. 188). There is also reference to *Mutjinga*, the Mother, the relation of men and women to the sacred, punishments for infringements, etc. Spiritual relations to clan land and a person's individual spirit are discussed.

0402 Maddock, Kenneth (1974) "Taxonomy and Kakadu Totemic Relationships." In *Australian Aboriginal Concepts*, edited by L.R. Hiatt, 121-133. Canberra: Australian Institute of Aboriginal Studies.
According to Spencer (0392), the Kakadu had totems which neither regulated marriage nor were hereditary. Using Spencer's own data as well as ethnographies from neighbouring Dalabon and Gunwinggu, and adapting a

structuralist mode of analysis, Maddock argues that an underlying social logic, albeit flexible, is in fact discernible.

0403 Maddock, Kenneth (1974) "Dangerous Proximities and their Analogues." *Mankind* 9,3: 206-17.
Using Gidjingali and Dalabon data, attempts to explain why certain places and objects are dangerous and restricted. Stresses it is owners of an estate who are often most at risk and sees the relationship as a means of separating ownership and control. This has a counterpart in the removal from men of sexual control over women of their own clan. Religious interdictions are modelled on sexual interdictions and thus dangerous places are a product of exogamy.

0404 Merlan, Francesca (1980) "Mangarrayi Semi Moiety Totemism." *Oceania* 51,2: 81-97.
Mangarai and Jungman subsection totemism had been known since Spencer's reports (0392) but this is the first attempt to try to comprehend this form of affiliation. Analyses indigenous views about relations between totems and social categories and suggests totemic affiliation is a symbolic complex which socializes the Dreaming, the country and people and that *marragwa* express the relationship between existents instituted by the Dreaming and living people.

0405 Stanner, W.E.H. (1936) "A Note on Djamindjung Kinship and Totemism." *Oceania* 6,4: 441-451.
Sketchy notes on totemism which locates totem centres, and refers to their mythical links and social affiliations.

0406 Stanner, W.E.H. (1936) "Murinbata Kinship and Totemism." *Oceania* 7,2: 186-216.
Examines the Murinbata adopting three new practices: subsections, sister's son's daughter marriage, and matrilineal 'non-cult' or 'social' totems. The latter is shown to have been meshing uneasily with existing forms of totemic inheritance. Also contains details of pre-existent totemic systems and the way these were connected with conception beliefs and patrilineal descent.

0407 Thomson, Donald F. (1975) "The Concept of 'Marr' in Arnhem Land." *Mankind* 10,1: 1-10.
Discusses the mana-like 'spiritual power' known as *'marr'*. *Marr* is distinct from strength, speed, skill, luck, heart, etc., and emanates directly from ancestors and objects, people and places associated with ancestors. Discusses *marr's* ability to compel humans, its dangerous manifestations (in corpses or sacred designs witnessed by inappropriate people) and its role in prompting the onset of ceremonies such as *Kunapipi*.

0408 Worsley, Peter M. (1967) "Groote Eylandt Totemism and Le Totémisme Aujourd'hui." In *The Structural Study of Myth and Totemism*, edited by E.R. Leach, 141-159. London: Tavistock Publications.
Critiques Lévi-Strauss' theories of myth and totemism (0098) using his data on the Andiljaugwa. He refuses to accept that totemic myths are cases of 'thinking

in concepts'. This indeed occurs in Aboriginal taxonomies, but myths are different. Gives historic, aesthetic, and personal ideosyncratic cases of the formulation of totems and concludes that, rather than revealing logical order, totemic schema are "agglomerative, arbitrary and fortuitous" (p.151).

See also: 0112, 0395, 0398, 0439, 0474, 0501, 0555.

Myth

0409 Allen, Louis A. (1976) *Time Before Morning: Art and Myth of the Australian Aborgines.* New York: Crowell. 304 pp.
Myths the author had collected in the north from Port Keats to Yirrkala. Classified into five categories: creation myths, myths pertaining to natural forces, myths concerned with gender, myths related to everyday life and myths associated with mortuary ritual. There is little in the way of interpretation, analysis or critical contextualization.

0410 Arndt, W. (1965) "The Dreaming of Kunukban." *Oceania* 35,4: 241-259.
The focus is a myth of *Kunukban*, a python/man, held by the Bulinara, Wardaman, Dagoman, Ngarinman, etc. The account is from one informant, and there are points at which one suspects the accuracy of the re-telling. An accompanying section introduces the 'wild-time' religion and some absurd reflections on the future of Aboriginal beliefs conclude the article. Among the first reports on religious life in this area.

0411 Barlow, Alex (1983) "Holding the Country: Carrying the Law." *Orana: Journal of School and Children's Librarianship* 19,2: 98-108.
Lightweight notes on the role of Arnhem Land myths.

0412 Berndt, Catherine H. (1968) "Myth and Mother-in-law: A Question of Meaning and Interpretation in Myth, an example from Aboriginal Australia." *Proceedings: VIIIth International Congress of Anthropological and Ethnological Sciences*, vol. II: Ethnology, 295-297. Tokyo: Science Council of Japan.
Brief interpretation of Gunwinggu myth of *Yirawadbad* the snake-man.

0413 Berndt, Catherine H. (1970) "Monsoon and Honey Wind." In *Échanges et Communications: Mélanges Offerts à Claude Lévi-Strauss*, edited by J. Pouillon and P. Maranda, 1306-1326. Paris: Mouton.
Based on the well-known *Wawalak* myth, focusing on Yolngu women's understanding and relating this to the *Wudal, Woial* or *Maiamaia* song cycle, on the one hand, and comparable myths from Western Arnhem Land on the other. The story is located within a series of mythic transformations, and some important recurring 'oppositions' and complementaries (*pace* Lévi-Strauss) are tentatively suggested.

0414 Berndt, Catherine H. (1979) *The Land of the Rainbow Snake: Aboriginal Children's Stories and Songs from Western Arnhem Land.* Sydney: Collins. 96 pp.
Twenty-seven children's myths told by older women from western Arnhem Land and translated for young readers. Useful to researchers despite the constraints imposed by the targeted market.

0415 Berndt, Catherine H. (1987) "Wawalag." In *The Encyclopedia of Religion*, edited by M. Eliade, Vol. 15, 358-361. New York: Macmillan.
Summarizes the story of the *Wawalak* sisters and examines some interpretations of the myth.

0416 Berndt, Catherine H. (1987) "Yulunggul Snake." In *The Encyclopedia of Religion*, edited by M. Eliade, Vol. 15, 541-543. New York: Macmillan.
Relates the python *Yulunggur* to territory demarcation, seasonal fertility and ritual.

0417 Berndt, Ronald M. (1948) "A 'Wonguri-'Mandjikai Song Cycle of the Moon-Bone." *Oceania* 19,1: 16-50.
Transcribes with literal and free translations the Yolngu (Wanguri linguistic group) Moon-Bone public song cycle, which also has a secret counterpart. Tells of Moon and his sister Dugong, who becomes discontented with their clay-pan home and says she will go to sea. Moon, in turn, decides to go into the sky, but he does not want to die. As the moon he will grow thin until he is only bone, will die in the ocean, but after three days will emerge alive again.

0418 Berndt, Ronald M. (1952) *Djanggawul: An Aboriginal Religious Cult of North-Eastern Arnhem Land.* London: Routledge and Kegan Paul. 320 pp.
The *Djanggawul* (two mythic sisters and their brother) are known throughout eastern and central Arnhem Land. The Yirrkala version of the song cycle is presented in free English translation. The 188 songs span from their arrival on the east coast of Arnhem Land to a rather abrupt ending - at central-northern Arnhem Land (continued in other versions). Transcriptions are not given. Avoids theoretical speculation, but briefly notes associated rituals.

0419 Berndt, Ronald M. (1966) "The Wuradilagu Song Cycle of Northeastern Arnhem Land." In *The Anthropologist Looks At Myth*, edited by J. Greenway, 193-243. Austin: University of Texas Press.
The *Wuradilagu* song cycle, transliterated with both interlinear and free translations, was recorded amongst the *Yirritja* moiety of the Yolngu. It is based on the actions of a mythic woman from Groote Eylandt, and the introduced exotic element is said to reflect the Yolngu view of Groote Eylandt women. The song is sung publicly, has no accompanying cult, but is relevant to mortuary and dispute-settling ritual. Emphasizes the way the song mirrors social organization and is paralleled in visual art.

0420 Berndt, Ronald M. (1987) "Other Creatures in Human Guise and Vice Versa: A Dilemma in Understanding." In *Songs of Aboriginal Australia*, edited by M. Clunies Ross, T. Donaldson and S.A. Wild, 168-191. Sydney: Oceania Monographs.
A Maung and Gunbalang 'gossip song' cycle first revealed by spirit familiars. (Goanna and Goose are the main characters). The cycle is recorded with transcription and literal and free translations. Songs are examined in light of the 'dilemma' of the Aboriginal humanizing of nature which has been the focus of debate about 'totemism' (Lévi-Strauss 0098). Suggests that it is only in human guise that mythic beings can assert intellectual significances.

0421 Berndt, Ronald M. (1987) "Djanggawul." In *The Encyclopedia of Religion*, edited by M. Eliade, Vol. 4, 382-383. New York: Macmillan.
Gives a version of the *Djanggawul* myth from Yirrkala, briefly compares it with other versions and highlights common features of the myth/rite cycle.

0422 Berndt, Ronald M. and Berndt, Catherine H. (1965) "Aborigines: Myths and Legends." In *The Australian Encyclopedia*, 2nd ed., Vol. 1, 53-5. Sydney: The Grolier Society.
A brief, uninspiring synopsis, with mainly Arnhem Land examples.

0423 Bozic, Streten and Marshal, Alan (1972) *Aboriginal Myths*. Melbourne: Gold Star Publications. 143 pp.
The source of these stories is 'Mulluk' of the Mullukmulluk people. The myths are re-told in an inauthentic manner, giving them a just-so story quality. There is no contextualization and the many photographs, all poorly related to the text, become pointless decoration. Of little value to serious scholars.

0424 Bradley, John (1988) *Yanyuwa Country: The Yanyuwa People of Borroloola tell the History of their Lands*. Richmond: Greenhouse Publications. 80 pp.
Three stories, transcribed and freely translated, dealing with the Dreaming foundations of Janjula country. The text is only the length of an average article, the remainder is taken up by the (non-Aboriginal) author's at best quaint illustrations. The translations are valuable, however, and opening the book is an insightful Aboriginal statement on 'The Dreaming'. The translator and community liaised closely throughout the production process.

0425 Buchler, Ira R. (1978) "The Fecal Crone." In *The Rainbow Serpent: A Chromatic Piece*, edited by I.R. Buchler and K. Maddock, 119-212. Paris: Mouton.
An obscure structuralist study of 'shit'. Most of the myths and ethnographic data (especially concerning incest) is from the Yolngu. The Rainbow Serpent is central to the analysis. Aborigines have chosen a python to be of mythic importance,we are told, because of snakes' keen sense of smell. This, in turn, is 'relevant' to the smell of excreta. The author concludes by confessing: "There is really no defensible way to tidy up all of this [article]"(p. 201).

0426 Capell, Arthur (1960) "Myths and Tales of the Nunggubuyu, S.E.
       Arnhem Land." *Oceania* 31,1: 31-62.
Recorded when Nunggubuju life was heavily influenced by missions and
government. Ten stories are presented, accompanied by interlineal and free
translations. Defines 'myth' as stories connected with sacred events, while those
related in a secular context are labelled 'tales'. There is no attempt to place the
myths in ritual context or, indeed, to do anything beyond providing translations.

0427 Capell, Arthur (1960) "The Wandarang and Other Tribal Myths of the
       Yabuduruwa Ritual." *Oceania* 30,3: 206-224.
A myth of Iguana belonging to the Wandaran. The myth is known, however, in
other areas and Capell looks at 3 variants giving the texts and interlinear and
free translations. The myth is further associated with the *Yabuduruwa*
ceremony, and to burial which is attributed to the primordial instigations of
Iguana. Both myth and ritual are linked to the social organization.

0428 Godelier, Maurice (1982) "Myths, Infrastructures and History in Lévi-
       Strauss." In *The Logic of Culture*, edited by I. Rossi, 232-261.
       Massachusetts: J.F. Bergin.
A neo-Marxist attempt to find the 'missing concept' in Lévi-Strauss (0097)
which once again takes up the Yolngu *Wawalak* myth. Accepts all Lévi-Strauss'
erroneous assumptions but seeks to understand why men are given a position of
prestige in religion. Develops the thesis of the primacy of kinship in this
society's infrastructure; relating mythology to the productive forces of society.
Little detailed analysis of the myth or the Yolngu, but theoretically significant.

0429 Hargrave, Susanne (1983) "Two Sister Myths: A Structural Analysis."
       Oceania 53,4: 347-357.
Interprets four Arnhem Land sister myths (*Wawalak, Djanggawul*, etc) using the
structuralist insights of Lévi-Strauss. Suggests the myths present events
validating social norms: namely the ritual control of male patrilineal groups and
the social value of women's reproductive power. The myths, says Hargrave, do
not focus on the relative status of men or women but rather on the perpetuity of
the social group which depends upon controlled relations between the sexes.

0430 Harney, W.E. and Elkin, A.P. (1949) *Songs of the Songmen: Aboriginal
       Myths Retold*. Melbourne: F.W. Cheshire. 173 pp.
A compromise between Harney's loose poetic interests and Elkin's attempt to
pull the work into acceptable anthropological form. None of the songs are exact
translations. They are organized to reflect a logical progression from
cosmogony, through the activities of ancestral heroes to songs related to various
stages of life (conception, childhood, death). Elkin's introduction, editorial
work and extensive notes did not really redeem the work.

0431 Heath, Jeffrey (1980) *Nunggubuyu Myths and Ethnographic Texts.*
       Canberra: Australian Institute of Aboriginal Studies. 556 pp.
Contains several hundred pages of transcriptions with translations of
Nunggubuju myths from Numbulwar Mission recorded in 1973-7. Useful
comments on the texts widen this book's potential audience - especially as some

of the myths are well known and frequently analysed for their 'theoretical' content. Also contain translations of descriptions of various rituals (*Kunapipi*, mortuary, circumcision, 'increase', *Mareiin*, magic, etc.).

0432 Knight, Chris (1983) "Lévi-Strauss and the Dragon: *Mythologiques* Reconsidered in the light of an Australian Aboriginal Myth." *Man* N.S. 18,1: 21-50.
Mainly a selective and questionable reinterpretation of the myth of the *Wawalak*. The thesis merges sociobiology and structuralist anthropology, arguing women's solidarity is regulated by menstrual synchrony among themselves and between women and nature (moon). Men's solidarity is maintained through rites symbolically incorporating women's biological processes. The *Wawalak* myth is interpreted in terms of its menstrual symbolism. Far fetched.

0433 Layton, Robert (1970) "Myth as Language in Aboriginal Arnhem Land." *Man* NS 5,3: 483-497.
A structuralist analysis of the Yolngu *Wawalak* and *Djanggawul* myths in the context of ritual action. Myth, it is said, provides the framework for social events. It is, following de Saussure, a *langue* - a system of interrelated communicative signs. Ritual, by comparison, is a *speech* form - a message communicated through mythic language. Their 'statements' are analytic and identify social events with mythic characters thus expressing the ideal of identity of worldly and Dreaming structures.

0434 Leeden, A.C. van der (1975) "Thundering Gecko and Emu: Mythological Structuring of Nunggubuyu Patrimoieties." In *Australian Aboriginal Mythology*, edited by L.R. Hiatt, 46-101. Canberra: Australian Institute of Aboriginal Studies.
Uses structuralist theory to analyse six Nunggubuju myths, their relation to patrimoieties and their expression of the balance of the forces of life and death. Emu is a trickster, employing experimental, dangerous behaviour to maintain life. Gecko, in contrast, is the conservative protector of life's status quo. This polarity is compared with the nature of the two moieties' religious orientation, one being essentially traditional purists, the other incorporating Macassan and European cultural objects as totemic symbols.

0435 McCarthy, Frederick D. (1953) "The Snake Woman, Jiningbirna." *Records of the Australian Museum* 23,3: 105-109.
Gives the myth and depicts associated stone arrangements and bark paintings.

0436 Maddock, Kenneth (1975) "The Emu Anomaly." In *Australian Aboriginal Mythology*, edited by L.R. Hiatt, 102-122. Canberra: Australian Institute of Aboriginal Studies.
Focuses on Dalabon myths, supplemented by other Arnhem Land (and South-Eastern) evidence. The flightless bird, the emu, is a taxonomic anomaly and emu myths, Maddock argues *à la* Lévi-Strauss, attempt to resolve the problem. Flightlessness (impeded movement) is mythologically associated with refusal to cooperate socially, while free movement is linked with cooperation.

0437 Maddock, Kenneth (1976) "Communication and Change in Mythology." In *Tribes and Boundaries in Australia*, edited by N. Peterson, 162-179. Canberra: Australian Institute of Aboriginal Studies.

Beginning with the Yolngu *Wawalak* myth, goes on to look at comparable Dalabon, Mangarai and Waljbiri myths. Detects a north-south continuity and transformation of structural relations between the sexes. Northern versions argue original female monopoly in now male dominated ritual. The southern Waljbiri maintain men have always controlled ritual. Medial tribes posit a primordial ritual equality. Maddock feels the differences do not reflect varying life situations but rather the way the myths "answer to each other."

0438 Maddock, Kenneth (1978) "Metaphysics in a Mythical View of the World." In *The Rainbow Serpent: A Chromatic Piece*, edited by I.R. Buchler and K. Maddock, 99-118. Paris: Mouton.

Bolung is the Dalabon Rainbow Serpent. The word is also an interchangable noun, referring to a series of attributes and to a phase in the cycle of 'reincarnation'. Three types of hypotheses could be formed. One, stressing the cyclical qualities of existence; the serpent's curvilinear shape corresponds with this. Two, one could look for an analogy between mythic history and present-day experiences. Three, attention could be directed to the grammatical peculiarities of the word *Bolung*.

0439 Merlan, Francesca (1987) "Catfish and Alligator: Totemic Songs of the Western Roper River, Northern Territory." In *Songs of Aboriginal Australia*, edited by M. Clunies Ross, T. Donaldson and S.A. Wild, 142-167. Sydney: Oceania Monographs.

The songs Catfish and Alligator from the Roper River area are contrasted in terms of their religious prominence, social affiliations and site-based contextualization. Addresses the question of *how* songs link totems with people and places and suggests this is achieved not only at the literal sense-making level but, primarily, that opacity encourages holistic interpretations which provide the foundation of socio-religious relationships.

0440 Mountford, Charles P. (1955) "The Lightning Man in Australian Mythology." *Man* 55: 129-30.

Brief notes on Arnhem Land sky beings associated with lightning and thunder.

0441 Munn, Nancy D. (1969) "The Effectiveness of Symbols in Murngin Rite and Myth." In *Forms of Symbolic Action: Proceedings of the 1969 Annual Spring Meeting of the American Ethnological Society*, edited by R.F. Spencer, 178-207. Seattle: University of Washington Press.

Focuses on the relationship between narrative codes and ritual action among the Yolngu. Relies on the ethnographies of Warner (0397) and Berndt (0481) for the well-known *Wawalak* myth and affiliated rites. Maintains that myth conveys body-destructive images saturated with negative feelings which rituals convert into feelings of well-being. Myth-ritual thus functions as a mechanism for social control by transferring individual subjective bodily feelings in terms of objective collective codes. .

0442 Petchkovsky, Leon   (1982)   "Images of Madness in Australian
       Aborigines." *Journal of Analytical Psychology* 27: 21-39.
A Jungian inquiry into the universality of Kingship archetypes in psychotic
processes. 21 case histories for Aboriginal psychoses are examined from notes
in Darwin hospital. Mythic data on incest associated with the *Djanggawul*,
Ngalyod and *Kunapipi* are examined in conjunction with case histories and the
kinship (not Kingship) scenario of incest. Disruption and retribution are
discerned as the common 'archetypes'. Intriguing but flattens mythic material
into a simplistic theoretical form.

0443 Robinson, Roland (1956) *The Feathered Serpent: The Mythological
       Genesis and Procreative Ritual of the Aboriginal Tribes of the Northern
       Territory of Australia.* Sydney: Edward and Shaw. 87 pp.
Material collected from Port Keats and Darwin to the far east of Arnhem Land
(also, briefly, the Aranda and Bidjandjadjara). The paraphrases are not so
liberal as to lose the original flavour and many of the myths complement other
accounts - for instance, those about *Kunmunggar, Mutinga* and *Kukpi* should be
compared with Stanner (0393). Others, such as "Barwal and the Macassars" add
to our meagre knowledge of post-Indonesian myths.

0444 Robinson, Roland (1967) *Legend and Dreaming: Legends of the Dream-
       Time of the Australian Aborigines.* Sydney: Edwards and Shaw. 48 pp.
Djauan, Rembarunga and other narratives collected by the author. Occasionally
refers to cults but mostly concerned with myths told in a public context. The
paraphrases are not too intrusive and the information useful. Thus, "The
Rainbow Serpent of the Plain" has interesting information on the transformative
role of the snake on the landscape. Nonetheless, limited in context and form.

0445 Rudder, John   (1980)   "The Song of the Turtle Rope." *Canberra
       Anthropology* 3,1: 37-47.
Analyses a Yolngu myth to reveal the richness of stories. At an esoteric level it
tells of *Mukarr* who used the first turtle harpoon rope. Some esoteric meanings
are then revealed for the key mythic symbols: rope, bark fibre, forked stick,
float and bones. The author then subjects the myths to structuralist and
functionalist interpretations, arguing that both of these, along with the Yolngu
esoteric exegesis, are necessary. The theoretical *bricolage* doesn't really work.

0446 Sims, Michael (1974) "Tiwi Cosmology." In *Australian Aboriginal
       Concepts*, edited by L.R. Hiatt, 164-167. Canberra: Australian Institute
       of Aboriginal Studies.
A brief account of Tiwi cosmological beliefs with a few notes on their
connection to land and society.

0447 Turner, David H. (1978) *Dialectics in Tradition: Myth and Social
       Structure in Two Hunter-Gatherer Societies.* Occasional Paper no. 36 of
       the Royal Anthropological Institute of Great Britain and Ireland.
       London: The Royal Anthropological Institute. 45 pp.
A Cree/Bickerton Is. Aborigines comparison studying dialectics in hunter-
gatherer societies. The *Nambirrirrma* myth is summarized and analysed (pp.

26-40) in a Lévi-Straussian manner but with a strong focus on territoriality and social relations, and tension between land ownership and land occupational usage. Suggests *Nambirrirrma* may symbolize a Macassan visitor. Compare (0448).

0448   Turner, David H.   (1988)   "The Incarnation of Nambirrirrma."   In *Aboriginal Australians and Christian Missions: Ethnographic and Historical Studies*, edited by T. Swain and D. Rose, 470-483. Adelaide: Australian Association for the Study of Religions.
An interpretation of the myth of *Nambirrirrma*, also analysed by the author in (0396) and (0447). Here, he argues the Bickerton Island narrative contains the structure of a 'Christ Event': an anti-Hegelian procession from anti-thesis through thesis to plurality (see 0112). New Testament passages are also examined in light of this model and the possibility of a mutual Aboriginal/Christian fulfillment is suggested. Highly original and likely to infuriate conservative scholars.

See also: 0097, 0119, 0120, 0125, 0374, 0378, 0387, 0390, 0393, 0397, 0410, 0449, 0450, 0455, 0459, 0467, 0474, 0476, 0481, 0482, 0493, 0494, 0495, 0502, 0504, 0506, 0534, 0545, 0551, 0554, 0556.

The Arts

0449   Allen, Louis A.   (1972)   *Australian Aboriginal Art: Arnhem Land*   USA: Field Museum Press. 43 pp.
An exhibition catalogue providing notes on religious significance. *Wawalak, Djanggawul, Laitjun-Banaitja* and other myths are re-told and linked with art. 'Nature myths' are discussed, and there are texts and artifacts associated with *Narra* rites, sorcery and mortuary practice. Finally, reflections on Macassan and European cultural contacts are given in spiritual terms. Commentary adds a few details to other published accounts.

0450   Arndt, W.   (1962)   "The Interpretation of the Delemere Lightning Painting and Rock Engravings." *Oceania* 32,3: 163-177.
The Wardaman rock painting depicts two brothers said to have fought for the favours of a woman. Arndt had found serious discrepancies between previous accounts and local Aboriginal interpretations. The mythical origins of the images are discussed and it is suggested that previously the site was used to produce rain. Other figures on the rock surface are also discussed.

0451   Arndt, W.   (1962)   "The Nargorkun-Narlinji Cult." *Oceania* 32,4: 298-320.
Illustrates and interprets six Djauan rock shelters. Brief explanations, relying heavily on information from local Aborigines, are given for 100 designs. The sites are related to relevant Dreaming narratives; their use in the education of youths; and an annual men's sickness ceremony. Concludes by discussing some

more general aspects of the history of the cult. By no means exhaustive. (See, 0478).

0452 Berndt, Catherine H. (1962) "The Arts of Life: An Australian
      Aboriginal Perspective." *Westerly* 1-3: 82-88.
A brief introduction to the place of art works in Aboriginal ceremonial life.
Segments of myths are given.

0453 Berndt, Ronald M. (1958) "The Mountford Volume on Arnhem Land
      Art, Myth and Symbolism: A Critical Review." *Mankind* 5,6: 249-261.
A scathing review of Mountford (0472) refuting it as a scientific and definitive
work on Arnhem Land art, myth and symbolism. Provides an awesome list of
inaccuracies, omissions, and simplifications. Berndt's clarifications are of
intrinsic value.

0454 Berndt, Ronald M. (1976) *Love Songs of Arnhem Land.* Chicago:
      University of Chicago Press. 244 pp.
The heart of this book is three song cycles taken from Goulburn Island and the
Rose River area traditions, as well as excerpts from the *Djarada*. The material
was collected at Yirrkala over some 3 decades before publication, and the
transcriptions and interlineal translations are given in appendices. The text itself
offers free translations, and explanatory chapters provide a general discussion of
the socio-ritual, procreative and personal role of sex in Arnhem Land thought.
The religious significance of the songs is stressed.

0455 Berndt, Ronald M. and Berndt, Catherine H. (1948) "Sacred Figures of
      Ancestral Beings of Arnhem Land." *Oceania* 18,4: 309-326.
A description of 10 Yolngu carved human figures. Although by no means
exhaustive, the article pays considerable attention to the ritual procedure of the
production of these works and their mythic interpretation. In particular they are
related to myth and ritual of the moieties - the *Wawalak* myths (associated with
Djungguan and *Kunapipi* ritual) of the *Dhuwa* and *Laitjun* and *Banaitja* myths of
the *Yirritja* moiety. See 0456.

0456 Berndt, Ronald M. and Berndt, Catherine H. (1949) "Secular Figures of
      Northeastern Arnhem Land." *American Anthropologist* 51,2: 213-222.
Yolngu human figures used in public ('secular') ceremonies. These are of two
kinds. The *Wuremu* figures have been identified as Dutch custom officials and
also as the spirits of deceased Macassans. The accompanying ceremony is
described. *Baijini* figures are similar. They are the first visitors (Europeans?
early Macassans?) and are at times located in mythic rather than historic
domains. Brief notes are provided on *Baijini* ceremonies.

0457 Berndt, Ronald M. and Berndt, Catherine H. (1965) "Aborigines: Music,
      Poetry, Song." In *The Australian Encyclopedia*, 2nd ed., Vol. 1, 56-61.
      Sydney: The Grolier Society.
Within a broader context of Aboriginal music, song and poety, offers a sampler
of Arnhem Land songs with a religious base: 'gossip songs', love-magic

(*Djarada*) songs, extracts from love-song cycles, mythic-songs, mortuary songs and extracts from the *Kunapipi* and *Djanggawul* cycles.

0458   Brandl, E.J.   (1973)   *Australian Aboriginal Paintings in Western and Central Arnhem Land: Temporal Sequences and Elements of Style in Cadell River and Deaf Adder Creek Art.*   Canberra: Australian Institute of Aboriginal Studies. 214 pp.
The analysis of rock art is supplemented by Dalabon and Rembarunga informantion on the religious significance of art. 'Totemic' beings and the Rainbow Serpent/All-Mother are discussed. Considers changes through time in art, such as reversals in rates of male/female figures, perhaps associated with fertility. Also contains some theoretical discussion of 'totemism' (cf. Lévi-Strauss, 0098) as manifest in rock art.

0459   Carroll, Peter J.   (1974)   "Mimi from Western Arnhem Land."   In *Form in Indigenous Art: Schematization in the Art of Aboriginal Australia and Prehistoric Europe*, edited by P.J. Ucko, 119-130.   Canberra: Australian Institute of Aboriginal Studies.
Mimi art has been frequently discussed but Carroll's paper, based on Oenpelli data, is particularly valuable for its *Mimi* stories - their exploits, camping places, hunting, singing and dancing, and their pets - as told by Aboriginal artists themselves. Focus is on barks of western Arnhem Land, but compares these with cave art.

0460   Clunies Ross, Margaret and Wild, Stephen A.   (1982)   *Djambidj: An Aboriginal Song Series from Northern Australia.*   Canberra: Australian Institute of Aboriginal Studies. 64 pp.
A book accompanying a record of the Blyth River region *Djambidj* song series which consists of songs relating to *Wangarr*. Some of the songs are central to mortuary ritual. There is a brief introduction to the *Djambidj* series in ethnographic and musicological terms, but most of the text is given to transcriptions, translations, and paraphrases combined with explanatory comments.

0461   Clunies Ross, Margaret and Wild, Stephen A.   (1984)   "Formal Performance: The Relations of Music, Text and Dance in Arnhem Land Clan Songs." *Ethnomusicology* 28,2: 209-235.
Djambidj is a clan song which is shared by a number of *Dhuwa* moiety groups. This article examines a performance within a *Larrgan* mortuary ceremony. Particularly concerned with dance effects, and musical and textual components of the mortuary rite. The process of integrating these various elements is addressed.

0462   Elkin, A.P.   (1952)   "Cave-Paintings in Southern Arnhem Land." *Oceania* 22,4: 245-255.
Develops Macintosh's interpretation of the cave art at Beswick Creek (0466), supplementing it with information on the cave at Tandandjal (some 14 miles east). Elkin's views rest heavily on information from Djauan people. The former cave is related to burial ritual and associated *Kunapipi* or *Yabuduruwa*

ceremonies. The latter is connected with the travels of mythic brolga and the *Mareiin* cult.

0463 Elkin, A.P. (1953-56) "Arnhem Land Music." *Oceania* 24,2: 81-109; 25,1-2: 74-124; 25,4: 292-342; 26,1: 59-70; 26,2: 127-152; 26,3: 214-230.
An extensive survey based on recordings made in 1949-1952. Not the work of an ethnomusicologist and hence the primary focus is upon the text of the songs and their ritual context. Divides recordings into three categories: secular, sacred and secret. Of interest is the discussion and map of the routes along which the various songs are distributed. The bulk of the article is taken up by texts and translations, but there are interspersed ethnographic comments.

0464 Elkin, A.P.; Berndt, Catherine H.; and Berndt, Ronald M. (1950) *Art in Arnhem Land*. Melbourne: F.W. Cheshire. 123 pp.
A valuable overview of Arnhem Land, mostly Yolngu, art carefully associating works with their religious contexts. A chapter is devoted to 'The Mythology and Sacred Emblems' - in particular the *Djanggawul*, *Wawalak* and *Laitjun-Banaitja*. Indonesian artistic/religious influences are well illustrated. Covers themes such as 'mortuary art', 'love magic and art', bringing belief and practice to the fore.

0465 Hoff, Jennifer and Taylor, Luke (1985) "The Mimi Spirit as Sculpture." *Art and Australia* 23,1: 73-77.
Mimi have been found in rock art thousands of years old and more recently as painted wood sculptures. This new manifestation is considered in relation to mythology. Brief, useful notes.

0466 Macintosh, N.W.G. (1952) "Paintings in Beswick Creek Cave, Northern Territory." *Oceania* 22,4: 256-274.
Descriptions, photographs, line drawings and interpretations of 81 figures. Interpretation is aided by Djauan informants. Argues that archaeological and verbal information indicates it was a site centre of women's religious activities with a Fertility Mother theme, the Mother herself being represented by the recess of the cave. For supplementary, sometimes contradicting interpretations, see Elkin (0462).

0467 Maddock, Kenneth (1970) "Imagery and Social Structure in Two Dalabon Rock Art Sites." *Anthropological Forum* 2,4: 444-463.
Depicts *Yirritja* moiety sites in Dalabon country. A substantial section relates the art to myths and rituals recalled by Aborigines then on Beswick Reserve. Myths are paraphrased and analysed in terms of binary themes, and parallels are established between rock art motifs, ritual practice and myth.

0468 Morphy, Howard (1978) "Rights in Paintings and Rights in Women: A Consideration of Some of the Basic Problems Posed by the Asymmetry of the 'Murngin System'." *Mankind* 11,3: 208-19.
Valuable consideration of the way Yolngu clan members inherit rights to *madayin* - sacred 'Law' which includes paintings. Distinguishes *rights* to produce designs from "ownership" and then discusses three types of rights:

rights within one's own clan, ideally handed down from one's father; rights to designs in one's "mother's" clan (*ngändi*); and rights in *märi* ("mother's mother's") clan paintings.

0469 Morphy, Howard (1981) "The Art of Northern Australia." In *Aboriginal Australia*, by C. Cooper; H. Morphy; J. Mulvaney; and N. Peterson, 53-65. Sydney: Australian Gallery Directors Council.
Meant to address the whole north but really is focused upon Arnhem Land. A good but brief look at aesthetic, social and religious aspects of art, arguing for an analysis of meaning in terms of total cultural patterns.

0470 Morphy, Howard (1989) "From Dull to Brilliant: The Aesthetics of Spiritual Power Among the Yolngu." *Man* NS 24,1: 21-40.
Considers the Yolngu criteria of aesthetic value, in particular the quality of *bir'yun* - 'brilliance' or 'shimmering' associated with both Ancestral power and beauty. Describes how cross-hatching produces a manifestation of the spiritual power or the *Wangarr* (Ancestral Beings). Argues that the experience of 'brilliance' transcends cultural boundaries and thus actually induces an affective state in ritual.

0471 Morphy, Howard (1989) "On Representing Ancestral Beings." In *Animals into Art*, edited by H. Morphy, 144-160. London: Unwin Hyman.
An insightful article analysing how the Yolngu transmit information about Ancestral Beings in art. The transformative abilities of Ancestors is noted and it is shown that, while figurative art represents their tangible forms, other less obvious elements (e.g. geometric designs) signify their fantastic aspects. This openness of symbolism enhances the engagements of the custodians of designs with the eternal events they have depicted.

0472 Mountford, Charles P. (1956) *Records of the American-Australian Scientific Expedition to Arnhem Land, I: Art, Myth and Symbolism*. Melbourne: Melbourne University Press. 513 pp.
A coffee-table book disguised as a scientific work. Berndt (0453) has said its commentary is inaccurate, superficial and highly selective; the art/mythology connection is poorly made; the ritual context of both art and myth is not adequately covered; and the author has not benefited from previous monographs on the subject (e.g. Warner 0397). Nice pictures, however.

0473 Moyle, Alice M. (1964) "Bara and Mamariga Songs on Groote Eylandt." *Canon* 17,3: 15-24.
Bara and *Mamaringa* are the totems of two prevailing winds which head moieties and which are also associated with the winds bringing Macassans. This article presents the songs with music and text, considering the history of cultural contact with Indonesian and Europeans and placing the songs in their social and ritual contexts.

0474 Tacon, Paul (1989) "Art and the Essence of Being: Symbolic and Economic Aspects of Fish Among the Peoples of Western Arnhem Land,

Australia." In *Animals into Art*, edited by H. Morphy, 236-250. London: Unwin Hyman.
Based on investigations of X-ray rock art depicting fish in the Kakadu National Park area. Myths from the region are briefly discussed to support the view that fish are intermediaries of the spirit of a 'clan well' which becomes the life essence of a human. The iconic value of fish is thus not primarily related to food value but to spiritual and philosophic concerns.

0475 Taylor, Luke (1989) "Seeing the 'Inside': Kunwinjku Paintings and the Symbol of the Divided Body." In *Animals into Art*, edited by H. Morphy, 371-389. London: Unwin Hyman.
Examines Gunwinggu X-ray art and levels of meaning inherent in an icon. Beyond overt representation are esoteric meanings encoded in abstract designs. The progressive revelations of the significance of art is stressed, as is the all-embracing range of information embodied in designs, spanning social, environmental and religious domains. Seeing the full 'inside' meaning of art is thus a revelation of the essence of the Law.

0476 Wells, A.E. (1971) *This Their Dreaming*. St. Lucia: University of Queensland Press. 76 pp.
Deals with two Aboriginal paintings, one from each moiety, painted for the Methodist church at Yirrkala. In doing so, secret-sacred iconography was transposed into a very different context, which the author largely ignores. Translations of the myths depicted in the panels are (deliberately?) truncated. Compare, however, with Berndt's study of a similar phenomena, (0530).

0477 Worsley, Peter M. (1954) "Material Symbols of Human Beings Among the Wanindiljaugwa." *Man* 54: 165-7.
Notes on Groote Eylandt 'dolls', noting their social and religious significances.

See also: 0161, 0387, 0409, 0418, 0420, 0430, 0439, 0481, 0498, 0517, 0518, 0519, 0520, 0522, 0530, 0531, 0533, 0547, 0548, 0549, 0550.

Ceremony

0478 Arndt, W. (1966) "Seventy Year Old Records and New Information on the Nargorkun-Narlinji Cult." *Oceania* 36,3: 231-8.
Corrects Arndt's earlier paper (0451) using photographic evidence from 1890. Contains mythic and ritual details of the 'sick country' based mainly on Djauan data.

0479 Bern, John (1979) "Politics in the Conduct of a Secret Male Ceremony." *Journal of Anthropological Research* 35,1: 47-60.
Focuses on the *Yabuduruwa* ceremonies (cf. Elkin 0483), performed in 1970. Argues the ceremony currently revolves around ownership of 'idological property'. Internal politicking is stressed and the cult is said to largely deny forms of White oppression. Much of the paper is wrong-headed, including the

insistence on religion as "practiced by men for the benefit of men" (p.47, cf. Langton 0203), but nonetheless contains useful data.

0480 Berndt, Ronald M. (1951) "Ceremonial Exchange in Western Arnhem Land." *Southwestern Journal of Anthropology* 7: 156-176.
Describes 6 ceremonies in which Aborigines from different communities meet for the sole purpose of exchanging goods. Discusses spectacular dancing, ritual and singing appropriate to the festive occasion. Includes *Rom* (see Wild 0492), *Wurbu, Njalaidj, Mamorung, Djamalag* and *Midjan* from various peoples but largely from a Gunwinggu perspective. Symbolic significance and Macassan influence are considered.

0481 Berndt, Ronald M. (1951) *Kunapipi: A Study of An Australian Aboriginal Religious Cult.* Melbourne: Cheshire. 223 pp.
A detailed study of the Yirrkala manifestation of the *Kunapipi*, a widely diffused cult, related to a common theme of a Great Mother. The myth and ritual of the *Kunapipi* are established in the first half of the volume, the remainder is given to a transcription with interlinear and free translations of the *Kunapipi* songs, divided into their 'sacred' and 'secular' forms. Concludes with some functionalist reflections on the role of the cult in a changing world.

0482 Berndt, Ronald M. (1987) "Gadjari." In *The Encyclopedia of Religion*, edited by M. Eliade, Vol. 5, 461-3. New York: Macmillan.
A concise overview of the cults and myths of the 'Old Woman' known variously as *Gadjeri, Kunapipi, Mumunga, Mutinga*, etc.

0483 Elkin, A.P. (1961) "The Yabuduruwa." *Oceania* 31,3: 166-209.
Contains a day-by-day account of Rembarunga *Yabuduruwa* ceremonial activities. Spencer and Gillen (0791) had identified this cult with the *Kunapipi*, but Elkin argues for their separate origin which has nonetheless led to a complementary arrangement. The *Yirritja* moiety is primarily responsible for the *Yabuduruwa* whilst the *Dhuwa* care for the *Kunapipi*. Concludes by looking at the wider context of the ritual and making some more general theoretical observations.

0484 Elkin, A.P. (1961) "Marain at Mainoru, 1949." *Oceania* 31,4: 259-293; 32,1: 1-15.
An account of a Rembarunga *Mareiin* ceremony. Part I of the article is a day by day account of ritual activity interposed with texts and translations. Topics covered include the display of *rangga* and body paintings, food taboo, myth dances, ritual bathing and the actual *rangga* rites. Part II interprets the data. Depicts *Mareiin* as similar to an "all souls" festival and attempts to place it in its social and religious context. Theoretically dull.

0485 Elkin, A.P. (1971) "Yabuduruwa at Roper River Mission, 1965." *Oceania* 42,2: 110-164.
Based on a film of a *Yabuduruwa* ritual performed by Nunggubuju (mainly) Mara, Wandaran, Alawa and Ngandi people. An introductory discussion of the context, themes and social arrangements of the ritual is followed by a scene by

scene description. The principal motifs were goanna, *Nagaran*, a giant culture-hero, and plum-bird. Discusses the social implications of the choice of motifs, but concedes the deeper symbolism remained unfathomed.

0486 Holmes, Sandra Le Brun (1965) "The Nagarren Yubidawara." *Milla wa-Milla: The Australian Bulletin of Comparative Religion* No. 5: 8-17.
A journalistic description of a *Yabuduruwa* ceremony held in the Roper River Mission environs. Does no more than describe the movements and body designs of the participants as their ceremony is being filmed. Compare with Elkin (0484) and Maddock (0488).

0487 Keen, Ian (1977) "Ambiguity in Yolngu Religious Language." *Canberra Anthropology* 1,1: 33-50.
A study of religious language in two Yolngu rituals: *Mareiin* and *Kunapipi*. Ambiguity in religious language is examined as a means to maintain identity whilst excluding others from the privilege of knowledge. In *Kunapipi*, people from a wide area participate, but women and neophytes are excluded from understanding esoteric meanings. In contrast, *Mareiin* songs not only separate men from women but also privilege specific men. Keen emphasizes this process is open-ended.

0488 Maddock, Kenneth (1979) "A Structural Analysis of Paired Ceremonies in a Dual Social Organization." *Bijdragen tot de Taal- Land- en Volkenkunde* 135: 84-117.
Focuses on the polarity and complementarity *Dhuwa* and *Yirritja* ceremonies - in particular in *Kunapipi* (Berndt 0481) and *Yabuduruwa* (Elkin 0483). Moiety organization is examined in terms of the roles of 'owner' and 'manager', and there are detailed structural analyses of song and silence, sacred waters and shelters, and the sequencing of the ritual. Some comparative data is given before offering concluding remarks on the unity of opposites.

0489 Maddock, Kenneth (1985) "Sacrifice and Other Models in Australian Aboriginal Ritual." In *Metaphors of Interpretation: Essays in Honour of W.E.H. Stanner*, edited by D.E. Barwick, J. Beckett and M. Reay, 133-157. Sydney: Australian National University Press.
Stanner (0393) had argued that *Punj* had striking formal resemblances with sacrifice. Maddock reviews the responses to Stanner's view before proceeding to test its adequacy and its applicability to Arnhem Land ceremonies. Highlights important dimensions of Arnhem Land ritual which cannot be identified with sacrifice, suggesting sacrifice is best seen as but one variation of a possible ritual combination still awaiting an appropriate explanatory model.

0490 Stanner, W.E.H. (1933) "Ceremonial Economics of the Mulluk Mulluk and Madngela Tribes of the Daly River, North Australia: A Preliminary Paper." *Oceania* 4: 156-175, 458-471.
A preliminary account of the *Merbok* inter-tribal exchange and the *Kue* 'sacramental' and legal exchange related to marriage, among the Mullukmulluk and Madngela in the Daly River Region. While not strictly a religious exchange,

Stanner emphasizes the symbolic significance of gift giving and the transmission of cults along exchange routes is also discussed.

0491   Thomson, Donald F.   (1949) *Economic Structure and the Ceremonial Exchange Cycle in Arnhem Land*. Melbourne: Macmillan. 106 pp.
Descriptions of movements of goods which are exchanged on ceremonial occasions. Notes these exchange traditions were established by totemic ancestors and codified in myth (p.34) but does not explore this dimension. Nor, in fact, does Thomson cover genuine ceremonial exchange. The title, therefore, refers to exchanges which occur incidentally to ritual. Disappointing.

0492   Wild, Stephen A., ed.   (1986) *Rom: An Aboriginal Ritual of Diplomacy*. Canberra: Australian Institute of Aboriginal Studies. 102 pp.
Documents and backgrounds the performance of an Gidjingali *Rom* ceremony in Canberra in 1982. Three brief articles provide context. L.R. Hiatt writes of *Rom* in Arnhem Land, B. Meehan and R. Jones document the process "From Anadjerramiya to Canberra", while M. Clunies Ross gives a synopsis of the Canberra performance itself. The ritual, while similar to mortuary ritual, is a 'trade ceremony' or 'ritual of diplomacy'. Ritual objects and associated bark paintings are tastefully displayed.

See also: 0169, 0172, 0378, 0393, 0397, 0418, 0427, 0431, 0433, 0441, 0451, 0455, 0456, 0462, 0467, 0494, 0496, 0534, 0544.

Initiation

0493   Bennie, Chris   (1980) "Aboriginal Inititation Rites and Myths: A Jungian Interpretation." *Sophia* 19: 9-19.
Drawing on ethnographic data from Stanner's (0393) study of Murinbata initiation, proceeds, after dismissing Freud, Róheim and Bettelheim, to develop a non-sexual psychoanalytic interpretation. 'Sexual' symbolism is said to relate to re-birth. Withdrawal and return to social life is equated with processes of individuation. An impoverished reading of Jung and, in particular, Stanner.

0494   Berndt, Ronald M.   (1951) "Subincision in a Non-Subincision Area." *The American Imago: A Psychoanalytic Journal for the Arts and Sciences* 8,2: 165-179.
Looks at subincision as a symbolic appropriation of women's genital and reproductive powers. Considers *Kunapipi* and the *Wawalak* in terms of their association with subincised phalli, then turns to the Gunwinggu, where circumcision is a recent innovation and subincision is known but not practiced. Here *Kunapipi* has been incorporated without the operation yet a substantiating myth is given which shows these people clearly know about the operation.

0495   Berndt, Ronald M.   (1952) "Circumcision in a Non-Circumcision Area." *International Archives of Ethnography* 46: 121-146.

Examines the response of the Gunwinggu to circumcision amongst neighbouring people. Myths indicating fear of circumcision are given, but it is said they have overcome this attitude and learned of the rites but not the full body of associated myths and songs. Argues these changes evince the internal dynamics of Aboriginal religions and hence the fluidity of pre-colonial Aboriginal traditions. Transcriptions with translations are given.

0496 Leeden, A.C. van der (1975) "Nunggubuyu Aboriginals and Marind-Anim: Preliminary Comparisons Between Southeastern Arnhem Land and Southern New Guinea." In *Explorations in the Anthropology of Religion: Essays in Honour of Jan van Baal*, edited by W.E.A. van Beek and J.H. Scherer, 122-146. The Hague: Martinus Nijhoff.

Postulating possible historical links, compares field material on Nunggubuju initiation and published accounts for the south of New Guinea. Stresses similarities and differences in ritual organization and descent procedures in these patrilineal societies. Suggests in both cases, under different ecological circumstances, ritual is directed towards territorial and local requirements of patrilineality. The actual data on the cults is illustrative rather than expository. See van Baal (0169).

0497 McCarthy, Frederick (1953) "A Circumcision Ceremony and Stone Arrangement on Groote Eylandt." *Records of the Australian Museum* 23,3: 97-103.

A ceremony witnessed in 1948. Contains descriptions of preliminary dances, but data is restricted to designs and behaviour and ignores social and religious significance. The circumcision rite proper contains some recognition of kin dynamics and rights and duties in initiation, but lacks detail.

See also: 0384, 0500.

Women

0498 Berndt, Catherine H. (1950) "Expression of Grief Among Aboriginal Women." *Oceania* 20,4: 286-332.

Examines socially approved means of expressing grief available to Tiwi and Yolngu women. Songs associated with circumcision, illness and death are transcribed and given literal and free translations. Some underlying themes of the songs explored are the speculations concerning the future of the deceased's spirit and the wish for the dead to return.

0499 Elverdam, Beth (1977) "Where Men and Women Have Separate Worlds - How Ritual is Used as a Mechanism of Socialization." *Temenos* 13: 56-67.

Considers how boys, socialized by their mothers, are inculturated into the realm of men. Drawing on the Berndts' Gunwinggu data (0378) and the insights of Victor Turner's studies of liminality, argues very much in line with the traditional hierarchical model of a male dominated religious life. While recognizing the bias inherent in anthropological data, the article does not come to terms with women's religiosity nor, for that matter, men's.

0500 Goodale, Jane C. (1971) *Tiwi Wives: A Study of the Women of Melville Island, North Australia.* Seattle: University of Washington Press. 268 pp.
Adds substantially to the ethnography of women's religious life. Discusses puberty rituals and menstruation taboos, beliefs concerning conception and pregnancy, and rituals associated with childbirth. There is a chapter on the *Kulama* (yam) ceremony which serves, among other things, as an initiation ritual for both men and women (see 0544). Death and funeral procedures are treated at length, including a full account of the *Pukimani* (mortuary ceremony). A final chapter pulls together the Tiwi socio-religious cosmology.

0501 Goodale, Jane C. (1986) "Production and Reproduction of Key Resources Among the Tiwi of North Australia." In *Resource Monographs: North American and Australian Hunter-Gatherers*, edited by N. Williams and E.S. Hunn, 197-210. Canberra: Australian Institute of Aboriginal Studies.
Argues the Tiwi classifiy the universe in terms of gender. The complementary roles of men and women are shown to reflect an ideological order in which the yam is the key unifying symbol. The *Kulama* ritual, in which a toxic yam is made edible is discussed as a clear expression of this ideology (cf. Goodale 0544). The *Kulama* yam is argued to symbolize all human life and its gender-based interrelatedness.

0502 Leeuwe, J. de (1964-5) "Male Right and Female Right among the Autochthons of Arnhem Land." *Acta Ethnografica* 13,1/4: 313-348; 14,3/4: 303-348.
A detailed examination of published ethnographies from across Arnhem Land (considering regional variations) in terms of the nature of sexual relationships. Stresses the priority of women in myths of early ritual life and considers the place of women indicated by Mother cults and the *Wawalak* and *Djanggawul* stories. Speculates on an historic gynaecrocracy.

See also: 0192, 0429, 0432, 0466.

Magic

0503 Berndt, Catherine H. (1964) "The Role of Native Doctors in Aboriginal Australia." In *Magic, Faith and Healing: Studies in Primitive Psychiatry Today*, edited by A. Kiev, 264-282. Glencoe: Free Press.
A detailed examination of western Arnhem Land healing in both its traditional and modern forms. The Gunwinggu *margidbu*'s initiation, powers, diagnostics and various forms of community support are discussed. Mission and government presence is described and the changing role of the *margidbu* illustrated. Argues their social skills are as important as their healing abilities, and that these are still called upon today.

0504 Berndt, Catherine H. (1982) "Sickness and Health in Western Arnhem Land: A Traditional Perspective." In *Body, Land and Spirit: Health and Healing in Aboriginal Society*, edited by J. Reid, 121-138. St. Lucia: University of Queensland Press.
A broad view of health in western Arnhem Land, particularly stressing religious foundations. Mythic themes related to dangerous places, sorcery, traditional healers and moral precepts are considered. Some mythic references dealing with more pragmatic aspects of illness are also offered. The holistic basis of health is emphasized and inversely, illness is argued to have a socio-moral dimension.

0505 Biernoff, David (1982) "Psychiatric and Anthropological Interpretations of 'Aberrant' Behaviour in an Aboriginal Community." In *Body, Land and Spirit: Health and Healing in Aboriginal Society*, edited by J. Reid, 139-153. St. Lucia: University of Queensland Press.
Reviews studies of Aboriginal 'abnormal' behaviour arguing they neglected traditional structures and processes as a means of maintaining and protecting land and Law. Stresses the role of sorcery in maintaining Nunggubuju social systems, and illnesses which result from mishandling sacred places, etc. Notes healers do not attempt to counter 'legitimate' illness, and that these have a logical place in the Aboriginal view.

0506 Cawte, John, ed. (N.D.) *Readings in Community Health*. Matraville: The Aboriginal Health Worker. 152 pp.
Readings from *The Aboriginal Health Worker* beginning with a section on 'primal religion'. Cawte's 'Snakes on a stick: Aboriginal Religion and Healing' considers some Yolngu stories but is confused. There are also two short pieces from L.A. Allen, both Arnhem Land myths in superficial detail.

0507 Eastwell, Harry D. (1973) "The Traditional Healer in Modern Arnhem Land." *The Medical Journal of Australia* No. 22: 1011-1017.
After 40 years of western medicine the traditional healer still remained. This article asked why and examines four cases of illness and traditional treatment in order to discern the functions of healers. Aboriginal diagnoses were 'incestuous relations', 'mystical', 'noxious spirit' and 'sorcery'. Argues that Aboriginal medicine has a strong sociological and psychological value but is technologically poor. Lacks detail and depth.

0508 Eastwell, Harry D. (1982) "Voodoo Death and the Mechanism for Dispatch of the Dying in East Arnhem, Australia." *American Anthropologist* 84,1: 5-18.
Argues for a common cause for both voodoo deaths and Aboriginal deaths brought on through suggestion. Describes the Aboriginal sequence for dispatching the dying and highlights the fact that they were kept away from water. Dehydration and the ritual nullification of thirst drives are given as the primary cause of death.

0509 McElroy, W.A. (1955) "PSI Testing in Arnhem Land." *Oceania* 26,2: 118-126.

Report on naïve tests carried out at Beswick and Delissaville in 1952 in order to measure Aboriginal psychokinesis. Suggests the Aboriginal view of time plus the need for bush communication could heighten abilities. The tests, made using techniques the author admits to be less than ideal, led to a result considerably worse than chance. Conjectures that this itself could be significant.

0510   Reid, Janice C.   (1978) "The Role of the *Marrnggitj* in Contemporary Health Care." *Oceania* 49,2: 96-109.
Estimates the value of traditional healers in modern health services by examining Yirrkala's three *marrnggitj*. Discusses the initiation of healers, their social function in counter-sorcery, and the factors influencing people's decision to consult a healer.   As the medicine-person's treatment is argued to be substantially psychotherapeutic, it is suggested that they do indeed have an important role in contemporary health care.

0511   Reid, Janice C.   (1983) *Sorcerers and Healing Spirits: Continuity and Change in an Aboriginal Medical System.* Canberra: Australian National University Press. 182 pp.
An important analysis of tradition and dynamics in Yolngu beliefs about sickness and health. Contains a detailed analysis of causes of sickness and death through sorcery and contact with places, rituals and spirits. The *marrnggitj* (healer) is discussed at length, and practices are interpreted in terms of the Yolngu understanding of life. The final chapter says change has been superficial and interrelations with Western and Christian beliefs are discussed. Currently the best book on Aboriginal healing.

0512   Reid, Janice C. and Manunggurr, D.   (1977) "We are Losing Our Brothers: Sorcery and Alcohol in an Aboriginal Community." *Medical Journal of Australia*, Special Supplement 2: 1-5.
Manunggurr, a senior member of a Yolngu community, adds an insider's views on sorcery, chronic alcohol consumption and fears that death cause in an Aboriginal community.

0513   Scarlett, Neville; White, Neville; and Reid, Janice C.   (1982) "'Bush Medicines': The Pharmacopeia of the Yolngu of Arnhem Land." In *Body, Land and Spirit: Health and Healing in Aboriginal Society*, edited by J. Reid, 154-191. St. Lucia: University of Queensland Press.
Focuses on physical causes and care of illness but briefly compares this with 'supernatural' agents of sickness.

0514   Simeon, George   (1980) "Tiwi Ethnomedicine and the Concept of *Tarni* (N. Australia)." *Anthropos* 75: 942-948.
Examines the Tiwi illness *tarni* and associated ethnomedical beliefs. Suggests *tarni* has undergone constant definitional changes, and notes that it became associated with the *Kulama* ceremony (see Goodale 0544). Considers sorcery and traditional healers in a changing environment and the increase in sorcery. *Tarni* , it is concluded, reflects the disruption to Tiwi understanding of health and harmony.

0515 Thomson, Donald F. (1961) "Marrngitmirri and Kalka - Medicineman and Sorcerer - in Arnhem Land." *Man* 61: 97-102.
Describes briefly the cult of the *marrngitmirri* ('medicineman'), the role of his *marrnggitj* or 'spirit familiar', and the cult of the *kalka* or sorcerer. Thomson argues, in contrast to Webb (0516), that the two cults did not occur among the same people and suggests their relative geographical distribution.

0516 Webb, T. Theodore (1936) "The Making of a Marrngit." *Oceania* 6,3: 336-341.
The *marrnggitj* of east Arnhem Land extract foreign bodies from patients and counter the sorcery of the *ragalk*. If death results they identify the culprit. The process of initiating a *marrnggitj* is described by paraphrasing two accounts given to the author.

See also: 0217.

Death

0517 Berndt, Ronald M. (1948) "Badu, Islands of the Spirits." *Oceania* 19,2: 93-103.
Badu is the Yolngu *Yirritja* moiety Isle of the dead. The *Badu* song-cycle's first song is translated and describes the spirits paddling their canoes. Male and female spirits are also illustrated by three sculptures. Concludes with some suggestion of historical contact between Arnhem Land, Torres Strait Islanders, and Macassans, the cultural borrowings involved, and the process of transposing history into myth.

0518 Clunies Ross, Margaret and Hiatt, L.R. (1974) "Sand Sculptures at a Gidjingali Burial Rite." In *Form in Indigenous Art: Schematization in the Art of Aboriginal Australia and Prehistoric Europe*, edited by P.J. Ucko, 131-146. Canberra: Australian Institute of Aboriginal Studies.
Analyses the construction of five sand sculptures during a *Larrgan* ceremony-the final phase of mortuary ritual in which bones are crushed and placed in a hollow log coffin. Previous descriptions saw them as totemic spirit homes. This paper suggests a more complex understanding is involved. The focus is on the rules for the selection of design, beliefs concerning the fate of the dead and the meaning of the sculptures.

0519 Goodale, Jane C. (1959) "The Tiwi Dance for the Dead." *Expedition* 2,1: 3-13.
An anecdotal description of mortuary poles commissioned by the author. There is little detail on the funeral songs and ceremonies, and one only wishes she had explained how dance themes of aeroplanes, buffaloes, boats, radios, telephones, cowboys and Indians and flags had been adapted into the Tiwi world-view (p.13). A lightweight and unsatisfying account.

0520 Goodale, Jane C. and Koss, Joan D. (1966) "The Cultural Context of
      Creativity Among Tiwi." *American Ethnological Society, Annual Spring
      Meeting, Proceedings* 175-191.
Considers Tiwi creative process by examining the construction of burial poles.
Death, pole construction, *Pukimani* rituals and concluding payment is chronicled
with plates. This is related to Tiwi appeasement of ghosts; their ideology and
standards of prestige; and their aesthetics. The relationship between tradition
and creativity is weighed and the possibility for change in burial pole art is
considered.

0521 Habenstein, Robert W. and Lamers, William M. (1963) *Funeral
      Customs the World Over.* Milwaukee: Bulfin. 854 pp.
Pages 357-368 on "Tiwi of North Australia" rely on the photographs and reports
of Goodale (0519, 0520). Adds nothing to her account.

0522 Keen, Ian (1974) "Yolngu Sand Sculptures in Context." In *Form in
      Indigenous Art: Schematization in the Art of Aboriginal Australia and
      Prehistoric Europe*, edited by P.J. Ucko, 165-183. Canberra: Australian
      Institute of Aboriginal Studies.
An analysis of 21 Yolngu sand sculptures associated with pollution caused by
contact with death and also, less frequently, by open wounds or sores. Relates
sculptures to 'smoke ceremonies' and 'washing ceremonies'. Since ceremonial
meaning is not determined in a one to one manner it must be understood as "a
condition of the syntactic relations between the elements" (p.182). Focuses on
the implications of ceremonies/sculptures for relationship with clans and the
land.

0523 Morphy, Howard (1984) *Journey to the Crocodile's Nest: An
      Accompanying Monograph to the Film Madarrpa Funeral at Gurak'wuy.*
      Canberra: Australian Institute of Aboriginal Studies. 160 pp.
Written to accompany a film, and a fine volume in itself. A general
ethnographic chapter is followed by an overview of Yolngu religious life, a
statement on their views on death and burial ceremonies and a three chapter
analysis of a funeral for a Madarrpa clan child. Morphy's interpretation focuses
not only on grieving for a loss, but also on the dynamic social role of
demonstrating and consolidating inter-group relationships.

0524 Morphy, Howard and Morphy, Frances (1987) "Waiting for the
      Djirrapuyngu." In *Australians to 1788*, edited by D.J. Mulvaney and J.P.
      White, 177-195. Sydney: Fairfax, Syme and Weldon.
Fictional reconstruction of nineteenth century Yolngu life but the details are
ethnographically sound. Set in the context of a man who has come for a
ceremony for the disposal of his mother's grandfather's bones. Mortuary
politics is an underlying theme and details of some ceremonial procedures are
given. Characterization is romanticized.

0525 Peterson, Nicolas (1976) "Mortuary Customs of Northeast Arnhem
      Land: An Account Compiled from Donald Thomson's Fieldnotes."
      Memoirs of the National Museum of Victoria 37: 97-108.

Detailed descriptive account of mortuary practice from death until final disposal in a hollow log coffin. Refers to body painting, the removal of hair, burial, the cleansing and distribution of the deceased's possessions, purifying the ceremonial grounds, exhumation, *marrnggitj* (see Thomson 0515), and final disposal. Notes the kin status of participants and sand sculptures and contains excellent photographic plates from the late 1930s.

0526 Reid, Janice C. (1979) "A Time to Live, A Time to Grieve: Patterns and Processes of Mourning Among the Yolngu of Australia." *Culture, Medicine and Psychiatry* 3: 319-46.
Suggests elaborate Yolngu mortuary rites facilitate the integration of the bereaved back into community life. Sequences from the anticipation of death to the initial and principal ceremonies and burial and purification are outlined in association with general literature on bereavement. Concludes that rites affirm the relationships with the living but also provide a context in which to resolve grief, sorrow and anger.

0527 Thomson, Donald F. (1939) "Two Painted Skulls from Arnhem Land, With Notes on the Totemic Significance of the Designs." *Man* 39:.1-3.
Briefly examines the role of designs painted on skulls in mortuary rituals.

0528 Williams, Nancy M. (1985) "On Aboriginal Decision-Making." In *Metaphors of Interpretation: Essays in Honour of W.E.H. Stanner*, edited by D.E. Barwick, J. Beckett and M. Reay, 240-269. Sydney: Australian National University Press.
The *raison d'être* of this article is to examine the neglected subject of Aboriginal decision-making. Of interest is the ten page case study "Death and Decision-Making" which revolves around the death of a member of a Yolngu community. Provides fresh insight into how people make important decisions regarding burial sites and the location of attendant phases of mortuary rites.

See also: 0372, 0384, 0395, 0397, 0460, 0461, 0498, 0500, 0531, 0534.

Change

0529 Berndt, Ronald M. (1952) "Surviving Influence of Mission Contact on the Daly River, Northern Territory of Australia." *Neue Zeitschrift für Missionswissenschaft* 8,2/3: 1-20.
A pioneering article examining the effects of the Daly River Mission (1887-1899) via recollections of the few remaining Mullukmulluk and Madngela. Claims there is little explicit influence but substantial covert impact. Includes segments of a Christian 'myth cycle' and the important note that Biblical figures had become Dreaming beings (p. 11). These stories are said to have been valued as they alluded to contemporary racial divisions and problems.

0530 Berndt, Ronald M. (1962) *An Adjustment Movement In Arnhem Land: Northern Territory of Australia*. Paris: Mouton.165 pp.

Analysis of a movement in which secret *rangga* were displayed in a memorial outside the Elcho Island Church. The history of the movement is described, followed by a detailed examination of the memorial's iconographic significance. Berndt claims the movement had two aims: to make certain traditional institutions appropriate to mission life; and to broaden Yolngu alliances to present a united front in negotiations with Europeans. Compare Morphy (0548).

0531 Berndt, Ronald M. (1965) "External Influences on the Aboriginal."
       Hemisphere 9,3: 2-9.
A brief but useful discussion of Macassan influence on northern traditions. Notes the location of Macassan and *Baijini* culture within the *Yirritja* moiety, and several songs are given in transcription and translation. Especially refers to mortuary songs and rituals replicating the departure of Macassan praus for *Badu*.

0532 Berndt, Ronald M. (1978-9) "Looking Back into the Present: A
       Changing Panorama in Eastern Arnhem Land." *Anthropological Forum*
       4,3-4: 281-296.
Examines change in Arnhem Land religious life. Distinguishes contact change from change due to internal dynamics. Both are facilitated by dreams. Contact change includes alterations to *Yirittja* moiety mortuary rituals; the Elcho Island Adjustment movement (see Berndt 0530); and the public display of previously secret segments of the *Djungguan* cult. Mission impact is also considered. Concludes people accomodate present change by reaffirming the value of their 'traditional' past.

0533 Berndt, Ronald M. and Berndt, Catherine H. (1947) "Discovery of
       Pottery in North-Eastern Arnhem Land." *The Journal of the Royal
       Anthropological Institute of Great Britain and Ireland* 77: 133-138.
A brief outline of Asiatic contact in Arnhem Land, some of which is recalled with a Dreaming quality. Transcriptions and translations from the *Baijini*-Macassan song-cycle are given, referring to rice cooking, etc.

0534 Borsboom, A.P. (1978) *Maradjiri: A Modern Ritual Complex in
       Arnhem Land, North Australia.* Nijmegen: Katholieke Universiteit. 240
       pp.
Bound version of a doctoral thesis analysing the public *Maradjiri* ritual associated with a Yolngu clan of Maningrida. Myths, song cycles and dances are discussed. Emphasis is upon the changing context of the ritual, originally used for mortuary purposes but since become a 'life symbolic rite'. Thus, whereas once a hair of the deceased was used, now a baby's hair or navel cord is substituted and is "ritually returned to this ceremony."

0535 Borsboom, A.P. (1986) "Continuiteit en Veran dering in Aboriginal
       Religie." In *Traditie in Verandering: Nederlandse Bijdragen aan
       Antropologisch Onderzoek in Oceanië*, edited by M. van Bakel; A.
       Borsboom and H. Dagmar, 223-245. Leiden: DSWO Press.
Examines the tension between the inevitability of change to Aboriginal religion and the concept of an eternal, immutable religious order. Based on field-

research with the Yolngu, tries to show how the skilful manipulation of one clan's Dreaming set can change the character of rites thus bringing them into accord with new conditions without undermining the concept of changelessness.

0536 Bos, Robert (1980) "Digeridoo Theology." *Nungalinya Occasional Bulletin* No. 8: 1-6.
Brief notes on Yolngu Christian cleansing ceremonies, initiation, memorial feasts, 'men of high degree' and iconography.

0537 Bos, Robert (1981) "Christian Ritual and the Yolngu Domain." *Nungalinya Occasional Bulletin* No. 13: 1-10.
Focus on Christian ritual at Galiwinku (Elcho Island) and Milingimbi. The Yolngu are said to perceive two domains: White and Aboriginal, and it is argued that Christianity is a part of the latter domain and is incorporated at a personal mythological level. This has been achieved by rejecting European church ritual and adopting Aboriginally appropriate rituals, especially as instigated by the Aboriginal minster Djiniyini Gondarra (0542).

0538 Bos, Robert (1988) "The Dreaming and Social Change in Arnhem Land." In *Aboriginal Australians and Christian Missions: Ethnographic and Historical Studies*, edited by T. Swain and D. Rose, 422-437. Adelaide: Australian Association for the Study of Religions.
Examines the 'Dreaming' and its ability to incorporate change. Theories of immutability are dismissed, as are those stating changes are appended to a unchanging core of tradition. The Yolngu incorporation of Christian ritual at Galiwinku is examined and it is suggested that the Dreaming is not a rigid doctrine stating that only what has always been can be legitimate, so much as it is saying that which is legitimate must always have been.

0539 Brady, Maggie (1989) "Number One for Action." *Australian Aboriginal Studies* No. 1: 62-3.
Briefly describes 'action' Christian liturgical dances in Arnhem Land and on Groote Eylandt.

0540 Brandl, Maria (1970) "Adaptation or Disintegration? Changes in the Kulama Initiation and Increase Ritual of Melville and Bathurst Islands, Northern Territory of Australia." *Anthropological Forum* 2,4: 464-479.
Published simultaneously with Goodale's paper (0544), likewise comparing her own data (1969) with Spencer's account of *Kulama* in 1914 (0392). Offers a general interpretation of the ritual as 'sacrifice' and notes the final sacrificial role of 'sharing' had been omitted. This, the author correctly concludes, does not say "very much about what the present day *Kulama* is" (p.478).

0541 Gondarra, Djiniyini (1986) "Overcoming the Captivities of the Western Church Context." In *The Cultured Pearl: Australian Readings in Cross-Cultural Theology and Missions*, edited by J. Houston, 176-182. Melbourne: The Joint Board of Christian Education.
An Elcho Islander, Gondarra is Moderator of the Northern Synod of the Uniting Church in Australia, and here presents his views on the needs of Aboriginal

Christians. Emphasizes the necessity for ecumenicalism and a liberation theology cognizant of traditional beliefs and values.

0542 Gondarra, Djiniyini (1986) *Series of Reflections of Aboriginal Theology.* Darwin: Bethel Presbytery. 35 pp.
A collection of Australia's best known Aboriginal theologians' papers. The first section is historical, giving an insider's view of missions to Arnhem Land, the Revival, and the Uniting Aboriginal and Islander Christian Congress. The remainder is theological, considering the nature of an Aboriginal Christianity, stressing ecumenicalism and the place of the church in sustaining Aboriginal identity. Social justice, Land Rights and racial harmony are emphasized throughout.

0543 Gondarra, Djiniyini (1988) "Father You Gave Us The Dreaming." *Compass Theology Review* 22: 6-8.
Theological reflections arguing the Aboriginal relation to land is spiritually compatible with Christian thought.

0544 Goodale, Jane C. (1970) "An Example of Ritual Change Among the Tiwi of Melville Island." In *Diprotodon to Detribalisation: Studies of Change Among Australian Aborigines*, edited by A.R. Pilling and R.A. Waterman, 350-366. Michigan: Michigan State University Press.
Compares her observations of the *Kulama* (wild yam) ceremonies with those of Spencer (0392). Suggests the ritual has remained remarkably constant but changes indicate a shift from a ceremony which was primarily concerned with teaching novices how to make a food edible to one concerned with removing illness. This reflects the introduction of European foods and disease. The ceremony is briefly described in relation to technology, social structure, psychological adaptation and Tiwi value-orientation.

0545 Mackinolty, Chips and Wainburranga, Paddy (1988) "Too Many Captain Cooks." In *Aboriginal Australians and Christian Missions: Ethnographic and Historical Studies*, edited by T. Swain and D. Rose, 355-360. Adelaide: Australian Association for the Study of Religions.
Wainburranga tells a Rembarunga Captain Cook narrative. Cook had two wives and lived in the Dreaming. He brought material goods with him and was peaceful. He had a fight with Satan and stuffed him into what is now Sydney's Cahill Expressway. Cook then left for home later to die from a spear wound. But new Captain Cooks came to take Australia. This myth is also related to relevant rituals.

0546 Maddock, Kenneth (1977) "Two Laws in One Community." In *Aborigines and Change: Australia in the '70s*, edited by R.M. Berndt, 13-32. Canberra: Australian Institute of Aboriginal Studies.
A study of changing world-views on Beswick Reserve. The community now has two 'Laws': the traditional law (the Dreaming), and the one introduced by Whites. The result is by no means syncretistic as Aborigines have sought to segregate the systems, maintaining old religious practices, but also adopting

European ways. Maddock sees 'two-Laws talk' as an expression of an ideology of cultural equality.

0547 Morphy, Howard (1974) "Yingapungapu - Ground Sculpture as Bark Painting." In *Form in Indigenous Art: Schematization in the Art of Aboriginal Australians and Prehistoric Europe*, edited by P.J. Ucko, 205-209. Canberra: Australian Institute of Aboriginal Studies.
Examines some Yolngu adaptations to the incongruencies between European culture and their traditional behaviour towards their dead. Pollution can extend to motor vehicles and planes that have contacted the corpse and some ingenious resolutions of this problem are described. Focuses on the use of bark paintings as a substitute for traditional mortuary ceremonies employing ground paintings.

0548 Morphy, Howard (1983) "'Now You Understand': An Analysis of the Way Yolngu Have Used Sacred Knowledge to Retain Their Autonomy." In *Aborigines, Land and Land Rights*, edited by N. Peterson and M. Langton, 110-113. Canberra: Australian Institute of Aborginal Studies.
A re-analysis of the 'Adjustment Movement' described by R.M. Berndt in 1962 (0530). Morphy attempts to explain why the Movement leaders revealed their sacred and secret *rangga*. Expands the Yolngu view of the relationship between sacred knowledge, designs, and land to show that revealing secret *rangga* to non-Aboriginal Australians demonstrated Yolngu ties to their land. This served as a symbolic basis for transactions with white Australians.

0549 Morphy, Howard and Layton, R. (1981) "Choosing Among Alternatives: Cultural Transformations and Social Change in Aboriginal Australia and French Jura." *Mankind* 13,1: 56-73.
Contests the view that indigenous populations respond to social change either by total resistance or by totally abandoning tradition. Examines Yolngu dynamics in adapting designs to a new context. Strategies are discussed for releasing secret designs for the market and displaying secret, land-based art as a negotiating tactic. Argues these adaptations were made to maintain cultural identity.

0550 Rose, Frederick (1947) "Malay Influence on Aboriginal Totemism in Northern Australia." *Man* 47: 129.
Note on Groote Eylandt totemic designs based on Macassan sails.

0551 Stanner, W.E.H. (1958) "Continuity and Change Among the Aborigines." *The Australian Journal of Science* 21,5a: 99-109.
An honest but ideologically dated look at the position of northern Aborigines in a changing world. Contains a section on the *Kunmunggar-Jinimin* myth comparing it with Christian myth, suggesting it is a belief fitted to a socially unsettled time and opposed to the non-millennial Mother-cult. Perhaps anticipates the eruption of the Jesus-*Jinimin* cult some five years later (see Petri and Petri-Odermann 0650).

0552 Stockton, Eugene D. (1985) "Mulinthin's Dream." *Nelen Yubu* 22: 3-11.

Mulinthin, a Murinbata man, had a dream which he later believed to be a revelation of Mary and Jesus. The text of his vision is transcribed and translated. Mulinthin, a sorcerer, was stricken and taken to Heaven where he saw God, Jesus, Mary, the dead and the fires of Hell. Jesus gave him *Malgarrin* songs and dances, which are still sung today, but not understood. Stockton's commentary relates to the church's response (or lack thereof) to the vision.

0553   Thomson, Donald F. (1939) "Proof of Indonesian Influence Upon the Aborigines of North Australia: The Remarkable Dog *Ngarra* of the Mildjingi Clan." *Illustrated London News* August 12th: 277-279.
The 'proof' is the construction of a totemic dog using wool and fabric associated with Macassans. Also a square-faced gin bottle *rangga*.

0554   Turner, David H. (1982) "Caste Logic in a Clan Society: An Aboriginal Response to Domination." In *Aboriginal Power in Australian Society*, edited by M.C. Howard, 32-54. St. Lucia, Queensland: University of Queensland Press.
Extends and takes issue with Lévi-Strauss' suggestion that the Indian caste system is a structural inversion of Australian Aboriginal clan organization. Turner argues an analysis of northern Aboriginal myths (from Warner 0397 and others) reveals they entertained the possibility of developing a caste-like relationship in dealing with the seasonal Macassan traders. An interesting, but conjectural analysis.

0555   Worsley, Peter M. (1955) "Totemism in a Changing Society." *American Anthropologist* 57,3: 851-861.
Looks at changes in Andiljaugwa totemism. Totems are discussed in three categories, two of which (wind totems and ship totems) show strong outside influence. Reference is made to myths explaining the division of humanity into Black and White, and songs related to themes such as flying boats and armies. Relates this to theoretical problems of totemism.

0556   Yule, Ian R., ed. (1980) *My Mother The Land*. Galiwin'ku: Christian Action Group. 44 pp.
Statements by Yolngu people lightly edited by Yule. Many intimate glimpses of the religious base of people's land identity, and references to the *Djanggawul* in particular. While not all speakers were Christian, a strong Christian voice is present. Monyu says God created the land (p. 30). Bunbatju says the *Djanggawul* are like God (p. 14), while Djiniyini's phrase, providing the title "The Land is my mother"(p. 8) belongs more to Church thought than to traditional religion.

See also: 0233, 0243, 0372, 0373, 0377, 0382, 0389, 0395, 0396, 0447, 0448, 0476, 0511, 0517, 0519.

Literature

0557 Craig, Beryl F. (1966) *Arnhem Land Peninsula Region (Including Bathurst and Melville Islands)*. Occasional Papers in Aboriginal Studies No. 8. Canberra: Australian Institute of Aboriginal Studies. 205 pp.
An extensive listing (1044 items) of published and unpublished pieces on the Central-North of Australia. Entries are uncritically annotated, describing the contents, and subject and tribal indexes are provided. Covers material up to 1965.

See also: 0252, 0453, 0489.

8

Kimberley

General

0558 Akerman, Kim (1979) "Honey in the Life of the Aborigines of the
        Kimberleys." *Oceania* 49,3: 169-178.
Notes on Worora,Wunambal and Ngarinyin honey culture. Covers themes such
as honey in myth, iconography, 'increase' and other ceremonies, totemism and
taboo.

0559 Basedow, Herbert (1918) *Narrative of An Expedition of Exploration in
        North-West Australia.* Adelaide: W.K. Thomas. 295 pp.
Superficial records, with some photographs, on ritual, art, etc. Considers
mission environment throughout the Kimberley.

0560 Benterrak, Kim; Muecke, Stephen; and Roe, Paddy (1984) *Reading the
        Country: Introduction to Nomadology.* Fremantle: Fremantle Arts Centre
        Press. 251 pp.
A book whose form attempts to let the country 'write itself' (p.230) and which
juxtaposes paintings, photographs, interviews and text. Territory is explored
with the guidance of Paddy Roe, a Nyigina man. Muecke writes in terms of a
'theory of place' and 'nomadology'. A fascinating attempt to penetrate the
Aboriginal understanding of place as it is mediated through stories.

0561 Berndt, Ronald M. (1979) "Traditional Aboriginal Life in Western
        Australia: as it was and is." In *Aborigines of the West: Their Past and
        Their Present*, edited by R.M. Berndt and C.H. Berndt, 3-27. Nedlands,
        W.A: University of Western Australia Press.
Provides a concise overview of religion throughout Western Australia.
Considers Dreaming, 'totemism', spirit children, initiation and death, categorized
by four regional forms. Also discusses the *Kunapipi/Gadjeri* cult in W.A. and its
association with *Kurrangara* as a *Wanderkulte* .

0562 Campbell, W.D. (1915) "An Account of the Aboriginals of Sunday
        Island, King Sound, Kimberley, Western Australia." *The Journal of the
        Royal Society of Western Australia* 1: 55-82.
Brief sections on Bard pearl shell pendant designs, initiation, mortuary practice,
myth and mission influence.

0563 Capell, Arthur (1952-3) "Notes on the Njigina and Warwa Tribes, N.W.
        Australia." *Mankind* 4,9: 351-360.
Brief notes, aimed primarily at linguists, on the Nyigina and Warwa peoples.
Sketchy comments on birth, initiation and death and several myth texts
accompanied by interlineal and free translations.

0564 Deakin, Hilton (1982) "Some Thoughts on Transcendence in Tribal
        Societies." In *Ways of Transcendence: Insights from Major Religions and
        Modern Thought*, edited by E. Dowdy, 95-109. Adelaide: The Australian
        Association for the Study of Religions.

The general theory of transcendence in 'tribal' religions is rather uninspired, but the author's Gwini and Andidja data is of use. Considers the Dreaming, the sacred boards of the *Mai-ange* cycle and sacred sites. Particularly interesting is the link made between the *Kurrangara* and *Julurru* rituals, two anti-European cults usually considered discrete.

0565 Kaberry, Phyllis M. (1935) "The Forest River and Lynne River Tribes of North-West Australia." *Oceania* 5,4: 408-436.
A general ethnography of the Jeidji, Wembria, Andidja, Arnga, Waladjangari and Wolyamidi. Some 10 pages discuss religion. Details are sketchy and often given as supplements to Elkin's (0081) reports. In some cases (e.g. pp. 431-2) adds interesting information more available to women researchers.

0566 Klaatsch, Hermann (1907) "Schlussbericht über meine Reise nach Australien in der Jahren 1904-7." *Zeitschrift für Ethnologie* 39: 635-690.
Considers a range of themes and areas in which the author did field work. The main section is on the Nyulnyul and examines *tjurunga* and initiation as well as suggesting they have no real totemism. Also considers Tiwi burial poles and makes less detailed observations on Port Keats and Tasmania. Unreliable.

0567 Koepping, Klaus-Peter (1987) "Ungarinyin Religion." In *The Encyclopedia of Religion*, edited by M. Eliade, Vol. 15, 134-138. New York: Macmillan.
Reviews existing ethnographies on Ngarinyin religion, relying particularly on Petri (0575) and Elkin (0604). Considers basic principles such as *Ungud* (Dreaming), *yayari* (personal life force), and cosmological heroes such as the *Wandjina*, *Ungud* the Rainbow Serpent/'Earth Mother', and others. Focuses on the Dreaming ancestors as instigators of social norms.

0568 Kolig, Erich (1987) *The Noonkanbah Story*. Dunedin: University of Otago Press. 159 pp.
In 1980, Noonkanbah received global publicity by resisting mining explorations. Kolig examines the community's history and relationship with their land. A chapter on "the Sanctity of the Land" explores land's religious basis by discussing the "Dreamtime heroes'" sojourns, particularly the *Marala-Marala* and *Danggaba*, locked in "a conflict of good and evil"(p.64). Other myths are related, as are beliefs about spirit children, and 'fertility magic'.

0569 Lommel, Andreas (1952) *Die Unambal: Ein Stamm in Nordwest-Australien*. Monographien zur Völkerkunde No. 2. Hamburg: Druck. 90 pp.
An important Wunambal ethnography from the Frobenius expedition of 1938. An overview of religion is in three categories. The first examines ancestral myths of *Ungud*, *Wandjina* and others, systems of totemism and initiation, death and the afterlife. Second, there is a long study of medicine men considering their powers, supernatural associations and initiation. Finally, the so-called 'wandering cults' are described, in particular the *Kurrangara*. Excellent plates.

0570 Lommel, Andreas (1969) *Fortschritt ins Nichts: Die Modernisierung der Primitiven Australiens: Beschreibung und Definition eines psychischen Verfalls.* Zürich: Atlantis. 197 pp.
The image of 'psychic decay' permeates this book. Early chapters consider cosmogony and other myths, ritual and *Wandjina* art and pp. 163-178 focus on adaptation and the rise of new cults, particularly the *Kurrangara* which, he argues, lost its significance with the next generation. Laments the disappearance of medicine men, and the emergence of new views of time looking pessimistically to the future. A gloomy false prophecy.

0571 Love, J.R.B. (1935) "Mythology, Totemism and Religion of the Worora Tribe of North-West Australia." *Australian and New Zealand Association for the Advancement of Science, Report* 22: 222-231.
Brief overview of Worora religious beliefs and practice, including sections on the relationship between myth and landscape, totemism and ritual.

0572 Love, J.R.B. (1936) *Stone-Age Bushmen of To-Day: Life and Adventure among Tribes of Savages in North-Western Australia.* London: Blackie. 220 pp.
A liberal Christian account of the Worora people, concluding Aboriginal traditions are akin to Church ceremony (eg. *Kurrangara* is like communion). The preceding text covers *Wandjina* art, myths, ritual 'cannibalism', death and funeral rites, conception, magic, healing, public ceremonies. A useful although not thoroughly researched, early supplement for the region.

0573 Peggs, Ada J. (1903) "Notes on the Aborigines of Roebuck Bay, Western Australia." *Folk-Lore* 14: 324-367.
All but unedited extracts from letters to the author's relative. Uninformed descriptions of 'corroborees', 'debil-debils' and a few legends collected from a boy. Superficial.

0574 Pentony, B. (1961) "Dreams and Dream Beliefs in North Western Australia." *Oceania* 32,2: 144-149.
Brief notes on Ngarinyin, Worora and Wunambal views on dreams as associated with spirits, magic, conception and totems.

0575 Petri, Helmut (1954) *Sterbende Welt in Nordwest-Australien.* Braunschweig: Albert Limbach. 352 pp.
This "Dying World of Northwest Australia", is, despite its title, an important, often neglected, monograph mainly on the Ngarinyin, but also Wunambal and Worora. Contains a detailed study of *Wandjina*, ritual and myth complexes, tracks of ancestral beings, totemism, magic, traditional healers and initiation (subincision and circumcision). There is also a fine section on the Nyigina, their totems and some detailed records of their myths.

0576 Rose, Deborah B. (1985) "Consciousness and Responsibility in an Australian Aboriginal Religion." *Nelen Yubu* : 3-15.
Ngarinman and Ngaliwurru religion considered in 4 sections. First examines principles upon which the cosmos is based. Second, discusses 'species

intersubjectivity' and consciousness. Third, considers concepts of responsibility towards the cosmos. Finally concludes religion permeates all aspects of life and hence there is no sacred/profane distinction. Rose postulates a mysticism of Immanence. Insightful.

0577 Shaw, Bruce (1981) *My Country of the Pelican Dreaming: The Life of an Australian Aborigine of the Gadjerong, Grant Ngabidj,1904-1977.* Canberra: Australian Institute of Aboriginal Studies. 202 pp.
Grant Ngabidj, a Gadjerong, gives his life account. Scattered references to religion, but 3 chapters make it a central theme. 'Law' covers Ngabidj's initiation giving a fine insider view of the process and the changes it awakes. 'The Spirit World' discusses ceremonies, spirit beliefs, including a few on the Christian God. *'Ngaranggani'* (Dreaming) contains a number of myths and a section on Boxer, the sorcerer (cf. Rowse 0657). Excellent insights.

0578 Shaw, Bruce (1983) *Banggaiyerri: The Story of Jack Sullivan.* Canberra: Australian Institute of Aboriginal Studies. 264 pp.
'Autobiography' of Jack Sullivan, born on Argyle Downs Station to a Djamindjung mother. Lightly edited by Shaw. A chapter on 'Gods, Devils and Clever Men' (pp.137-166) gives a clear view of the heritage of both traditional and Catholic religious worlds. Cosmogonies of a synthetic nature are described, as are Dreaming stories, ritual, healing, sorcery, 'devils', *Djanba* (Meggitt 0881) and Boxer, the clever man from Queensland (cf. Rowse 0657). Very authentic.

0579 Shaw, Bruce (1986) *Countrymen: The Life Histories of four Aboriginal men as told to Bruce Shaw.* Canberra: Australian Institute of Aboriginal Studies. 325 pp.
Thoughtful recollections of Mandi Munniim, Jeff Djanama, Banggaldun Balmirr and Bulla Bilinggiin. Part two, 'Law', is a fine series of insights into religious life by men who had much contact with the Catholic Mission at Kununurra. *Djanba* (cf. Meggitt 0881) are discussed at length. There are also a range of myth fragments, some, such as "Djawaleng, Black Man and Gadia, White Man" and "Boxer" (cf. Rowse 0657), having important synthetic elements.

See also: 0581, 0582, 0606, 0613, 0620, 0660.

Philosophy and Totemism

0580 Hernández, Theodore (1941) "Social Organization of the Drysdale River Tribes, North-West Australia." *Oceania* 11,3: 211-232.
Observations from the far north-west, then inaccessible to professional anthropologists. Contains 9 pages on aspects of totemism, covering themes such as origins of totemic objects, spirit-children, dream totems, horde and clan totems, rituals and totemic centres. Rather anecdotal.

0581 Kaberry, Phyllis M. (1938) "Totemism in East and South Kimberley, North-West Australia." *Oceania* 8,3: 265-288.

Attempts to unravel some theoretical problems involved in totemism. Accepts Radcliffe-Brown's view that totems are drawn from species and objects of social value. Examines Wolyamidi, Lungga and Djaru 'totemism', covering cosmologies, 'increase' ceremonies, and cult, conception, moiety, subsection and dream totems. Concludes with a revised definition of totemism as uninspiring as its predecessors.

0582 Petri, Helmut (1948) "Seelenvorstellungen und Totemismus in Nördlichen Dampierland N.W. - Australien." *Studium Generale* 1,4: 237-48.
Considers concepts of the soul and totemism within the broader context of Bard, Djaui, and Ninambur religious traditions. Examines spirit children beliefs, the central role of *Wandjina* sites and relevant myth segments. Based on research of the 1938-9 Frobenius expedition.

See also: 0081, 0104, 0560, 0571, 0576.

Myth

0583 Blundell, Valda J. and Layton, Robert (1978) "Marriage, Myth and Models of Exchange in the West Kimberleys." *Mankind* 11,3: 231-45.
Examines exchange (women, goods and ritual objects) among the Worora, Wunambal, Ngarinyin and Unggumi. Statements about exchange are compared with recorded marriages on the one hand and concepts of exchange in mythology on the other. Myths, pertaining to the *Wandjina* etc., are shown not to simply sanction social norms of exchange, but rather to transpose ideals of exchange to a realm of meaning with layers of symbolic significance.

0584 Capell, Arthur (1939) "Mythology in the Northern Kimberley, North-West Australia." *Oceania* 9,4: 382-404.
Postulates Kimberley mythology is composed of 3 diffusionary layers. The first is the cult of the dead, rather obscure, with no iconographic aspects. The second, which Capell feels is fairly ancient and comes via Timor, is the *Wandjina* cult, associated with cave art. The third from the south-east brought the Rainbow Serpent myths and also the *Maianjari* and recently, the *Djanba* cult. In part based on an analysis of the linguistics of myths.

0585 Capell, Arthur (1960) "Language and World View in the Northern Kimberley, Western Australia." *Southwestern Journal of Anthropology* 16,1: 1-14.
Very brief notes on Ngarinyin cosmogony.

0586 Capell, Arthur (1972) *Cave Painting Myths: Northern Kimberley.* Oceania and Linguistic Monographs No. 18. Sydney: University of Sydney. 173 pp.
Wandjina and other myths of the Ngarinyin, Worora, Wunambal, and Unggumi, collected in 1938-9. Following a general introduction, the myths are

transcribed, translated literally, and paraphrased. A few linguistic and socio-religious notes are added. The brief ethnographic introductions to each chapter provide some contextual information including references to ritual practices accompanying myths.

0587 Dickey, Anthony (1976) "The Mythical Introduction of 'Law' to the Worora Aborigines." *University of Western Australia Law Review* 12: 350-367; 480-498.
Attempts to present Worora Law in a manner comprehensible to lawyers. Four paraphrased texts on the introduction of Law are given. The basic theme concerns a primordial man, *Ngyarri*, who produced the first sacred boards which were stolen so that a Lawless people might have Law. The role of boards as repositories of sacred Law is discussed. Also considers *Wandjina* and other traditions.

0588 Elkin, A.P. (1930) "The Rainbow-Serpent Myth in North-West Australia." *Oceania* 1,3: 349-352.
Very brief account of Rainbow Serpent myths from the southern Kimberley.

0589 Hernández, Theodore (1961) "Myths and Symbols of the Drysdale River Aborigines." *Oceania* 32,2: 113-127.
Speaks of the ignorance of Aborigines (like all 'primitives') concerning their own beliefs. Reluctantly agrees to call their 'religion' whatever pertains to the supernatural, then primarily paraphrases myths, although there are sections on bull-roarers and other objects. At times does no more than describe a mythic being's appearance. Condescending and superficial.

0590 Love, J.R.B. (1946) "A Tale of the Winking Owl: A Worora Bird Legend." *Mankind* 3,9: 258-261.
A paraphrase of the Worora myth with very few contextual notes.

0591 Nangan, Joe and Edwards, Hugh (1976) *Joe Nangan's Dreaming: Aboriginal Legends of the North-West.* Melbourne: Thomas Nelson. 64 pp.
Stories and pencil drawings from Joe Nangan, a Nyigina man who was a pastoral worker and a *maban* or traditional healer. Edward's rendering is over-edited, and there is no contextualization. Little more than a book of just-so stories. Disappointing.

0592 Petri, Helmut (1938-40) "Mythische Heroen und Urzeitlegende im Nördlichen Dampierland, Nordwest-Australien." *Paideuma* 1: 217-240.
An account of Bard, Ninambur and Djaui mythology from the Frobenius Expedition of 1938-9. *Kalalong, Mino,* and *Djamara,* 3 totally anthropomorphous beings, are said to personify the esoteric truths re-enacted in initiatory and fertility ritual. Other myths of part-animal, part-human beings are also given. Contains a few transcriptions with literal translations. *Djamara* is said to be comparable to the South-Eastern All-Fathers, and *Ungud* to the northern Kimberley.

0593   Roe, Paddy   (1983)   *Gularabulu: Stories from the West Kimberley*, edited
       by S. Muecke. Fremantle: Fremantle Arts Centre Press. 98 pp.
A delightful collection of stories by Paddy Roe, a Nyigina man. Not myths as
such but stories giving intimate observations of the working of spiritual powers.
A *maban* (healer) kills his wife and is arrested but escapes by turning into a cat
and, later, an eaglehawk. *Maban* are prominent, but there are 'devils', 'monster
birds' and the mysterious *Worawora* woman. Muecke transcribes the stories
giving priority to reflecting Aboriginal speech patterns.

0594   Worms, Ernest A.   (1940)   "Religiöse Vorstellungen und Kultur einiger
       Nord-westaustralischen Stämme in fünfzig Legenden." *Annali Lateranensi*
       14: 213-282.
Nyulnyul, Karadjeri, Walmadjari, Bard, Ninambur, Jauor and other's myths .
Beginning with the 'Two Old Men' (cf. Worms 0728), 50 different stories are
paraphrased of anthropomorphic beings, the moon's exploits, 'evil' spirits,
dwarfs, serpents and other animals, and a range of narratives concerning kinship
tensions. Suffers from lack of contextualization.

0595   Worms, Ernest A.   (1945)   "*Djamar*, the Creator: A Myth of the Bad
       (West Kimberley, Australia)." *Anthropos* 45: 641-658.
Djamar is alleged to be the "creator, the great Supreme Being" (p.642) of the
Bard. Tells of his arrival, his introduction of rites and the sacred boards
associated with him. His myth is given with interlineal and free translations.
Lacks critical interpretation and glosses over clearly introduced iconographic
elements. Informants' commentary notes are also included, as are songs of
Djamar's relation to other cult heroes. See (0596).

0596   Worms, Ernest A.   (1952)   "Djamar and His Relation to Other Culture
       Heroes." *Anthropos* 47: 539-560.
Continues 0595 adding information on the relation of the Bard to *Djamar* and his
sons. Intriguingly, yet inadequately, associates *Djamar* with other beings in the
context of social change. Thus *Galalan* and *Minau* were overthrown by *Djamar*
who was being usurped by *Djanba* (see Lommel 0646, Meggitt 0881). Also
contains a brief note on *Kurrangara*, which is compared and equated with
Kunapipi cults (Berndt 0481).

See also: 0104, 0160, 0410, 0563, 0568, 0571, 0600, 0601, 0602, 0605, 0608,
       0610, 0611, 0631, 0641, 0642, 0652, 0724.

The Arts

0597   Adam, Leonhard   (1958)   "Anthropomorphe Darstellungen auf
       australischen Ritualgeräten." *Anthropos* 53: 1-50.
Although considering examples from elsewhere in Australia, focuses mainly on
the Kimberley region in a study of *tjurunga* designs and decorations. Items are
described and depicted in plates, and mythic associations and ritual roles of

tjurunga are discussed. Historic issues are raised through a comparison with works from Papua New Guinea.

0598 Berndt, Ronald M. and Berndt, Catherine H. (1950) "Aboriginal Art in Central Western Northern Territory." *Meanjin* 9,3: 183-8.
Brief notes on Nyinin *Tjarada* ('love magic'), myths, public ceremony and Mother cult, accompanied by crayon drawings.

0599 Blundell, Valda J. (1974) "The Wandjina Cave Paintings of Northwest Australia." *Arctic Anthropology* Supplement 11: 213-223.
The significance of Worora, Ngarinyin and Wunambal *Wandjina* art is related to the way clan members ensure the continuing processes of life. Patrilineal clans roam beyond their spiritual territories and have access to other areas through marriage, etc. The caves serve as important places for reinforcing clan solidarity. Also shows the sites have mortuary and other significances. One of the better studies of the religious function of rock art.

0600 Blundell, Valda J. (1982) "Symbolic Systems and Cultural Continuity in Northwest Australia: A Consideration of Aboriginal Cave Art." *Culture* 2,1: 3-20.
Examines Worora, Ngarinyin and Wunambal *Wandjina* art as a set of symbols facilitating cultural continuity in the face of change. Locates the art in the socio-religious order, giving relevant myth segments. Pressures of change, from pre-history to new cults, are noted, and the tension between innovation and an ideology of changelessness developed. Immutability is symbolized by the mouthlessness of *Wandjina*. The ambiguity of symbols allow novel factors to be accomodated.

0601 Crawford, I.M. (1968) *The Art of the Wandjina: Aboriginal Cave Paintings in Kimberley, Western Australia.* Melbourne: Oxford University Press. 144 pp.
Based on expeditions to *Wandjina* galleries long after rituals had been discontinued. There are, however, accounts of relevant myths, such as those dealing with the exploits of *Wandjina*, although literal transcriptions are not given. The well-illustrated survey of sites and the variety of art forms and styles depicted, make this a pleasant introduction.

0602 Crawford, I.M. (1987) "Wandjina." In *The Encyclopedia of Religion*, edited by M. Eliade, Vol. 15, 329-331. New York: Macmillan.
Considers *Wandjina* paintings, their mythic significance and their association with both human and natural fecundity.

0603 Davidson, Daniel S. (1953) "The Possible Source and Antiquity of the Slate Churingas of Western Australia." *American Philosophical Society, Proceedings* 97,2: 194-213.
Considers origins of Kimberley *tjurungas* in terms of continent-wide diffusions. Little insight into their meaning.

0604 Elkin, A.P. (1930) "Rock-Paintings of North-West Australia." *Oceania* 1,3: 257-279.
A descriptive account of *Wandjina* cave paintings in Ngarinyin and Worora country. These are compared with Sir George Grey's observations in 1838, and supplemented by comments by local Aborigines. The connection between *Wandjina, Ungud* the Rainbow Serpent, rituals to produce rain and the fertility of humans and other species is discussed. Little detail on the mythological content of these paintings.

0605 Layton, Robert (1985) "The Cultural Context of Hunter-Gatherer Rock Art." *Man* N.S. 20,3: 434-53.
Developing hermeneutic concepts from Ricoeur, treats both myth and art as texts reflecting the structure of culture. Variations in art and myth are thus symptomatic of variance in cultural systems. Examines rock art and myth of the Worora, Wunambal and Ngarinyin, suggesting art and myth have complementary roles in totemic tradition. The latter have a richer structure but the fixed locative nature of the former can signal ownership of estates through totemic allegiance.

0606 Lewis, Darrell and Rose, Deborah B. (1988) *The Shape of the Dreaming: The Cultural Significance of Victoria River Rock Art.* Canberra: Aboriginal Studies Press. 79 pp.
Contains descriptions of the Victoria River people's construction of the cosmos, Dreaming ancestors and their form-changing activities, and the ancestors' role as the creators of art. Rock art is shown to be inherently ambiguous in meaning and hence significant in linking a changing world with an ideology of an unchanging Dreaming. Socio-geographical and moral aspects of art are also explored.

0607 Lommel, Andreas (1958) "Fünf neue Felsbildstellen in Nordwest-Australien." *Zeitschrift für Ethnologie* 83: 1-33.
Describes five groups of rock paintings in the Kimberley, providing mythological interpretations.

0608 Love, J.R.B. (1930) "Rock Paintings of the Worrora and Their Mythological Interpretation." *Journal of the Royal Society of Western Australia* 16: 1-24.
An account of the rock art of the Worora relying heavily on informant interpretations. Contains myths of how the *Wandjina* shaped the earth, mentions other mythic figures and comments on conception sites. Provides information on maintenance of art. Speculations on origins and significance of certain iconic elements are dated. Largely superceded by the work of Capell (0586).

0609 Playford, Philip E. (1960) "Aboriginal Rock Paintings from the Western Kimberley Region, Western Australia." *Journal of the Royal Society of Western Australia* 43,4: 111-122.
Description of various Kimberley rock art sites, with notes on mythical significance of each.

0610 Schulz, Agnes S. (1956) "North-West Australian Rock Painting." *Memoirs of the National Museum of Victoria, Melbourne* no. 20: 7-57 + plates.
Data from the Frobenius Expedition of 1938. The many plates are the strongest part of this work but it also attempts to provide mythic background to rock art. A brief introduction to *Ungud* and *Wandjina* is followed by myths associated with each gallery. H. Petri supplied many of the notes but the detail varies greatly and is never entirely adequate.

0611 Worms, Ernest A. (1955) "Contemporary and Prehistoric Rock Paintings in Central and Northern North Kimberley." *Anthropos* 50: 546-566.
Covers *Wandjina* art and *Ungud* paintings by Ngarinyin, Gwini and Andidja peoples, as well as *Menhirs* and miniatures or *Gira Gira*. The latter are associated with a totally speculative thesis of a pygmoid race once occupying the Kimberley, but there is a useful Bard myth, with transcription, interlineal and free translation, of the 'Killing of the Dwarfs.' Some data on the myths and functions of rock art, but a very incomplete exposition in this regard.

0612 Worms, Ernest A. (1957) "The Poetry of the Yaoro and Bad, North-Western Australia." *Annalie Lateranensi* 21: 213-229.
These Jauor and Bard songs, given in transcription with metre, literal and free translations are all public and known by men, women and children. Some, however, were formerly associated with 'magic fertility rites'. All relate to economic activities - hunting, carving, etc.

See also: 0160, 0165, 0410, 0627.

Ceremony

0613 Petri, Helmut (1952) "Rituelle Vermehrungs-Handlungen in den Kimberleys (Nordwest-Australien)." *Paideuma* 4: 189-200.
Data from the 1953-5 Frobenius Expedition presenting a general view of Ngarinyin 'increase' ritual. Emphasizes a world-view stressing a wholeness humans must maintain. Develops the role of rock art in spiritual life and considers some myths and beliefs associated with the *Wandjina*. Various forms of 'totemism' - conception, dream, etc. - are discussed along with beliefs in spirit children. Supplements this with the beliefs of neighbouring Nyigina. A solid overview.

See also: 0586, 0631, 0637, 0643, 0648, 0774.

Birth

0614 Akerman, Kim (1977) "Notes on 'Conception' Among Aboriginal Women in the Kimberleys, West Australia." *Oceania* 48,1: 58-63.

Brief notes on when Kimberley women consider conception to begin and what they consider causes it.

0615   Kaberry, Phyllis M.   (1936)   "Spirit-Children and Spirit-Centres of the North Kimberley Division, West Australia." *Oceania* 6,4: 392-400.
Contrasts her evidence from the Forest River region with reports from Central Australian 'spirit-children.' The Kimberley differ in that a) spirit centres are not totemic sites, b) spirit-children are not essences of ancestors and c) the father, not the mother, finds the child. Discusses relevant myths, the process of 'finding' and the cognizance of the procreative role of sexual intercourse.

0616   Kaberry, Phyllis M.   (1968)   "Virgin Birth." *Man* N.S. 3,2: 311-13.
Summarizes Kimberley views on procreation in a rebuttal of Leach (0175).

0617   Worms, Ernest A.   (1957)   "Mythologische Selbstbiographie eines australischen Ureinwohners." *Wiener Völkerkundliche Mitteilungen* 5,1: 40-48.
Baibab, a Bard, died in 1955. This spiritual auto-biography is in 3 sections, each with substantial footnotes to relevant mythic, ritual and linguistic details. Baibab's pre-existence is explained, followed by his coming into being - how he entered a pond with spirit children and announced his identity to his father. Finally, Baibab's old age is related. An intriguing approach but too brief.

Initiation

0618   Elkin, A.P.   (1936)   "Initiation in the Bard Tribe, North-West Australia." *Journal and Proceedings of the Royal Society of New South Wales* 69: 190-208.
Based on one ceremony supplemented by oral data. Begins with preliminary *Kundaldja* ceremonies, and describes tooth-avulsion, some intermediary rituals, and circumcision. This is followed by the *Djaminagga*, focusing on the bullroarers, subincision, cicatrization and other rituals. Detailed, and frequently identifies the kin status of performers. Concludes with observations on the significance of the rites.

0619   Hardman, Edward T.   (1889)   "Notes on Some Habits and Customs of the Natives of the Kimberley District, Western Australia." *Royal Irish Academy, Proceedings* 1(series 3): 70-5.
Contains brief notes on circumcision and subincision.

0620   Lommel, Andreas   (1949)   "Notes on Sexual Behaviour and Initiation, Wunambal Tribe, North-Western Australia." *Oceania* 20,2: 158-164.
A rather disjointed article nonetheless containing useful information. Notes data is coloured by mission influence. Focuses primarily on initiation of men and, to a lesser extent, women. Brief references are given to defloration, circumcision, subincision and cicatrices. There are also summaries of myths associated with

circumcision and defloration. Contains sections on love magic, women's rituals and conception beliefs.

0621 Petri, Helmut (1979) "Pre-Initiation Stages Among Aboriginal Groups of North-West Australia." In *Aborigines of the West: Their Past and Their Present*, edited by R.M. Berndt and C.H. Berndt, 224-233. Nedlands, W.A.: University of Western Australia Press.
Considers the education of boys and, to a lesser extent, girls at Njangomada prior to initiation. The influence of mission and cattle station is emphasized. Discusses training in dance and ceremonial singing and the processes of selecting youths ready for initiation.

0622 Watson, Eliot L.G. (1924) "The Sacred Dance: Corroboree of Natives of North-west Australia." *English Review* 38: 817-827.
Description of some more obvious aspects of a pre-initiatory ceremony.

0623 Worms, Ernest A. (1938) "Die Initiationsfeiern einiger Küsten- und Binnenlandstaemme in Nord-Westaustralien." *Annali Lateranensi* 2: 147-174.
While noting common themes, provides separate sections on the initiations of the Karadjeri, Walmadjari, Djaru, Jauor, Nyulnyul and Bard. Suggests eight grades of initiation over a period of many years and discusses rites of blood-letting, circumcision and subincision as well as food taboos, etc. The response of women to men's initiation is mentioned and there is some brief material on mythology.

See also: 0592, 0634, 0640.

Women

0624 Berndt, Catherine H. (1950) *Women's Changing Ceremonies in Northern Australia*. L'Homme: Cahiers d'Ethnologie, de Geographie et de Linguistique, 1. Paris: Hermann. 87 pp.
An important study of women's ceremonies in the Victoria River Downs district. Religious life is shown to be resilient but nonetheless changing due to the pressures of European employment and culture. The bulk of the book is an ethnography of the *Tjarada*, *Yawalyu* and *Djamunari* ceremonies. Increasingly, women are said to be using these rituals merely as magic to attract lovers and to neglect other aspects associated with ancestral activities.

0625 Kaberry, Phyllis M. (1939) *Aboriginal Woman: Sacred and Profane*. London: George Routledge. 294 pp.
A pioneering book refuting the equation of women with profane life, using ethnographic data from throughout the Kimberley. Establishes women are part of a broad 'totemic' cosmology, and discusses in detail the contexts of women's rites of passage (pre-puberty, menstruation, birth), their knowledge of magic, and their secret *Yilpinji* ceremonies. Women's religious life confirms the wider

thesis that women play an essential, active and valued part in the overall well-being of Aboriginal societies.

Magic

0626 Akerman, Kim (1979) "Contemporary Aboriginal Healers in the South Kimberley." *Oceania* 50,1: 23-30.
Kimberley communities which have lost their 'doctors' look to healers from the Western Desert. Describes six cases of healing involving Walmadjari, Kukatja and Mangala doctors. Briefly mentions symptoms and methods of diagnosis. Treatments such as 'tapping', massaging, sucking and the insertion of *maban* (quartz crystals) are mentioned, and there are references to the relationship between traditional healing and Western health services.

0627 Akerman, Kim and Bindon, Peter (1986) "Love Magic and Style Changes within one Class of Love Magic Objects." *Oceania* 57,1: 22-32.
Focuses on small 'bullroarer' love magic charms. 'Male' and 'female' sides of 5 of these are described and there are notes on their background and ritual use. Notes a shift from traditional graphic totemic forms to more realistically erotic and universal styles. This is more marked on the 'female' face of the charms, perhaps indicating a higher regard by men for the sacredness of their own iconography.

0628 Cawte, John E. (1963) "Tjimi and Tjagolo: Ethnopsychiatry in the Kalumburu People of North-Western Australia." *Oceania* 34,2: 170-190.
Ethnopsychiatry: Aboriginal (mainly Gwini, Andidja and Wolyamidi) and Western. Aboriginal 'psychopathology' is subdivided into sorcery (*tjagolo*), evil beings (*tjimi*), ghosts, and omens. There is a brief examination of local definitions of mental disorder, healing and the training of traditional doctors. The Western interpretations of Aboriginal psychic disorders are superficial.

0629 Coate, H.H.J. (1966) "The Rai and the Third Eye: North-West Australian Beliefs." *Oceania* 37,2: 93-123.
Consists mainly of interlineal and free translation of Ngarinyin views on the *'Rai'* and the 'third eye'. These are not Ngarinyin doctrines but belong to more southern Kimberley peoples - Umida, Nyigina and others. *Rai* are spirits of the dead who teach the arts of initiation and give the 'third eye' and other powers. The translations provide fresh and direct insights.

0630 Worms, Ernest A. (1942) "Die Goronara-Feier im australischen Kimberley." *Annali Lateranensi* 6: 207-235.
Considers a range of sorcery rites, the prosecution of 'murderers', their detection and the role of the traditional healers. 'Pointing the bone' is discussed, as are magic death ceremonies. Also discusses initiation grades and briefly mentions so-called phallic worship. Rain-making ceremonies are described and there is mention of culture heroes. Includes data for the Nyulnyul, Jauor, Djaberdjaber, Karadjeri, Djaru, Walmadjari and Bard.

See also: 0209, 0218, 0569, 0612.

Death

0631 Berndt, Ronald M. (1975) "Life and Death: A Lungga (Gidja) Mythic Corollary." In *Explorations in the Anthropology of Religion: Essays in Honour of Jan van Baal*, edited by W.E.A. van Beek and J.H. Scherer, 122-146. The Hague: Martinus Nijhoff.

Mainly transcriptions with translations and notes from two Lungga song cycles. The *Djadu* is the local form of the *Gadjari* (Meggitt 0851) or *Dingari* and deals with the Mother. The *Bururu* concerns the spirits of the dead. Both selections deal with death - *Djadu* denying that physical death is death while *Bururu* recognizes death as a pre-requisite for ongoing life.

0632 Kaberry, Phyllis M. (1935) "Death and Deferred Mourning Ceremonies in the Forest River Tribes, North-West Australia." *Oceania* 6,1: 33-47.

A useful account of attitudes towards death in the Northern Kimberley. Mentions 'clever men' who are in close contact with the spirits of the dead, the methods of uncovering the sorcery that has caused death, tree-exposures and the fate of the human spirit. Most valuable is a description of mourning ceremonies focusing on the *durdu* - a paperbark package containing the bones of the deceased.

0633 Mjöberg, Eric (1915) *Bland vilda djur och folk I Australien*. Stockholm: Albert Bonnier. 524 pp.

Besides a minor reference to a public ceremony (pp.331-3), the main section of note is chapter 22 which describes the announcement of an illness, and the subsequent grieving, death and burial in the Noonkanbah area. The author was an unwelcome intruder and his data is uninformed.

See also: 0226, 0592.

Change

0634 Akerman, Kim (1979) "The Renascence of Aboriginal Law in the Kimberleys." In *Aborigines of the West: Their Past and Their Present*, edited by R.M. Berndt and C.H. Berndt, 234-242. Nedlands, W.A.: University of Western Australia Press.

Discusses religious revival in the region between Balgo and Looma where Walmadjari influence holds sway. The new *Julurru* cult is briefly mentioned and the spread of the *Worgaia* traced. More attention is paid to the revitalization of initiation. Reasons are given for the revival and it is argued that the changes mark the emergence of a new religious base adapted to changed contexts.

0635 Berndt, Ronald M. (1951) "Influence of European Culture on Australian Aborigines." *Oceania* 21,3: 229-235.

A critique of Lommel (0646), based on field research in adjacent regions. Finds Lommel's inferences regarding to the decline of spirit-child dreams unfounded. Argues the 'new' *kurrangara* was firmly established throughout northern Australia, although concedes elements of a Western nature may have been added. Claims Lommel's rendering of Aboriginal eschatology is unreliable. Berndt's criticisms mostly miss their mark.

0636 Koepping, Klaus-Peter (1988) "Nativistic Movements in Aboriginal Australia: Creative Adjustment, Protest or Regeneration of Tradition." In *Aboriginal Australians and Christian Missions: Ethnographic and Historical Studies*, edited by T. Swain and D. Rose, 397-411. Adelaide: Australian Association for the Study of Religions.

Questions the assumption that Aboriginal religions are immutable by suggesting our definitions of intellectual opposition have been too narrow. Re-examining numerous ethnographies and particularly those of the Kimberley (eg. Petri, Lommel, and Kolig) reveals a different picture. The *Kurrangara* and *Worgaia* cults are examined and are understood as a kind of 'ethno-genesis' which could lead to a form of pan-Aboriginality.

0637 Kolig, Erich (1971) "Quo Vadis, Australian Aboriginal Religion?" *International Committee on Urgent Anthropological and Ethnological Research*, Bulletin no. 13: 99-113.

A brief overview of changes in the southern Kimberley religious life. Old traditions are said to have vanished while immigrants from the desert have brought   new   complexes,   especially   the   *Wandji*   and *Gauwaruwaru/Djularga/Ngamandjimandji*. Notes tendency to break locality-based cults to form larger aggregates. Also considers *Dingari-Worgaia* relationships, their sacred objects. See, for more detail, 0644.

0638 Kolig, Erich (1972) "Bi:n and Gadeja: An Australian Aboriginal Model of the European Society as a Guide in Social Change." *Oceania* 43,1: 1-18.

Bi:n (Aborigines) and *Gadeja* (Europeans) are polarities for Walmadjari Aborigines. Kolig argues Aboriginal speculations about European society rest heavily on an assumption of alleged similarities in social concepts, activities, behaviour and values. This position is embedded in a myth exploring the spread of *Gadeja* from the edge of the cosmos to subdue *Bi:n*. Because of the perceived similarity of the two cultures, says Kolig, Aborigines see systematic attempts to 'assimilate' as unnecessary.

0639 Kolig, Erich (1973) "Tradition and Emancipation: An Australian Aboriginal Version of Nativism." *Newsletter: Aboriginal Affairs Planning Authority* 1,16 supplement: 1-42.

Based on research in Fitzroy Crossing and surrounding areas, discusses creative movements directed towards accomodating Western society. Considers a wide range of phenomena but of especial interest are sections on "Resurrection of the 'Law'"and "New Style Religion" which examine the influx of desert culture, the new social base to religion, and the *Worgaia* and other cults.

0640 Kolig, Erich (1979) "Djuluru: Ein Synkretistischer Kult Nordwest-Australiens." *Baessler-Archiv* 27: 419-448.
The first published account of the cult of *Julurru* (see 0883) based on observations in the Fitzroy Crossing area but also attempting to trace the cult's origins. Considers a range of syncretistic elements - the images of policemen, prisoners, soldiers, war, gunfire, devils and houses; and looks at historical antecedents of these images. Some songs are transcribed, not all with translations. Briefly places this in context of Aboriginal forms of religious revival.

0641 Kolig, Erich (1979) "Captain Cook in the Western Kimberley." In *Aborigines of the West: Their Past and Their Present*, edited by R.M. Berndt and C.H. Berndt, 274-282. Nedlands, W.A.: University of Western Australia Press.
Examines 'Captain Cook' as a new cult hero in the west Kimberley. The myth portrays Cook as a liar who declared Australia unpopulated and hence open for settlement. This was the White Law, but Australia was occupied by a people who predated Whites and who thus had an older Law. Kolig sees the narrative as a political myth devised to revitalize Aboriginal traditions. See Rose (0652).

0642 Kolig, Erich (1980) "Noah's Ark Revisited: On the Myth-Land Connection in Traditional Aboriginal Thought." *Oceania* 51,2: 118-132.
Noah's ark now rests in the southern Kimberley. Kolig examines this story in order to detail the land-myth connection. Suggests a process in which myth becomes *arbitrarily* superimposed upon geographic sites. The 'ark' does not look like an ark and so the myth hardly explains its shape. Many apparently spectacular sites, furthermore, lack mythic explanations. Myth thus seems to precede land affiliation and requires other explanations.

0643 Kolig, Erich (1981) "Woagaia: Weltanschaulicher Wandel und neue Formen der Religiosität in Nordwest-Australien." *Baessler-Archiv* 29: 387-422.
Worgaia among the Walmadjari of Fitzroy Crossing is geared to the socio-political situation of contemporary Aborigines. Considers *Worgaia* as a new religious development, documenting in detail the myth, ritual and ceremonial objects and grounds. The social organization of the cult is noted and the ritual illustrated. Makes comparative statements about *Worgaia* as compared with the *Molonga*, Red-ochre and other cults.

0644 Kolig, Erich (1981) *The Silent Revolution: The Effects of Modernization on Australian Aboriginal Religion*. Philadelphia: Institute for the Study of Human Issues. 192 pp.
An important monograph based on research throughout the southern Kimberleys. Suggests that Western economies, in particular large cattle stations, have begun to transform Aboriginal religion from its localized totemic form into a force capable of unifying a wide range of people. Throughout, the interdependence of social, economic and religious forces is stressed, in both their traditional and post-contact manifestations.

0645 Kolig, Erich (1988) "Mission Not Accomplished: Christianity in the Kimberleys." In *Aboriginal Australians and Christian Missions: Ethnographic and Historical Studies*, edited by T. Swain and D. Rose, 376-396. Adelaide: Australian Association for the Study of Religions.
An attempt to explain why Christianity has failed to become established in the Kimberley. The exception of the community at Looma is noted, as are the localized versions of the Noah's ark myth, and the Jesus-*Jinimin* cult (see 0650). Argues Western secularizing processes have meant Christianity has been presented as divorced from and irrelevant to the 'real' world.

0646 Lommel, Andreas (1950) "Modern Culture Influences on the Aborigines." *Oceania* 21,1: 14-24.
Looks at the effects of Western culture on the Ngarinyin, Worora and Wunambal during 1938-9. Argues psychic disturbances have upset the dream-based religious functions of medicine men and would-be fathers searching for spirit-children, and that disruptions have led to the formation of the *Kurrangara* cult, associated with myths of *Nguniai* and his son *Djanba*. Suggests this cult incorporates European imagery, and has a millennial view of time. See Berndt (0635) and Meggitt (0881).

0647 O'Donovan, Dan (1988) "Marie Minga: Theologian in Paint." *Nelen Yubu* 34: 3-12.
An exegisis of two Christian paintings by Marie Minga, a Djaru woman. The paintings are of the 'Lunga' tree and the local red hill in conjunction with Christian symbols, and of God in association with a traditional serpent. The reading is that of a Christian employing the findings of comparative studies of symbolism in the Eliadian and Jungian traditions.

0648 Petri, Helmut (1950) "Kurangara: neue magische Kulte in Nordwest-Australien." *Zeitschrift für Ethnologie* 75: 43-51.
According to Petri, *Kurrangara* was a new magic/poison cult associated with the *Djanba* (see Meggitt 0881), who bring drought, disease and death. Intergroup organization and trade patterns are discussed, together with the sociological factors making the cult attractive. Places the cult in the context of post-European occupation of the area.

0649 Petri, Helmut (1960) "Neue Magische Geheim kulte in Nordwest Australien." *Congrès International des Sciences Anthropologiques et Ethnologiques 3c. Session, Brussels, 1948*, 182-4.
Brief comments on *Kurrangara*.

0650 Petri, Helmut and Petri-Odermann, Gisela (1964) "Nativismus und Millenarismus im Gegenwärtigen Australien." In *Festschrift für Ad. E. Jensen*, 461-466. München: K. Renner.
Refutes the view that Aborigines lack millennial movements. Describes a syncretistic *Jinimin* (= Jesus) myth in which *Jinimin* had revealed (during a *Wanadjara* ceremony) that he had both black and white skin, and that the land belonged to Aborigines. In the future, differences between Aborigines and

Whites would disappear if the people clung to the 'old law'. Also refers to a Dreaming Noah's ark. For a slightly edited English translation, see (0245).

0651 Petri, Helmut and Petri-Odermann, Gisela (1970) "Stability and Change: Present-Day Historic Aspects Among Australian Aborigines." In *Australian Aboriginal Studies: Modern Studies in the Social Anthropology of the Australian Aborigines*, edited by R.M. Berndt, 248-276. Nedlands, Western Australia: University of Western Australia Press.
Describes changes to traditions between 1954 and 1966. Suggests that liberal mission policies led to syncretism in the *Jinimin* -Jesus movement and the 'cargoistic' stories about Noah's ark. Underlying these are strong anti-White sentiments. Relevant aspects of the associated *Worgaia* cult are also described in this fascinating ethnographic account.

0652 Rose, Deborah B. (1984) "The Saga of Captain Cook: Morality in Aboriginal and European Law." *Australian Aboriginal Studies* no. 2: 24-39.
A Captain Cook Saga from Ngarinman country, examined in light of Yarralin people's view of moral Law. The saga depicts European actions as being based upon immoral Law and explores the implications of this problem. Whilst not a myth the story transcends history in that it is shown to be descriptive, analytical and predictive about life under a Law of oppression.

0653 Rose, Deborah B. (1986) "Christian Identity Versus Aboriginal Identity in the Victoria River District." *Australian Aboriginal Studies* no. 2: 58-61.
Focuses on the rejection of the value of land by the Pentecostal Christians, who opposed traditional Ngarinman affiliations. Also considers the social implications of conversion which removes people from kin-based ritual responsibilties. Aboriginal people are said to be concerned by this Christian message and to have made a conscious decision not to join the 'god mob'.

0654 Rose, Deborah B. (1988) "Jesus and the Dingo." In *Aboriginal Australians and Christian Missions: Ethnographic and Historical Studies*, edited by T. Swain and D. Rose, 361-375. Adelaide: Australian Association for the Study of Religions.
Analyses the disjunction between Pentecostal and Aboriginal cosmologies in the Victoria River area. The respective cosmologies are presented and distilled into two forms of relation: "either-or" and "both-and", further located under the two key (abbreviated) cosmological principles - "Jesus" and "Dingo." There is, finally, some reflection on the appeal of the Pentecostal message to Aborigines as a cosmology which encapsulates the processes of conquest.

0655 Rose, Deborah B. (1988) *Ned Kelly Died for Our Sins*. The 1988 Charles Strong Memorial Lecture. Adelaide: Charles Strong. 28 pp.
Tries to establish what is central to Aboriginal responses to invasion. Examines a Ngarinman narrative in which Ned Kelly and Captain Cook are both represented. Suggests Aborigines see Cook as the archetypal immoral European while Kelly is viewed as a Christ-like figure who fights for the oppressed.

Finally maintains these stories have attracted scant attention because they do not flatter European's self-images but rather suggest it is Whites who are in need of change.

0656   Rose, Deborah B. (1989) "Ned Lives!" *Australian Aboriginal Studies* No. 2: 51-59.
An attempt to discern the historic origins of the Ned Kelly narrative in 0655.

0657   Rowse, Tim (1987) "Were You Ever Savages?: Aboriginal Insiders and Pastoralists' Patronage." *Oceania* 58,2: 81-99.
Primarily a reading of the life of Jack Sullivan, noting his place in the Aboriginal cultural revival of the Kimberley. The section "The Supernatural on the Frontier" considers the *Djanba*, *Balga* and *Wadjarra* cults allegedly brought by 'Boxer' from Queensland, and discusses *Djanba* songs and stories in the context of adjustment to Whites intrusion. (cf. Shaw, 0578).

See also: 0106, 0242, 0243, 0244, 0564, 0569, 0570, 0577, 0578, 0579.

Literature

0658   Craig, Beryl F. (1968) *Kimberley Region: An Annotated Bibliography.* Australian Aboriginal Studies No. 13. Canberra: Australian Institute of Aboriginal Studies. 205 pp.
887 items, including unpublished and very brief publications from the Kimberley, up to 1967. Annotations are not critical, but rather point-form summaries of themes covered. Contains subject and tribal indexes.

0659   Kolig, Erich (1981) "The Rainbow Serpent in the Aboriginal Pantheon: A Review Article." *Oceania* 51,4: 312-316.
Reviews Buchler (0425), Maddock (0438) and Mountford (0132), and briefly adds some interesting observations from Fitzroy Crossing extending, supplementing and countering their arguments.

9

South-West

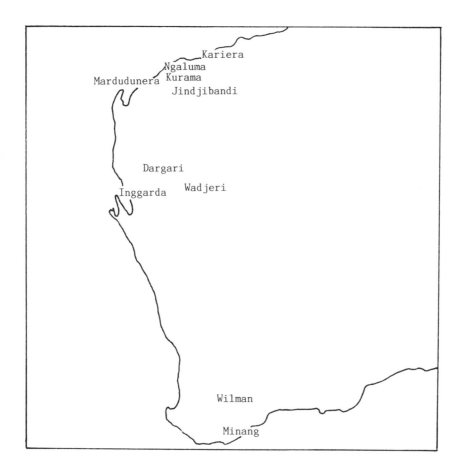

Kariera
Ngaluma
Mardudunera Kurama
Jindjibandi

Dargari
Inggarda Wadjeri

Wilman
Minang

General

0660 Bates, Daisy (1985) *The Native Tribes of Western Australia*, edited by I. White. Canberra: National Library of Australia. 387 pp.
Research from 1904 to 1912, through an amazingly chequered history, was published over 7 decades later. White's editorial work has turned a huge, meandering manuscript into a very useful volume. Contains chapters on initiation, totems, religion and magic, diseases, remedies, death and burial, dances, songs and ceremonies. Details, such as descriptions of initiation in the Broome district, are invaluable. Turn of the century theoretical agendas are evident throughout.

0661 Berndt, Ronald M. (1973) "Aborigines of South-Western Australia: The Past and the Present." *Journal of the Royal Society of Western Australia* 56,1 and 2: 50-55.
Brief summary of literature on initiation, myth, ritual, magic and death; with good bibliography.

0662 Berndt, Ronald M. (1979) "Aborigines of the South-West." In *Aborigines of the West: Their Past and Their Present*, edited by R.M. Berndt and C.H. Berndt, 81-89. Nedlands, W.A.: University of Western Australia Press.
Contains a very brief discussion of initiation, myth, ritual and death (pp.84-86) for this virtually unstudied region.

0663 Brandenstein, C.G. von (1970) *Narratives from the North-West of Western Australia in the Ngarluma and Jindjiparndi Languages*. Canberra: Australian Institute of Aboriginal Studies. 3 Vols., 448 pp.
60 Ngaluma and Jindjibandi narratives with transcription, interlineal and general translations. Texts cover a fascinating range of subjects, including magical incantations and beliefs, initiation practice and 'increase' rituals - including one for the introduced disease of small-pox. A wide range of Dreaming myths and myth fragments add to the value of this authentic reference.

0664 Clement, E. (1904) "Ethnographical Notes on the Western-Australian Aborigines." *Internationales Archiv für Ethnographie* 16: 1-29.
Kariera and neighbouring people described in a general ethnography containing brief notes on *taketa* (traditional healers), beliefs associated with death, and circumcision rites. nf the latter, various stages of the ceremony are superficially listed. Little insight.

0665 Hammond, J.E. (1933) *Winjan's People: The Story of the South-West Australian Aborigines*. Perth: Imperial. 84 pp.
Hammond was born in 1856 and knew many Aborigines and some languages of the South-West. His notes were edited. This book adds to our meagre information for the area with chapters on 'corroborees', 'treatment of sickness' and 'rites and beliefs', but the detail is poor.

0666 Hassell, Ethel (1936) "Notes on the Ethnology of the Wheelman Tribe of Southwestern Australia", selected and edited by D.S. Davidson. *Anthropos* 31: 679-711.
A sober account of Wilman life by a pioneer woman whose data begins from1870. Covers birth ritual, ceremonial meetings, the piercing of the nasal septum, public 'corroborees', the *man carl* ceremony coinciding with burning the land, beliefs in evil spirits, traditional medicine, magic and medicine-men, and mortuary ceremonies. Objectively reported but fragmentary. (See, 0677).

0667 Oldfield, Augustus (1865) "On the Aborigines of Australia." *Ethnological Society of London, Transactions* 3: 215-298.
A very early report, mostly on the Western Australian coast, with useful information, imperfectly recorded. Considers 'Heaven divinities' as well as 'evil spirits' and more probable themes. Not all may be due to error. The evil *horned* spirit (p.229) and the story of the primordial black and white tribes in conflict indicate post-contact influence. With careful handling can be a useful source.

0668 [Radcliffe-] Brown, A.R. (1913) "Three Tribes of Western Australia." *The Journal of the Royal Anthropological Institute of Great Britain and Ireland* 43: 143-194.
Account of an expedition to the Kariera, Ngaluma and Mardudunera in 1911. Focuses on social organization and there are only brief notes on Ngaluma and Mardudunera religion. Kariera totemism, initiation ceremonies, and procreation beliefs receive more attention and the later famously analysed eaglehawk and crow myth is recorded (0107). Data was collected through translators and he did not witness the ceremonies described.

0669 Salvado, Rosendo (1977) *The Salvado Memoirs: Historical Memoirs of Australia and Particularly of the Benedictine Mission of New Norcia and of the Habitats and Customs of the Australian Natives*, translated and edited by E.J. Stormon. Nedlands: University of Western Australia Press. 300 pp.
First appeared in 1851, and is here translated and provided with an introduction and an anthropological evaluation by R.M. Berndt (Appendix II). Salvado's observations are clearly biased, and there are inaccuracies. Nonetheless, this is one of the most important documents on the Aborigines of the South-West, with chapters on religious beliefs, mortuary practice, medicine men, birth customs, the soul and a few mythic figures.

0670 Withnell, John G. (1901) *The Customs and Traditions of the Aboriginal Natives of North Western Australia*. Roebourne, S.A.: Libraries Board. 37 pp.
An early general account of the Pilbara region briefly covering birth, initiation, iconography, ritual, magic, mortuary practice and mythology. Inevitably, lacking in ethnographic detail and rigour.

See also: 0019, 0561.

Philosophy and Totemism

0671 Brandenstein, C.G. von (1970) "The Meaning of Section and Section
      Names." *Oceania* 41,1: 39-49.
Examines the significance of section names in the Pilbara region. Concludes
names and affiliated totems reveal the section system is an aspect of a taxonomy
based on two pairs of opposed elements or temperaments. They are a) cold-
blooded (temperament) or abstract (element): warm-blooded (temperament) or
concrete (element); and b) active: passive. Begins a comparison with
Empedoclean philosophy developed in 0674.

0672 Brandenstein, C.G. von (1972) "The Phoenix 'Totemism'." *Anthropos*
      67: 586-594.
Despite Lévi-Strauss (0098), argues Kariera section names reveal the ashes of
'totemism' could re-emerge in a new form transcending old problems.
Totemism is based on two pairs of opposites (active/passive: cold-blooded/hot-
blooded) and the 4 resultant categories are described. An original mind creating
the divisions is postulated and variations on that theme outlined.

0673 Brandenstein, C.G. von (1974) "Die Weltordnung der Frühzeit nach den
      vier Wesensarten (Neuentdeckungen auf dem Gebiet des Totemismus)."
      Zeitschrift für Religions- und Geistesgeschichte 26,3: 211-221.
Reviews theories of Australian totemism, offers data from the Kariera and, as in
0674 derives a parallel to Greek elemental theory of dry + warm = fire; dry +
cold = earth; moist + warm = moist air; moist + cold = water. Compares
Aboriginal concepts with Greek philosophers in a highly speculative but
intriguing paper.

0674 Brandenstein, C.G. von (1974) "Identical Principles Behind Australian
      Totemism and Empedoclean 'Philosophy'." In *Australian Aboriginal
      Concepts*, edited by L.R. Hiatt, 134-145. Canberra: Australian Institute of
      Aboriginal Studies.
Using structuralist techniques, briefly recapitulates his findings that Australian
Kariera totemism is a classification of the universe using the polarity of 4 basic
qualities. (See, 0671). An ingenious analysis of Empedoclean philosophy so that
the 4 elements - fire, air, earth and water - are correlated with Aboriginal
totemic classification. The two systems, he says, are identical.

Myth

0675 Clarke, J.; Dix, W.C.; Durtch, C.E.; and Palmer, K. (1978) "Aboriginal
      Sites on Millstream Station, Pilbara, Western Australia." *Records of the
      Western Australian Museum* 6,2: 221-257.
A survey recording site data including those with paintings and engravings.
Pages 248-256 (by Palmer) considers two important myths: the 'Two Men',
which follows their travels down the Fortescue River, and an ætiological myth

about one particular pool. Sites associated with myths are noted, based on details from a Kurama and a Jindjibandi informant.

0676 Hallman, Sylvia J. (1975) *Fire and Hearth: A Study of Aboriginal Usage and European Usurpation in South-West Australia.* Canberra: Australian Institute of Aboriginal Studies. 158 pp.
Three chapters scour records for references to fire-related myths and rituals. The burning of the deceased's body and reference to a water-dwelling serpent form an earth-water polarity in chapter 12. Chapter 13 searches out the role of fire in the movement from sky to earth, while 14 examines crystals as the embodiment of fire in 'magical' thought. A quasi-structuralist obsession with polarities.

0677 Hassell, Ethel (1934-5) "Myths and Folktales of the Wheelman Tribe of South-Western Australia", selected and revised by D.S. Davidson. *Folk-Lore* 45: 232-248, 317-341; 46: 122-147, 268-281.
22 myths collected by the author from 1870 onwards. Most stories deal with the ætiological activities of animals with a 'just-so' story flavour. The first instalment focuses on sky myths and provides an account of a world flood. Over-edited, with no indication of original style. Nonetheless, an important addition for the little-studied Wilman. (See 0666)

0678 Mathews, R.H. (1909) "Folklore Notes from Western Australia." *Folk-Lore* 20: 340-2.
A few myth fragments from a correspondent from southern Western Australian coast.

0679 Palmer, Kingsley (1976) "Aboriginal Oral Tradition from the South-West of Western Australia." *Folk-Lore* 87,1: 76-80.
Brief account of Minang folklore.

See also: 0663, 0681.

The Arts

0680 Campbell, W.D. (1911) "The Need for an Ethnological Survey of Western Australia." *Natural History and Science Society of Western Australia Journal* 3,2: 102-9.
Describes rock art at Port Hedland and, in more detail, *tjurunga* from the Kurnalpi district. Illustrates boards with no exegesis but some notes on their association with powers of traditional healers and their use in initiation ceremonies. Very sketchy.

0681 Palmer, Kingsley (1977) "Stone Arrangements and Mythology." *Mankind* 11,1: 33-8.
Gives Pilbara Aborigines' myths for stone arrangements. Dispels the notion that these myths are of minimal worth simply because they are not associated with

frequently visited sites and rituals. It is feasible that myths were *imposed upon* stones originally arranged for non-religious reasons. The myths should not, therefore, be considered as survivals of a lost religious era but a vital and relevant aspect of Aboriginal religious life.

0682 Petri, Helmut (1951) "Felsgravierungen aus Nordwest-Australien." *Zeitschrift für Ethnologie* 76,1: 70-93.
Discusses Kariera rock art. No informants could be found who understood the works and comparisons are made with similar motifs from better studied regions in order to conjecture the significance of the designs.

0683 Virili, Fulgenzio L. (1983) "An Essay of Interpretation of Some Ritual Representations Among the Prehistoric Petroglyphs of the Pilbara, Western Australia." In *The Intellectual Expressions of Prehistoric Man: Art and Religion*, edited by A. Beltron et al., 445-456. Italia: Edizioni del Centro/Editoriale Jaca Book Spa.
A superficial account, based on published reports and field research, which does little more than argue that petroglyphs had some ritual significance, in all probability related to the mythical understanding of the environment.

0684 Wright, Bruce J. (1986) *Rock Art of the Pilbara Region, North-West Australia*. Occasional Papers in Aboriginal Studies No. 11. Canberra: Australian Institute of Aboriginal Studies. 78 pp. + plates.
Describes and illustrates 13 areas in the Pilbara where rock engravings are found. Establishes some possibilities for the religious significance of this art. Most interesting is his review of theories relating these figures to *Kurrangara* cults. Some data is provided that supports the hypothesis that explicitly sexual works are *Kurrangara* petroglyphs.

See also: 0675, 0689.

Birth

0685 [Radcliffe-] Brown, A.R. (1912) "Beliefs Concerning Childbirth in Some Australian Tribes." *Man* 12: 180-182.
Brief notes on Kariera, Ngaluma and Jindjibandi conception beliefs.

Magic

0686 Gray, Dennis (1979) "Traditional Medicine on the Carnarvon Aboriginal Reserve." In *Aborigines of the West: Their Past and Their Present*, edited by R.M. Berndt and C.H. Berndt, 169-183. Nedlands, W.A.: University of Western Australia Press.
Based on work with *maban*-men or *jamadji* (doctors) at Carnarvon Reserve, emphasizing the role of traditional healing in a contact situation. 7 case studies are examined and traditional practice is compared with Western medical

treatment and diagnosis. Gray argues the *maban* has persisting value because of his access to the patient's emotional and social situations which are integral to the wider context of healing.

Death

0687 Gray, Dennis (1976) "Aboriginal Mortuary Practice in Carnarvon." *Oceania* 47,2: 144-156.
Basing his analysis on interviews, observations and active participation in funerals, suggests the assumption that death results from malevolent intent through sorcery still exists for the (predominently Wadjeri) Aborigines of Carnarvon. European technology has, nonetheless, necessitated changes: motor vehicles allow for large gatherings, introduced foods have led to abandoning traditional food taboos, European names make taboos of the deceased's name problematic, etc.

See also: 0226.

Change

0688 Beier, Ulli and Johnson, Colin (1985) "The Aboriginal Novelist Who Found Buddha." *Quadrant* 29,9: 69-75.
Interview with the famous Aboriginal novelist Colin Johnson, who became a Buddhist, and who was a Buddhist in his 'last life'. Considers the relationship between Buddhist and Aboriginal thought.

0689 Brandenstein, C.G. von and Thomas, A.P. (1974) *Taruru: Aboriginal Song Poetry from the Pilbara.* Adelaide: Rigby. 91 pp.
80 *Tabi* songs from 11 Pilbara language groups. These 'individual' songs reflect with immediacy the impact of cultural change. Religious themes are strongly presented in these delightful, skilfully translated, songs. Particularly illuminating is the impression of European technology against traditions of spiritually-based power. Also contains transliterations and extensive endnotes.

0690 Fazeldean, Mick et al. (1987) "Aboriginal and Christian Healing: An interview with Mick Fazeldean, Western Australia." In *The Gospel is Not Western: Black Theologies from the Southwest Pacific*, edited by G.W. Trompf, 95-106. New York: Orbis Books.
Interview with an Aboriginal healer born and initially trained in the Pilbara. Argues there is one source of healing only, and that Aborigines were for all intents and purposes practising Christians without knowing it. Interview questions focus on the practice of healing, processes of diagnosis and the physical experiences whilst curing, and contains comparative comments from other healers from the Pacific.

0691 Gray, Dennis (1978) "A Revival of the Law: The Probable Spread of Initiation Circumcision to the Coast of Western Australia." *Oceania* 48,3: 188-201.
The people of Carnarvon reserve, although of Wadjeri, Dargari and Inggarda descent, have developed a new identity as 'the mob'. Coastal religious traditions had largely died and the mob felt the need to re-establish the 'Law' to strengthen the community, reduce social problems and contain younger men. Increased mobility made it possible to adopt the Law of other groups in the Pilbara and Western Desert, including circumcision.

0692 White, Isobel M. (1980) "The Birth and Death of a Ceremony." *Aboriginal History* 4,1: 33-41.
Pieces together notes by Daisy Bates concerning a ceremony of the Aborigines of King George Sound emerging in response to contact in 1801 with Captain Matthew Flinders' marines. Unlike Christianity, military drill provided Aborigines with a form of ritual which meshed with their own views of ceremonial practice. A brief description of a *Koorannup*-like ceremony depicts the Aborigines emulating the visitors. Brief but tantalising.

See also: 0686, 0687.

10

Western Desert

General

0693 Basedow, Herbert (1904) "Anthropological Notes Made on the South Australian Government North-West Prospecting Expedition, 1903." *Transactions and Proceedings and Report of the Royal Society of South Australia* 28: 12-51.

A superficial collection of observations from east of the Musgrave Ranges west to the Mann Ranges. Notes healing and disease, 'corroborees' (described in meaningless detail), and burial. A long, illustrated second section is devoted to art, and provides notes which offer some Aboriginal exegesis but more often the author's own guesses.

0694 Berndt, Ronald M. (1972) "The Walmadjeri and Gugadja." In *Hunters and Gatherers Today: A Sccioeconomic Study of Eleven Such Cultures in the Twentieth Century*, edited by M.G. Bicchieri, 177-216. New York: Holt, Rhinehart and Winston.

A general account of the people at Balgo Hills mission. Dreaming tracks criss-crossing the country are used as a theme to illustrate the fabric of desert life. Rites of passage are briefly discussed but a richer account is given of the mythic character of *Ganabuda* (or *Gadjeri*, see Meggitt, 0851), the old Mother or group of women. The associated *Dingari* and *Kurrangara* rituals are also discussed.

0695 Berndt, Ronald M. and Berndt, Catherine H. (1942-5) "A Preliminary Report of Field Work in the Ooldea Region, Western South Australia." *Oceania* 12,4: 305-330; 13,1: 51-70; 13,2: 143-169; 13,3: 243-280; 13,4: 362-375; 14,1: 30-66; 14,2: 124-158; 14,3: 220-249: 14,4: 338-358; 15,1: 49-80; 15,2: 154-165; 15,3: 239-275.

Covers a range of elements in the religious life of the Antakirinya, Bidjandjadjara, Kokata and Ngalia. The final installment is a detailed description of an initiation. Also covers magical rites, love chants, conception beliefs, initiation, death, totemism, myth, ritual and many others themes. Worthy of note is the section devoted to Aboriginal women. This fragmented ethnography deserves careful attention and contains a store of valuable information.

0696 Berndt, Ronald M. and Berndt, Catherine H. (1951) *From Black to White in South Australia*. Melbourne: Cheshire. 313 pp.

Brief notes on initiation, myth, ritual and magic, and some references to changing contexts. Draws heavily on research in Ooldea. (See 0695).

0697 Eylmann, Erhardt (1908) *Die Eingeborenen der Kolonie Sudaustralien*. Berlin: Dietrich Reimer. 494 pp.

A little-known volume based on field-research during 1896-1900. Contains information on South Australian Aboriginal life, from birth through initiation and death, to totemism, magic, dreams, spirit beliefs and myths. Useful only insofar as it offers an early ethnographic account for the region.

0698 Gould, Richard A. (1969) *Yiwara: Foragers of the Australian Desert*. New York: Charles Scribner. 239 pp.

A non-technical introduction to Nganajara life containing a fairly detailed description of an initiation, somewhat marred by the interpretative interjections. There is, further, an account of an 'increase' ritual focusing on the importance of the sacred site and notes on 'how to get rid of ghosts' and the practice of revenge sorcery.

0699 Hamilton, Annette (1982) "Descended from Father, Belonging to Country: Rights to Land in the Australian Western Desert." In *Politics and History in Band Society*, edited by E. Leacock and R. Lee, 85-108. Cambridge: Cambridge University Press.
Drawing primarily on Bidjandjadjara data, argues a differentiation must be made between economic and religious affiliations with land. Within the religious sphere there has been a shift over time from place-based rights to father-based rights. This is interpreted in terms of a qualified Marxist view of pre-capitalist society and men's ideological ritual attitudes towards economic production in which women, who provide the labour, feature primarily by their absence.

0700 Heermann, Ingrid (1981) *Die Traumzeit lebt weiter: Eine Ausstellung des Linden-Museums Stuttgart.* Stuttgart: Linden-Museum. 95 pp.
A catalogue for an exhibition of Aboriginal artifacts supplemented by the author's own contacts with Bidjandjadjara, Pintubi and other peoples. Substantial sections on cosmology, myth, ritual, art, initiation and magic, and the text is richly illustrated.

0701 Mountford, Charles P. (1962) *Brown Men and Red Sand: Journeyings in Wild Australia.* Sydney: Angus and Robertson. 192 pp.
Popularistic book with references to Bidjandjadjara ritual, magic, myths, etc.

0702 Myers, Fred R. (1980) "The Cultural Basis of Politics in Pintupi Life." *Mankind* 12,3: 197-214.
Investigates the relationship between Pintubi cultural constructs and political life. Draws heavily on the role of Dreaming Law, and the way it impinges on the male life cycle. 'Holding' (*Kanyininpa*) is shown to be a dominant symbol - the authority of the elders is simultaneously a responsibility to 'carry' the Law and to 'look after' those who follow. Hierarchy can thus exist within an egalitarian society. Rejects the view that male religious knowledge is the ideology of a gerontocracy.

0703 Myers, Fred R. (1986) *Pintupi Country, Pintupi Self: Sentiment, Place and Politics Among Western Desert Aborigines.* Washington: Smithsonian Institution Press. 334 pp.
A very rich ethnography of the Pintubi focusing on the issue of how a culture maintains itself through time while placing a high value on individual autonomy. An excellent chapter on "The Dreaming: Time and Space" portrays an ontology of immutability in which 'egalitarian' negotiations take place. A pioneering chapter on the emotions links these to the landscape and the Dreaming. A chapter on initiation explores the tension between ritual 'hierarchy' and equality. Insightful.

0704 Odermann, Gisela (1957) "Das Eigentum in Nordwest-Australien."
      Annali Lateranensi 21: 30-97.
Nyangumarda data is used to discuss the notions of property, shown to be based
on totemic sites and taught through myth. Highlights the importance of ritual
knowledge and the means by which this is transferred through time.

0705 Petri, Helmut (1956) "Dynamik im Stammesleben Nordwest-Australien."
      Paideuma 6,3: 152-168.
Report from the Frobenius Expedition of 1954-5 to the Nyangumarda, Julbaridja
and neighbouring peoples. A range of topics is briefly covered, including myths,
mythological routes, Dreaming ancestors, myth-ritual complexes, initiation rites
(circumcision and subincision) and others. A *tour de force* lacking detail

0706 Scrobogna, Bruno (1980) *Die Pintubi am Ende der Steinzeit*. Berlin:
      Safari bei Ullstein. 246 pp.
An introduction to traditional and contemporary Pintubi life which relies heavily
on photographic records and has journalistic sections on myth and ritual.

0707 Tonkinson, Robert (1974) *The Jigalong Mob: Aboriginal Victors of the
      Desert Crusade*. Menlo Park, California: Cummings. 166 pp.
A well-regarded study of cultual contact between Aborigines and missionaries at
Jigalong. Emphasizes how these Aborigines have retained a tradition-oriented
life-style in the face of Western culture. Provides an overview of Mandijildjara
beliefs and practices and shows how the Jigalong mob, while accepting certain
aspects of White culture, have rejected Christianity in order to retain their
traditional religious values.

0708 Tonkinson, Robert (1978) *The Mardudjara Aborigines: Living the
      Dream in Australia's Desert*. New York: Holt, Rhinehart and Winston.
      149 pp.
A careful and detailed ethnography of the peoples Tonkinson refers to
collectively as the Mardudjara. Covers themes such as conception beliefs,
initiation, the afterlife, myth, ritual and magic. Some data was recorded from
Jigalong settlement, but it is significant that a substantial part comes from desert
Aborigines who had minimal or no contact with Whites. The book ends by
examining problems of cultural adaptation.

0709 Tonkinson, Robert (1987) "Mardudjara Religion." In *The Encyclopedia
      of Religion*, edited by M. Eliade, Vol. 9, 196-201. New York: Macmillan.
A brief overview of the religious life of the 'Mardudjara' (Manjildjara,
Gardudjara and others). Discusses the Dreaming, totemic affiliations, men's
initiation, women's ceremonies, myth rituals and sacred objects. Concludes by
exploring the process of change.

See also: 0003, 0660, 0723, 0784, 0785, 0786, 0787, 0893.

Philosophy and Totemism

0710 Barden, Garrett (1973) "Reflections of Time." *The Human Context* 5,2: 331-344.
Examines Western Desert social systems as a means of ordering experience in a manner denying time. The Dreaming is discussed as an ideology ignoring the present. Myth is examined as hierophony in its relation to the temporal world. Considers the impact of Christianity on time perception and especially the Judæo-Christian view of history, as well as the general effect of the presence of European society. Thematically important but often too summary.

0711 Piddington, Ralph (1932) "Totemic System of the Karadjeri Tribe." *Oceania* 2,4: 373-400.
An early study, nonetheless after considerable White contact, of the totemic systems of the Karadjeri near Lagrange Bay. After a brief discussion of the social context of totem allocation, there is a purely descriptive listing of 'increase' sites and rites and totemic myths.

See also: 0112, 0699, 0702, 0703, 0704, 0712, 0720, 0729, 0731, 0732, 0745, 0746, 0760.

Myth

0712 Bain, Margaret S. (1978-9) "No Pitjantjatjara Transformation." *Anthropological Forum* 4,3-4: 308-326; + "Comment" by W.H. Douglas, 327-330.
Munn (0818) argued both Waljbiri and Bidjandjadjara myths evinced a transformation from subject to object. Bain critiques Munn with regard to the Bidjandjadjara, suggesting Munn's duality of ancestral subjects and geographic and cultural objects, necessitating further a duality of time (Dreaming and present), is misconceived. Rather the relation of 'subjects' and 'objects' should be phrased as one of identity in which temporal divisions become unimportant.

0713 Berndt, Ronald M. (1941) "Tribal Migrations and Myths Centring on Ooldea, South Australia." *Oceania* 12,1: 1-20.
Mainly recounts Antakirinya myths concerning the wanderings of two cultural heroes - the *Wati Kutjara* (more detailed than Tindale 0726 cr Mountford 0733), but there are also myths of personified mammals, birds and serpents. Argues the myths provide evidence of diffusion of Aboriginal cultural elements from north-west Australia, south along the coast and then eastwards into the Desert. The myths give detailed accounts of routes.

0714 Berndt, Ronald M. (1970) "Traditional Morality as Expressed Through the Medium of an Australian Aboriginal Religion." In *Australian Aboriginal Studies: Modern Studies in the Social Anthropology of the Australian Aborigines*, edited by R.M. Berndt, 216-247. Nedlands, W.A.: University of Western Australia Press.

Uses structuralist techniques but basically restates the functionalist view that myths serve as guides for correct behaviour. The ten myth sections discussed come from the Walmadjari, Kukatja, Mardudjara, and others, and are analysed in terms of outcomes to immoral acts. Berndt argues people learn of the inevitable repercussions of behaviour through these myths.

0715 Berndt, Ronald M. (1973) "Mythic Shapes of a Desert Culture." In *Festschrift zum 65. Geburtstag von Helmut Petri*, edited by K. Tauchmann, 3-31. Köln: Böhlau.
Focuses on Walmadjari and Kukatja-Mardudjara myths associated with *Dingari*, a transitional relative of the *Kunapipi/Gadjeri*. The mythic sections lack contextualization. The emphasis is on the wandering nature of the *Dingari*. *Wati Kutjara* mythemes are also given (cf. Berndt, 0713) and some general comments on the symbolism of mythic shapes are made.

0716 Capell, Arthur (1949-50) "Some Myths of the Garadjeri Tribe, Western Australia." *Mankind* 4,2: 46-61; 4,3: 108-125; 4,4: 148-162 .
Transcriptions, interlineal translations and free interpretations of 10 Karadjeri myths. The myths belonged to initiated men and cover themes such as the bullroarer being forbidden to women, the origins of 'increase' rites and the exploits of the two cultural heroes *Gagamara* and *Gumbar*. The introductory narrative and textual notes are geared primarily to linguists.

0717 Harney, W.E. (1957) *The Story of Ayers Rock*. Melbourne: Bread and Cheese Club. 24 pp.
These stories dealing with *Uluru* sites are carelessly and superficially recorded. Narratives included are 'the battle of the Serpent People'; *Mutidjula*, relating to a rock hole and mythic figures associated with it; and 'the cult-path of the Kangaroo-rat man', which Harney claims is a version of the northern *Kunapipi* or 'Earth Mother' cult. Hopelessly confused. (Cf. Layton, 0719).

0718 Harney, W.E. (1963) *To Ayers Rock and Beyond*. London: Hale. 192 pp.
More unreliable Ayers Rock information. See 0717.

0719 Layton, Robert (1986) *Uluru: An Aboriginal History of Ayers Rock*. Canberra: Australian Institute of Aboriginal Studies. 139 pp.
Relates 5 Jangkundjara myths - the Pythons, the Blue-Tongued Lizards, the Red Lizard, the Hare Wallabies, and the Two Boys. Each is accompanied by pictures of parts of *Uluru* (Ayers Rock) with which they are associated. The style is deliberately simple and yet, whilst obviously not exhaustive, the account is sound. Some socio-ecological aspects of the myths are explored.

0720 Liberman, Kenneth B. (1980) "Two World-Creative Carpet Snakes from the Australian Desert." *Folklore and Mythology Studies* 4: 6-16.
Using a Two Carpet Snake Dreaming as an illustration of the Kuwarra way of understanding places, proceeds to argue theirs is as precise and 'objective' as Western ideas of space and time. The myth of the Snakes is given and the

relationship between myth and landscape is underlined, drawing inspiration from phenomenological thought. Promising but unsatisfying.

0721 McCarthy, Frederick D. (1961) "The Story of the Mungan or Bagadjimbiri Brothers." *Mankind* 5,10: 420-425.
An account of a myth concerning two brothers from the Njamal, making comparisons with a Karadjeri version (in Piddington 0732) and the related *Wati Kutjara* myth (see Tindale 0726). Each of these myths is shown to be associated with the introduction of circumcision and there are some suggestions as to the evolution of the narrative.

0722 Mountford, Charles P. (1965) *Ayers Rock: Its People, their Beliefs and their Art.* Sydney: Angus and Robertson. 208 pp.
The 100-plus plates are the strongest part of this book. The introductory sections on the Bidjandjadjara, not all of which are entirely accurate, are followed by 8 myths related to specific features of the rock. There are short chapters on art and sacred objects of the area. The descriptions are weakest when concerned with the social and ritual context of beliefs.

0723 Mountford, Charles P. (1976) *Nomads of the Western Desert.* Adelaide: Rigby. 628 pp.
An infamous book withdrawn from sale due to protests from the Bidjandjadjara, who felt about 20 of the 737 plates were unsuitable for public display. Ethics aside, the photographs related to Bidjandjadjara myths are superb. Unfortunately, the accompanying commentary is far less impressive. Detailed descriptions are conspicuously absent, and some of the myths are very highly abridged.

0724 Petri, Helmut (1965) "Kosmogonie unter farbigen Völkern der westlichen Wüste Australiens." *Anthropos* 60: 469-479.
Considers Western Desert cosmogony in the context of Schmidt's (0995) advocacy of the doctrine of an Aboriginal Supreme Being and Worm's (0595) claim that *Djamar* is of this kind. Discusses beliefs from other regions by way of comparison.

0725 Piddington, Ralph (1930) "The Water-Serpent in Karadjeri Mythology." *Oceania* 1,3: 352-354.
Brief account of some Karadjeri myths about the serpent *Bulaing*.

0726 Tindale, Norman B. (1936) "Legend of the Wati Kutjara, Warburton Range, Western Australia." *Oceania* 7,2: 169-185.
A detailed record of Dreaming sites of the *Wati Kutjara* (Two Men). westwards from the Western Australia border. Their travels gave rise to certain topographical formations as well as introducing various sacred objects and ritual practices. Tindale comments the characters are more human than in other Central Australian myths, and dubiously conjectures the myth may have an historical base. See Mountford 0733.

0727 Tindale, Norman B. (1959) "Totemic Beliefs in the Western Desert of Australia: Part I: Women Who Became the Pleiades." *Records of the South Australian Museum* 13,3: 305-322.
Mandjindja, Pindiini, Bidjandjadjara, Ngadajara and Jangkundjara material on the myth of the women associated with Pleiades and the Morning Star. They climbed the sky to avoid the attentions of a man and his son, and set their dogs on them. The appearance of the Pleiades in autumn is associated with the season of pups and 'increase' ceremonies. A brief description of the spectacular cave *Owalinja* where 'increase' ceremonies are held is also given.

0728 Worms, Ernest A. (1949) "An Australian Migratory Myth." *Primitive Man* 22,1-2: 33-38.
A Karadjeri myth of the Two Wandering Men genre (cf. Berndt 0713).

See also: 0443, 0704, 0706, 0730, 0733, 0734, 0735, 0737, 0741, 0743, 0744, 0747, 0763, 0818, 0820.

The Arts

0729 Berndt, Ronald M. (1985-6) "Identification of Deity Through Land: An Aboriginal Point of View." In *Visible Religion: Annual for Religious Iconography*, Vol. 4-5 'Approaches to Iconography', edited by H.G. Kippenberg, 266-279. Leiden: E.J. Brill.
Speaks of an Aboriginal 'holy trinity' of 1) land, 2) Dreaming beings alive within the land, and 3) all species and elements which are tangible expressions of mythic beings. These connections are discussed in the context of 11 Kukatja *Daragu* designs, each described briefly. The *Daragu* are shown to be the primary vehicle by which deities are made visibly present, but visibility in this case means designs which primarily refer to the land.

0730 Berndt, Ronald M. and Berndt, Catherine H. (1952-4) "A Selection of Children's songs from Ooldea, Western South Australia." *Mankind* 4,9: 364-376; 4,10: 423-434; 4,12: 501-508.
144 children's songs with interlineal translations and explanations. All songs were recorded at 'play about' *Inma* ('corroborees') and all are said to be of Dreaming origin. All were sung by boys between the ages of four and seventeen, i.e., prior to their being taken to preliminary initiation rites. This data was collected in 1941 and should be read in conjunction with the authors' earlier report from Ooldea (0695).

0731 Ellis, Catherine J. (1984) "Time Consciousness of Aboriginal Performers." In *Problems and Solutions: Occasional Essays in Musicology Presented to Alice M. Moyle*, edited by J.C. Kassler and J. Stubington, 149-185. Sydney: Hale and Iremonger.
Examines theories of the phenomenology of time perception, then extends these to examine Bidjandjadjara rules and structures for organizing time in ritual. The focus is both on the a-temporality of 'Dreaming' and the metre of song. Suggests

these people have 'perfect time' (analogous to 'perfect pitch') employed to manipulate perceptions of time to permit and facilitate a reflection upon the timelessness of their religious beliefs.

0732 Ellis, Catherine J. (1985) *Aboriginal Music: Cross-Cultural Experiences from South Australia.* St. Lucia: University of Queensland Press. 236 pp.
Music, myth and spiritual experience are said to belong to a common level of learning, and Ellis advocates learning of Aboriginal culture through these modes. The structure of Bidjandjadjara music is examined to uncover how it produces the 'feeling of iridescence' (p.108) and obliterates the flow of time. The educational theory and practice of using this music in a cross-cultural context is discussed. Borders on pop-psychology but raises interesting questions.

0733 Mountford, Charles P. (1937) "Aboriginal Crayon Drawings from the Warburton Ranges in Western Australia Relating to the Wanderings of Two Ancestral Beings, the Wati Kutjara." *Records of the South Australian Museum* 6,1: 5-28.
Crayon drawings obtained from two elderly Ngadajara men are reproduced. The symbolism employed is analysed and the drawings are related to sites and to *Wati Kutjara* mythology. See Tindale (0726).

0734 Mountford, Charles P. (1937) "Aboriginal Crayon Drawings: II, Relating to Totemic Places in South-Western Central Australia." *Transactions and Proceedings of the Royal Society of South Australia* 61: 226-240.
Describes 17 crayon drawings by 4 Bidjandjadjara men. Explanations of their meaning (ascertained with the help of T.G.H. Strehlow) and, in some cases, relevant myths, are provided. The drawings relate to totemic centres and exploits of 9 ancestors: Kangaroo, Ice Man, Woman, Wild Cat, Emu, Bell Bird, Mulga, Seed Man, Yellow Goanna and Snake. Some comparisons are made with Aranda drawings in Mountford, 0831.

0735 Mountford, Charles P. (1938) "Aboriginal Crayon Drawings: III. The Legend of the Wati Jula and the Kunkarunkara Women." *Transactions and Proceedings of the Royal Society of South Australia* 62,2: 241-254.
12 Ngadajara crayon drawings relating to *Wati Jula* are accompanied by explanations as to how they relate to both ancestors and sites. The myth belongs to the 'shade' moiety and substantial comparisons are made with the *Wati Kutjara* myth (see Tindale 0726) and drawings (see Mountford 0733) of the 'sun' moiety. Both ancestors are associated with a group of women called *Kunkarunkara*; in both cases they are transformed into stellar constellations.

0736 Mountford, Charles P. (1962) "Sacred Objects of the Pitjantjatjara Tribe, Western Central Australia." *Records of the South Australian Museum* 14,2: 397-411.
Records 21 *Kulpidji* (sacred boards) of the Bidjandjadjara, 17 associated with the totemic site of the mulga-seed (*Kulpidji*), another 3 with a region 20 miles west of Ayers Rock. The designs are depicted, their meanings stated, and to a limited degree, related myths are noted. Design motifs and methods of

engraving are mentioned and the use of limited graphic forms to produce a rich variety of mythic themes is emphasized.

0737 Mountford, Charles P. and Tonkinson, Robert (1969) "Carved and Engraved Human Figures from North Western Australia." *Anthropological Forum* 2,3: 371-390.
Describes 5 Mandjindja and Mardudjara carved and engraved figures representing *Ngajunangalgu* spirit beings. These were associated with 'dream-spirit' rituals and other rituals of recent origin. The *Ngajunangalgu* myths refer to malicious beings who devour humans. They are related to the *Wati Kutjara* (see Tindale, 0726), also depicted in the engravings. Mostly devoted to describing in detail the mythic significance of the figures.

0738 Moyle, Richard M. (1979) *Songs of the Pintupi: Musical Life in a Central Australian Society.* Canberra: Australian Institute of Aboriginal Studies. 183 pp.
Although concerned primarily with the musical aspects of Pintubi song there is much here for those interested in its ceremonial form. The chapter "Categories of Songs", for example, gives a balanced introduction to public ceremonies, love magic, women's-songs, initiation, sorcery, healing and other classifications of ceremonies. Also contains data on the ownership, acquisition and exchange of rituals/songs.

0739 Payne, Helen E. (1978) "The Integration of Music and Belief in Australian Aboriginal Culture." *Religious Traditions* 1,1: 8-18.
Drawing primarily on Bidjandjadjara evidence, seeks to show how the melodic line and interval structure of songs identifies chants with specific ancestors. An ancestor can be felt, 'smelt' or touched in the 'contour' of music. It is this ability to re-actualize Dreaming beings which allows music to draw on supernatural forces at sites within the physical environment. Thus, both meaning *and* structure are of importance to ritual.

0740 Tindale, Norman B. (1963) "Totemic Beliefs in the Western Desert of Australia: Part 2: Musical Rocks and Associated Objects of the Pitjantjatjara tribe." *Records of the South Australian Museum* 14,3: 499-514.
Describes the *kondala* rocks which are arranged and decorated with blood and said to be the voice of the ancestors (when struck). Considers their role in men's and women's ceremonies, and their place in secular, initiatory and 'increase' ceremonies.

See also: 0700, 0722, 0743, 0752, 0757, 0758, 0826, 0842.

Ceremony

0741 Harney, W.E. (1960) "Ritual and Behaviour at Ayers Rock." *Oceania* 31,1: 63-76.

Information from two Luridja men about Ayers Rock. Focuses on the *Kerungera* ritual of the northern 'sun-over' moiety. The account moves, site by site, along the northern circumference of the rock, indicating totemic affiliation, and briefly describing ritual behaviour. The southern part of the rock is very briefly related to relevant myths but not the accompanying rituals. Unreliable. Cf. Strehlow (0824).

0742 Palmer, Kingsley (1983) "'Owners' and 'Managers': Ritual Cooperation and Mutual Dependence in the Maintenance of Rights to Land." *Mankind* 13,6: 517-530.
Drawing on field research among the Walmadjari and Kukatja, examines the relationship between patrimoieties, rituals and land ownership. Shows members of both moieties ('owners' and 'managers'), are essential to any ritual performance. The inheritance of ritual, and land rights and responsibilities is discussed, and the intricacies illlustrated by a brief case study of 4 men and their respective land custodianship duties.

0743 Petri, Helmut (1966) "'Badur' (Parda-Hills), ein Felsbilder- und Kultzentrum im Norden der westlichen Wüste Australiens." *Baessler-Archiv* 14: 331-370.
The rock art of *Badur* belongs to the Karadjeri and contains secret works associated with 'two heroes'. Although no longer the centre of ritual activity, this is said to be the place of the oldest *Kurrangara* law in the region. Relates ancestral wanderings, noting possible confusion in informants' story lines, and the present coexistence of two Laws - the older *Wandji* and the more recent *Mideidi*. A somewhat tortured exposition.

0744 Petri, Helmut (1967) "'Wandji-Kurang-gara', ein Mythischer Traditionskomplex aus der Westlichen Wüste Australiens." *Baessler-Archiv* 15,1: 1-34.
Develops Petri's article on *Badur* (0743) and discusses revivals of the *Wandji* traditions in the area from Port Hedland to Broome, noting new post-European elements. The revival had co-ordinated components from various neighbouring groups and entailed a changed mythic line, illustrated by map. Mythic wanderings are given in detail and accompanied by ritual details. Includes an outline of initiation ceremonies.

0745 White, Isobel M. (1981) "Generation Moieties in Australia: Structural, Social and Ritual Implications." *Oceania* 52,1: 6-27.
Adds White's own data to the literature on generation moieties throughout the Western, and, to a lesser extent, Central Desert. In some cases the moieties are argued to be *the* most important basic division of communities, and their significance for both social and ritual life is documented. Concludes by re-affirming Stanner's view (0109) that the succession of generation moieties provides a cyclic foundation for the Aboriginal view of time.

See also: 0706, 0715, 0731, 0738, 0739, 0740, 0748, 0761, 0762, 0772.

Birth

0746 Berndt, Ronald M. (1940) "Aboriginal Sleeping Customs and Dreams, Ooldea, South Australia." *Oceania* 10,3: 286-294.
Some brief notes on the travel of spirits during dreams and 'Dream totemism'.

0747 Piddington, Ralph (1957) *An Introduction to Social Anthropology*, Vol. II. Edinburgh: Oliver and Boyd. 819 pp.
An appendix to volume II, "The Rationalizations of Yuari", notes Yuari had engaged in an incestuous - by Karadjeri standards - marriage and manipulated traditional myth and procreation beliefs to justify his practice. Views of procreation beliefs and the nature of cultural change are most dated.

0748 Sackett, Lee (1977) "Confronting the Dreamtime: Belief and Symbolism in an Aboriginal Ritual." *Ethnos* 42,3-4: 156-179.
Yet another attempt to answer the question of ignorance of physiological paternity. Presents the beliefs of people at Wiluna in regard to the origin of children and analyses a *Djabija* ('increase') ceremony, developing both indigenous exegesis and theoretical models. Apparently phallic and uterine symbolism is noted, likewise that Aborigines reject such interpretations. The answer offered is an infinite qualification.

0749 Tonkinson, Robert (1970) "Aboriginal Dream-Spirit Beliefs in a Contact Situation: Jigalong, Western Australia." In *Australian Aboriginal Studies: Modern Studies in the Social Anthropology of the Australian Aborigines*, edited by R.M. Berndt, 277-291. Nedlands: University of Western Australia Press.
Looks at how dream-spirit beliefs of the Mardudjara help them maintain religious traditions in a contact situation. Examines the role of these beliefs in rituals and curative magic, and goes on to argue that dream-spirits provide settled Aborigines with a link to ancestral sites through their capacity to travel during dreams. Also illustrates their creative role in the construction of new ceremonial forms.

0750 Tonkinson, Robert (1974) "Semen Versus Spirit-Child in a Western Desert Culture." In *Australian Aboriginal Concepts*, edited by L.R. Hiatt, 81-92. Canberra: Australian Institute of Aboriginal Studies.
Drawing on evidence from Jigalong, argues adult male Aborigines only thought of procreation in spiritual terms. Semen is deemed irrelevant and pregnancy is said to be possible without intercourse. There is also evidence for a denial of physiological maternity. Weighs the evidence in the context of the controversy surrounding this issue.

See also: 0858.

Initiation

0751 Jones, Ivor H. (1969) "Subincision Among Australian Western Desert Aborigines." *British Journal of Medical Psychology* 42: 183-190.
Like Cawte et al. (0860), attempts to locate the meaning of subincision. Considers Law, contraception, hygiene, stimulation and symbolism as possible reasons among the people of the Warburton Range United Aborigines Mission. 'Law' was the only explicitly recognized reason. Inconclusive.

0752 Mountford, Charles P. (1938) "Contrast in Drawings Made by an Australian Aborigine Before and After Initiation." *Records of the South Australian Museum* 6,2: 111-114.
Shows drawings of a Ngadajara youth before subincision were concerned with Western cultural items; after subincision with traditional Law. Argues this indicates the cohesive power of ceremonies.

0753 Piddington, Ralph (1932) "Karadjeri Initiation." *Oceania* 3,1: 46-87.
Emphasizes the differences between the 'southern' and 'northern' Karadjeri initiations. These areas differ regarding the rite of circumcision and correlatively, they have different associated mythologies, in turn traced back to variations in their respective cosmologies. Brief references also to rites of passage in the lives of women and to ceremonies restricted to older men.

0754 Sackett, Lee (1978) "Punishment in Ritual: 'Man-Making' Among Western Desert Aborigines." *Oceania* 49,2: 110-127.
Points out studies of Aboriginal ritual have tried to re-construct a pristine pre-contact situation. Suggests initiation needs to be understood in the context of present life-styles. Today, initiation is no longer a reward for youths at Wiluna, who are seen as disinterested in tradition. To change this, men enforce initiation, but it is now a form of punishment to control unruly lads.

0755 Tindale, Norman B. (1935) "Initiation Among the Pitjandjara Natives of the Mann and Tomkinson Ranges in South Australia." *Oceania* 6,2: 199-224.
Detailed description of a Bidjandjadjara initiation which retained much of the traditional nomadic ceremony. Although imperfect and incomplete, there are useful quotations of initiatory songs - alas not always with translations. Concludes at the removal of the foreskin and hence does not mention later rituals. Contains some details on social groupings and interactions, but these are not always satisfactory.

See also: 0189, 0190, 0623, 0695, 0744, 0772.

Women

0756 Berndt, Catherine H. (1989) "Retrospect and Prospect: Looking Back Over 50 Years." In *Women, Rites and Sites: Aboriginal Women's Cultural Knowledge*, edited by P. Brock, 1-20. Sydney: Allen & Unwin.
Drawing on her experiences at Ooldea, Oodnadatta and Point McLeay, argues that women handled their ceremonial roles with authority and confidence. The discussion is located in the broader context of social change and its effects on Aboriginal relation to and knowledge of sacred and significant sites. Little actual detail of women's role in religious life is given, however.

0757 Ellis, Catherine J. (1970) "The Role of the Ethnomusicologist in the Study of Andagarinja Women's Ceremonies." *Miscellanea Musicologica* 5: 76-208.
Part III is a valuable discussion of an Antakirinya women's secret Emu ceremony. Contains explanations of events and designs used in the ritual and the layers of meaning residing within the text. A full description, with explicit photographs, of the ceremony is offered. Ellis highlights meanings more accessible to the ethnomusicologist and also thus the need for multidisciplinary approaches to Aboriginal women's ritual life.

0758 Ellis, Catherine J. and Barwick, Linda (1989) "Antikirinja Women's Song Knowledge 1963-72: Its Significance in Antikirinja Culture." In *Women, Rites and Sites: Aboriginal Women's Cultural Knowledge*, edited by P. Brock, 21-40. Sydney: Allen & Unwin.
Based on data recorded among Antakirinya from Port Augusta to Oodnadatta and from 1963-1972. The relationship between songs and sites is discussed, as is the relationship between men's and women's songs. Argues women release strong ancestral powers through their ceremonies, maintaining the country and the balance of species. Finally, some changes in performance over the research period are examined.

0759 Gibson, Jen (1989) "Digging Deep: Aboriginal Women in the Oodnadatta Region of South Australia in the 1980s." In *Women, Rites and Sites: Aboriginal Women's Cultural Knowledge*, edited by P. Brock, 60-75. Sydney: Allen & Unwin.
Brief sections on contemporary Dreaming and mortuary traditions of the people at Oodnadatta.

0760 Hamilton, Annette (1980) "Dual Social Systems: Technology, Labour and Women's Secret Rites in the Eastern Desert of Australia." *Oceania* 51,1: 4-19.
Takes issue with those who argue women's secret cults pose no real opposition to male ideological dominance. Her survey of Western Desert data suggests that although men have a model of their religious hegemony, a number of features have hindered this from becoming a reality. These are the nature of women's labour, certain ambiguities in the relationship between totemic affiliations and

sites and, importantly, the presence of an autonomous women's secret religious life.

0761 Payne, Helen E. (1984) "Residency and Ritual Rights." In *Problems and Solutions: Occasional Essays in Musicology Presented to Alice M. Moyle*, edited by J.C. Kassler and J. Stubington, 264-278. Sydney: Hale and Iremonger.
For Bidjandjadjara women, visualizing sites acts as a mnemonic aid in recalling the sequences of their ceremonies. This association between country and ritual results from women's participation in ceremonies supervised by their elders. There is thus a process of induction into the deeper levels of meaning of song/land relationships. The effects of women's residence on the receipt, transmission and maintenance of ritual rights and responsibilities is discussed.

0762 Payne, Helen E. (1989) "Rites for Sites or Sites for Rites?: The Dynamics of Women's Cultural Life in the Musgraves." In *Women, Rites and Sites: Aboriginal Women's Cultural Knowledge*, edited by P. Brock, 41-59. Sydney: Allen & Unwin.
A convincing examination of Bidjandjadjara women's song knowledge which seeks to overthrow the academic assumption that ownership of songs is identical with ownership of land. Rather, the fluidity of the process and politicking involved is emphasized. Some sites have many songs, and new songs for rites can be dreamt, hence a 1:1 relationship of site:song is unrealistic. Also includes sections on relationships between men and women's rites, and changes over time.

0763 White, Isobel M. (1975) "Sexual Conquest and Submission in the Myths of Central Australia." In *Australian Aboriginal Mythology*, edited by L.R. Hiatt, 123-142. Canberra: Australian Institute of Aboriginal Studies.
A somewhat simplistic discussion of violent sexual encounters in desert mythology. Although there are differences between women and men's myths, both are said to reflect the sexual values of male dominance. This is linked to feminist studies and a dilemma for those who would uplift the lot of Aboriginal women: to do so would necessitate undermining the religious order they hold so reverently.

See also: 0197, 0695, 0699.

Magic

0764 Odermann, Gisela (1958) "Heilkunde der Njanomada, Nordwest Australien." *Paideuma* 6: 411-428.
A general overview of Nyangumarda healing processes. Mythical traditions associated with *Djanba* are given, along with processes of sorcery, but most is devoted to healing, including the training of children as healers, therapeutic magic, and the practice and function of traditional doctors. A list of medical terms is provided, along with remedies and particular treatments to be used after circumcision, subincision and cicatrization.

0765 Tonkinson, Myrna (1982) "The Mabarn and the Hospital: The Selection
      of Treatment in a Remote Aboriginal Community." In *Body, Land and
      Spirit: Health and Healing in Aboriginal Society*, edited by J. Reid, 225-
      241. St. Lucia: University of Queensland Press.
Examines factors linfluencing choice between the *maban* (traditional healer) and
European health service at Jigalong (convenience, privacy, community support,
etc.), and concludes that the *maban* is more readily understood, is given credit
for remarkable cures and alone is capable of countering sorcery. Describes the
maban's training, treatment, diagnosis, clientele and payment.

See also: 0221, 0626, 0630.

Death

0766 Berndt, Ronald M. and Johnston, T. Harvey (1942) "Death, Burial and
      Associated Ritual at Ooldea, South Australia." *Oceania* 12,3: 189-208.
A brief description of sorcery causing death is followed by various cases of
burial among the Antakirinya. Also discusses inquests to determine cause of
death and consequent revenge expeditions, as well as beliefs concerning the fate
of the spirit.

0767 Elkin, A.P. (1937) "Beliefs and Practices Connected with Death in
      North-Eastern and Western South Australia." *Oceania* 7,3: 275-299.
A brief, incomplete overview of mortuary beliefs and practices from the
Mandjindja in the west and the Pangkala in the south. Based on Elkin's own
observations in 1930 (in which no deaths and only one burial occurred) as well
as the reports of earlier ethnographers. Covers burial, inquest, ritual
cannibalism, mortuary song, 'soul' concepts, revenge expeditions etc. Very
summary.

See also: 0226, 0759.

Change

0768 Rose, Frederick G.G. (1965) *The Wind of Change in Central Australia:
      The Aborigines at Angus Downs, 1962.* Berlin: Akademie. 382 pp.
Looks at change among the Bidjandjadjara at Angus Downs from a materialist
perspective. Argues ideology is more resilient than the economic base upon
which it was originally founded. This is attributed to a time lag in
superstructural change. Some religious innovations are noted, however.
Interesting are references to pearlshell cult objects incised with playing card
motifs and to cargoistic ideology.

0769 Rose, Frederick G.G. (1968) *Australia Revisited: The Aborigines' Story
      from Stone Age to Space Age.* Berlin: Seven Seas. 277 pp.

Pages 239-250 have brief details on new iconography and ceremony, an alleged would-be cargo-cult, and the impact of Christianity.

0770 Sackett, Lee (1977) "Liquor and the Law." In *Aborigines and Change: Australia in the '70s*, edited by R.M. Berndt, 90-99. Canberra: Australian Institute of Aboriginal Studies.
How do the Aboriginal people of Wiluna (predominantly Mardudjara) cope with a phenomenon like alcohol which has no Dreaming sanction? To amend the Law to regulate alcohol consumption would undermine its primordial authority, but by retaining the Law in its pristine state there is no way to regulate drunkenness, which, by disrupting ritual life, will in turn destroy the Law. A dilemma more academic than Aboriginal.

0771 Tonkinson, Robert (1982) "Outside the Power of the Dreaming: Paternalism and Permissiveness in an Aboriginal Settlement." In *Aboriginal Power in Australian Society*, edited by M.C. Howard, 115-130. St. Lucia: University of Queensland Press.
Looks at problems arising at Jigalong from government policies of self-determination. In previous eras it was possible to separate 'Whitefella' power, focused in the 'mission', and Aboriginal power, seen as residing in the Dreaming, tapped by ritual processes and personified by the 'camp'. Policy changes attempted to merge the two spheres by inducing Aborigines to take responsibility for the 'mission' domain. Examines strategies adopted to resolve this problem.

0772 Wallace, Noel M. (1977) "Change in Spiritual and Ritual Life in Pitjantjatjara (Bidjandjadjara) Society, 1966 to 1973." In *Aborigines and Change: Australia in the '70s*, edited by R.M. Berndt, 74-89. Canberra: Australian Institute of Aboriginal Studies.
Attempts to determine the degree and nature of change to Bidjandjadjara ritual life from 1966-1973. Emphasis is placed upon initiation ceremonies, but there are also discussions of 'Red Ochre Business', 'increase' rituals and a note on *Yaritjiti*. Concludes the imposed withdrawal of children from traditional religious activities has led to a diminished quality of ritual involvement in spiritual life.

See also: 0637, 0638, 0639, 0643, 0707, 0744, 0749, 0754, 0765.

Literature See 0248.

11

Central Desert

Mudbara

Kukatja   Djingilu

Waramanga

Wagaja

Waljbiri

Gaididja

Aljawara

Luridja

Aranda

Anmatjera

Kokata

General

0773   Bjerre, Jens (1956) *The Last Cannibals*. London: Joseph. 192 pp.
Contains superficial, voyeuristic observations of Waljbiri initiation (male and female), conception beliefs, ritual and magic.

0774   Capell, Arthur   (1952)   "The Wailbri Through Their Own Eyes."
         Oceania 23,2: 110-132.
An early study of the Waljbiri relying heavily on Aboriginal texts, which are transcribed and translated.   Focuses on religious themes, such as initiation, medicine men, rain-making, the Dreaming, rituals and myths, which are covered very briefly and at best are supplementary to the later works of Meggitt (0799) and Munn (0840).

0775   Chewings, Charles (1936) *Back in the Stone Age: The Natives of Central
         Australia*. Sydney: Angus and Robertson. 161 pp.
Dated, superficial observations, mainly of Aranda.   Contains references to myths, magic, conception beliefs and mourning.

0776   Gillen, Francis J. (1896) "Notes on Some Manners and Customs of the
         Aborigines of the McDonnel Ranges Belonging to the Arunta Tribe." In
         Report of the Work of the Horn Scientific Expedition to Central Australia,
         edited by W.B. Spencer, Vol. 4, 161-186. London: Dalau.
Gillen's first publication on the Aranda.   Contains information on rites of passage, 'increase' ceremonies, magic and sorcery, *tjurunga*, etc.   In light of Spencer and Gillen's later critique of All-Father beliefs, perhaps the most interesting reference is to the emu-footed *Ulthaana* ('spirit'), a sky-dweller to whom peoples' spirits ascend upon death (p.183).

0777   Gillen, Francis J. (1901) "The Natives of Central Australia." *Royal
         Geographical Society of Australasia, South Australian Branch,
         Proceedings* 4: 17-28.
Contains brief notes on Aranda myth, initiation and magic.

0778   Mathews, R.H. (1901) "Ethnological Notes on the Aboriginal Tribes of
         the Northern Territory." *Proceedings and Transactions of the Royal
         Geographical Society of Australasia, Queensland* 16: 69-90.
Mainly on Central Desert regions of the Northern Territory (and briefly the Central-North) and includes notes from correspondents on initiation, ritual cannibalism, etc.   Superficial.

0779   Meggitt, Mervyn J. (1962) *Desert People: A Study of the Walpiri
         Aborigines of Central Australia*.   London: Angus and Robertson
         Publishers. 338 pp.
An excellent ethnography of the northern Waljbiri.   The focus is on social relationships, and religious phenomena are examined from this perspective. Important religious themes fall outside the scope of the book, but not to be overlooked are chapters with titles such as 'Moieties and Descent Lines'

containing much information on ritual organization. The final two chapters, 'Initiation' and 'Death', contain data on the social processes involved in the rituals.

0780   Meggitt, Mervyn J. (1987) "Walbiri Religion." In *The Encyclopedia of Religion*, edited by M. Eliade, Vol. 15, 323- 327. New York: Macmillan.
A concise overview of Waljbiri religion, largely summarizing 0779. Discusses the concept of Dreaming, the geographic focus of religious life, initiation into lodge cults, the spiritual components of individuals, and death. Neglects Waljbiri women's religious life.

0781   Michaels, Eric (1985) "Constraints on Knowledge in an Economy of Oral Information." *Current Anthropology* 26,4: 505-510.
The introduction of television to central Australia is considered in light of traditional Waljbiri concepts of access to knowledge. Contains a useful discussion of *Kumunjayi* (tabooed names), sacred/secrecy and the place of Dreaming in the process of knowing. Develops a model of society based upon the transmission of information along Dreaming communication tracks.

0782   Penniman, T.K. (1929) "The Arunta Religion." *Sociological Review* 21,1: 20-37.
A summary of Aranda traditions from Spencer and Gillen (0790), arguing that it is based on an impersonal, mana-like numinous force, the misuse of which is governed by taboo. Considers *tjurungas*, cults, totemism, morality, etc. A rather pointless extrapolation from published accounts.

0783   Pink, Olive (1933) "Spirit Ancestors in a Northern Aranda Horde Country." *Oceania* 4,2: 176-186.
Sketchy details of the ancestral significance of certain features of the Aranda landscape. Based on information from one man on a two week "walk-about."

0784   Róheim, Géza (1932) "Psycho-Analysis of Primitive Culture Types." *The International Journal of Psycho-Analysis* 13,1&2: 1-224.
Róheim's first report on the Aranda, Luridja, and Bidjandjadjara, emphasizing psychoanalytic procedures with children and the relationship between sexual practice and castration anxiety. Totemism is discussed in this context (pp.57-73). Rituals are said to reveal two types of symbolic activities: a dance followed by incest, and masturbation followed by dance. "It is all so simple"(p.65).

0785   Róheim, Géza (1932) "Animism and Religion." *The Psychoanalytic Quarterly* 1: 59-112.
Do Aborigines have a religion? Aranda, Bidjandjadjara, Pintubi, Jumu and Luridja 'animism' is discussed and Róheim then concludes (wrongly) that Aboriginal religious life is more an aesthetic pleasure than a 'devout duty' and hence is not truly 'religion'. This is because they have not developed their superego and are still relatively free of the unresolved fears of castration needed to create a fully fledged religion.

0786 Róheim, Géza (1974) *The Riddle of the Sphinx or Human Origins.* New York: Harper Torchbooks. 286 pp.
First published in 1934. Postulates an ontogenic theory of religion based on Aranda, Luridja, Pintubi and other evidence. Aboriginal religion springs from the trauma of witnessing parents copulating and Aboriginal myths, spirits, magic, dreams and, at length, totemism, are all interpreted according to this thesis. The Milky Way, *Waniga*, 'double devils' etc., all relate to the primal scene. Behind the theory is some worthy data.

0787 Róheim, Géza (1974) *Children of the Desert: The Western Tribes of Central Australia: Vol. I,* edited by W. Muensterberger. New York: Basic Books. 262 pp.
A posthumous publication based on notes Róheim thought would form his *magnum opus.* Discusses Aranda, Luridja, Pintubi, Bidjandjadjara, and others. Deals with some religious aspects of sex; *Alknarintja* (lit. 'eyes-turn-away'), threatening androgynous women, are dealt with, as is *Ilindja*, men's love magic. The theoretical approach is Freudian, although this is not always intrusive.

0788 Schmidt, Wilhelm (1908) "Die Steilung der Aranda unter den australischen Stämmen." *Zeitschrift für Ethnologie* 40: 866-901.
Criticizes the *a priori* nature of theories about the Aranda's relative primitiveness and argues in fact (and equally *a priori*) that they reveal a complex historical development. Considers their "atheism", conception beliefs and totems in a veiled Christian diffusionist *apologia.*

0789 Schulze, Louis (1891) "The Aborigines of the Upper and Middle Finke River: Their Habits and Customs, with Introductory Notes on the Physical and Natural-History Features of the Country." *Transactions of the Royal Society of South Australia* 14,11: 210-246.
A missionary's view of the "indolent", "lazy" and "mentally inferior" Aranda (p.219), containing brief notes on sorcery, superstition, "witch-craft" and religion. Useless.

0790 Spencer, W. Baldwin and Gillen, F.J. (1899) *The Native Tribes of Central Australia.* London: Macmillan. 669 pp.
Remains a frequently consulted and valuable source. The bulk is devoted to Aranda religion. Contains chapters on marriage customs and ceremonies, initiation, the *Engwura* fire ceremony, Dreaming myths, medicine men, *kurdaitcha* practice, 'Peculiar Native customs' (which contains a few passing references to women's religious life), and mortuary practice. The descriptions are extensive, detailed and unsensationalistic. Contains many plates of ceremonies. (Cf. 0792).

0791 Spencer, W. Baldwin and Gillen, F.J. (1904) *The Northern Tribes of Central Australia.* London: Macmillan. 784 pp.
Beginning with the Aranda, this book surveys northwards and thence eastwards to the Gulf of Carpentaria. Most detailed on the Waramanga, (especially their fire ceremony), but Gaididja, Anmatjera, Djingilu, Wakaya, Waljbiri, etc., were also studied. There is a wealth of information on totems, *tjurunga*, 'increase'

rites, initiation, magic and clever men, myths, mortuary practice, etc., and over 300 plates. Despite language barriers, it contains pioneering research.

0792 Spencer, W. Baldwin and Gillen, F.J. (1927) *The Arunta: A Study of a Stone Age People*. London: Macmillan. 646 pp.
Written by Spencer (Gillen had died) to oppose the counter-opinion of Aranda religion presented by Strehlow (0794). Relies heavily on one surviving old informant. Chapters on totemism, magic, mortuary practices, *tjurunga*, 'increase' and initiation ceremonies add new material but it is the chapters on the Dreaming (Chaps. 12-14, see also appendix D) which are directed against Strehlow, correctly denying *Altjira* refers to an Aranda God. A mine of information.

0793 Stirling, Edward C. (1896) "Anthropology." In *Report of the Horn Scientific Expedition to Central Australia*, edited by W.B. Spencer, Vol. 4: 1-157. London: Dalau.
A wide-ranging report on the Aranda, Luridja, Gaididja and others, with sections on religious themes such as initiation, totemic organization, rituals, ritual paraphenalia, revenge sorcery, etc. Uneven but provides some useful early data for this region.

0794 Strehlow, Carl (1907) *Die Aranda- und Loritja-Stämme in Zentral-Australien*, 5 vols. Frankfurt: Baer.
A mine of scholarly information largely neglected in Aboriginal studies. Although Strehlow did not witness Aranda and Luridja ceremonies (forbidden on the mission), his linguistic skills by far exceed those of Spencer and Gillen (0790) and others working in the area at that time. Themes covered include totemic myths, lists of totems, totemic cults and ceremonies, conception, initiation, mortuary beliefs and practices, men's and women's magic and medicine. Contains many transcriptions and translations of myths.

0795 Strehlow, T.G.H. (1947) *Aranda Traditions*. Melbourne: Melbourne University Press. 181 pp.
A valuable book containing three large, minimally connected, essays. In the first Strehlow's fine linguistic skills are applied to myths chosen to cover a broad range of themes. Part two focuses on the diversity and variation within Aranda traditions. Finally, there is an important section on 'Tjurunga Ownership' which classifies the frequently oversimplified concept of *tjurunga* and places it within a wider socio-religious context.

0796 Strehlow, T.G.H. (1956) *The Sustaining Ideals of Australian Aboriginal Societies*. Adelaide: Aborigines Advancement League. 15 pp.
Written for the general reader arguing Aboriginal cultures offer many insights into principles of co-operation, mutuality and tolerance that might help a war-torn world. Draws on evidence from Aranda, considering cosmology and totemism, and principles of 'differentiation and co-ordination'. Insightful for its time, and to some extent anticipating current opinion (e.g. Turner 0112).

0797 Strehlow, T.G.H. (1957) "La Gémellité de l'âme humaine dans les croyances en Australie Centrale." *La Tour Saint-Jacques* 11/12: 14-23.
A general introduction to Aranda beliefs and practices considering 'totemic reincarnation', *tjurunga*, magic and other themes better covered in 0795.

0798 Strehlow, T.G.H. (1978) *Central Australian Religion: Personal Monototemism in a Polytotemic Community.* Adelaide: Australian Association for the Study of Religions. 64 pp.
First published as an article in 1964 and is a concise study of Aranda religious life. Briefly describes the chief mythological beings, then shows that although an individual's religious life focuses on a single totem, community unity is maintained by a common spiritual ancestry. Concludes with a plea for a study of Aboriginal society in order to evolve a more enlightened way of facing a convergent human destiny.

0799 Thurnwald, Richard (1927) *Die Eingeborenen Australiens und der Südseeinseln.* Religionsgeschichtliches Lesebuch, Heft 8. Tübingen: J.C.B. Mohr. 48 pp.
Brief selections from C. Strehlow (0794).

0800 Winthuis, Joseph (1928) *Das Zweigeschlecht erwesen bei den Zentralaustraliern und anderen Völkern: Losungsversuch der ethnologischen Hauptprobleme äuf Grund primitiven Denkens.* Leipzig: Hirschfeld. 297 pp.
As androgyny is a very neglected topic in Aboriginal studies, this book, based on the author's fieldwork with the Aranda and Luridja, is of value despite its dated theoretical understandings. Considers 'dual-sex-beings' in art, sacred ritual objects, myth, ritual and totemic traditions. Pioneering, but see, to a lesser extent, Róheim (0787).

See also: 0049, 0056, 0062, 0063, 0066, 0840, 0845, 0865.

Philosophy and Totemism

0801 Chatwin, Bruce (1987) *The Songlines.* London: Jonathan Cape. 293 pp.
An intelligent travel narrative centred in Alice Springs. Chatwin talks with locals and explores publications in an effort to ascertain the nature of songlines criss-crossing the desert. Postulates Aborigines express the universal human disposition to mark out territory and organize a nomadic life through songlines. Not always strictly accurate, at times highly speculative and unacknowledgedly fictious, but nonetheless lucid and thought provoking.

0802 Frazer, James G. (1899) "Observations on Central Australian Totemism." *The Journal of the Anthropological Institute of Great Britain and Ireland* 28: 281-286.
A paper applauding Spencer and Gillen's book (0790) and reaffirming their theory of totemism which Frazer had independently invented. The theory is

totemism originated as a system of co-operative magic to secure a plentiful supply of natural commodities. Of historical interest only.

0803 Glowczewski, Barbara (1987) "Totem, rêve et langage: les Warlpiri du désert central australien." *Ann. Fondation Fyssen* 3: 59-67.
Briefly considers the absence of a nature/culture distinction in Waljbiri language and how all concepts are preserved in *Jukurrpa* (Dreaming) as dream or totem.

0804 Lang, Andrew (1904) "A Theory of Arunta Totemism." *Man* 4: 67-69.
Dull critique of Spencer and Gillen (0808).

0805 Lang, Andrew (1910) "The 'Historicity' of Arunta Traditions." *Man* 10: 118-121.
[Mis]uses Aranda myth to discover possible origins of totemic segmentation.

0806 Nieuwehnhuis, Anton W. (1927) *Die Psychologische Bedeutung des Gruppen-totemismus in Australien.* Leiden: Brill. 50 pp.
Drawing heavily on Aranda data, this booklet examines the 'psychological' dimensions of group totemism. Considers local groups in totemism, associated beliefs, and in particular, the significance of birds. Dated conceptions permeate this essay.

0807 Pink, Olive (1936) "The Landowners in the Northern Division of the Aranda Tribe, Central Australia." *Oceania* 6,3: 275-305.
Examines Aranda land ownership *vis à vis* 'ancestral totemic clans'. Clans are composed of people of common athough indirect descent, from a Dreaming ancestor affiliated with the land and specific totemic species. Covers themes such as totemic myths, conception beliefs, "reincarnation" and the allocation of totems within the context of Aranda marriage regulation. Compare Strehlow (0809).

0808 Spencer, W. Baldwin and Gillen, F.J. (1899) "Some Remarks on Totemism as Applied to Australian Tribes." *The Journal of the Anthropological Institute of Great Britain and Ireland* 28: 275-280.
Draws out some theoretical implications of 0790 in light of Frazer's theories (see 0802). Suggests Aranda totemism is the most primitive in Australia; that totemic groups of the Aranda are *not* exogamous and hence that the social aspect of totemism was a later addition. Totemism thus is a magical institution for securing species proliferation. Totally dated.

0809 Strehlow, T.G.H. (1970) "Geography and the Totemic Landscape in Central Australia: A Functional Study." In *Australian Aboriginal Studies: Modern Studies in the Social Anthropology of the Australian Aborigines*, edited by R.M. Berndt, 92-140. Nedlands, W.A.: University of Western Australia Press.
Focuses on how the totemic view of geography provides the foundations for social authority and control among the Aranda. Examines links between geography, totemism, subsistence, social organization, authority, and punishment. Supernatural beings were transformed into the landscape and people in turn were 'reincarnations' of these beings. The sacred site therefore

became a geographic foundation of both sacred and secular authority and did away with the need for conspicuous governmental institutions.

0810 Thomas, Northcote W. (1904) "Arunta Totemism: A Note on Mr. Lang's Theory." *Man* 4: 99-101.
Response to Lang (0804).

See also: 0078, 0079, 0113, 0781, 0786, 0796, 0798, 0815, 0816, 0837, 0838, 0839, 0840, 0855, 0872, 0895.

Myth

0811 Glowczewski, Barbara (1983) "Viol et involabilité: un myth territorial en Australie centrale." *Cahiers de Littérature Orale* 14 spéc: 125-50.
Analyses the myth of *Wadaingnula*, the Pintubi stranger who violated Waljbiri women and was killed by them. Considers related ceremonies (esp. *Gunadjari* kinship and sites, and discusses the sexual symbolism in this and other myths, such as those associated with the serpent *Yarrapiri* (cf. Mountford 0817).

0812 Leonhardi, M. Freiherr von (1907) "Über einige religiöse und totemistische Vorstellungen der Aranda und Loritja in Zentralaustralien." *Globus* 91,18: 285-90.
Consists substantially of quotations from letters by Carl Strehlow which undermine the views of Spencer and Gillen (esp. 0790). Claims (mistakenly) the latter had misunderstood Aranda informants and hence missed the significance of *Altjira* as a High-God. Also critiques their views on 'reincarnation' and other points.

0813 Maegraith, Brian G. (1932) "The Astronomy of the Aranda and Luritja Tribes." *Transactions of the Royal Society of South Australia*, 56: 19-26.
Contains brief details on Aranda and Luridja stellar myths, covering three regions: the area of the Southern Cross, the constellation of Scorpio, and the Milky Way and adjacent areas.

0814 Merz, Richard (1978) *Die Numinose Mischgestalt: Methodenkritische Untersuchungen zu tiermenschlichen Erscheinungen Altägyptens, der Eiszeit und der Aranda in Australien.* Berlin: Walter de Gruyter. 306 pp.
A comparative study of religious powers manifest through beings of mixed human/animal form among the ancient Egyptians and the Aranda. The extensive Aboriginal section (pp.90-209) is based primarily on the writings of Spencer and Gillen (0790), Carl Strehlow (0794) and T.G.H. Strehlow (e.g. 0795). Besides considering the state of research on Aranda myth, examines stories of ancestors, such as *Altjira*, in terms of their reference to mixed forms.

0815 Morton, John (1987) "Singing Subjects and Sacred Objects: More on Munn's 'Transformations of Subjects into Objects' in Central Australian Myth." *Oceania* 58,2: 100-118.

A re-analysis of Munn 0818, supplemented by Aranda data, to suggest three polarities: between earth's surface and depth, male and female, and life and death. A cycle in which the Dreaming 'depths' are alienated during early life and thence revealed during initiation are advocated and the life-cycle is depicted as homologous with a cycle from earth's depths to surface/sky and back to earth. Rich, high risk, analysis. (See 0816).

0816 Morton, John (1989) "Singing Subjects and Sacred Objects: A Psychological Interpretation of the 'Transformation of Subjects and Objects' in Central Australian Myth." *Oceania* 59,4: 280-298.
Continues 0815. Develops a psychoanalytic framework for exploring the relationships between communication, the body and the landscape in Aranda belief and ceremony. These are seen in terms of the human life-cycle which is said to be oriented towards reconciling a range of oppositions: male and female, earth and sky, life and death, consciousness and unconsciousness, language and speech. Eclectic and slightly lacking in focus.

0817 Mountford, Charles P. (1968) *Winbaraku and the Myth of Jarapiri.* Adelaide: Rigby,.116 pp.
Follows the route of the serpent *Yarrapiri* through Waljbiri country. The illustrations occupy over half the book and the text consists of brief notes on the mythology and topography of the route. Some songs are given in English but with no indication as to whether they are translations of texts. Descriptive without being analytical and the photographs are somewhat repetitious for the general reader.

0818 Munn, Nancy D. (1970) "The Transformation of Subjects into Objects in Walbiri and Pitjantjatjara Myth." In *Australian Aboriginal Studies: Modern Studies in the Social Anthropology of the Australian Aborigines,* edited by R.M. Berndt, 141-163. Nedlands, W.A.: University of Western Australia Press.
A classic study of Waljbiri and Bidjandjadjara myth. Examines the process whereby ancestors (subjects) turned into geographical objects. Deposited in the landscape, therefore, are essences which give birth to humans as subjects once again. This bi-directional transformation means each generation must renew its self-objectification. People thus orient themselves to the world through objects, and objects become socializing agents mediating the individual and collective life.

0819 Newsome, A.E. (1980) "The Eco-Mythology of the Red Kangaroo in Central Australia." *Mankind* 12,4: 327-333.
Aranda totemic sites of red kangaroos are listed and mapped and this is compared with the distribution and habitats of the species. Where the kangaroo ancestors travelled overland is shown to correspond to ecologies suitable to this species. When traversing lands which cannot support kangaroos the ancestors used supernatural modes of movement - underground or airborne.

0820 Róheim, Géza (1934) "Primitive High Gods." *The Psychoanalytic Quarterly* 3,1: 1-133.

Analyses Aranda sky beings in terms of psychoanalytic theory. *Altjira* is argued to have demonic qualities. Related myths, such as that connected with the Milky Way, are transcribed and given an interlineal translation. Refers to connection of sky beings with medicine men and initiation. Concludes the myths revolve around infantile response to 'the primal scene' - Sky Father and Mother Earth are parents in the act of coition.

0821 Strehlow, Carl (1907) "Einige Sagen des Arandastammes in Zentral-
        Australien." *Globus* 92,8: 123-6.
Moon and other myths with transcription and German translation.

0822 Strehlow, T.G.H. (1933) "Ankotarinja, An Aranda Myth." *Oceania* 4,2:
        187-200.
Translations of Aranda myth and songs recounting the exploits of *Ankota* who is decapitated by a *tjurunga* and whose severed head returns home to become a part of the present landscape. The ritual re-enactment of *Ankota's* exploits are described and illustrated. The article confines itself to revealing the essential unity of myth, ritual, song and sacred objects.

0823 Strehlow, T.G.H. (1965) "Aborigines: Myths and Legends: Central
        Australian Myths." In *The Australian Encyclopedia*. 2nd ed., Vol. 1, 55-
        6. Sydney: The Grolier Society.
Describes main features and translates two myths.

0824 Strehlow, T.G.H. (1969) "Mythology of the Centralian Aborigine." *The
        Inland Review* 3,11: 11-17; 3,12: 19-20, 25-28.
Written for the tourist but nonetheless offers useful data on *Uluru* (Ayers Rock), Corroboree rock, Simpson's Gap, Standley Chasm, etc., based on Aranda traditions. Secret data is not included. Emphasizes the influence of cosmogonies on the significance of the entire landscape.

0825 Thomas, Northcote W. (1905) "The Religious Ideas of the Arunta."
        Folk-Lore 16: 428-433.
Points out contradictions between Gillen (0776) and Spencer and Gillen (0790), the latter omitting reference to *Ulthaana* who comes closer to the form of South-East sky heroes. Contains extracts of a letter from Carl Strehlow criticizing Spencer and Gillen's views on *Altjeringa*, etc.

See also: 0120, 0125, 0437, 0443, 0795, 0826, 0831, 0832, 0851.

The Arts

0826 Amadio, Nadine and Kimber, Richard (1988) *Wildbird Dreaming:
        Aboriginal Art from the Central Desert of Australia*. Melbourne:
        Greenhouse Publications. 144 pp.
Contains some lovely plates of Luridja, Waljbiri, Pintubi and Bidjandjadjara art from Papunya, but the text is poor. Part I, by Amadio, is "in no way a book for

academics" (p.7), yet begins with quotations from Lévi-Strauss, Eliade, Jung and Merleau-Ponty, who are not popularized but bastardized into a pop-psychology of Aboriginal art. Kimber's section is better but says little. Both authors focus on myth in art.

0827 Anderson, Christopher and Dussart, Françoise (1988) "Dreaming in Acrylic: Western Desert Art." In *Dreamings: The Art of Aboriginal Australia*, edited by P. Sutton, 89-143. Ringwood: Viking.
Despite its title, this article, while addressing Western Desert examples, draws mainly on Waljbiri (Central Desert) traditions from Yuendumu. Provides a serviceable account of interrelations between art, social groups and religious life, but in terms of exegesis does not have the depth of, for instance, Munn's work (0840).

0828 Dubinskas, Frank A. and Traweek, Sharon (1984) "Closer to the Ground: A Reinterpretation of Walpiri Iconography." *Man* NS 19,1: 15-30.
Attempts to strip Munn (0840) of her 'dualistic' 'structuralistic' orientation in order to circumvent her alleged embeddedness in Western thought. Nonetheless, relies heavily on Munn's categories throughout: her interpretations of *Jukurrpa* (Dreaming) and *guruwari* (designs), and her examples of sand stories, dreaming designs and 'increase' ceremonies. It is difficult to conceive how the authors' could recreate Waljbiri understanding through a 'misconstructed' ethnographic text.

0829 Ellis, Catherine J. (1964) *Aboriginal Music Making: A Study of Central Australian Music*. Adelaide: Libraries Board of South Australia. 373 pp.
Begins with brief notes on Aranda religious beliefs before presenting a range of song cycle sections. Insights into meaning and ritual context are drawn from published and unpublished material by T.G.H. Strehlow. There are comparisons with songs from elsewhere in Australia and a concluding chapter looks at Aboriginal songs in mission and settlement contexts.

0830 Ellis, Catherine J. (1969) "Structure and Significance in Aboriginal Song." *Mankind* 7,1: 3-14.
Examines the communication process in Aranda music. A basic series of notes identifies a song with an ancestor and it is this melodic contour which identifies a song. In total, songs convey emotional and spiritual experiences associated with a totemic ancestor and site. Strategies for ensuring accurate and efficacious songs are discussed. Less convincing are spectaculations on the effects rhythms have on brain functions.

0831 Mountford, Charles P. (1937) "Aboriginal Crayon Drawings Relating to Totemic Places belonging to the Northern Aranda Tribe of Central Australia." *Transactions and Proceedings of the Royal Society of South Australia* 61: 84-95.
Records 17 Aranda crayon drawings by Padika who would only explain their meaning in the presence of T.G.H. Strehlow, who acted as interpreter. The stories refer to totemic centres related to nine ancestral beings. Padika's

interpretations are recorded and similar myths from existing literature are noted. Comments are made on the style of the drawings and their relation to those of *tjurunga*.

0832 Mountford, Charles P. and Walsh, Gwen (1943) "A Stone Tjurunga of Unusual Form from the Aranda Tribe of Central Australia." *Mankind* 3,4: 113-115.
Brief notes on the mythic significance of the design on a *tjurunga*.

0833 Moyle, Richard M. (1983) "Songs, Ceremonies and Sites: The Agharringa Case." In *Aborigines, Land and Land Rights*, edited by N. Peterson and M. Langton, 66-93. Canberra: Australian Institute of Aboriginal Studies.
An important study of Dreaming track ownership. Focuses on a portion of Aljawara land called Agharringa country. Although Moyle's research centres on music, he reminds that all songs are associated with ceremonies on the one hand, and with ancestral events which occurred at specific places on the other. The song-ceremony owners thus also own the sites associated wtih the Dreaming myth (but cf. 0762)..

0834 Moyle, Richard M. (1984) "Jumping to Conclusions." In *Problems and Solutions: Occasional Essays in Musicology Presented to Alice M. Moyle*, edited by J.C. Kassler and J. Stubington, 51-58. Sydney: Hale and Iremonger.
Examines how the Kukatja co-ordinate men's and women's activities in the *Kurtitji* ceremonies for initiating youths. The women's calls and shuffling dances do not coincide with the accompanying men's singing and Moyle argues that synchronism in fact exists in the silences between calls and dance movements. A brief synopsis of the ceremony is given.

0835 Moyle, Richard M. (1986) *Alyawarra Music: Songs and Society in a Central Australian Community*. Canberra: Australian Institute of Aboriginal Studies. 271pp.
Considers both the musical and ceremonial nature of songs. Useful introductory chapters on Aljawara religious concepts, ownership of ceremonies and dreaming tracks are followed by classifications and descriptions of ritual contexts of songs. *Yawalyu* (women's ceremonies) are covered in detail and there is an solid chapter devoted to initiation. There are also brief notes on 'increase' ceremonies, public rituals and 'charms'.

0836 Munn, Nancy D. (1962) "Walbiri Graphic Signs: An Analysis." *American Anthropologist* 64,5: 972-984.
Three Waljbiri figure types are described: the site-path, associated with ancestral travels in the country; the actor-item related to activities in the camp and ceremonial ground; and the trail-footprint referring either to animals or the marks of shape-changing ancestors. The implications of this approach are not realized here, but see 0839 and 0840.

0837 Munn, Nancy D. (1964) "Totemic Designs and Group Continuity in Walbiri Cosmology." In *Aborigines Now: New Perspectives in the Study of Aboriginal Communities*, edited by M. Reay, 83-100. Sydney: Angus and Robertson.
Discusses the relationship between totemic designs and country, dreams and Dreaming in the maintenance of Waljbiri socio-cultural order. Establishes a series of polarities in the iconography - inside: outside, dreams: waking life, conception: birth, life: death - all of which are metaphorical projections of the relationship between the ancestral past and the present. Waljbiri identity is thus maintained through totemic designs and their Dreaming affiliation.

0838 Munn, Nancy D. (1968) "Visual Categories: An Approach to the Study of Representational Systems." *American Anthropologist* 68,4: 936-950.
Waljbiri totemic designs are said to combine elements in such a way as to classify totemic species in terms of similarities and differences (cf.Lévi-Strauss, 0097). Studying these, it is argued, opens the way for cross-cultural investigation of art in terms of structural configurations rather than stylistic dimensions. Speculative and programmatic.

0839 Munn, Nancy D. (1973) "The Spatial Presentation of Cosmic Order in Walbiri Iconography." In *Primitive Art and Society*, edited by A. Forge, 193-220. London: Oxford University Press.
Examines key motifs in a Waljbiri 'world theory' based on the polarity of 'coming out' and 'going in'. The circle is the fertile site where the ancestral essences 'went in', and is associated with women's childbearing bodies. In contrast, the line is masculine and conveys mobility in space along trails between sites. Time too is involved as the past is made available to the present through the coming out and going in cycle. There is thus a continuity between the inside and outside of country and its past and present.

0840 Munn, Nancy D. (1973) *Walbiri Iconography: Graphic Representation and Cultural Symbolism in a Central Australian Society*. Ithaca: Cornell University Press. 234 pp.
Provides an intelligent but sometimes dubious analysis of Waljbiri 'sand stories', men's and women's designs and key concepts in Waljbiri religious thought. Polarizes the social, procreative, symbol-fabricating role of men and the personal, biological, family maintenance role of women. At the iconographic level, this is represented in the binary relationship of the circle (representing the female/camp) and the line (equals male/trade). Design imagery thus forms a basis for the maintenance of the "experience of unity and differentiation in the social order."

0841 Peterson, Nicolas (1981) "Art of the Desert." In *Aboriginal Australia*, by C. Cooper; H. Morphy; J. Mulvaney; and N. Peterson, 43-51. Sydney: Australia Gallery Directors Council.
Very much in the tradition of Munn (0840), summarizing Desert (mainly Waljbiri and Aranda) art, but adding little that is new. Accurate, nonetheless.

0842   Stanton, John E. (1987) "Tjurungas." In *The Encyclopedia of Religion*, edited by M. Eliade, Vol. 14, 539-542. New York: Macmillan.
Brief overview of the mythic origin, human manufacture and ritual use of *tjurunga*. Aranda data is central to his exposition.

0843   Strehlow, T.G.H. (1964) "The Art of Circle, Line and Square." In *Australian Aboriginal Art*, edited by R.M. Berndt, 44-59. Sydney: Ure Smith.
Stresses Aboriginal art is always religious and provides a general discussion of central Australian, particularly Aranda, belief and ritual. Examines how a simple repertoire of artistic motifs can be used in a variety of artistic forms (ground painting, body decoration, totem poles and *tjurunga*) to depict totemic emblems. Concludes with comments on the diffusion of central Australian iconography and its fate in a colonial context.

0844   Strehlow, T.G.H. (1965) "Aborigines: Music, Poetry, Song: Central Australian Songs." In *The Australian Encyclopedia*. 2nd ed., Vol. 1, 61-2. Sydney: The Grolier Society.
Brief samples of Aranda song and a classification of chants.

0845   Strehlow, T.G.H. (1971) *Songs of Central Australia*. Sydney: Angus and Robertson. 775 pp.
A unique, monumental book dealing with Aranda songs. The third section (some 400 pages) considers the essentially religious nature of the songs. Subjects include charms to heal and injure, 'increase' ceremony songs, commemorative songs, initiation songs, love charms, women's songs and chants dealing with death. No one could seriously question Strehlow's linguistic skills and if there is any fault to be found with this volume it is its intrusive and unnecessary comparisons with early Germanic, Scandinavian and English poetry.

0846   Wild, Stephen A. (1984) "Warlpiri Music and Culture: Meaning in a Central Australian Song Series." In *Problems and Solutions: Occasional Essays in Musicology Presented to Alice M. Moyle*, edited by J.C. Kassler and J. Stubington, 186-203. Sydney: Hale and Iremonger.
Analyses a Waljbiri yam *Purlapa* (public ritual) in terms of song text, rhythm, accompaniment, melody and performance. Looks at three 'themes' in the songs: their non-developmental character, their context as an arena allowing for individual assertiveness, and their inherent male/female relationship. Argues music embodies fundamental characteristics of the wider culture.

0847   Wild, Stephen A. (1987) "Recreating the *Jukurrpa*: Adaptation and Innovation of Songs and Ceremonies in Warlpiri Society." In *Songs of Aboriginal Australia*, edited by M. Clunies Ross; T. Donaldson; and S.A. Wild, 97-120. Sydney: Oceania Monographs.
While set in the context of European-Waljbiri contact, the author devotes less attention to specifically European-influenced change than to the process of innovation within traditional cosmology. Rights to land are discussed along with the taxonomy of ritual song, before examining how new songs and rituals are

received from the Dreaming. The final pages consider new religious movements in the region.

See also: 0161, 0166, 0795, 0817.

Ceremony

0848 Kimber, R.G. and Smith, M.A. (1987) "An Aranda Ceremony." In *Australians to 1788*, edited by D.J. Mulvaney and J.P. White, 221-237. Sydney: Fairfax, Syme and Weldon.
Based largely on stories told to Richard Kimber by Walter Smith, an Arabana man instructed in Aranda ritual. The style is popularized and the events in narrative range from fires signalling the time for ceremonies, through to travel to the ritual ground and a non-description of 'an Aranda ceremony'. The focus is more on the political and economic demands made by collective ceremonial life and detail is notable by its absence.

0849 Malinowski, Bronislaw (1912) "The Economic Aspect of Intichiuma Ceremonies." In *Festskrift tillegrad Edvard Westermark*, 81-108. Helsingfors.
"Savages", says Malinowski, play at work and economics thus requires exciting motivation. Aranda *Intichiuma* (based on Spencer and Gillen 0790) actually involve a great deal of economic activity and hence totemic ceremonies are a highly developed form of labour. Appeals to Durkheim's early (pre-0079) view of religion as constrained thought and behaviour to suggest totemic ideas educate in economic utility. Very unsatisfying.

0850 Meggitt, Mervyn J. (1955) "Notes on the Malngjin and Gurindji Aborigines of Limbunya, N.W. Northern Territory." *Mankind* 5,2: 45-50.
Brief notes on initiation, *Gadjeri* (see Meggitt 0851), rain-making and other rituals.

0851 Meggitt, Mervyn J. (1966) *Gadjari Among the Walbiri Aborigines of Central Australia*. The Oceania Monographs No. 14. Sydney: The University of Sydney. 129 pp.
A comprehensive study of the Waljbiri *Mamandabari* or *Gadjeri* related to both the Arnhem Land *Kunapipi* (see Berndt 0481) and Aranda *Ingkura* (Spencer and Gillen 0790). Meggitt details the similarities and differences (pp.78-93). The *Mamandabari* myth is related in detail followed by a full description of the then annual ritual of the Northern Waljbiri at Lajamanu (Hooker Creek). The final section is an appendix containing some important Waljbiri myths.

0852 Morton, John (1987) "The Effectiveness of Totemism: 'Increase Ritual' and Resource Control in Central Australia." *Man* NS 22: 453-474.
A re-analysis of published accounts of Aranda 'increase' rites, marrying Durkheim with Lacan to suggest the rites' main consequences are psychological

rather than environmental/ecological. Rites as a form of sacrifice and the symbolic death of the ancestral father are stressed as means for controlling reproduction within the social and natural worlds. All are expressions of individual autonomy within the constraints of ancestral authority.

0853   Peterson, Nicolas (1969) "Secular and Ritual Links: Two Basic and Opposed Principles of Australian Social Organisation as Illustrated by Walbiri Ethnography." *Mankind* 7: 27-35.
Argues the Waljbiri distinguish between secular rights, transmitted through women, and ritual rights, inherited through men. Discusses beliefs about procreation and people's dual patri and matri spirits and then articulates the tension between the two types of rights in *Banba* (Lodge ceremonies), initiation and Fire ceremonies. Contrary to previous opinion, maintains patrilines act as a corporate group only in the domain of ritual.

0854   Peterson, Nicolas (1970) "Buluwandi: A Central Australian Ceremony for the Resolution of Conflict." In *Australian Aboriginal Studies: Modern Studies in the Social Anthropology of the Australian Aborigines*, edited by R.M. Berndt, 200-215. Nedlands, W.A.: University of Western Australia Press.
Ceremonies involving self-inflicted burns were first recorded by Spencer and Gillen (0855). Peterson provides an analysis of a Waljbiri version, known as *Buluwandi*. Its mythology relates to a stork, who at various stages transforms into a snake, owl, cockatoo and bird. Throughout the description, emphasis is on social interaction. Suggests the ritual is a means for resolving conflict of interests between patrikin and matrikin over the bestowal of women.

0855   Spencer, W. Baldwin and Gillen, F.J. (1897) "An Account of the Engwurra or Fire Ceremony of Certain Central Australian Tribes." *Proceedings of the Royal Society of Victoria* 10: 17-28.
Briefly documents the Aranda *Engwurra* fire ceremony. It is said to be instigated to test the endurance of young men and to impart secrets to them. Much of the paper is taken up with discussion of totem inheritance and the relationship between totems and mythic ancestors, sacred objects and rites. Skirts important issues. (See 0790; chapters 8 and 9 for a fuller account.)

0856   Wild, Stephen A. (1977-8) "Men as Women: Female Dance Symbolism in Walbiri Men's Rituals." *Dance Research Journal* 10,1: 14-22.
Examines Waljbiri rites employing female symbolism. In particular, *Gadjeri* (see 0851) and the circumcision Blood Dance are discussed. Concludes that when men dance in women's styles it is part of a symbolic celebration of the complementarity of sex roles and, futher, a partial symbolic appropriation of women's procreative and nurturing roles. This is done by ritually inducting novices into the spiritual domain of fertility.

See also: 0172, 0741, 0745, 0784, 0811, 0833, 0835, 0846.

Birth

0857 Crawley, Marjorie (1983) "Aboriginal Beliefs and Reincarnation."
   Religious Traditions 6:1-29.
Attempts to argue for an Aranda doctrine of 'reincarnation' primarily through
the writings of T.G.H. Strehlow (0795, 0798). To some extent the issue is
semantic, but there is also a misplaced concern to align Aranta and Indian
thought - thus "*karma* is applicable for the individual Aranda man. For him, life
is determined according to the activities and choices he exercized in his previous
existence as the ancestor"(p.17). Such speculation is hardly credible.

0858 Fry, H. K. (1933) "Body and Soul: A Study from Western Central
   Australia." *Oceania* 3,3: 247-256.
A sketchy attempt to generalize regarding Pintubi, Luridja, and Aranda views of
the origins of the human body and the place of sexual intercourse as a
contributing factor. The evidence is incomplete and there is little on the origins
of the spirit.

See also: 0180, 0181, 0615, 0853, 0879.

Initiation

0859 Cawte, John E. (1968) "Further Comment on the Australian Subincision
   Ceremony." *American Anthropologist* 70: 961-964.
Corrects Singer and De Sole (0190) with Waljbiri photographic evidence.

0860 Cawte, John E.; Djagamara, N.; and Barrett, M.J. (1966) "The Meaning
   of Subincision of the Urethra to Aboriginal Australians." *British Journal
   of Medical Psychology* 39: 245-253.
Tests theories of the function of subincision against the opinions of Waljbiri men.
The theories are: Law; hygene; rite of passage; sign of rank; source of ritual
blood; sexual stimulation; to alter urinary position; contraception; and to
simulate women's genitals. Some of these are flatly rejected (contraception),
some acknowledged, while others are only weakly asserted (female simulation).
Custom or Law are the main reasons given and several relevant myths are
related.

0861 Hawte, Ian V. (1954) "An Account of the Ngalia Initiation Ceremonies
   of Yuendumu, Central Australia." *Royal Society of South Australia,
   Transactions* 77: 175-181.
Brief description of overt action in Waljbiri initiation.

0862 Spencer, W. Baldwin and Gillen, F.J. (1897) "Notes on Certain of the
   Initiation Ceremonies of the Arunta Tribe, Central Australia."
   Proceedings of the Royal Society of Victoria 10: 142-174.
Divides Arunta initiation into 4 types. The first, briefly mentioned, is the tossing
ceremony, *Alkirakiwuma*. The second, *Lartna* or circumcision, is documented

in detail and while meaning is not well understood, the quality of observation is high. Thirdly, subincision or *Ariltha* ceremonies are described. The fourth rite, *Engwurra* or fire ceremony is omitted, referring to 0855.

See also: 0189, 0779, 0834, 0835, 0879.

Women

0863 Bell, Diane (1981) "Women's Business is Hard Work: Central Australian Aboriginal Women's Love Rituals." *Signs: Journal of Women in Culture and Society* 7,2: 314-337.
Examines the implications of Gaididja women's *Yilpinji* (love) rituals for understanding gender relations. Suggests women have a distinct and autonomous ritual tradition related to country and mythology. Emphasizes that *Yilpinji* rituals support 'correct' marriages but not men's individual marriage agendas. In a changing context, however, autonomy is undermined by the White norm of male political domination.

0864 Bell, Diane (I982) "Women's Changing Role in Health Maintenance in a Central Australian Community." In *Body, Land and Spirit: Health and Healing in Aboriginal Society*, edited by J. Reid, 197-224. St. Lucia: University of Queensland Press.
Argues that while Gaididja women's traditional ceremonies focused on the well-being of society during life crises - birth, death, menarche, etc. - today they focus on resolution of conflict in larger groups and their nurturing role now draws on different aspects of their ritual repertoire. Locates health within the parameters of Dreaming and considers women's rites of passage and *Yawalyu* rituals.

0865 Bell, Diane (1983) *Daughters of the Dreaming.* Melbourne and Sydney: McPhee Gribble and George Allen & Unwin. 297 pp.
An important study of Waljbiri and Gaididja women, discussing Dreaming, *Yawalyu* ceremonies and women's healing and 'love magic' practices. Also analyses the reciprocal roles of women and men and their co-operation in following a single Law. There is a good study of the neglected topic of the responsibility of women in the initiation of young boys. Depicts the relations between the sexes as an ever-shifting, negotiable balance in which women's rituals are central.

0866 Bell, Diane and Ditton, Pam (1980) *Law: The Old and the New: Aboriginal Women in Central Australia Speak Out.* Canberra: Aboriginal History. 129 pp.
Based on transcripts of Aboriginal women speaking on their Law in contemporary central Australian communities. The sections on customary Law has useful references to women's ritual status and the effect of contact upon it. Useful data on Aboriginal women's evalution of the socio-religous value of the new (Western) Law.

0867 Dussart, Françoise (1988) "Notes on Warlpiri Women's Personal Names." *Océanistes* 86,1: 53-60.
The first exploration of Aboriginal women's names, using data from the Waljbiri. Explains the link between names and Dreaming, the revelation of names in dreams and their acquisition by other means. Suggest names are manifestations of ancestors which locate individuals within the ancestors' socio-religious realm. The process of naming is thus seen as a *rite de passage.*

0868 Glowczewski, Barbara (1981) "Affaire de femmes ou femmes d'affaires: Les Walpiri du Central Australien." *Journal de la Society des Oceanistes* 37,70-1: 77-91.
Develops a model of women's roles in maintaining Waljbiri society and cosmology. Considers women's participation in the regulation of society through land affiliations, kinship and totemic systems; their fertility cults, their participation in the initiation of males, and their reciprocal role with men in mortuary ritual and in versions of the *Gadjeri* myth. (Cf. Bell 0865).

0869 Glowczewski, Barbara (1983) "Death, Women and 'Value Production': The Circulation of Hair Strings among the Warlpiri of the Central Australian Desert." *Ethnology* 22,3: 225-289.
Argues goods created by Waljbiri women play a determining role in social reproduction and analyses this by looking at the place of hair string in the period after death. Shows that men's ceremonies would be meaningless without women's complementary ceremonies. Hair string keeps sons, daughters, etc., socially alive, even when they are physically dead and in this process women are essential.

0870 Hellbusch, Sigrid (1941) "Die Frauen bei den Aranda." *Zeitschrift für Ethnologie* 73: 71-87.
A paper derived from notes taken by a missionary (Wettengel) about Aranda women's life. Contains information on bodily scarification, conception beliefs, naming, ritual paraphenalia, initiation, and myths. References to matriarchy are certainly confused.

0871 Róheim, Géza (1933) "Women and Their Life in Central Australia." *Journal of the Royal Anthropological Institute of Great Britain and Ireland* 63: 207-265.
Contains some pioneering information on Aranda and Luridja women including their magic, myths, ideas on conception, taboos, songs and ceremonies. Some women's songs are translated. Róheim's analysis, however, is entirely at odds with current opinion. He argues women are virtually devoid of religion and that their beliefs primarily concern fearful demons symbolizing an incestuous desire for their fathers.

0872 Yeatman, Anna (1983) "The Procreative Model: The Social Ontological Bases of the Gender-Kinship System." *Social Analysis* 14:3-30. "Comments" and "Reply" 16(1984): 3-43.

A thought-provoking article relying heavily on Waljbiri data. Examines myth, kinship and gender, or, more accurately, argues these all belong to one domain of inquiry. Her thesis is that gender classification arises out of a specific type of social ontology which she calls "the procreative model", i.e. a model of social life which is based on the idea of parentage. Attempts to show the domains of myth, kinship and gender belong together and are grounded in that ontology.

See also: 0192, 0835, 0840, 0878, 0912.

Magic

0873 Barrett, M.J. (1964) "Walbiri Customs and Beliefs Concerning Teeth." *Mankind* 6,3: 95-100.
Brief notes on the role of the snakes *wilki ngarunu*, which cause toothache. Includes a version of the associated Waljbiri myth and some chants and other techniques used in the cure of toothache. See Strehlow (0882).

0874 Byrne, P.M. (1896) "Notes on the Customs Connected with the use of So-Called Kurdaitch Shoes of Central Australia." *Royal Society of Victoria, Proceedings* 5,8: 65-68.
Notes on revenge sorcery .

0875 Cawte, John E. (1965) "Aboriginal Medicine Men: Stone-Age Relic?" *Sandorama* Dec: 19-21.
Brief notes on Waljbiri doctors.

0876 Cawte, John E. (1965) "Ethnopsychiatry in Central Australia: I: 'Traditional' Illnesses in the Eastern Aranda People." *The British Journal of Psychiatry* 3: 1069-1077.
An examination of mental illnesses of the Aljawara, Waljbiri, Waramanga, Gaididja and Aranda. Argues that despite 50 years of contact traditional illnesses are still important. Explanations of sickness and in particular the role of 'assistant totems' and *wilaiba* ('devil animals') are discussed. Adding 'assimilation' disorders to traditional ones, Cawte concludes this is a 'sick society'.

0877 Cawte, John E. and Kinson, M.A. (1964) "Australian Ethnopsychiatry: The Walbiri Doctor." *The Medical Journal of Australia* 2: 977-983.
A useful overview of Waljbiri healers discussing *mabanba*, small beings dwelling in the doctor's body and give him power. Traditional causes of illness are detailed, including the activities of several kinds of malevolent spirits; sorcery; the moral warnings of *millelba*; and the *Djanba* who, contrasting with the northern Waljbiri view (Meggitt 0881) are men who carry out judicial incantations and executions.

0878 Devanesen, Dayalan (1985) "Traditional Aboriginal Medicine and the Bicultural Approach to Health Care in Australia's Northern Territory."

In *Alcohol and Drug Use in a Changing Society: Proceedings of the 2nd National Drug Institute*, edited by K.P. Larkins, D. McDonald and C. Watson, 33-41. Canberra: Alcohol and Drug Foundation.
Brief notes on Waljbiri healers and women's ceremonies in a changing context.

0879 Gillen, Francis J. (1900) "Magic Amongst the Natives of Central Australia." *Australian and New Zealand Association for the Advancement of Science, Report* 8: 109-123.
Compressed notes on Aranda magic and related beliefs and practices. Magic - "the attempt to produce results by the aid of some occult or superhuman agency" (p.109) here subsumes spirit and conception beliefs, the process of birth, childhood and initiation as well as the more obvious themes of sorcery, disease and *Kurdaitcha*. Training, healing and associated totems are mentioned, and men and women's love magic described. Useful despite its age and prejudices.

0880 Kitching, H.S. (1961) "Observations of Customs Associated with Kadaitja Practices in Central Australia." *Oceania* 31,3: 210-214.
A brief paper on the role of *Kurdaitcha* which dispels a few erroneous views in the literature.

0881 Meggitt, Mervyn J. (1955) "Djanba Among the Walbiri, Central Australia." *Anthropos* 50: 375-403.
A response to issues surrounding *Djanba* cults reported by Lommel (0646), Petri (0218), and Worms (0596). A description of the malevolent beings, their homes, associated myths, attributes and habits, is followed by an account of their role as killers and the attempts of traditional doctors to counter their harm. Concludes by stressing that Waljbiri *Djanba* are dissociated with the Kimberley rituals, and neither usurp traditional roles nor predict a radical change in world order.

0882 Strehlow, T.G.H. (1964) "Commentary on the Magic Beliefs Described in M.J. Barrett's 'Walbiri Customs and Beliefs Concerning Teeth'. *Mankind* 6,3: 100-105.
Additional notes to Barrett (0873). Indicates internal contradiction in Barrett's informants' account, attributed to the breakdown in traditional religious life. Adds translation for Barrett's recordings and offers comparative observations from Aranda evidence.

See also: 0209, 0864.

Change

0883 Glowczewski, Barabara (1984) "Manifestations Symboliques D'une Transition Économique: Le 'Juluru', Culte Intertribal du 'Cargo'." *L'Homme* 23,3: 7-35.
One of two published accounts of a most innovative religious cult (see Kolig 0640). Notes its dual origin from a dream of a Port Hedland man about a shipwreck and from a Broome woman's dream following bombings. The two

versions are shown to be linked with the establishment of a new Law embodied in three 'tables' representing food, transport and books of Law. This cargoistic orientation is located in the wider process of mobilizing inter-'tribal' confederations.

0884 Kunoth-Monks, Rose (1987) "Church and Culture: An Aboriginal Perspective." In *The Gospel is Not Western: Black Theologies from the Southwest Pacific*, edited by G.W. Trompf, 38-41. New York: Orbis.
A conservative view of the relationship between Christian and traditional religious life by an Aboriginal woman raised under the Hermannsburg mission régime. Refers specifically to Aranda and Anmatjera contexts. Distinguishes religious and social aspects of traditional religious life and claims only the former is incompatible with Christianity.

0885 Swain, Tony (1988) "The Ghost of Space: Reflections on Warlpiri Christian Iconography and Ritual." In *Aboriginal Australians and Christian Missions: Ethnographic and Historical Studies*, edited by T. Swain and D. Rose, 452-469. Adelaide: Australian Association for the Study of Religions.
Examines concepts of time, space and place in Waljbiri Christian rituals and designs. Traditional art forms are shown to be concerned with specific places and to some extent Christian beliefs are re-interpreted in this way. But the Western Christian notion of a universal belief system and the consequent view of space are demonstrated to have intruded into some domains. Argues that the Waljbiri have tried to ally the ideas of universal traditions with localized ones.

See also: 0847, 0864, 0866.

L. Literature See 0248

12

Lake Eyre

Marulta

Wongkanguru

Jauraworka

Wongkumara

Dieri

Maljangapa

Arabana

Adnyamathanha

Gujani

Pangkala

Ngadjuri

Kaurna

Narangga

General

0886 Berndt, Ronald M. (1953) "A Day in the Life of a Dieri Man Before
Alien Contact." *Anthropos* 48: 171-201.
In this "Day in the Life of a Dieri Man" he grows up, undergoes *Malgara*
(initiation), makes love with several women, goes through various other rituals,
marries twice, has a large family and, quite understandably, visits the traditional
doctor. Despite the misleading title, this text, transcribed with interlineal and
free translations, provides an interesting brief oral autobiography with emphasis
on religious matters.

0887 Gason, Samuel (1874) *The Dieyerie Tribe: The Manners and Customs of
Australian Aborigines.* Adelaide.
"A more treacherous race I do not believe exists." "Some... customs are
altogether so obscene and disgusting, I must, even at the risk of leaving my
subject incomplete, pass over." While Gason is hardly a sympathetic observer,
this work contains early, sometimes salvagable, information on Dieri 'creation'
beliefs, tooth avulsion, circumcision and subincision rites, 'increase' ceremonies,
mortuary practice, sorcery, rain-making rituals and traditional doctors.

0888 Gregory, J.W. (1906) *The Dead Heart of Australia: A Journey around
Lake Eyre in the Summer of 1901-1902 with some Account of the Lake
Eyre Basin and the Flowing Wells of Central Australia.* London: John
Murray. 384 pp.
Contains a range of observations on totemism, religion and mythology, all
couched in the context of turn of the century evolutionary and diffusionary
debates. Valuable, however, is chapter XIII, an eye-witness account of the
Molonga cult in this area, and comparisons with Roth (0315), Spencer and Gillen
(0791, pp. 719-20), and Siebert's correspondence allowed the author to attempt
to plot its movement and to highlight changes in ritual.

0889 Hercus, Luise A. (1987) "Looking for Ditji-mingka." *Records of the
South Australian Museum* 21,2: 149-156.
Ditji-mingka was an important Dieri site, referred to by Reuther (0891) and
Gason (0887). The site and myth were still known in the 1930s (Fry 0900) and
Hercus re-visited the site only to find it had been destroyed by dynamite.
Considers some of the implications of such a loss and the interrelation between
sites, myths, rituals and living custodians. A text with interlineal and free
translation accompanies the paper.

0890 Horne, G. and Aiston, G. (1924) *Savage Life in Central Australia.*
London: Macmillan. 184 pp.
A general account of the Wongkanguru and neighbouring peoples. The
information on beliefs is superficial and confused, while rituals are discussed
emphasizing the sensational aspects of magic, bone-pointing, cannibalism and
burial. Little of original value is to be found. The title reflects the book's
mood.

0891 Reuther, J.G. (1981) *The Diari*, translated by Rev. P.A. Scherer. Canberra: Australian Institute of Aboriginal Studies, microfiche no.2. 13 vols.

Missionary Reuther spent 18 years with the Dieri. His unique 13 volume work remained unpublished until the appearance of this English translation. Volume 10 (254 pp) is *Diari Religion: Myths and Legends*, dealing extensively with stories of the *Muramura* (some 30 myths), while vol. 11 *The Supernatural Beings and the Spirit-World of the Australian Aborigines* considers *Muramura*, 'devils', 'witchdoctors', the soul, dreams, sorcery and taboos. Volumes 12 and 13 are concerned with *Toas* and their meaning (cf. Jones and Sutton, 0908).

0892 Siebert, Otto (1910) "Sagen und Sitten der Dieri und Nachbarstämme in Zentral-Australien." *Globus* 97,3: 44-50; 97,4: 53-9.

Gives a range of myths, rituals and other traditions of the Dieri and neighbouring Gujani, Jauraworka, Wongkumara and Arabana, supplementing earlier accounts given to Howitt (0938). Of fundamental importance is the section on the *Molonga* cult, reported by others (eg. Roth 0315) but here first revealed to be a millennial movement which climaxes with *Kanini* destroying all the Whites.

0893 Taplin, G., ed. (1879) *The Folklore, Manners, Customs and Languages of the South Australian Aborigines: Gathered from Inquiries made by Authority of the South Australian Government.* Adelaide: Government Printer. 174 pp.

The bulk of this volume supplies responses to a questionnaire. Questions relate to totems, sorcery, mortuary rites, life after death, beliefs in gods and demons, legends, initiation, healing, cannibalism and other 'peculiar customs'. The data is predictably uneven but in some instances fills important ethnographic gaps. The majority of tribes are in the Lake Eyre/Adelaide area, but bordering peoples from the South-East and Western Desert are also surveyed.

0894 Tiechelmann, C.G. (1841) *Aborigines of South Australia: Illustrative and Explanatory Notes of the Manners, Customs, Habits and Superstitions of the Natives of South Australia.* Adelaide: South Australian Wesleyan Methodist Auxilliary Society. 13 pp.

Written to reveal the difficulties of, and directions for future evangelization, this unsympathetic pamphlet nonetheless briefly provides some very early information on celestial and earthly myths, beliefs concerning the soul, healing and causes of death.

See also: 0003, 0063.

Philosophy and Totemism

0895 Elkin, A.P. (1934) "Cult-Totemism and Mythology in Northern South Australia." *Oceania* 5,2: 171-192.

Examines totemic affiliations of the Luridja, Southern Aranda, Wongkanguru, Jauraworka, Arabana, Marulta and Dieri. Distinguishes associations based on birth with those of inheritance, to determine what gives a person ritual rights and responsibilities. Recounts several myths and associated 'increase' rituals. Concludes suggesting some dated views on the functions of totemic myths.

Myth

0896 Berndt, Ronald M. (1940) "A Curlew and Owl Legend from the Narunga Tribe, South Australia." *Oceania* 10,4: 456-462.
Recounts a Narangga myth in which Owl-man's dogs eat Curlew-man and his wife's children, the myth providing an aetiology for the behaviour of both owls and curlews. Draws on comparative material to show similar myths are widespread throughout Australia. Conjectures that such information can be used to unravel historical changes in religious beliefs.

0897 Berndt, Ronald M. (1987) "Muramura Darana." In *The Encyclopedia of Religion*, edited by M. Eliade, Vol. 10, 157-159. New York: Macmillan.
Briefly relates *Darana* mythic associations with rainmaking as maintained primarily by the Dieri.

0898 Boehmer, Julius (1928) "Die Sudaustralischen Dieri und Otto Siebert; Anmerkungen zu P.W. Schmidt, Der Ursprung der Gottesidee, Teill, 2 Aufl." *Anthropos* 23: 316-320.
Adds two alleged examples of Dieri High Gods to Schmidt's thesis (0995).

0899 Davis, Christine; Coulthard, Clifford; and Coulthard, Desmond (1986) *The Flinders Ranges: An Aboriginal View.* Adelaide: Department of Environment and Planning. 19 pp.
An Adnyamathanha reading of the Flinders Ranges. Contains contemporary Aboriginal versions of myths recounted in formal English: e.g. 'The Eagle, Crows and Magpies', 'Creation of Mt. Chambers by the Purple-Backed Wren', 'Moon Man', 'An Old Man and His Daughter', etc. Truncated, public myths only. Useful supplement for this region.

0900 Fry, H.K. (1937) "Dieri Legends." *Folk-Lore* 48:187-206; 269-287.
Myths told by an old Dieri man brought up on Kopperamanna mission station. They are mostly transcribed with interlineal translations and placed in social or religious contexts. There are gaps in the translation and the want of free translations is felt. The myths, dealing with Pigeon, Sun cave, Lizard, Charcoal, Red Ochre, Rat, Moon and other subjects, are treated unsensationalistically.

0901 Hercus, Luise A. (1971) "Arabana and Wangganguru Traditions." *Oceania* 42,2: 92-109.
Lake Eyre itself contains no major totemic sites. It nonetheless has important mythic associations and the mysterious *Warana* are said to dwell on the island at its centre. The *Warana* are not Dreaming ancestors, and although 'timeless' they

have had encounters with humans in living memory. Gives texts with interlineal and free translations of some Arabana-Wongkanguru informants' accounts of past encounters with these beings.

0902 Hercus, Luise A. (1980) *The Story of Gudnangamba.* Adelaide: D.J. Woolman. 26 pp.
A myth relating to Mound Springs which also appeared in Howitt and Siebert (0903). The story of the ancestor *Djarda-njudlu* and a serpent, revolves around magic and subsequent destruction. The Arabana-Wongkanguru text is transcribed with interlineal glosses and an as literal as possible free translation. Useful notes are offered on the text giving background and data on mythical beings, etc.

0903 Howitt, Alfred W. and Siebert, Otto (1904) "Legends of the Dieri and Kindred Tribes of Central Australia." *The Journal of the Anthropological Institute of Great Britain and Ireland* 34: 100-129.
Myths collected by Siebert on Howitt's request, relating to the *Muramura*, a mythical people of great power of the Lake Eyre Basin. The myths range from their origins, their transformation and perfection of humans, to the *Muramura's* wanderings over an area of some 700 miles. The documentation, while lacking verification in ritual contexts, is careful and useful.

0904 Howitt, Mary E.B. (1902) "Some Native Legends from Central Australia." *Folklore* 13: 403-417.
A collection of Dieri, Wongkanguru, Jauraworka and Arabana myths selected from the collection of Rev. Siebert. Focuses on the *Muramura* - beings of human form with superhuman powers, who perfected humans from shapeless forms, named totemic species and established ceremonies. A. Howitt and Siebert provide contextual notes for the myths.

0905 Tindale, Norman B. (1937) "Two Legends of the Ngadjuri Tribe from the Middle North of South Australia." *Transactions and Proceedings of the Royal Society of South Australia* 61: 149-153.
Two Ngadjuri myths. In one, a woman and her human/dog companions' cannibalistic ways are the cause of the murder which gave rise to the first sunset. The other is a variant of a widely distributed myth. In this case Crow through envy causes Eagle to injure his foot and is subsequently smoked in a cave, thus producing crows' characteristic feather and eye colour.

0906 Tindale, Norman B. (1987) "The Wanderings of Tjirbruki: A Tale of the Kaurna People of Adelaide." *Records of the South Australian Museum* 20: 5-13.
Based on notes taken between 1928-64 with Kaurna men. *Tjirbruki* was was noted as a great hunter of kangaroos. Tindale examines him in the contexts of conservation themes and rules established to protect important food resources, as well as observing his wanderings in relation to trade processes and the continuation of exchange systems through time.

0907 Tunbridge, Dorothy (1988) *Flinders Ranges Dreaming*. Canberra:
      Aboriginal Studies Press. 177 pp.
Translates over 50 Dreaming stories at the request of Adnyamathanha people
who feared their loss. The narratives are brief, often incomplete myth segments,
and the translations are stylistically ordered in a very Western way - particularly
annoying is the translation of *wadu* as "A long time ago..." or "Once upon a
time..." The introduction is fair, the photographs of relevant sites superb.

See also: 0889, 0891.

The Arts

0908 Jones, Philip and Sutton, Peter (1986) *Art and Land: Aboriginal
      Sculptures of the Lake Eyre Region*. Adelaide: South Australia Museum/
      Wakefield Press. 144 pp.
The catalogue of a superb exhibition of Dieri *Toas* collected by Rev. Reuther
between 1890 and 1905. Explains how these 'direction markers' refer to the
Muramura and the sites they visited during the Dreaming. Intriguing is the
question of whether these were a post-mission advent. Rightly emphasizes we
are seeing "the continuing metamorphosis and transformation of Aboriginal
artistic [and religious] traditions"(p.61).

0909 Stirling, Edward and Waite, Edgar R. (1919) "Description of Toas, or
      Australian Aboriginal Direction Signs." *Records of the South Australian
      Museum* 1,2: 105-155 + plates.
An abstract from a manuscript by Rev. Reuther. Repeats Reuther's error that
the Dieri used *'Mura'* to refer to a single Supreme Being. *'Mura*'s' attributes are
discussed, and his creation of the *Muramura* ('demigods'). The *Toas* are said to
indicate locality by their topographic references or by reference to *Muramura*
associated with particular sites. 322 *Toas* are illustrated and provided with brief
inadequate, descriptions. Cf. Jones and Sutton (0908).

See also: 0891.

Initiation

0910 Beckett, Jeremy (1967) "Marriage, Circumcision and Avoidance Among
      the Maljangaba of North-West New South Wales." *Mankind* 6,10: 456-
      464.
Focuses on Maljangapa recollections of traditional social organization with
particular emphasis on sibling avoidance relationships. The second section
begins with a description of the *Milia* or circumcision ceremony where the
author shows that ritual social relations reflect secular social relations. Behind
both spheres he perceives a rivalry for the bestowal of women in marriage.

Women

0911 Hercus, Luise A. (1989) "The Status of Women's Cultural Knowledge: Aboriginal Society in North-East South Australia." In *Women, Rites and Sites: Aboriginal Women's Cultural Knowledge*, edited by P. Brock, 99-119. Sydney: Allen and Unwin.
A valuable consideration of women's religion throughout the Lake Eyre Basin. Clarifies the process of Dreaming inheritance and the means of transmitting sacred knowledge. Women are said to have had access to practically all ceremonial and ancestral sites, and to have become traditional healers. Further refers to post-contact change, including the *Molonga* cult (cf. Hercus, 0918) and other 'revivalist movements'.

0912 Jacobs, Jane M. (1989) "'Women Talking Up Big': Aboriginal Women as Cultural Custodians, a South Australian Example." In *Women, Rites and Sites: Aboriginal Women's Cultural Knowledge*, edited by P. Brock, 76-98. Sydney: Allen & Unwin.
The extent of Adnyamathanha, Kokata and Pangkala women's sacred knowledge in a post-colonial era is discussed and the resistance of Aboriginal men to women 'talking up big' about religious matters noted. Suggests men have only come to see themselves as rightful spokespersons since White researchers and government officials deemed them thus. No solid data is given to prove things were once otherwise, however.

0913 Mountford, Charles P. and Harvey, Alison (1941) "Women of the Adnjamatana Tribe of the Northern Flinders Ranges." *Oceania* 12,2: 155-162.
Brief notes on Adnyamathanha woman's life, including conception ideology, pregnancy and childbirth rituals, and ceremonies at the onset of menstruation.

See also: 0197, 1046.

Magic

0914 Berndt, Ronald M. (1987) "Panaramittee Magic." *Records of the South Australian Museum* 20: 15-28.
Mountford had claimed that a rock-engraving located in Ngadjuri territory was a Panaramittee 'crocodile head'. Berndt recalls evidence from a man of that region who said it represented a 'magic spirit stick'. While not totally denying the previous interpretation, Berndt relates its magical significance, and places it in contexts of the society, myths and theory and technique of sorcery.

0915 Berndt, Ronald M. and Vogelsang, T. (1941) "The Initiation of Native-Doctors, Dieri Tribe, South Australia." *Records of the South Australian Museum* 6,4: 369-380.
A Dieri text, transcribed with interlineal and free translations, on the making of the *kunki* or traditional doctor. The process of seeing the spirits is related - the

seclusion, meditation, use of tobacco, etc., until the spirit manifests itself. The 'rebirth' of the healer is noted, together with his accompanying paraphenalia and powers. Also contains data on the *Kutji* spirit that produces the powers.

0916 Pounder, Derrick J. (1985) "A New Perspective on Kadaitja Killings."
        Oceania 56,1: 77-82.
Suggests forensic evidence indicates deaths attributed to sorcery may often have resulted from covert physical assault.

See also: 0215.

Death

0917 Basedow, Herbert (1913) "Burial Customs in the Northern Flinder's
        Ranges of South Australia." *Man* 13: 49-53.
Archaeological evidence for platform burial and mutilation of dead bodies in Northern Flinders Ranges area.

See also: 0767.

Change

0918 Hercus, Luise A. (1980) "'How We Danced the Mudlungga': Memories
        of 1901 and 1902." *Aboriginal History* 4: 5-31.
Wongkanguru men recall the *Molonga* ceremonies which they learned in 1901 and 1902. The men's statements are transcribed with interlineal and free translations. Describes the event as a "new and exciting ceremony" but finds no support for the views of Siebert (0892) and Eliade (0023) that it was anti-European. Adds little information to the meaning of the cult.

See also: 0888, 0892, 0908, 0911, 0912.

Literature See 0249.

13

South-East

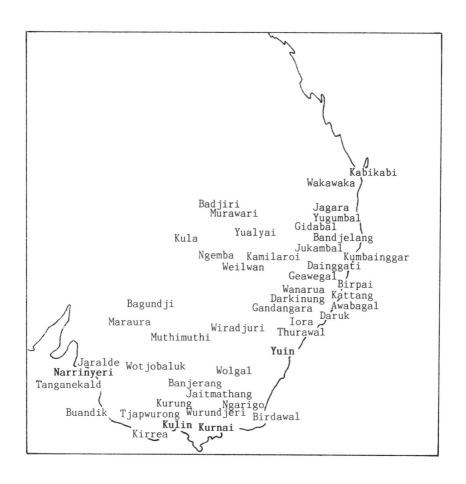

Kabikabi
Wakawaka

Badjiri
Murawari
Jagara
Yugumbal
Gidabal
Bandjelang
Jukambal
Kumbainggar
Dainggati
Geawegal
Birpai
Wanarua
Darkinung
Kattang
Gandangara
Awabagal
Iora
Daruk
Wiradjuri
Thurawal
Yuin

Yualyai
Kula
Ngemba
Kamilaroi
Weilwan

Bagundji
Maraura
Muthimuthi

Jaralde
Narrinyeri
Wotjobaluk
Wolgal
Tanganekald
Banjerang
Jaitmathang
Kurung
Ngarigo
Buandik
Tjapwurong
Wurundjeri
Birdawal
Kulin
Kurnai
Kirrea

General

0919 Bennett, Gordon (1964) *The Earliest Inhabitants: Aboriginal Tribes of the Districts: The Blacks of Dungog, Port Stephens and Gresford.* Dungog: Chronicle. 33 pp.
Notes on the Awabagal, mainly from Howitt (0983). Terrible.

0920 Beveridge, Peter (1861-4) "A Few Notes on the Dialects, Habits, Customs and Mythology of the Lower Murray Aborigines." *Transactions and Proceedings of the Royal Society of Victoria* 6: 14-24.
Pages 18-21 contains notes on religious beliefs.

0921 Beveridge, Peter (1883) "Of the Aborigines Inhabiting the Great Locustrine and Riverine Depression of the Lower Murray, Lower Murrumbidgee, Lower Lachlan, and Lower Darling." *Journal and Proceedings of the Royal Society of New South Wales* 17: 10-74.
A catalogue weighted towards material culture. Mourning is discussed and there are brief myth fragments related to the sun, moon and stars. Traditional doctors are briefly and superficially mentioned and there is an absurd report of the author's spying on a secret ceremony. Lacks insight.

0922 Booney, Frederic (1884) "On Some Customs of the Aborigines of the River Darling, New South Wales." *The Journal of the Anthropological Institute of Great Britain and Ireland* 13: 122-136.
Account of Bagundji and neighbouring traditions, with a brief and confused description of initiation (pp.126-9); and discussions of sickness; the use of quartz in sorcery; traditional healers (both men and women) and traditional remedies (pp.130-133); and burial and mourning (pp.133-6). Piecemeal and only of use to fill in details for the region.

0923 Braim, Thomas H. (1846) *A History of New South Wales from its Settlement to the Close of the Year 1844.* 2 volumes. London: Richard Bentley. 320 pp + 344 pp.
Chapter 6 of volume 2 is a missionary's lament, describing 'Customs and Traditions'. Interesting is a long extract from Assistant Protector Parker which mentions a new ceremony with a theme of death and rebirth and an early statement for an Aboriginal High God. Other beings and ceremonies are described by Braim himself. A very early report.

0924 Brayshaw, Helen (1986) *Aborigines of the Hunter Valley: A Study of Colonial Records.* Scone, N.S.W: Scone & Upper Hunter Historical Society. 109 pp.
An overview based on written and archaeological sources for the Kamilaroi, Geawegal, Wanarua, Darkinung, Kattang and Awabagal. The chapter on ritual life covers initiation and burial rites but by no means makes an exhaustive survey. A final chapter superficially considers carved (ceremonial) trees, cave paintings and the sites of burials and *Bora* grounds. A first introduction only.

0925 Cameron, A.L.P. (1885) "Notes on Some Tribes of New South Wales." *The Journal of the Anthropological Institute of Great Britain and Ireland* 14: 344-370.
An overview of New South Wales emphasizing the Wiradjuri with whom the author had more acquaintance. Contains a brief but useful account of initiation and comments on clever men and their role as healers. Also describes burial, beliefs in the afterlife and deities. Lastly, there are a few summary versions of legends. Almost certainly influenced by European notions .

0926 Cawthorne, W.A. (1925-6) "Rough Notes on the Manners and Customs of the Natives." *Proceedings of the Royal Geographical Society, South Australian Branch* reprint : 1-31.
The manuscript, written in 1844, was based on observations of the people bordering the southern coast and the Murray River. Describes several 'corroborees' with no explanation of meaning. Initiation and circumcision are likewise discussed. Contains a section on 'Religion-Burial-Mourning-Superstitions, etc.'. Myths and beliefs are given but some, such as the belief in an eternal collective rebirth, are unlikely.

0927 Collins, David (1975) *An Account of the English Colony in New South Wales: With Remarks on the Dispositions, Customs, Manners, etc., of the Native Inhabitants of that Country.* Vol. I. Sydney: A.H. and A.W. Reed. 649 pp. 1st ed. 1798.
While inevitably flawed, the 62 page appendix on the Iora was the first publication on Aboriginal culture. Particularly valuable are the descriptions of the rites of burial/cremation and initiation. The latter is discussed at length and accompanied by etchings. Collins was not allowed full knowledge of the proceedings and offers little in the way of exegesis, but as our only eighteenth century account of Aborigines, this work is very valuable.

0928 Dawson, James (1881) *Australian Aborigines: The Languages and Customs of Several Tribes of Aborigines in the Western District of Victoria, Australia.* Melbourne: George Robertson. 111. + civ pp.
Dawson provides the best eyewitness account we have for western Victoria (Tjapwurong, Kirrea, etc.). Religion, as such, is not mentioned, but there are frequent references to 'native superstitions', for example, those relating to cleanliness, names, disease, death and ghosts. The brief references to 'Korroborae' reveals Dawson saw little of the rapidly disappearing ritual life. Predictably superficial.

0929 Dunbar, G.K. (1943-4) "Notes on the Ngemba Tribe of the Central Darling River, Western New South Wales." *Mankind* 3,5: 140-148; 3,6: 172-180.
Dunbar's recollections of his youth in Ngemba territory. Whilst initiation, death, and 'legends', receive brief commentaries, 'religion' is disposed of in a paragraph, and the religious aspects of 'medicine men' sadly is also omitted.

0930 Enright, W.J. (1939) "Notes on the Aborigines of the North Coast of N.S.W." *Mankind* 2,7: 193-195; 3,9: 264-5.

Brief notes on Kumbainggar and Kattang myth, rite and ceremonial grounds.

0931 Eyre, Edward J. (1845) *Journals of Expeditions of Discovery into Central Australia and Overland from Adelaide to King George's Sound, in the years 1840-1...* 2 Vols. London: T. and W. Boone. 448 + 512 pp.
Volume 2 contains a 9 chapter section on 'Manners and Customs of the Aborigines of Australia'. Having sketched some variations in initiation, gives an account of the rites in the Adelaide district including, briefly, those for women. Funeral ceremonies and disposal of the dead are also described. Religious beliefs are said not to exist, but descriptions of a Sky-Father (*Nooreele*) are given as are other beliefs and ritual practices.

0932 Fison, Lorimer and Howitt, Alfred W. (1967) *Kamilaroi and Kurnai: Group-Marriage and Relationship, and Marriage by Elopement.* The Netherlands: Anthropological Publications. 372 pp. 1st ed. 1880.
In essence, an Australian validation of L.H. Morgan's theories of the origin of the family. Fison's section on the Kamilaroi contain an appendix on totem names, but Howitt's part on the Kurnai has more on religion. Contains data on initiation, mortuary practice and beliefs, magic, spiritual beings and an appendix on the *turndun* (bull-roarer). Howitt's understanding of the secret ceremonies was then limited.

0933 Flanagan, Roderick J. (1888) *The Aborigines of Australia.* Sydney: George Robertson. 167 pp.
Based on secondary sources and adds nothing not available in other early accounts. Rambling.

0934 Fraser, John (1892) *The Aborigines of New South Wales.* Sydney: Charles Potter. 102 pp.
Ignoring some far-fetched statements about the origins of Aborigines, this book is useful. Considers ideas about causes of death, various preparations and disposals of the corpse, funerals and beliefs about ghosts and spirits, mourning and revenge. A long section on *Bora* (pp. 6-21) describes the ceremonial grounds, body painting, tooth avulsion, etc., but does not penetrate initiatory beliefs. Strangely, traditional healers and mythology are *not* included in the survey.

0935 Gundert, H. (1878) "Die religiösen Vorstellungen der Australier." *Evangelische Mission-Magazin* 27: 114-120.
Based on observations of Rev. Günther at the Wellington Mission and the writings of Manning (0985), gives a Christian reading of Kamilaroi and other religions, with emphasis on the role of *Baiami* and upon initiation ceremonies.

0936 Gunson, N. ed. (1974) *Australian Reminiscences and Papers of L.E. Threkeld.* Australian Aboriginal Studies No. 40. Canberra: Australian Institute of Aboriginal Studies. 2 Vols, 176 + 382 pp.
First printed in 1853-55 in *The Christian Herald* and opens: "The Aborigines of New South Wales, like most ignorant savage tribes, are remarkably superstitious..." Nonetheless, offers a very early account derived using

reasonable linguistic facilities. Contains notes on mortuary practice and belief, initiation ceremonies, sorcery, the arts, spirits, lack of belief in a Supreme God and sacred places. Gunson's commentary helps unravel the errors and half-truths.

0937 Hale, Horatio (1846) *Ethnography and Philology.* Volume of the United States Exploring Expedition During the Years 1838, 1839, 1840, 1841, 1842, under the Command of Charles Wilkes. Philadelphia: Lea and Blanchard. 666 pp.
Pages 110-2 contain brief but very early and significant references to the*Baiami* cult in the Wellington Mission area.

0938 Howitt, Alfred W. (1904) *The Native Tribes of South-East Australia.* London: Macmillan. 819 pp.
Deservedly a classic for this region. The wealth of data was collected by Howitt over a 40 year period and with the help of 59 correspondents. Contains major sections on magic, medicine men, burial practices and initiation. The most controversial section of the book remains the discussion of the 'All-Fathers' of South-Eastern Australia (pp.488-508). While Howitt was not without theoretical bias the book is for its time balanced, careful and critical. A mine of information although inevitably uneven.

0939 James, Ken (1978) *Aborigines in the Werribee District.* Geelong: Campbell Wilson. 47 pp.
Kulin religon is reconstructed from accounts of Massola (0986) and Howitt (0938). Adds nothing.

0940 Kelly, Caroline T. (1935) "Tribes on Cherburg Settlement, Queensland." *Oceania* 5,4: 461-473.
An attempt to salvage information about the traditional life of the various tribes gathered together at Cherburg government settlement. Contains brief descriptions of totems and their affiliation with moieties and 'increase' ceremonies, as well as some notes on the significance of dreams, food taboos and a few legends.

0941 Locke, William (1876) "Notes on the Language and Customs of the Tribe Inhabiting the Country known as Kotoopna." In *The Aborigines of Victoria: With Notes Relating to the Habits of the Natives of Other Parts of Australia and Tasmania...,* by R. Brough Smyth. Vol. 2, 289-299. Melbourne: John Currey.
Brief notes on 'corroborees', afterlife, traditional healers, etc.

0942 McKiernan, Bernard (1911) "Some Notes on the Aborigines of the Lower Hunter River, N.S.W." *Anthropos* 6: 885-892.
Very superficial comments on religion, based on White Australian reminiscences.

0943 Macpherson, Peter (1883) *The Religion of the Aborigines of Australia as Preserved in their Legends and Ceremonies.* Singleton: Argus. 21 pp.

A centennial reflection on knowledge about (mainly) South-Eastern religious beliefs. Of 'Demons and Devils', the bunyip takes the main place and is said to be the alligator [sic]. *'Baiami'*, is derived from *ba* and *fa* said to be the roots of 'Father' in all languages. Notes on 'the mystic triad' and 'the mystic fire' make the nonsense complete.

0944   Mann, John F.   (1884)   *Notes on the Aborigines of Australia.*   Sydney: Government Printer. 37 pp.
Sections on religion (pp.14-24) rely on Manning (0985), and others, and considers mythology, 'corroborees', songs, *Boras*, traditional healers and disposal of the dead. Mostly South-Eastern and less useful than the author's very imperfect sources.

0945   Massola, Aldo   (1971)   *The Aborigines of South-Eastern Australia As They Were.*   Melbourne: Heinemann. 166 pp.
Geared towards a popular readership. Religious themes such as totemism, myth, ritual, iconography, magic and mortuary practice are represented, but the research is superficial. The many plates provide an interesting commentary on both Aboriginal life and European perceptions of that life.

0946   Mathew, John   (1887)   "Mary River and Bunya Bunya Country." In *The Australian Race: Its Origins, Languages, Customs, Place of Landing in Australia, and the Routes by which it Spread itself over that Continent,* by E.M Curr, Vol. 3, 152-209. Melbourne: John Ferres.
Contains brief references to Kabikabi religious life, including a description of initiation (not witnessed), death ritual, 'corroborees' and traditional doctors.

0947   Mathew, John   (1910)   *Two Representative Tribes of Queensland: With an Inquiry Concerning the Origin of the Australian Race.*   London: Fisher Unwin. 256 pp.
Based on acquaintance with the Kabikabi and Wakawaka from 1866 to 1872. Sets out an ethnography with emphasis on religion; initiation, curing, death, mortuary practice, religion and magic are all considered. The myths presented have some transcriptions with interlineal translations. The quality is above average for its time, although there are many loose references (such as that these people had a concept cognate to the Indian *Atman* [p.169]).

0948   Mathews, R.H.   (1904)   "Ethnological Notes of the Aboriginal Tribes of New South Wales and Victoria." *Journal of the Royal Society of New South Wales* 38: 203-381.
This extensive article (later released as a book) contains much material on social organization, language and religion throughout the South-East. Initiation is detailed, including higher grades and the initiation of girls. Magic, sorcery and mortuary practice are covered and there are substantial pieces on myths given in a style above average for the time. In some respects better than Howitt's more exhaustive book of the same year (0938), and with some important divergencies.

0949   Mathews, R.H.   (1907)   *Notes on the Aborigines of New South Wales.*   Sydney: Government Printer. 40 pp.

A pamphlet condensing the author's previous articles. A *Bora* ceremony in southern Queensland is described with particular attention to ground plans, sand sculptures and tree carvings. There is also a *Yaroma* (human-like malevolent beings) story, and notes on iconography, bullroarers, initiation songs (without translations), and a medley of 'curious beliefs'. Adds little. Rambling and disjointed.

0950 Meyer, H.E.A. (1846) *Manners and Customs of the Aborigines of the Encounter Bay Tribe: South Australia.* Adelaide: George Dehane. 15 pp.
A brief, crude account of the people of the lower Murray River and Encounter Bay. The more public rites of circumcision are described as nocturnal fighting and entertainment. That they are "deeply sunk in superstition"(p.8) is proven by reference to traditional methods of sorcery, magic and healing. Mentions some of their "more or less immoral and obscene"(p.11) myths. Some material salvageable, however.

0951 Morgan, John (1852) *The Life and Adventures of William Buckley: Thirty Two Years a Wanderer Amongst the Aborigines of the Unexplored Country Round Port Phillip.* Hobart: A. MacDougall. 238 pp.
Buckley learned suprisingly little in 32 years living with the Aborigines of southern Victoria. There are intertwined in this narrative early descriptions of 'corroborees', disposal of the dead, 'superstitious ceremonies' and mythic figures. James Morril's experiences in north Queensland are bound with Buckley's (pp. 194 ff.). Truncated and disappointing accounts.

0952 Parker, Katherine L. (1905) *The Euahlayi Tribe: A Study of Aboriginal Life in Australia.* London: Archibald Constable. 156 pp.
Heavily influenced by the theories of Andrew Lang, hence giving priority to 'the All-Father [*Baiami*]'. Virtually the entire book is devoted to Yualyai religion - totemism, 'medicine men', and other forms of healing, *Bora* rites, myths and mortuary practice. The interesting chapter on women's rites of passage was pioneering and presents a picture of women's initiation more extensive than other accounts would lead us to believe existed.

0953 Petrie, Constance C. (1932) *Tom Petrie's Reminiscences of Early Queensland.* Brisbane: Queensland Book Depot. 323 pp. 1st ed. 1904.
Tom Petrie knew Jagara and other languages of southern Queensland. His reminiscences date back to 1837. Religion is prominent in the first 8 chapters of the book. Discusses 'corroborees', sorcery, mortuary practice, naming and initiation. For their time, the descriptions are remarkably good, and are presented without sensationalism.

0954 Ridley, William (1873) "Report on Australian Languages and Traditions." *Journal of the Anthropological Institute of Great Britain and Ireland* 2: 257-291.
In two parts. The first is based on the author's research with the Kamilaroi and provides brief descriptions of their 'Supreme Creator' *Baiami*, myths concerning stars, *Boras*, rites for the deceased and the practices of 'clever men'. The second

part is derived from secondary sources on the Wiradjuri and covers similar themes. A serviceable account.

0955 Ridley, William (1875) *Kámilarói and other Australian Languages*. 2nd ed. Sydney: Government Printer. 172 pp.
Primarily a philological work on the Kamilaroi, Kabikabi and Jagara. The final part is a general ethnography of these areas. Most influential was his advocation of *Baiami* as "a ray of true light which has passed down through many generations" (p. vi) - i.e. as a Supreme Being. Also considers other spiritual beings and stellar myths, provides transcriptions and translations of myths and *Bao-illi* songs, and discusses *Bora* and mortuary rituals.

0956 Ryan, J.S., ed. (1964) *The Land of Ulitarra: Early Records of the Aborigines of the Mid-North Coast of New South Wales*. Armidale: University of New England. 241 pp.
Covers material from the Bandjelang in the north along the coastal regions to the Birpai in the south and contains chapters on initiation, magic and mythology. The text is largely composed of extended quotations from earlier writers such as Mathews, Enright, Colley and lesser known authors. A useful localized collection which adds little but saves labour.

0957 Smith, Mrs. James (1880) *The Booandik Tribes of South Australian Aborigines: A Sketch of their Habits, Customs, Legends and Language*. Adelaide: Goverment Printer. 139 pp.
A general account of the Buandik by a woman who had spent 35 years evangelizing them. Contains brief superficial sections on birth, death, totems, myths, sorcery and healers. More interesting are records of Aboriginal recollections of the first Whites providing some glimpses into the processes and pressures for religious change.

0958 Smyth, R. Brough (1876) *The Aborigines of Victoria: With Notes Relating to the Habits of the Natives of Other Parts of Australia and Tasmania...* 2 vols. Melbourne: John Currey. 483 + 456 pp.
A thorough compilation gathering most of the published and correspondent information available at that time. The focus is on Victoria but other regions (including Tasmania) are brought in. Volume 1 contains substantial chapters on death and burial, and mythology, while other religious themes are less conspicuously covered under the headings of 'Education' (initiation) or 'Daily Life: Dances '('corroborees', etc.). An indispensible source of early data from this region.

0959 Steele, J.G. (1984) *Aboriginal Pathways in Southeast Queensland and the Richmond River*. St. Lucia: University of Queensland Press. 366 pp.
A detailed reconstruction of the Aborigines of the area centred on Brisbane. 21 separate regions are in turn analysed. Available information on myth and ritual is drawn upon, often with quotations from inaccessible primary sources or photographs. Particularly strong on the archaeology of *Bora* grounds. The fragmentary regional presentation mitigates against any extensive thematic investigations, however.

0960 Stone, A.C. (1911) "The Aborigines of Lake Boga, Victoria." *Proceedings of the Royal Society of Victoria* 23,11: 433-468.
An attempt to salvage some of the traditions of the Kurung at a time when their old life was largely disturbed. Contains brief notes on medicine, burial, sorcery and some paraphrased legends.

0961 Turbet, Peter (1989) *The Aborigines of the Sydney District Before 1788.* Kenthurst, N.S.W.: Kangaroo Press. 160 pp.
Collects the terribly inadequate data on the Iora, Daruk, Thurawal, Gandangara and Darkinung into a serviceable account faithful to the sources (particularly Mathews, various; Howitt, 0938; and Gunson, 0936) but failing to do more than bring them together. Considers funerals, inquests, the fate of the spirit, totems, the All-Father, and other ancestral beings, initiation, clever men, and myths.

0962 Watson, F.J. (N.D.) "Vocabularies of Four Representative Tribes of South Eastern Queensland..." *Supplement to Journal of the Royal Geographical Society of Australasia (Queensland)* 48,34: 1-115.
Covers the Kabikabi, Wakawaka, Jagara and Yugumbal language groups and includes 'Notes on the Manners and Customs' (pp.87-98). Superficial comments on rites and 'superstitions', but an interesting record of Captain Cook and Captain Flinders 'corroborees' (pp.96-7).

0963 Wyndham, W.T. (1889) "The Aborigines of Australia." *Journal and Proceedings of the Royal Society of New South Wales* 23: 36-42.
A general account of the Jukambal with especial reference to religion. Sympathetic even though the author was barred from many ceremonies. Refers to 'the Supreme Being' *Baiami* and his powers, the *Bora* ceremonies, the practice of curing, sorcery, mortuary ritual and beliefs in afterlife. Lacks detail but adds to the available information for this region.

See also: 0019, 0020, 0044, 0054, 0893, 1054, 1060, 1061.

Philosophy and Totemism

0964 Howitt, Alfred W. (1889) "Further Notes on the Australian Class System." *Journal of the Anthropological Institute of Great Britain and Ireland* 18: 31-70.
In the context of advocating an original Australian society with moieties which intermarried as entire groups, Howitt discusses the origins of totem names. Pages 51-59 consider, confusedly, the relation of totems and social demarcation, and records some totemic myths collected by the author.

0965 Radcliffe-Brown, A.R. (1918 and 1923) "Notes on the Social Organisation of Australian Tribes." *The Journal of the Royal Anthropological Institute of Great Britain and Ireland* 48: 222-253; 53: 424-447.

Based on field research ranging from the Jaralde to the Murawari. Much of the data is sketchy, based on brief encounters in areas highly influenced by European contact. The focus is on social organization but under this heading, the subject of totemism is considered, albeit briefly. Useful primarily in attempting to reconstruct the social base of religious life in the South-East.

0966 Radcliffe-Brown, A.R.   (1929)   "Notes on Totemism in Eastern Australia." *The Journal of the Royal Anthropological Institute of Great Britain and Ireland* 59: 399-415.
Based on three week's research on the north coast of N.S.W. from the Jukambal to the Birpai. Contains a number of myth extracts associated with 'increase' rites. Having noted that myths are associated with both sites owned by 'hordes' and with rites, enquires as to whether this constitutes a form of 'totemism'. The question - answered in the affirmative - is to some extent semantic. Anticipates some of Lévi-Strauss' critique (0098).

0967 Schmidt, Wilhelm   (1910)   "Die soziologischen Verhältnisse der südostaustralischen Stämme." *Globus* 97,10: 157-160; 97,11: 173-176; 97,12: 186-189.
Treats sociological relationships of the Aborigines in the South-East in terms of the absence and presence of what he calls 'marriage totemism'. Considers also the significance of sex-totemism, mythology and other religious beliefs and practices, all within an obsolete diffusionary paradigm.

See also: 0102.

Myth

0968 Berndt, Ronald M.   (1940)   "Some Aspects of Jaralde Culture, South Australia." *Oceania* 11,2: 164-185.
Based on information from two old men and devoted to the legends of *Ngurunderi*, previously reported by Cawthorne (0926), Meyer (0950) and Taplin (0893). Recounts the wanderings of *Ngurunderi* in considerable detail and takes care to relate these to the local typography. Argues geography and socio-economic facets are essential to understanding the myth. Some diffusionist suggestions are rather conjectural.

0969 Blows, Mieke (1975) "Eaglehawk and Crow: Birds, Myths and Moieties in South-East Australia." In *Australian Aboriginal Mythology*, edited by L.R. Hiatt, 24-45. Canberra: Australian Institute of Aboriginal Studies.
Re-examines the arguments of Radcliffe-Brown (0107) and Lévi-Strauss (0098) about the nature of the opposition of Eaglehawks and Crows in Aboriginal myths, using secondary source data from the South-East. Argues his predecessors were mistaken in seeing the birds primarily as mythic representations of moiety oppositions. Rather the myths indicate the conflict between fathers and sons.

0970 Calley, Malcolm J.C. (1958) "Three Bandjalang Legends." *Mankind* 5,5: 208-213.
Three Bandjelang stories revealing the stress of Aboriginal life - in particular between a man and his mother's brother and his elder brother. They are episodes concerning a *Njimbun* or little person; 'the Gaunggan', a womanizer; and events in the life of a neophyte. Draws out kinship tensions underlying myths.

0971 Dunlop, W. (1898) "Australian Folklore Stories." *The Journal of the Anthropological Institute of Great Britain and Ireland* 28: 22-34.
Myths recorded by Dunlop in 1850 and edited by his daughter. The four myths are entitled The Bunyip, The Great Fire Bird, Revenge Approved and A Cannibal Story, and come from unspecified regions of South-Eastern Australia. The renderings are highly Europeanized. Of little use to scholars.

0972 Hartland, E.S. (1898) "The 'High Gods' of Australia." *Folk-Lore* 9: 290-329.
A long critique of Andrew Lang's thesis that Aborigines had a Supreme Being belief. Claims Lang dismisses as mere 'mythology' evidence which does not fit his thesis. Draws on other ethnographies which undermine Lang's position. Also argues these beliefs were a response to missionary teachings. Takes the beings in turn (*Baiami, Daramulun, Bunjil*, etc.) noting their limited powers and status. See Lang (0982).

0973 Hartland, E.S. (1899) "Australian Gods: Rejoinder." *Folk-Lore* 10: 46-57.
The stale end of the Hartland (0972)/Lang (0973) debate.

0974 Harvey, Alison (1943) "A Fishing Legend of the Jaralde Tribe of Lake Alexandrina, South Australia." *Mankind* 3,4: 108-112.
Paraphrases the Jaralde myth known as *neilun* ('netting') concerning the activities of fishing bird-humans. Their travels are noted and mapped. Suggests a historical migratory origin to the myth, even though it has a current educational function.

0975 Hemming, S.J. (1988) "Ngurunderi: A Ngarrindjeri Dreaming." *Records of the South Australian Museum* 22(2): 191-3.
Brief comments on various published accounts of the myth and contemporary Narrinyeri knowledge. (Cf. Berndt, 0968).

0976 Hercus, Luise (1971) "Eaglehawk and Crow: A Madimadi Version." *Mankind* 8,2: 137-140.
The text, with interlineal and free translations, of a Muthimuthi version of Eaglehawk and Crow by the last speaker of the language. (Cf. Blows, 0969).

0977 Hoddinott, W.G. (1978) "The Languages and Myths of the New England Area." In *Records of Times Past: Ethnohistorical Essays on the Culture and Ecology of the New England Tribes*, edited by I. McBryde, 52-64. Canberra: Australian Institute of Aboriginal Studies.

A thoroughly researched outline of language and myth in the New England area. Reconstructs myth fragments dealing with shape-changing beings and aetiological stories concerning moon and fire. Most interesting are the references to *Grumerungung* and *Yuludara*, figures of an All-Father type. The latter is also known as *Birugan* and later emerges as 'Christ' in Bandjelang myths (see Calley, 1055).

0978 Holmer, Nils M. and Holmer, Vanja E. (1969) *Stories From Two Native Tribes in Eastern Australia*. Uppsala: A.-B. Lundequistska Bokhandeln. 64 pp.
A welcome collection of Kattang and Dainggati texts which include ghost stories, myth fragments, 'corroboree' songs, etc. Especially useful in indicating changes to traditional beliefs. Thus spirits become associated with the devil (p.16) and old myths are blended with the story of Christ (pp.34-6). Compare Calley (1055) and Robinson (0994).

0979 Howitt, Alfred W. (1884) "On Some Australian Beliefs." *The Journal of the Anthropological Institute of Great Britain and Ireland* 13: 185-198.
Beliefs and mythic traditions collected by Howitt among the Kurnai, Wurundjeri, Wolgal, Jaitmathang, Ngarigo, etc. Covers themes considered in more detail in 0938. Examines the human spirit's ascent to the sky; the so-called 'Supreme Spirit', a benevolent/malevolent sky being (in particular *Daramulun* and *Bunjil*); and the connection between traditional healers and the sky realm.

0980 Howitt, Alfred W. (1906) "The Native Tribes of South-East Australia." *Folk-Lore* 17: 174-189.
In a very brief statement Andrew Lang argued Howitt had provided evidence that All-Fathers accompany the most 'primitive' forms of Australian social organization (matrilinal descent, lacking sections or sub-sections). Howitt counters this claim. A relic of a fruitless debate.

0981 Jung, Karl E. (1877) "Mythen und Sagen der Australier." *Die Natur* 38: 523-6.
Narrinyeri myths of creation, flood and *Ngurunderi*.

0982 Lang, Andrew (1899) "Australian Gods: A Reply." *Folk-Lore* 10: 1-46.
An animated reply to Hartland (0972) claiming he misses the mark. Nonetheless concedes Hartland's critique that the term 'Supreme Being' has unfortunate connotations. Offers a theory of how these people come upon a belief in an All-Father and attempts to counter Hartland's ethnographic data and accusations of missionary infiltration. A dead debate. See Hartland (0973).

0983 McKeown, Keith C. (1938) *The Land of Byamee: Australian Wild Life in Legend and Fact*. Sydney: Angus and Robertson. 229 pp.
A horrible book attempting to 'restore' to Wiradjuri and other myths a breath of life, but instead finally suffocating them.

0984 Maddock, Kenneth (1987) "All-Father." In *The Encyclopedia of Religion*, edited by M. Eliade, Vol. 1, 212-213. New York: Macmillan.

Brief description of *Baiami* et al., with comments on the authenticity of the literature on these figures.

0985 Manning, James (1882) "Notes on the Aborigines of New Holland." *Journal and Proceedings of the Royal Society of New South Wales* 16: 155-173.
Written in 1845, and hence an extremely early report. Concerned to argue Aborigines have a belief in a Supreme Being. Describes *Baiami* with the full Christian trappings - a crystal throne, a Moses-like prophet, and a fiery hell. Also contains descriptions of initiation ceremonies. The comments by J.F. Mann at the end of the paper explore the possibility of Christian influence. Interesting data in a highly confused state.

0986 Massola, Aldo (1968) *Bunjil's Cave: Myths, Legends and Superstitions of the Aborigines of South-East Australia.* Melbourne: Landsdowne. 208 pp.
Myths collected in Victoria and, understandably, divorced from their religious contexts. Also contains supplementary data from older published and unpublished accounts. Divided into two sections. The first presents myths from six areas, the second focusing on traditions about the sky realm. The renditions are heavily paraphrased and popularized and the photographs are horribly inappropriate.

0987 Mathews, R.H. (1899) *Folklore of the Australian Aborigines.* Sydney: Hennessey, Harper. 35 pp.
A pamphlet of myths from throughout New South Wales, mainly the Kamilaroi and Wiradjuri. They are: 1. The Arrival of the *Thurrawal*; 2. Destruction of the Eaglehawk; 3. The Journey to *Kurrilwan* (Baiami's home); 4. The *Kurrea* (snake monster) and the Warrior; 5. *Thoorkook* and Baiami's Sons; 6. The *Wareenggary* (7 sisters) and *Karambal* (a man): *Bunjil* and *Koombangary*; and 7. The Hereafter.

0988 Mathews, R.H. (1909) "The Wallaroo and the Willy-Wagtail: A Queensland Folk-Tale." *Folk-Lore* 20: 214-216.
Brief account, in English, with no commentary.

0989 Norledge, Mildred (1968) *Aboriginal Legends from Eastern Australia: The Richmond-Mary River Region.* Sydney: A.H. and A.W. Reed. 62 pp.
Myths from the Gidabal and other peoples of the north-eastern corner of New South Wales as transmitted by men no longer engaged in traditional ritual life. While these add to our meagre knowledge for the region, the myths are over-edited and lack authenticity. Story headings such as: 'The Bean Trees that are sacred to the Witches' warn that this is hardly ethnographically reliable.

0990 Parker, Katherine L. (1930) *Woggheeguy: Australian Aboriginal Legends.* Adelaide: F.W. Preece. 98 pp.
... and yet more Aboriginal Legendary Tales - or Woggheeguy (see, 0991) which sadly the author translates as 'fairy tales'. Collected at the end of the last century from the Kamilaroi and other people. The translations largely hide the original,

and the main value of the stories - dealing mostly with various species and their Dreaming activities - is as a supplement to this poorly documented region.

0991 Parker, Katherine L. (1978) *Australian Legendary Tales: Being the Two Collections 'Australian Legendary Tales' and 'More Australian Legendary Tales'*. Sydney: The Bodley Head. 191 pp.
The latest reissue of two books appearing in 1896 and 1898. The pair were among the earliest collections of their kind and were the first major collections by a woman researcher. To say these myths are overly Europeanized perhaps misses the real point. As Wandjuk Marika says in the new Introduction, it is through such books that modern Aboriginal descendants of the original tellers of these stories are reclaiming their identity - Parker's personality intrusion and all!

0992 Radcliffe-Brown, A.R. (1930) "The Rainbow-Serpent Myth in South-East Australia." *Oceania* 1,3: 342-347.
Salvages scraps of information about this widespread mythic figure. Based on a brief field-excursion in New South Wales and perusal of earlier ethnographies. Attempts to reconstruct the ritual significance of the serpent, but succeeds only in showing the impossibility of that task.

0993 Robinson, Roland (1958) *Black-Feller, White-Feller*. Sydney: Angus and Robertson. 151 pp.
The second section of this book mainly contains stories from Percy Mumbulla, an Aborigine born at Wallaga Lake Mission. Robinson has worked the stories into standard prose. There are avenging sorcerers, 'bunyips', something of the order of 'Big Foot', wild sirenesque women, and malevolent beings who take the form of animals. An intimate glimpse of some Aboriginal beliefs in the mid twentieth century.

0994 Robinson, Roland (1965) *The Man Who Sold His Dreaming*. Sydney: Currawong. 143 pp.
Suffers from poor documentation and over-editing but was willing to accept the stories of settled Aborigines as worthy of collection. They range from myths with firm traditional foundations through a range of stories showing the application of traditional values to modern contexts ('Gold and Grog and Pretty Stones' has almost a cargoistic mood to it) to full-blown syncretisms such as 'The Aboriginal Jesus' (cf. Calley, 1055). A valuable collection.

0995 Schmidt, Wilhelm (1912-1955) *Der Ursprung der Gottesidee: Eine historisch-kritische und positive Studie*. 12 Vols. Münster: Aschendorff. Vol. 1, 510 pp.; vol. III, 1155 pp.; vol. VI, 600 pp.
Aboriginal data is extensively represented in this massive work. It is constantly evoked in volume I where Andrew Lang's argument for an Australian High God is defended. In volume III some 550 pages (pp.565-1114) are devoted to an exhaustive analysis of High-Gods in the South-East, while volume VI (pp.311-367) again takes up Australian data. This book has been almost totally neglected, at least partially because of the author's thinly veiled Christian apologetics. Valuable if used with caution.

0996 Tindale, Norman B. (1935) "The Legend of Waijungari, Jaralde Tribe, Lake Alexandrina, South Australia, and the Phonetic System Employed in its Transcription." *Records of the South Australian Museum* 5,3: 261-274.
A Jaralde myth is transcribed with interlineal and free translations. The myth tells how a newly initiated man, *Waijungari*, is seduced by the two wives of another man and how, to escape revenge, he went to the sky, becoming the planet Mars. The significance of local topography is discussed.

0997 Tindale, Norman B. (1937) "Native Songs of the South-East of South Australia." *Transactions and Proceedings of the Royal Society of South Australia* 61: 107-120.
17 songs obtained from Milerum, a Tanganekald man, each transcribed and given interlineal translations and further information based on Milerum's commentary. The songs have a wide range of subjects, from Dreaming stories to those related to social and personal issues. Also includes a sorcery song, songs of ancestral heroes and one dealing with the supernatural understanding of a small-pox epidemic. A useful collection.

0998 Tindale, Norman B. (1938) "Prupe and Koromarange: A Legend of the Tanganekeld, Coorong, South Australia." *Transactions of the Royal Society of South Australia* 62,1: 19-24.
Brief transcription with interlineal and free translations of the myth of *Prupe* and *Koromarange*, very human-like Tanganekald ancestors.

0999 Tindale, Norman B. (1939) "Eagle and Crow Myths of the Maraura Tribe, Lower Darling River, New South Wales." *Records of the South Australian Museum* 6,3: 243-61.
Transcribes, with interlineal and free translations, the Maraura story of *Wa:ku* (crow) and *Ka:nau* (Eagle). Crow seeks two classificatory mother-in-laws as wives and, failing this incestuous liaison, kills his sister's son and is turned into a bird by Eagle. Suggests the myth is possibly rooted in history (a dubious thesis at best) and maps the distribution of similar myths throughout the continent.

1000 Unaipon, David (ND) *Native Legends*. Adelaide: Hunkin, Ellis and King. 15 pp.
Possibly the first collection by an Aborigine of their traditions, in this case Narrinyeri. We are not told what editing was involved, but the language suggests a shadow writer may have taken considerable editorial licence. The stories (e.g. totemism, and tales of dragonflies, cockatoos, lizards, etc.) are horribly fairytale-like, and the value of the book is largely as an instance of either cultural transformation or editorial vandalism.

See also: 0144, 0145, 0436, 0964, 0966, 1004.

The Arts

1001 Clegg, John K. (1971) "A ? 'Metaphysical' Approach to the Study of
         Aboriginal Rock Painting." *Mankind* 8,1: 37-41.
A tentative and conjectural reconstruction of the relationship between art and
myth. The Woronora site, south of Sydney, depicts 21 animals. Most are in
their natural level (subterranean, ground, middle, upper). This, combined with
the size of pictures, is said to indicate mythical significance. Next, direction of
figures is said to reflect mythic reversals parallel to Maddock's finding of myth
transformation from northern to central Australia (0131).

1002 Clegg, John K. (1985) *Prehistoric Pictures As Evidence About Religion.*
         Sydney: Private Publication. 59 pp.
A small, limited distribution, publication with an ambitious and important
agenda. Attempts to interpret changes in art over a period of 5,000 years as
indicative of changes in religion. Sturt's Meadows (western New South Wales)
and Sydney region art works are compared in terms of style and subject matter.
Concludes that while change in religion is revealed, little can be said about the
content of that change.

1003 Donaldson, Tamsin (1987) "Making a Song (and Dance) in South-East
         Australia." In *Songs of Aboriginal Australia*, edited by M.Clunies Ross,
         T. Donaldson & S.A. Wild, 14-42. Sydney: Oceania Monographs.
Focuses on seven variations of a song written by a Ngemba man and also contains
interesting ethnological and classificatory data on ritual in the South-East. The
origin and early meanings of 'corroboree' are discussed (pp.19-22) and there is a
breakdown of Ngemba taxonomy of songs and dances (pp.25-9). Argues that
although of recent origin, the song was written in conformity with the style of
'corroboree' songs for the region.

1004 Elkin, A.P. (1949) "The Origin and Interpretation of Petroglyphs in
         South-East Australia." *Oceania* 20,2: 119-157.
Discusses rock carvings from the Sydney environs attempting to shed light on
their ceremonial significance. Maintains, by reference to early literature and his
own field enquiries, that the carvings primarily represent significant
mythological beings and were visited by men of 'high degree' as well as being
the focus of wider ceremonial activity. Insights from recollections of Aborigines
themselves greatly add to the value of this paper.

1005 Etheridge, R. (1918) *The Dendroglyphs, or 'Carved Trees' of New
         South Wales*. Sydney: Government Printer. 104 pp + plates.
A catalogue of carved trees found in association with the dead and on initiatory
grounds. Besides illustrating the carvings and describing their distribution, there
is cautious speculation, reviewing the literature, of the meaning of these trees and
their place in ritual practice. Descriptions of the carved designs are
frustratingly, but inevitably, inadequate.

1006 Howitt, Alfred W. (1887) "Notes on Songs and Song-makers of Some Australian Tribes." *Journal of the Anthropological Institute of Great Britain and Ireland* 16: 327-335.
Some references to religious origin and use of Kurnai and Wurundjeri songs.

1007 Lane, K.H. (1978) "Carved Trees and Initiation Ceremonies on the Nambucca River." In *Records of Times Past: Ethnohistorical Essays on the Culture and Ecology of the New England Tribes*, edited by I. McBryde, 222-234. Canberra: Australian Institute of Aboriginal Studies.
Describes dendroglyphs in the Nambucca River area. Oral tradition support the thesis that they were associated with initiation grounds, although this does not rule out a mortuary significance. Most interesting are the views of an old Kumbainggar man initiated at one of the sites. His exegisis includes not only traditional themes but also Christian interpretations.

1008 McCarthy, Frederick D. (1941-9) "Records of Rock Engravings in the Sydney District." *Mankind* 3,2: 42-56; 3,6: 161-171; 3,8: 217-225; 3,9: 266-272; 3,11: 322-329; 4,2: 61-69.
Illustrates and discusses 40 groups of rock engravings in the Sydney district. Each contains interpretations providing varying degrees of conjecture regarding the religious, or other, significances of the art - for example, several groups are associated with the culture hero *Daramulun*. Whilst such reasoning is always open to question, adds to our knowledge of an ethnographically barren region.

1009 Mathews, R.H. (1897) "Bullroarers used by the Australian Aborigines." *The Journal of the Anthropological Institute of Great Britain and Ireland* 27; 52-60.
Descriptions of construction and use of bull-roarers, based on the author's observations supplemented by other published accounts. Refers to its mythic association with *Daramulun*, etc., and place in initiation.

See also: 0163, 0997, 1012.

Ceremony

1010 Beckler, Hermann (1868) "Corroberri: Ein Beitrag zur Kenntnis der Musik bei den australischen Ureinwohnern." *Globus* 13: 82-4.
Description of public ceremony witnessed near Darling Downs.

1011 Sabine, Nigel (1978) "The Paddymelon Stone: An Increase Centre of the Gumbaynggir Tribe, Nymboida." In *Records of Times Past: Ethnohistorical Essays on the Culture and Ecology of the New England Tribes*, edited by I. McBryde, 218-221. Canberra: Australian Institute of Aboriginal Studies.
Includes some Kumbainggar oral traditions.

See also: 1003.

Initiation

1012 Black, Lindsay (1944) *The Bora Ground: Being a Continuation of a Series on the Customs of the Aborigines of the Darling River Valley and of Central New South Wales.* Part IV. Sydney: F.H. Booth. 64 pp.
Attempts to shed some light on Wiradjuri and Kamilaroi *Bora* grounds by reviewing published accounts, albeit with a lack of comprehensiveness. Most of the plates are devoted to the dendroglyphs (carved trees) with no exegesis. Introductory and incompletely researched.

1013 Cambage, R.H. and Selkirk, H. (1920) "Early Drawings of an Aboriginal Ceremonial Ground." *Journal and Proceedings of the Royal Society of New South Wales* 54: 74-78.
The earliest known plan for a initiation ground, at Moreton Bay, drawn by John Oxley in 1824.

1014 Cohen, Philip (1897) "Description of the 'Gaboora'." *The Australian Anthropological Journal* March 31: 83-4; April 30: 97-8; May 31: 115-7.
Notes on an initiation in the Hastings River district, 1838. One of the earliest descriptions but the understanding is confined to observable behaviour patterns: the duties of 'head wizards', the handling of neophytes, the preparation of grounds, etc. A translation of a ritual leader's words is imaginative but hardly authentic.

1015 Enright, W.J. (1899) "The Initiation Ceremonies of the Aborigines of Port Stephens, N.S.Wales." *Journal and Proceedings of the Royal Society of New South Wales* 33: 115-124.
A short description of Kattang initiation ceremonies (*Keeparra*) to which the author was admitted after an introduction from R.H. Mathews. Covers organization of participants, early public rituals, the preparation of the youths, the bullroarer, the removal of bodily hair, the return to camp and the food taboos following initiation.

1016 Fraser, John (1882) "The Aborigines of New South Wales." *Journal and Proceedings of the Royal Society of New South Wales* 16: 193-233.
Describes the life stages of the Kamilaroi and others: youth, manhood and old age. The most valuable section is on initiation (pp. 204-220) giving a lengthy account of *Bora* and associated rites, and some insight and some wild conjectures on the association of *Bora* with cults of the Ancient Near East.

1017 Gunn, Donald (1908/9) "The Last Bora on the Weir River." *Queensland Geographical Journal* 24,10: 88-91.
The Aborigines danced "in the altogether" (p.96). It gets no better.

1018 Howitt, Alfred W. (1884) "On Some Australian Initiation Ceremonies." *The Journal of the Anthropological Institute of Great Britain and Ireland* 13: 432-459.

Attempts to provide a detailed account of initiation indicating some of the meanings of the rites. Refers to Wolgal, Ngarigo, Jaitmathang, and Wurundjeri traditions and considers the assemblage of participants, and the ceremonies in 3 phases: i) the procession leading to ii) the 'magic camp' and iii) the return. The dances and sand figures related to *Daramulun* and *Baiami* are stressed. The final discussion of the 'object of the ceremonies' is anything but satisfying.

1019 Howitt, Alfred W. (1885) "The Jeraeil or Initiation Ceremonies of the Kurnai Tribe." *Journal of the Anthropological Institute* 14: 301-325.
A pioneering description of initiation among the Kurnai. The ceremony had fallen into disuse and was revived, at least partially, on Howitt's behalf. Evidence of ritual modification is apparent. The description spans from the period of early preparations and negotiations through the various phases of the rite. The account is detailed, climaxing in the revelation of the bullroarer and the myth of *Mungan-ngaur*.

1020 Mathews, R.H. (1894) "Aboriginal Bora Held at Gundabloui in 1894." *Journal and Proceedings of the Royal Society of New South Wales* 28: 98-129.
A description of a *Bora* in northern central N.S.W., from notes provided by a police officer primed by Mathews. Covers the various stages, from 'mustering the tribes' to establishing the camps; the making of the *Bora* grounds and the ground sculptures and tree designs (illustrated); the initiation of boys, through sacred revelations, education and bodily ordeals. Concludes by comparing his description with previous accounts.

1021 Mathews, R.H. (1894-5) "The Bora, or Initiation Ceremonies of the Kamilaroi Tribe." *Journal of the Anthropological Institute of Great Britain and Ireland.* 24: 411-427; 25: 318-339.
The first part is based on data provided by a police officer. Mathews subsequently travelled into Kamilaroi country to collect the supplementary material of part II. The new material is located under the same headings as the first: Mustering of Tribes; the Camp; the *Bora* Ground; Preliminary Ceremonies; Surrendering the Boys to the Head-men; Departure of the Boys; and Return of the Boys. A collection of notes offering little insight.

1022 Mathews, R.H. (1895-6) "The Burbung of the Wiradthuri Tribes." *The Journal of the Anthropological Institute of Great Britain and Ireland* 25: 295-318; 26: 272-285.
Part I is devoted to the preliminary Wiradjuri initiation activities: summoning participants, preparing the *Burbung* grounds, and staging initial rituals. Part II focuses on the withdrawal of neophytes, secret bush ceremonies - noting the novices' ordeals, body painting and singing, their education in sacred matters, the revelation of the bullroarer - and the return to the community. The description is detailed and sober, but lacks detail on the significance of rites.

1023 Mathews, R.H. (1896) "The Bunan Ceremony of New South Wales." *American Anthropologist* 9:327-344.

A description of initiation for the people east of the Wiradjuri, salvaged from descriptions and *Bunan* ground remains. The latter are mapped and the recollections of ceremonies, from the sending of messages for gathering to the youth's gradual rejoining the community are described. Notes kinship of guardians, bodily designs, bullroarers, *Daramulun* the All-Father, tooth avulsion, etc.

1024 Mathews, R.H. (1896) "The Keeparra Ceremony of Initiation." *The Journal of the Anthropological Institute of Great Britain and Ireland* 26: 320-340.
An account of the *Keeparra* ceremonies of the extremely altered coastal Aborigines communities from Newcastle to the Macleay River. The organization of ceremonies, the use of bull-roarers, the departure of the women and the bush ceremonies, the revelations of sacred designs, clever men's magic, and the return of the neophytes are each described.

1025 Mathews, R.H. (1897) "The Bora of the Kamilaroi Tribes." *Proceedings of the Royal Society of Victoria* 9: 137-173.
This *Bora* was largely performed by the same peoples who performed the ceremony a little over a year earlier in Mathews 1020 and 1021. The article format is identical. Of note are novel ground sculptures: a train, a bullock dray and four aces! One of Mathew's fuller and more richly described accounts of initiation.

1026 Mathews, R.H. (1897) "The Burbung of the Darkinung Tribes." *Proceedings of the Royal Society of Victoria* Vol. 10: 1-12.
Describes Darkinung initiation from reminiscences of two old initiated men. Include discussion of ground sculptures and tree carvings, organization of ceremonies, rituals leading up to the revelations of *Daramulun* and the bull-roarers, education in the bush, tooth avulsion and post-initiatory taboos. Mathews tends to fill in uncertain details with data he has collected elsewhere.

1027 Mathews, R.H. (1897) "The Wandarral of the Richmond and Clarence River Tribes." *Proceedings of the Royal Society of Victoria* 10: 29-42.
Using mainly Bandjelang evidence, provides the first ethnographic account of *Wandarral* ceremonies many years after social disruption in the region. The ceremonial grounds, with the inverted *warrangooringa* stumps, the organization of the intertribal ceremonies, the smoke ordeal and the gradual reincorporation into the society are described. Sketchy and lacking detail.

1028 Mathews, R.H. (1897) "The Burbung of the New England Tribes, New South Wales." *Proceedings of the Royal Society of Victoria* 9: 120-136.
An account of the initiation ceremonies in the New England region. Stresses local variation and common general forms. The grounds are described, as is the marking of trees and the sculptures of the All-Father. There is constant commentary on the movements of the various group involved (neophytes, women, leaders etc.).

1029 Mathews, R.H. (1897) "The Burbung, or Initiation Ceremonies of the Murrumbidgee Tribes." *Journal and Proceedings of the Royal Society of New South Wales* 31: 111-153.
Complements his earlier papers on northern Wiradjuri initiations (1022) considering more southerly manifestations and organizing his account in much the same manner.

1030 Mathews, R.H. (1898) "The Victorian Aborigines: their Initiation Ceremonies and Divisional Systems." *American Anthropologist* 11: 325-343.
Survey, comparing and contrasting, briefly, known facts about initiation and social organization. With map of distribution.

1031 Mathews, R.H. (1898) "The Group Divisions and Initiation Ceremonies of the Barkunjee Tribes." *Journal and Proceedings of the Royal Society of New South Wales* 32: 241-255.
Contains a brief account of Bagundji initiation rites emphasizing variations throughout their region. Discusses *Kuranda* - the plucking of body hair, circumcision and *Tumba* which he associates with the Kamilaroi *Bora*. Concludes with some general remarks valid for the entire region.

1032 Mathews, R.H. (1898) "Initiation Ceremonies of Australian Tribes." *Proceedings of the American Philosophical Society* 37: 54-73.
Anticipated as being his final piece in his study of New South Wales initiatory rites and hence providing a map of the state subdivided into nine regions, with a key to his various publications for each region. A useful guide to his widely dispersed papers on initiation. Also considers the *Burbung* ceremonies of the Kumbainggar.

1033 Mathews, R.H. (1899-1900) "The Walloonggurra Ceremony." *Queensland Geographical Journal* NS 15: 67-74.
Sketchy, and in places superficial, account of Kumbainggar and Bandjelang initiation. Discusses the gathering, preliminary public rituals, the departure of women, the main grounds, 'disgusting' food and drink, a traditional healer doing 'jugglery', the revelation of the bull-roarer, final rituals and the gradual return to society.

1034 Mathews, R.H. (1900) "The Toora Ceremony of the Dippil Tribes of Queensland." *American Anthropologist* 2,1: 139-144.
The *Toara* of the Kabikabi and others near the Queensland/New South Wales border. The grounds, inverted ceremonial tree stumps etc., are noted and the rituals of initiation are given in a brief and inadequate form. Process of smoking youths, tooth avulsion, combat/hunting training, and bullroarer revelation are mentioned. A truncated summary of overt behaviour.

1035 Mathews, R.H. (1900) "The Origin, Organisation and Ceremonies of the Australian Aborigines." *Proceedings of the American Philosophical Society* 39: 556-578.

Brief and unsatisfactory generalizations and comparisons of the South-East and Tasmania.

1036 Mathews, R.H. (1900-1) "The Murrawin Ceremony." *Queensland Geographical Journal* NS 16: 35-41.
Describes a Dainggati initiation. The gathering of 'tribes', construction of ritual grounds, early public rituals, removal of boys from women, ordeals of authority, phallic rites (eg. threatened ritual sodomy) and the revelation of bullroarers and sacred tree designs are described. Not exhaustive and no hint is given as to the deeper significance of the ritual.

1037 Mathews, R.H. (1901) "Initiation Ceremonies of the Wiradjuri Tribes." *American Anthropologist* 3,2: 337-341.
A western supplement to his earlier studies of Wiradjuri initiation (1022, 1029), focusing mainly on the sand sculptures.

1038 Mathews, R.H. (1904) "Die Multyerra-Initiations-Zeremonie." *Mitteilungen der Anthropologischen Gesellschaft in Wien* 34: 77-83.
Describes Kula ceremonies with relatively detailed descriptions of the physical details of tooth avulsion and other practices and the use of the bullroarer; and the various stages, from organizing the gathering to the separation of neophytes and later reaggregation into the community. Aboriginal interpretations of their actions not considered.

1039 Mathews, R.H. (1905) "Some Initiation Ceremonies of the Aborigines of Victoria." *Zeitschrift für Ethnologie* 6: 872-879.
Patchy data continuing the author's sweeping studies of initiation in the South-East. These, from the Victorian area bordering on New South Wales, are the *Wonggumuk* and *Kannety* ceremonies of unnamed 'tribes'. His usual sequence of gathering the tribes, preparation, separation, initiation and reintroduction to society is followed. Very incomplete accounts.

1040 Mathews, R.H. (1907) "Initiation Ceremonies of the Murawarri and other Aboriginal Tribes of Queensland." *Proceedings of the Royal Geographical Society of Australia, Queensland* 22: 1-10.
A short account of the *Multyerra* ceremony of the Murawari and Badjiri. Discusses invitations being sent, preparation of grounds, 'mustering' of men, women and children, separation and segregation, tooth avulsion, teaching, a smoke ceremony as the boys are reintroduced to their mothers and the gradual return to society. Descriptive and devoid of all Aboriginal exegesis.

1041 Mathews, R.H. (1909-10) "Initiation Ceremonies of Some Queensland Tribes." *Queensland Geographical Journal* NS 25: 103-118.
Account of initiation in the south-eastern corner of Queensland, pieced together from data from old men who had passed through the rites long ago. Discusses two rites: *Toara* is described along the author's usual division of summoning tribes, establishment of the grounds, separation of boys, revelations and the return to camp. The *Bundandaba* ceremony, a further rite of passage, is given in a truncated form.

1042 Mathews, R.H. (1910) "Die Bundandaba - Zeremonie in Queensland." *Mitteilungen der Anthropologischen Gesellschaft in Wein* 40: 1-4.
A brief account of the concluding part of the initiatory ceremony from the New South Walses border.

1043 Mathews, R.H. (1916-18) "Initiation Ceremony of the Birdhawal Tribe." *Queensland Geographical Journal* NS 32-3: 89-97.
A thin account of the Birdawal *Dyerrayal* which makes unpenetrating comparisons with Mathews' previous publications on initiation. Emphasis is placed upon the practice of throwing small bundles of sticks and bark over the novices as they are separated from their mothers and on the role of women in men's rituals. Much is clearly missing from this account.

1044 Mathews, R.H. and Everitt, M.M. (1900) "The Organisation, Language and Initiation Ceremonies of the Aborigines of the South-East Coast of N.S. Wales." *Journal and Proceedings of the Royal Society of New South Wales* 34: 262-281.
A reconstruction of traditional life from town dwelling men and women on the south coast of New South Wales. The actual intiation described is very abbreviated. Particulary interesting is the acknowledgement of women's role in initiation and the description of their activities while the men are secluded.

1045 Schmidt, Wilhelm (1923) *Die geheime Jugendweihe eines australischen Urstammes: mit einem Abriss der soziologischen und religionsgeschichtlichen Entwicklung der südostaustralischen Stämme.* Paderborn: Ferdinand Schöningh. 73 pp.
Considers the initiation ceremonies of the South-East, and in particular those of the Kurnai as reported by Howitt (0938, 1019) in terms of diffusionist theory. Historical interest only.

See also: 0927, 0934, 0949, 1005.

Women

1046 Gale, Fay (1989) "Roles Revisited: The Women of Southern South Australia." In *Women, Rites and Sites: Aboriginal Women's Cultural Knowledge*, edited by P. Brock, 120-135. Sydney: Allen & Unwin.
Draws on published sources and the author's research at Point McLeay to argue for a revised view of Aboriginal women's status. Notes their powerful position as Dreaming beings, their prominent position in religious domains and their active roles in the present day. Given this thematic concord, suggests the view that these women were subservient chattels could only reflect a failure in scholarship.

See also: 0197, 0952, 1044.

Magic

1047 Berndt, Ronald M. (1947) "Wuradjeri Magic and 'Clever Men'." *Oceania*
       17,4: 327-365; 18,1: 60-86.
A valuable and detailed piece of 'reconstruction' anthropology based on
information from two elderly Wiradjuri men. Covers making of clever men;
displays of magical powers; magic used to cure, evade enemies, hunt, make rain
and attract lovers; sorcery; and spirits and totems associated with clever men.
The inevitable shortcomings of the article are due to the lack of living
practitioners of these arts.

1048 Cassidy, Sarsfield (1896) "The Aboriginal Doctors of Australia."
       American Medico-Surgical Bulletin August 15: 182-185.
Brief, tolerant views on Aboriginal clever men, seemingly based on observations
in the South-East.

1049 Howitt, Alfred W. (1887) "On Australian Medicine Men: Or Doctors and
       Wizards of Some Australian Tribes." *Journal of the Anthropological
       Institute of Great Britain and Ireland* 16: 23-58.
Data on the Kurnai, Wiradjuri, Wotjobaluk, and Wurundjeri covering both
'doctors', who heal, and 'wizards' who see spirits, make rain, etc. Includes
discussion of their supernatural powers - e.g. seeing human spirits, travel to sky,
taking animal form, use of quartz, etc. - their role in both causing and curing
illness, and the processes of initiating these men. Useful data, albeit collected
well after European disruption.

1050 Massola, Aldo (1965) "Some Superstitions Current Amongst the
       Aborigines of Lake Tyers." *Mankind* 6,5: 211-214.
Very brief notes from the peoples gathered at Lake Tyers. A typical entry is
"The Pigeon. If a pigeon flies over a boy's head, the boy will stop growing. If a
pigeon coos at night, it foretells a death"(p.212). Frustratingly sketchy.

See also: 0215, 0221, 1004.

Death

1051 Haglund, Laila (1976) *An Archaeological Analysis of the Broadbeach
       Aboriginal Burial Ground*. St. Lucia: University of Queensland Press.
       118 pp.
Broadbeach revealed some 150 skeletons buried within the last millennium. The
evidence suggested marked continuity of tradition, nonetheless with room for
variations. The ceremonies were elaborate and in stages, employing fire, ochre
and ritual meals. Draws on anthropological studies for the area to supplement
the picture and the divergencies between written and archaeological evidence
provides for a range of speculative possibilities.

1052 Mathews, R.H. (1909) "Some Burial Customs of the Australian Aborigines." *Proceedings of the American Philosophical Society* 48: 313-318.
Notes, with informant explanations, of manufactured objects found at burial sites.

1053 Pardoe, Colin (1988) "The Cemetery as Symbol: The Distribution of Prehistoric Aboriginal Burial Grounds in Southeastern Australia." *Archaeology in Oceania* 23,1: 1-16.
A useful attempt to analyse the symbolic significance of the Aboriginal ceremonial ground. Focusing on the Murray River area, the cultural and economic roles of cemeteries are examined. It is argued that these cemeteries indicate a higher than the Aboriginal 'normal' concern with social exclusion and a preoccupation with boundary maintenance. The interrelation of religion and subsistence concerns is stressed.

See also: 0229, 1005.

Change

1054 Beckett, Jeremy (1958) "Marginal Men: A Study of Two Half Caste Aborigines." *Oceania* 29,2: 91-108.
Contains a few general notes on religious life in the far west of New South Wales. Includes interesting glimpses of initiation, failed attempts to become a 'clever man' and conversion to Christianity. One informant equates the passion with Eaglehawk and Crow myths, the other feels he has a religious message to proclaim in which God's (*Guluwiru*) people are led astray by Eaglehawk and Frog.

1055 Calley, Malcolm J.C. (1964) "Pentecostalism Among the Bandjalang." In *Aborigines Now: New Perspectives in the Study of Aboriginal Communities*, edited by M. Reay, 48-58. Sydney: Angus and Robertson.
Pentecostalism was attractive to the Bandjelang and pentecostal 'initiations' and emphasis on healing and magical power had many similarities with traditional religious life. Syncretistic myths are given. Indicates some peculiarities of Bandjalang pentacostalism, especially the solitary nature of their 'baptism of the spirit' which is associated with the solitary initiation of 'clever men'. An important, pioneering study of religious change.

1056 Flood, Bernard (1985) "Aspects of Popular Religion Among Catholic Murris of Moree." *Nungalinya Occasional Bulletin* no. 29: 1-19.
Attempts to assess Catholicism amongst the Aborigines of Moree. Examines Aboriginal Catholic concepts of God, sacrament (baptism, marriage, eucharist) and views on death, and concludes that although there is no overt reference to traditional beliefs, their religious attitudes are nonetheless more Aboriginal than Catholic. Not convincing, however.

1057   Kelly, Caroline T. (1944) "Some Aspects of Culture Contact in Eastern Australia." *Oceania* 152: 142-153.
Based on observations on unidentified reserves in Queensland and New South Wales and includes a half a dozen pages on the influence of Christianity on Aboriginal culture. Contains glimpses of the contrasts between traditional 'rule' and Christian 'rule'. The focus is on death and healing, but there is mention of syncretistic beliefs, the merging of Christian and Aboriginal myth, and attempts to locate Christian events in the local landscape.

1058   Lang, Andrew (1907) "Australia: Prayer. A Reply to 'Man', 1907.2." *Man* 7: 67-69.
Defends Parker (0952) against Marett (1059).

1059   Marett, R.R. (1907) "Australia: Prayer." *Man* 7: 2-3.
Suggests Parker's account (0952) contains mission influence.

1060   Reay, Marie (1945) "A Half-Caste Aboriginal Community in North-Western New South Wales." *Oceania*, 154: 296-323.
Looks at the remains of traditional Weilwan (and other) Aboriginal life in the context of race conflict and social problems such as alcoholism, assault, and sexual offences. The final eight pages examine views upon the origin and cure of disease, medicine-men, death and ghosts (*guwa*). Largely a reconstructionist approach, but there is some attempt to come to grips with the dynamics of religion in transition.

1061   Reay, Marie (1949) "Native Thought in Rural New South Wales." *Oceania* 20,2: 89-118.
A useful survey of cultural change in north-western New South Wales. Covers a variety of areas and 'tribes' in conditions ranging from predominantly Aboriginal communities to major settled towns. Looks at changing views of magic, traditional healing, death, ghosts, mortuary practice, cosmology and ritual. Refers to attempts to amalgamate God with *Baiami*, at times seen as two incarnations of one mythological figure.

1062   Swain, Tony (1990) "A New Sky Hero From A Conquered Land." *History of Religions* 29,3: 195-232.
A detailed examination of early accounts of the South-East arguing they indicate radical religious change. Considers the belief in All-Fathers, the emphasis on a distant, unknown sky paradise, and the concept of 'evil' in the context of colonial race relations, arguing these 'abberrant' beliefs replicate principles of invasion. Also examines millennial expectations, pessimistic eschatologies and the presence of symbols of European culture (bullocks, trains, playing cards, horses and White people) in the cults of the All-Father.

1063   Thomas, Gaboo Ted (1987) "The Land is Sacred: Renewing the Dreaming in Modern Australia." In *The Gospel is Not Western: Black Theologies from the Southwest Pacific*, edited by G.W. Trompf, 90-94. New York: Orbis.

Written by a Yuin 'elder' involved in neo-traditional revivals. Advocates the Aboriginal capacity to 'feel' sacred places and a range of syncretistic ideas. God is equated with *Darama*, Noah's Ark is localized and the Yowie (Australian Bigfoot) is identified as a spirit involved in initiation, etc. Set in the context of a desire to renew the Dreaming.

1064 Thomas, Northcote W. (1905) "Baiame and the Bell-Bird." *Man* 5: 49-52.
Besides arguing *Baiami* once was a bird of the 'Eaglehawk and Crow' type, examines early references to Aboriginal All-Fathers and dates early missions to these regions.

See also: 0144, 0145, 0244, 0962, 0972, 0973, 0977, 0978, 0982, 0985, 0993, 0994, 1007, 1025.

Literature

1065 Massola, Aldo (1971) *Bibliography of the Victorian Aborigines from the Earliest Manuscripts to 31 December, 1970.* Melbourne: Hawthorn Press. 95 pp.
Despite the title, few manuscripts are listed. Most of this book is an unannotated but classified listing, poorly organized and incomplete.

1066 Reed, Les and Parr, Ed (ND) *The Keeping Place: An Annotated Bibliography and Guide to the Study of the Aborigines and Aboriginal Culture in Northeast New South Wales and Southeast Queensland.* Lismore, N.S.W.: North Coast Institute for Aboriginal Community Education. 157 pp.
1440 entries to published and unpublished sources on the Aborigines of the coastal South-East. Contains brief, uncritical annotations and an index referencing many subthemes to 'religion and magic' (e.g. after-life beliefs, 'increase' rituals, mythology, totemism, women's rituals, etc.).

See also: 0249.

14

Tasmania

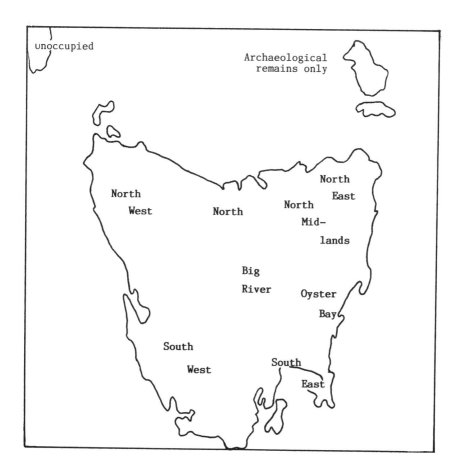

General

1067 Calder, J. E. (1875) *Some Account of the Wars, Extirpation, Habits, etc.,
       of the Native Tribes of Tasmania*. Hobart: Henn. 115 pp.
Terribly superficial snippets on mortuary practice, etc.

1068 Giglioli, Enrico H. (1874) *I Tasmaniani: cenni storici ed etnologici di un
       popolo estinio*. Milano: Fratelli Treves. 456 pp.
Explorers' reports on Tasmanian Aborigines with brief notes on spirit beliefs,
'superstitions' and myths, together with some truncated transcriptions and
translations (pp. 429ff.)

1069 Kabo, Vladimir R. (1975) *Tasmaniitsy i Tasmaniiskaia Problema*.
       Moscow: Navka. 198 pp.
"Tasmanians and the Tasmanian Problem" is an evolutionary study of Tasmanian
Aboriginal society. A chapter on religion (pp. 154-170) discusses good and
'evil', life and death, day and night, 'reincarnation', initiation, magic, myth, and
'shamanism'. Stresses continuity with mainland religion but likewise argues that
it represents an earlier stage. While theoretically dated (in the West, but not in
the Marxist-Leninist study of religion), it does add to a poorly studied region.

1070 Plomley, N.J.B. (1977) *The Tasmanian Aborigines: A Short Account of
       them and some aspects of their Life*. Launceston: Author's publication. 72
       pp.
A few notes on religion, derived from G.A. Robinson's journals.

1071 Roth, H. Ling (1899) *The Aborigines of Tasmania*. 2nd ed. Halifax: F.
       King. 228 + ciii pp. 1st ed. 1890.
An examination of virtually all available published data on a people then deemed
to be extinct. The section entitled 'religion' is largely written in the negative.
Useful information, however, can be found in other sections which discuss
taboos, medicine, myths, mortuary rituals and 'corroborees'. Ritual practice is
poorly documented and initiation is dismissed in a quarter of a page. Nearly all
Roth's sources lacked linguistic skills and the combination of ignorance and
Victorian orientation result in a frustratingly sketchy account.

1072 Vögler, Gisela (1972) *Die Tasmanier: Versuch einer ethnographisch-
       historischen Rekonstruktion*. Wiesbaden: Franz Steiner. 381 pp.
The most ambitious attempt to date to reconstruct Tasmanian Aboriginal
traditional life in all its aspects, based on a thorough examination of published
sources and relying heavily on ethnographic analogy from the rest of Australia
and interpretations of cultural remains. Given the poverty of sources, this
examination of initiation, totemic ritual, and other aspects of Tasmanian religion
is welcome, despite its unavoidable inadequacies.

See also: 0049, 0069, 0070, 0071, 0566, 0958, 1075.

Myth

1073 Cotton, Jackson (1979) *Touch the Morning: Tasmanian Native Legends.*
   Hobart: O.B.M. 56 pp.
The stories were collected by the author's ancestors who allegedly learned them
from Aborigines. Authenticity is claimed for the myths but they totally lack a
genuine air.

1074 Worms, Ernest A. (1960) "Tasmanian Mythological Terms." *Anthropos*
   55:1-16.
A wild attempt, relying mainly on Roth (1071), to linguistically reconstruct
Tasmanian Aboriginal beliefs. Only around 30 terms were known to the author,
which he attributes to deficiency in the Tasmanian cosmology. Argues they had
lost Supreme Beings to a stronger tradition of Spirits of the Dead. Ten
mythemes are examined in more detail - including the Isle of the Dead, ghosts,
spirits of various 'natural phenomena', etc. The linguistic liberties taken are
astounding.

Literature

1075 Müller, F. Max (1892) *Anthropological Religion.* London: Longmans,
   Green. 464pp.
Pages 428-435 review the evidence in Roth (1071), observing one can conclude
anything one wishes about Tasmanian religion: that they are irreligious, dualistic,
nature worshippers, devil devotees or monotheists, and much more. Set within a
general critique of the reliability of accounts of 'savage' religion.

1076 Plomley, N.J.B. (1969) *An Annotated Bibliography of the Tasmanian
   Aborigines.* Royal Anthropological Institute Occasional Paper No. 28.
   London: Royal Anthropological Institute of Great Britain and Ireland. 143
   pp.
A listing of books and articles referring to Tasmanian Aborigines, most briefly,
but not critically annotated. Covers the period up to 1965. Little reference to
religion. No index.

Author Index

* One and two digit numbers in *italics* refer to the page numbers of the narrative chapters where a particular author whose work is listed in the bibliography is mentioned. All other names are located in the General Subject Index

* Four digit numbers in plain-type refer to entry numbers in the bibliography.

* Four digit numbers contained within parentheses indicate that the *annotation* of an entry refers to the author in question.

Abbie, A.A., 0001.
Adam, Leonhard, 0150, 0152, 0597.
Akerman, Kim, *42;* 0558, 0614, 0626, 0634.
Akerman, Kim and Bindon, Peter, 0627.
Allen, Louis A., 0409, 0449.
Amadio, Nadine and Kimber, Richard, 0826.
Anderson, Christopher and Dussart, Françoise, 0827.
Arndt, W., 0410, 0450, 0451, 0478.

Baal, J. van, 0169.
Bain, Margaret S., 0712.
Barden, Garrett, 0710.
Barker, Graham, 0170.
Barlow, Alex, 0411.
Barrett, M.J., 0873.

Basedow, Herbert, 0002, 0183, 0371, 0372, 0559, 0693, 0917.
Bates, Daisy, *54;* 0003, 0660.
Beckett, Jeremy, *42, 48, 60;* 0297 0300, 0301, 0302, 0910, 1054.
Beckler, Hermann, 1010.
Beier, Ulli and Johnson, Colin, 0688.
Bell, Diane, *24, 38, 39, 57, 62;* 0192, 0863, 0864, 0865.
Bell, Diane and Ditton, Pam, 0866.
Bendann, E., 0224.
Bennett, Gordon, 0919.
Bennett, Samuel, 0004.
Bennie, Chris, *35;* 0493.
Benterrak, Kim; Muecke, Stephen; and Roe, Paddy, *24, 31;* 0560.
Bern, John, *21, 22;* 0193, 0373, 0479.
Berndt, Catherine H., *31, 39;* 0116, 0117, 0118, 0153, 0194, 0195, 0196,

Title Index

Entries
* *Italicized* titles are used for books.
* Plain-type indicates articles.

Tribes and Places Index

Entries
* *Italicized* words are Aboriginal 'tribes' or Islander names for Torres Strait Islands.

* Plain-type is used for the names of places, such as towns, rivers, islands or well known sites. The states and territories of Australia (excepting Tasmania) are not indexed. References to other countries are located in the General Subject Index.

Numbering
* One and two digit numbers in *italics* refer to page numbers of the narrative chapters.

* Four digit numbers in plain-type refer to entry numbers in the bibliography.

General Subject Index

Entries
* *Italicized* words are Aboriginal words.
* Plain-type is used for the remaining entries.

Numbering
* One and two digit numbers in *italics* refer to page numbers of the narrative chapters.
* Four digit numbers in plain-type refer to entry numbers in the bibliography.

Aborigines Protection Society, *7*.
Adam and Eve, 0365.
Adaptive cults, 0009.
Adjustment Movement, *52*; 0233, 0239, 0246, 0530, 0532, 0548.
Aeroplanes, *54*.
Aesthetics, 0469, 0470, 0520, 0785.
Ætology, 0675, 0677, 0977.
Affections, 0103, 0110, 1063.
Afterlife, 0011, 0045, 0054, 0071, 0312, 0360, 0385, 0518, 0596, 0708, 0766, 0925, 0926, 0941, 0961, 0963, 0979, 0987, 1066.
Agriculture, *47*.
Alchemy, 0092.
Alcohol, 0770, 0994, 1060.
Alkirakiwuma, 0862.
Alknarintja, 0787.

All-Father, *49, 52, 56, 59*; 0009, 0067, 0116, 0185, 0244, 0592, 0776, 0825, 0931, 0938, 0952, 0961, 0977, 0980, 0982, 0984, 1008, 1032, 1028, 1062, 1064.
All-Mother, *34, 49, 50, 51, 56*; 0116, 0158, 0169, 0392, 0401, 0458, 0551, 0631.
Altjeringa, 0002, 0825.
Altjira, 0002, 0792, 0812, 0814, 0820.
Ancestral Beings, 0012, 0066, 0142, 0223, 0264, 0266, 0269, 0282, 0324, 0398, 0407, 0430, 0470, 0471, 0529, 0568, 0575, 0596, 0615, 0630, 0705, 0735, 0739, 0758, 0814, 0830, 0831, 0961, 0997, 0998, 1046.
Androcentrism, 0198, 0203.